PERILOUSMISSIONS

CIVIL AIR TRANSPORT AND
CIA COVERT OPERATIONS IN ASIA

WILLIAM M. LEARY

Smithsonian Institution Press

Washington and London

Passages from *Street without Joy* by Bernard Fall, ©1961 by Stackpole Books.
Reprinted with permission from Stackpole Books, Harrisburg, Pennsylvania 17105.

Library of Congress Cataloging-in-Publication Data
Leary, William M. (William Matthew), 1934–
    Perilous missions : Civil Air Transport and CIA covert operations in
Asia / William M. Leary.
        p.   cm.
    Originally published: University, Ala. : University of Alabama, c 1984.
    Includes bibliographical references and index.
    ISBN 1-58834-028-7 (alk. paper)
    1. Civil Air Transport—History.   2. United States. Central Intelligence Agency—
History.   3. Asia—History—1945.   I. Title.

    UC333 .L4 2002
    358.4'13432'0973—dc21

                                                                            2001058196

British Library Cataloguing-in-Publication Data is available

A Smithsonian reprint of the edition published by University of Alabama Press in 1984

Manufactured in the United States of America
08 07 06 05 04 03 02   5 4 3 2 1

To my parents
William and Beatrice Leary

Contents

Preface

In the preface to the first edition of this volume, I wrote the following:

> I first encountered CAT during the winter of 1952–53 while serving in the U.S. Air Force at Kadena Air Base, Okinawa. My duties in operations included filing flight plans, logging arrivals and departures, and arranging parking and servicing for transient aircraft. Pot-bellied CAT C-46s often came through Kadena, usually parking in front of the operation building. From time to time, however, word came down from on high that an arriving CAT flight would be handled by an odd group of civilians who inhabited a far corner of the airfield. Questions about these unusual arrangements were silenced with knowing looks.
>
> Many years later, youthful curiosity grew into historical interest about American aeronautical activity in East Asia. *The Dragon's Wings* (University of Georgia Press), the first volume in a proposed trilogy, appeared in 1976 and detailed the affairs of the China National Aviation Corporation, a pioneering Sino-American airline. The present study deals with CAT—the Civil Air Transport. Fate and the availability of adequate documentation permitting, a final volume will tell the story of Air America.

While I am yet to complete the third volume of the trilogy, the past fifteen years has seen information come to light about the later activities of the CIA's air proprietaries in Asia. Much more is known, for example, about CAT's participation in a major CIA covert operation that was aimed at overthrowing the government of Indonesia. Concerned about President Sukarno's leftist leanings, President Dwight D. Eisenhower in November 1957 approved a special political action program to support dissident groups on Sumatra and the Celebes in a rebellion against the central government. Although CAT pilots flew arms and ammunition from the CIA's supply base on Okinawa to rebel forces on Sumatra, resistance soon collapsed on that island.

CAT played an even larger role during fighting in the Celebes in 1958. The airline's PBY flew search-and-rescue missions, while CAT pilots conducted air strikes in unmarked B-26s that had been provided by the U.S. Air Force. On

May 17, 1958, Allen L. Pope was shot down during an attack on Ambon. Pope, who previously had flown 57 airdrop missions over Dienbienphu in 1954, survived. His capture and identification as a CAT pilot brought an end to the CIA's Indonesian adventure. Condemned to death, Pope was later released by Sukarno, thanks to the efforts of Attorney General Robert Kennedy.[1]

CAT also supported a CIA covert operation to assist Tibetan forces in their struggle against Chinese occupation. The intelligence agency had been asked by the Eisenhower administration to provide secret aid to resistance forces at "the roof of the world." The CIA, in turn, directed CAT to perform the hazardous overflight missions. CAT's participation in the project, code-named ST-BARNUM, began in 1958 when the U.S. Air Force turned over a C-118 to the airline for the long-distance flights. The operation expanded the following year, with CAT crews manning "sanitized" air force C-130s. During the monthly phases of the full moon, a small group of C-130s would launch from Takhli Royal Thai Air Force Base, north of Bangkok, for the lengthy flight over India, China, across the high Himalayas, and into Tibet. It took some six to seven hours to reach the drop zone. After delivering a cargo of men and arms to the waiting Tibetans, the C-130s would then complete the round trip to their base in Thailand.

Between November 1959 and May 1960, when the project ended, CAT flew some 35 to 40 missions and delivered some 400 tons of cargo to the resistance fighters of Tibet. Although no aircraft were lost, there were several close calls. James Glerum, former head of the CIA's Special Operations Group and familiar with the CIA's many aerial activities in the 1950s and 1960s, has called ST-BARNUM "the most professional of all Agency overflight programs." It was, he added, a complete success "in terms of the planning and effectiveness against the operational parameters, which left little or no margin for error."[2]

While CAT crews were conducting the challenging missions to Tibet, the CIA was making organizational changes in its Asian air proprietary. In March 1959, the CIA changed the name of CAT, Inc., to Air America. This was done primarily to avoid confusions about the air proprietary's operations in Japan. By the early 1960s, there were a plethora of company identities under the Pacific Corporation, which was the interface between the secret and open worlds. These included Air America, which operated in Southeast Asia and Japan; Air Asia, which designated the giant maintenance complex on Taiwan; Southern Air Transport, based in Japan; and Civil Air Transport, which flew commercial routes between Seoul and Bangkok. No matter what the name, however, there was a single aircrew seniority list. A pilot, for example, might wear his Civil Air Transport hat and fly a load of tourists into Bangkok, where he would put on his Air America baseball cap and make an airdrop to forces engaged in fighting in Laos.[3]

Civil Air Transport, the international flag carrier of the Republic of China, prospered as a commercial airline. In 1960, it acquired a Convair 880—"the

Mandarin Jet"—to fly premier passenger service on Far Eastern routes. Individuals who flew the Mandarin Jet have fond memories of the superior quality of service aboard this lavishly appointed airliner—and of course were completely unaware of the real ownership of the company. The Convair was replaced in January 1968 by a Boeing 727, leased for Southern Air Transport. On February 16, 1968, the Boeing crashed during an instrument approach to Taipei, killing 21 of the 63 people on board. The accident became a *cause célèbre* among the international pilot community after two CAT pilots were charged with criminal manslaughter. (Ernest K. Gann's *Band of Brothers* was loosely based on this episode.) In the aftermath of the accident, CAT gave up its passenger air routes to China Airlines.

Air America became a vital component of the CIA's expanding war in Laos during the 1960s. In the largest paramilitary operation ever undertaken by the agency, a handful of case officers directed native forces in a decade-long battle against major North Vietnamese units. Air America provided the essential transportation infrastructure for this growing "secret war." By 1970, the airline had some two dozen twin-engine transports, another two dozen short-takeoff-and-landing (STOL) aircraft, and some 30 helicopters dedicated to operations in Laos. There were more than 300 pilots, copilots, flight mechanics, and airfreight specialists flying out of Laos and Thailand. During the year, Air America air-dropped or landed 46 million pounds of foodstuffs—mainly rice—in Laos. Helicopter flight time reached more than 4,000 hours a month in 1970. Air America crews transported tens of thousands of troops and refugees, flew emergency medevac missions, and rescued downed airmen throughout Laos, inserted and extracted road-watch teams, flew nighttime airdrop missions over the Ho Chi Minh Trail, monitored sensors along infiltration routes, conducted a highly successful photoreconnaissance program, and engaged in numerous clandestine missions using night-vision glasses and state-of-the-art electronic equipment. The airline's civilian crew members paid a high cost for operations in this combat environment. In all, 100 Air America personnel died in Laos between 1960 and 1974.[4]

Air America also provided transport for the CIA's extensive activities in South Vietnam. Most of the airline's flying consisted of routine operations, but even a "milk run" could suddenly turn deadly. On 14 January 1966, for example, an Air America C-47 left Saigon to pick up passengers in Vi Thanh. Although no opposition was expected, Vietcong gunners shot down the aircraft as it approached the field. Pilot William R. Prunner and copilot Johnny Yong Hoe Chang survived the crash only to be executed by the Vietcong. Air-freight specialist Nguyen Van Thai was led away from the wreckage with a rope around his neck and was not seen again.

The agency's airline took part in the numerous, often chaotic, evacuations that marked the collapse of the South Vietnamese regime in 1975. Indeed, one of the most enduring images of the war's final days was a photograph of an Air America helicopter perched atop the Pittman Apartments in Saigon as CIA officer O. B. Harnage reached down to help evacuees onboard.

Even before the end of the war in Southeast Asia, the CIA had decided to end the relationship with its air proprietary. On 21 April 1972, Director of Central Intelligence (DCI) Richard Helms concluded that the CIA no longer needed a large covert airlift capability in Asia and ordered the agency to divest itself of ownership and control of Air America and related companies. The air proprietary went out of business on 30 June 1976, returning more than $20 million to the U.S. Treasury.

Air America's public image fared poorly in the post-Vietnam era. In the 1990 movie, *Air America*, the war in Laos is portrayed as a struggle for the area's opium fields. The CIA and its native allies, the movie alleges, were centrally involved in the drug trade. Air America pilots in the film are portrayed as skilled in landing damaged airplanes, but basically as a wildly unprofessional menagerie of party animals, including a few borderline psychotics.

The CIA, which had remained silent through the years about the role of its air proprietary, finally recognized the contributions of CAT and Air America with a unit citation in June 2001. Signed by DCI George Tenet, it read:

> During the hottest days of the Cold War, the aircrews and ground personnel of Civil Air Transport and Air America gave unwavering service to the United States of America in the worldwide battle against communist oppression. Over the course of four decades, the courage, dedication to duty, superior airmanship, and sacrifice of these individuals set standards against which all future covert air operations must be judged. From the mist-shrouded peaks of Tibet, to the black skies of China, to the steaming jungles of Southeast Asia, the legendary men and women of Civil Air Transport and Air America always gave full measure of themselves in the defense of freedom. They did so despite often outdated equipment, hazardous terrain, dangerous weather, enemy fire, and their own government bureaucracy. Their actions speak eloquently of their skill, bravery, loyalty, and faith in themselves, each other, and the United States of America.[5]

William M. Leary
Athens, Georgia

Notes

1. See Kenneth Conboy and James Morrison, *Feet to the Fire: CIA Covert Operations in Indonesia, 1957–1958* (Annapolis, Md.: Naval Institute Press, 1999).

2. On the Tibetan project, see John Kenneth Knaus, *Orphans of the Cold War: America and the Tibetan Struggle for Survival* (Public Affairs, 1999), and Roger E. McCarthy, *Tears of the Lotus: Accounts of the Tibetan Resistance to the Chinese Invasion, 1950–1962* (McFarland, 1997). On Cat's role, see William M. Leary, "Secret Mission to Tibet," *Air & Space* (December 1997/January 1998), 12:62–71.

3. On the corporate confusion, see William M. Leary, "The Aircraft of Air America," *Airliners* (summer 1993), 6:14–20.

4. William M. Leary, "CIA Air Operations in Laos, 1955–1974, *Studies in Intelligence* (winter 1998/1999), 71-86. This article can also be found at www.odci.gov/csi/studies/winter99-00/art7.html.

5. Information on the awards ceremony can be found at www.air-america.org.html.

Prologue

The first rays of the rising sun glanced off the silver wings of the twin-engined aircraft that circled lazily in the tropical sky. Tired after seven hours in the air, the amphibian's crew nevertheless remained alert for a signal from the ground. Suddenly, a green light flashed the Morse code letter "A." The pilot immediately turned to the south-southwest, reversed course, then set the PBY-5A down in a calm sea, about one mile from the shoreline.

As the aircraft tossed gently in the warm waters of Lembeh Strait, off the northeastern tip of Celebes Island, the crew used binoculars to scan the deserted beach. A few anxious minutes went by before nineteen men emerged from the jungle, dragging behind them several wooden boats. The distant figures pushed off through the surf and rowed quickly toward the unmarked aircraft.

The crew remained wary, weapons within easy reach, until a man stood up in one of the boats and shouted: "Hello from Jack Harjono." The tension eased out of the fliers as they completed the prescribed ritual: "Greetings from Val Mac and Sam."

The nineteen Indonesians scrambled aboard. The pilot headed the PBY-5A into the wind and applied full power to the idling engines. The aircraft skimmed across the water, rose on the step, then lifted off into the early morning sky. Ahead lay ten hours of tedious flight to Clark Air Force Base in the Philippines.

The date was October 25, 1951. Civil Air Transport (CAT) had performed another successful mission for its secret owner, the Central Intelligence Agency.[1]

The airline with the unusual pedigree traced its origins to 1946, when Claire L. Chennault and Whiting Willauer formed a company to haul relief supplies and other cargo in war-ravaged China. The two men sought profit and adventure, and they wanted to encourage the development of an anti-

Communist, Western-oriented regime. After an arduous struggle to establish their airline in the face of political and operational adversity, Chennault
and Willauer became caught up in the civil war that convulsed China in the
late 1940s. Both their sentiments and pocketbooks were on the side of the
Nationalist government, and they used CAT in paramilitary fashion to support the declining fortunes of Chiang Kai-shek and his doomed followers.

In the final stages of the conflict, the Central Intelligence Agency contracted with CAT to airlift arms secretly to anti-Communist groups on the
periphery of China. Although the effort came far too late to achieve worth-
while results, it led to close ties between CAT and the CIA and to the
agency's eventual purchase of the airline.

The Korean War marked an explosive growth of the CIA's paramilitary
forces and brought the widespread use of CAT to support a series of covert
operations through the Far East. At the same time, the CIA struggled to
develop policy guidelines to govern the first of what would become a vast
complex of air proprietaries. The later aerial empire of the CIA in East Asia,
at its peak during the Vietnam War, evolved from the modest beginnings
with CAT.

The story of this unique aeronautical enterprise begins with Chennault
and Willauer and their plans for an airline in postwar China.

1 Origins of CAT

Major General Claire L. Chennault left China in summer 1945 in the midst of controversy. The acerbic warrior, at odds with his superiors for decades, believed that his leadership of the Fourteenth Air Force had merited a third star and command of all air units in the theater. As the general's supporters pointed out, despite massive logistical problems, the Fourteenth Air Force had compiled an impressive record against the Japanese. In three years of combat, American fliers claimed some 2,600 enemy aircraft destroyed and 2,230 million tons of shipping sunk or damaged. Washington, however, had a different perspective. "Everyone agrees," Air Force commander Henry H. Arnold had written in 1943, "on his exceptionally able tactical control of operations and his combat successes." But Chennault did not "exercise the necessary administrative and executive control of his present units to warrant independence." Arnold never changed his mind, and an embittered Chennault retired shortly before Japan surrendered.[1]

Anger, disappointment, and frustration seemed to plague Chennault's career. Perhaps it had something to do with his French Huguenot heritage — they were a people known for passionate dissent. Born in Texas in 1890, Chennault grew up amid the woods, bayous, and lakes of northeastern Louisiana. His mother died when he was five. When Chennault was ten, his father married Lottie Barnes, a grade school teacher whom Chennault later recalled with affection for fostering his ambition and love of learning.[2]

Chennault entered Louisiana State University in 1908, the year his beloved stepmother died. After two years, he left Baton Rouge to teach in a one-room school in rural Louisiana. Other posts followed: he taught English at a business college in Biloxi, Mississippi, and he was assistant director of physical training at the YMCA in Louisville, Kentucky. Family responsibilities and limited resources finally forced Chennault to abandon the teaching profession. American entry into World War I in April 1917 found him married, with three children, and working in a tire factory in Akron, Ohio.[3]

Chennault, who as a boy had dreamed of a military career, entered Officers' Training School at Fort Benjamin Harrison, Indiana, in August 1917. Emerging ninety days later as a freshly minted lieutenant in the Infantry Reserve, he was assigned to duty with the Ninetieth Division in San Antonio, Texas. San Antonio's Kelly Field was the center of training for military aviators. Chennault had been caught up in the romance of flight ever since he had first seen a Curtiss pusher biplane at the Louisiana State Fair in 1910. He made up his mind to become an aviator and volunteered for the Air Service but was turned down because of his age and marital status. It took nearly two years of persistent effort—a quality Chennault would amply demonstrate throughout his later career—before the determined young man entered flight school and won his wings.[4]

In fall 1920 Chennault secured a regular commission in the newly organized Air Service. A variety of assignments followed over the next seventeen years, including command of the Nineteenth Pursuit Squadron in Hawaii, 1923–26, which he recalled as "my happiest time in the Air Corps," and instructor at the Air Corps Tactical School, Maxwell Field, Alabama.[5]

A man who always seemed to be marching to the beat of a different drummer and tended to be passionate in his commitments, Chennault championed fighters at a time when most contemporaries believed that the future lay with bombers. He wrote treatises on pursuit tactics (*The Role of Defensive Pursuit*, 1935), led an acrobatic team to demonstrate his theories, and stepped on the toes of superiors. His career languished. Passed over for promotion, a frustrated Chennault retired as a captain in April 1937, partially deaf from long hours in open cockpits and suffering from chronic bronchitis.[6]

Retirement opened a new and crucial phase in Chennault's career. Through the efforts of Roy Holbrook, an American friend with the Chinese government, he obtained a three-month contract to make a confidential survey of the Chinese Air Force (CAF). He had barely begun his assignment when the Marco Polo Bridge incident of July 7, 1937, plunged China and Japan into full-scale war. Volunteering his services to the Nationalist government, Chennault assumed duties with an air force that his survey had revealed to be in deplorable condition. Throughout the summer, in the face of overwhelming Japanese superiority, Chennault made do as best he could, even leading Chinese air units into battle on occasion. By October, however, the air war had been lost.[7]

Chennault retreated with the government into the interior, opened a flight training school at Kunming, and began the seemingly hopeless task of rebuilding the Chinese Air Force. He shared with Nationalist leaders the dark days of 1938–39, a time when China seemed bereft of friends and hope. His loyalty would long be remembered.[8]

American economic assistance to China began in 1940. As Washington's relations with Japan worsened, President Franklin D. Roosevelt entertained a number of esoteric schemes to counter Tokyo's aggressive behavior. One of these involved the use of "volunteer" American aviators, recruited from the military services with official sanction, to protect the land supply route from Burma to China. Chennault, an early advocate of the plan, took command of the American Volunteer Group (AVG) in summer 1941.[9]

Overcoming difficulties that would have daunted a less determined man, Chennault had the AVG ready for action on the eve of Pearl Harbor. Over the next seven months, the Flying Tigers, as the AVG came to be known, earned a reputation as the most effective Allied fighter group in the Far East, destroying some three hundred enemy planes at a cost of twelve aircraft and four pilots lost in aerial combat. During a time of deep despair, when news from abroad sounded like a litany of disaster, the success of Chennault's young fliers in their shark-nosed P-40s gave hope to Americans. For many, the craggy-faced, square-jawed leader of the AVG seemed the very symbol of determined resistance.[10]

Recalled to active duty as a brigadier general in April 1942, Chennault had no sooner taken command of American air units in China when he became embroiled in a controversy with his superiors that would last throughout the war. In part, the problem turned on personality. Theater commander Joseph W. Stilwell shared in full measure Chennault's talent for combat leadership, but neither man claimed tact and diplomacy as strong suits. "Vinegar Joe" Stilwell, Theodore White recalls, "was pure Yankee; strait-laced; crisp in diction; whatever [Chief of Staff] George Marshall and the United States needed of him, he would do." From the beginning, Stilwell had reservations about his subordinate. "Chennault," Stilwell wrote to General Marshall in October 1942, "has decided limitations. Within his sphere he is superior, but his administration is terrible and his judgment of men is weak."[11]

Chennault and Stilwell were soon at odds over matters of high strategy. An impassioned advocate of air power, Chennault wanted to use the theater's limited resources to fight an air war against Japan. Stilwell disagreed, emphasizing the need to train Chinese ground forces to open a land supply route to China and defend the Fourteenth Air Force's advanced bases. Always prone to overstatement, Chennault argued long and loud that Stilwell lacked appreciation for air power. Stilwell made no secret of his conviction that Chennault had a grossly inflated concept of the ability of air power to affect the course of the war.[12]

Under normal circumstances, the strategic view of the senior military commander would determine the course of events; but the China theater was not normal. Chennault's emphasis on air power had the enthusiastic support of Chiang Kai-shek. President Roosevelt, unable to provide any significant logistical support for China, also found Chennault's views seductive. Following the Trident conference of May 1943, Roosevelt ordered an emphasis on air power. The result was disaster. As Stilwell had predicted, the Japanese reacted promptly and vigorously, overrunning Chennault's forward bases in East China. His strategy discredited, Chennault's influence faded in Washington.

Chennault may have been a thorn in the side of his American superiors, but his relations with Chiang Kai-shek remained excellent throughout the war, perhaps because he deferred to the generalissimo, showed no interest in China's internal politics, and rarely criticized the Chinese war effort. Even below the highest levels of government, however, Chennault got along much better with Chinese than did most of his countrymen. As General Albert C. Wedemeyer, Stilwell's successor, later observed, "General Chennault enjoyed the confidence and respect of the Chinese officials, both military and civil, and the Chinese people loved and respected him also. Actually he was a national hero, and I believe deservedly so."[13]

Before his departure from Kunming in summer 1945, Chennault had extensive discussions with Lung Yun, governor of Yunnan province, and Dr. Y. T. Miao, prominent businessman and government economist, about postwar possibilities in the area. The Yunnanese officials, anxious to preserve a measure of independence from the central government, suggested that Chennault return to China and head a provincial airline that would serve as Yunnan's link to the outside world. The line would carry tin, Yunnan's main export, to ports in Indochina, developing a tourist traffic on the return trip. Chennault was sufficiently interested in the project to approach several subordinates about joining the airline in managerial positions.[14]

Chennault, however, was not the only one interested in China's postwar aeronautical development. One of the general's wartime associates, Whiting Willauer, also had plans to exploit air transportation opportunities in the war-ravaged country.

Whiting Willauer would have been comfortable in Elizabethan England, where he happily would have set sail in quest of greater glory for country and self, profit, and adventure. Impetuous, intelligent, hardworking, and fiercely loyal to friends, he belonged on the quarterdeck with Drake and Hawkins. He once boasted that he was not afraid of anything. "Yes, you are," his wife replied, "you're afraid of being afraid."[15]

Born in New York City on November 30, 1906, Willauer grew up with upper-middle-class values, though sometimes lacking upper-middle-class affluence. His father, Arthur Ebbs Willauer, was a prominent architect who died when Willauer was six years old, leaving his mother, Katherine Whiting Willauer, to raise four young children, among whom Whiting was the oldest.[16]

Willauer attended private schools in New York, St. Albans in Washington, and the Stone School. He was a good student, as a yellowed report card from St. Albans testifies: "Head of his form: a splendid record." His home life did not go as well. His mother remarried, and Willauer did not care for his stepfather. In 1918 Katherine Willauer Witridge died while working in a hospital during the great influenza epidemic.[17]

The strongest female influence in young Willauer's life—an influence enhanced by his mother's untimely death—was his grandmother, Daisy Day Whiting. A fiercely independent woman, she became a pioneer interior decorator after her husband had lost the family's money. When interviewed in 1953 about his early life, Willauer barely mentioned his mother, but he recalled with admiration the grandmother who had trained him to handle money and pointed him toward a legal career.[18]

The other major influence on Willauer, especially during his impressionable early teenage years, was his uncle, Kenneth Whiting. Handsome, dashing, and hard-drinking, Whiting was a career naval officer who had made a reputation in submarines before moving on to aviation. He won his wings in 1914, fought for development of the air arm, and led the first American naval aviation detachment to Europe in 1917. "After the war," a naval historian has written, "more than any other single officer, he helped plan the U.S. Navy's first carriers, served in, and commanded them." Willauer remembered that a visit at age twelve to a Loening aircraft factory with Uncle Ken spurred an already strong desire to become a naval aviator. But both his uncle and grandmother later encouraged the young man to think about a nonmilitary career. The navy, Commander Whiting said, was not the place to be in the postwar era of disarmament.[19]

Willauer graduated from the Stone School at age sixteen, and the family decided to send him to Exeter for a year before entering college. Exeter led to Princeton, where Willauer blossomed. The school brought out with special intensity the dual aspects of his nature. The active, competitive Willauer excelled on the athletic field, playing fullback on the varsity football team; the reflective, romantic Willauer responded to the intellectual influence of Professor Robert Root, a noted Chaucerian scholar. In his last year at Princeton, Willauer was captain of the lacrosse team while writing his senior thesis, "Platonic Influences in Shelley." He graduated with honors in 1928.[20]

Willauer loved the sea and during summer vacations taught sailing at the West Chop Club on Martha's Vineyard. On a trip to Nantucket in 1929, he met Louise Russell. Attractive, strong-willed, and affluent (her maternal grandfather was a founder of Union Carbide), Louise had rebelled against parental wishes, gone to secretarial school instead of college, and was working for a newspaper on the island. After the usual fits and starts of young love, they were married on June 21, 1930. The newlyweds moved to Cambridge while Willauer completed his last year at Harvard Law School. Louise attended Radcliffe for a time but had to drop out while awaiting the arrival of Whiting Russell Willauer, the first of three children. He was born on May 24, 1931, the day before his father's final examinations.[21]

Willauer did well at Harvard, graduating sixty-fifth in a class of 408. He joined the prominent Boston firm of Bingham, Dana & Gould, specializing in the investigation and trial of transportation cases. Restless in private practice and entertaining thoughts of a political career, he left Boston in January 1939 and took a position in Washington with the Civil Aeronautics Board. Later in the year, he transferred to the Department of Justice and worked on cases involving political corruption. He soon was one of three lawyers in the department assigned to subversive activities. "It was during this work," he recalled, "that my eyes were first really opened to the techniques of international subversion. Although it is true that the major enemy in those days seemed to be the Nazis . . . we also got a fairly good beginning into an indoctrination as to the aims and methods of the Communist conspiracy." In January 1941 he became special counsel to the Federal Power Commission, assigned to work on the proposed St. Lawrence Seaway.[22]

The early months of 1941 saw rising international tensions as the United States edged closer to confrontations with Germany and Japan. Willauer, who held a reserve commission in naval intelligence, volunteered for active duty but failed the physical examination because of a history of frequent dislocations of the right shoulder stemming from a lacrosse injury and a recent incidence of pleurisy (later diagnosed as embolism). Distressed at the prospect of remaining behind a desk during times of crisis, Willauer contacted an old Exeter-Princeton roommate, Howard F. Corcoran, about a job with the newly formed China Defense Supplies, Incorporated (CDS).[23]

CDS had been formed in spring 1941 as the official Chinese counterpart agency to coordinate lend-lease activities after President Roosevelt had declared China eligible for American assistance. T. V. Soong, China's sometime foreign minister, headed CDS, aided by David M. Corcoran (Howard's brother) and a group of Americans. Thomas G. Corcoran, oldest of the Corcoran brothers and formerly a close personal adviser to President Roosevelt, was the organization's political mentor.[24]

Willauer joined CDS in July 1941 and assisted in setting up Chennault's American Volunteer Group. He spent most of the war years in China on a variety of field assignments, mainly dealing with the logistical problems of

Chennault's Fourteenth Air Force. Willauer enjoyed the excitement and sense of purpose provided by his wartime duties. "I am one of TV's [Soong] staff," he wrote to his wife in 1943, "considered as a part of the operating machinery with the right to make decisions and to take action which will have tangible results. . . . I, like everyone, must have a sense of accomplishment some of the time to be happy. Also I must admit that the minor sense of personal danger some of the time, such as during air raids, or flying the hump, seems to give a good reaction. In a strange way it makes living seem more useful." Willauer later told his wife that he would not be content in a desk job in a law office after the "heady medicine" of the war years. "Indeed," he concluded, "I shall have a hell of a time going back into anything much less exciting than the war job."[25]

In May 1944 Willauer became director of the Far East and Special Territories Branch in the Foreign Economic Administration. Concerned with economic intelligence, procurement of strategic materials, and postwar planning, he spent the summer of 1945 in the Philippines, trying to restore that nation's economy. Willauer also thought about his own future. He hoped one day to be able to work "in important international things" for the government. "I shall have to have some money for that," he confided to his wife, "and I think if I could pile up about a quarter of a million to a half-million due to some fortunate set of circumstances I would have the necessary financial prerequisite."[26]

In search of adventure, a sense of accomplishment, and enough money to finance the life he desired, Willauer returned to the United States in fall 1945 and became involved in the Corcoran brothers' plans to take advantage of postwar entrepreneurial opportunities around the world. Willauer wanted to start an airline in China, and he needed financial backing. In September 1945 Thomas and David Corcoran and William S. Youngman, a partner in Thomas Corcoran's Washington law firm, formed Rio Cathay– S.A., a Panamanian corporation, for the purpose of pursuing business ventures in China and South America. Rio Cathay arranged with Pennsylvania Central Airlines (PCA) for a fee of $50,000 to fund preliminary work on Willauer's airline scheme. A letter of instruction to Willauer set forth the original scope of the venture: "You will, for the account of PCA, make in China a survey of the possibilities of ownership or operation by PCA of a civilian freight and passenger airline in China (including Manchuria), Burma and French Indo-China. The survey shall cover, among other things, technical, commercial, competitive and legal factors, and prospective relationships with lines entering China from other countries."[27]

While making arrangements for the trip to China, Willauer approached General Chennault and suggested that he join the Rio Cathay group. The general told Willauer about his own plans for a postwar airline in Yunnan

Province. That scheme, however, seemed less promising following the over-throw of Governor Lung Yun, Chennault's key supporter. Also, the central government no doubt would oppose Yunnan's bid for greater autonomy. After some discussion, they decided to merge the two ventures. Rio Cathay then secured $35,000 from PCA for Chennault. The necessary financial arrangements completed, the two men headed for Shanghai, China's commercial Mecca, before year's end.[28]

Wracked by inflation, hopelessly corrupt and cynical, postwar Shanghai struggled to resume its role as foremost outpost of Western capitalism in Asia. Old China hands recalled a city of skyscrapers and broad avenues, hovels and narrow lanes, heady affluence and desperate poverty. These contradictory realities remained constant, but the war had brought dramatic changes. The end of extraterritoriality had made Chinese government authority more evident, even though foreign taipans scoffed at the inefficiency of oriental administration. Above all, American influence was ubiquitous. The stars and stripes flew from the mastheads of great warships crowding the Whangpoo River, a "U.S. Navy Hamburger Stand" did a booming business on The Bund, the French Club was now an American officers' club, and General Wedemeyer occupied Sir Victor Sassoon's quarters at the Cathay Hotel. New Year's Day 1946 brought a symbolic change of the imperial guard when traffic flow in the city switched from the left to the right side of the street.[29]

After arranging for temporary offices and housing in the overcrowded metropolis, Chennault and Willauer left in early January 1946 for a survey of Chungking and Kunming. Air transport seemed a natural field for development. China's inadequate road and railroad systems had been ravaged by nearly a decade of war. Air was the only means available for rapid movement of people and important cargo, and demand far exceeded supply. "Every other form of transport is stalled," Willauer reported. There was a passenger waiting list of fifty thousand in Kunming; even though willing to pay the full round trip air fare to Shanghai, plus a black market premium, people were unable to obtain seats.[30]

Chennault had no difficulty in arranging meetings with important Chinese officials to discuss plans for a new air service. T. V. Soong, now president of the Executive Yuan, was interested; General Chou Chih-jou, director of the National Aeronautical Commission, and Yu Fei-peng, minister of communications, promised support. Most important, Chennault had the sympathetic ear of Madame Chiang Kai-shek, his wartime patron. "We have been promised the full cooperation of Madame Chiang," Willauer noted with pleasure following a luncheon meeting with the influential wife of China's president.[31]

Events during his first weeks in China filled Willauer with optimism. "We have been enthusiastically received everywhere with our idea of really making an overall approach to the Air Transport problem," he wrote in mid-January. China's needs were so great that the opportunity for additional air service was undeniable. Indeed, improvement of civilian air transport was "one of the most important steps to be taken to hold the country together politically and economically." An enormous amount of work would be required to establish an airline. "But after all," Willauer told his wife, "that is not much bigger than the old jobs during the war, and I feel confident that out of the process big things will come, both for China and for those with whom we are working."[32]

This initial optimism soon faded as Chennault and Willauer learned more about the realities of Chinese politics. Two airlines already were entrenched in China. The China National Aviation Corporation (CNAC), 80 percent owned by the Chinese government and 20 percent by Pan American Airways, operated approximately thirty aircraft, while the smaller Central Air Transport Corporation (CATC), entirely owned by the government, had a dozen C-47s in service. Both companies, backed by powerful political interests within the factional Nationalist government, had plans to expand service and objected to increased competition. CNAC officials, especially vociferous in guarding the airline's premier position in the field, argued that competition at this stage would likely hinder the orderly development of air transportation services in China.[33]

Potential competition certainly was not lacking. Indeed, the Ministry of Communications (MOC) was awash in applications from private and semiofficial groups to establish new airlines. Most applicants could be fended off on the ground that CNAC and CATC were China's chosen instruments in the field of air transport, but some interests were too powerful to be so easily thwarted. The government, for example, was under great pressure to permit operations by the Great China Aviation Corporation, an organization backed by a coalition of influential businessmen and politicians.[34]

Strong opposition to the two Americans also appeared from elements in the central government who viewed with hostility non-Chinese ownership of transportation facilities. Chennault, Willauer, and their supporters were well aware that nationalism was a volatile issue, part of a general antiforeign bias in postwar China, that was capable of generating considerable popular sentiment. Some proponents of Chinese control no doubt acted out of principle, but more cynical observers saw other motives on the part of certain individuals who sought to inflame public opinion against foreigners. As Willauer pointed out, "Government ownership gives a wonderful fund of political patronage."[35]

Finally, there existed considerable doubt that China's depleted reserves of foreign exchange could support additional aeronautical enterprises. Arthur N. Young, financial adviser to the government, strongly opposed any increase in civil aviation, arguing that its expansion "threatens to involve foreign exchange costs beyond what China can afford to allocate." He recommended that all airline flying be limited to the current level of five hundred thousand miles a month, representing an annual cost of $10 million in foreign exchange.[36]

What proved to be the key for operations in China came at 10:00 A.M., February 6, when Colonel Ralph W. Olmstead, director of operations for the United Nations Relief and Rehabilitation Administration (UNRRA), asked Chennault and Willauer to draft a proposal for an airline to carry UNRRA relief supplies that were piling up in coastal ports. Twenty-four hectic hours later, Olmstead had in hand the draft of a contract with "Chennault Airlines" to transport relief supplies to inland points and operate a commercial cargo service on the return portion of the trip. UNRRA, through its Chinese counterpart the Chinese National Relief and Rehabilitation Administration (CNRRA), would provide funds to purchase the necessary aircraft and equipment. Chennault and Willauer would operate the service and contribute working capital and their management skills. Olmstead recommended approval of the scheme to his superiors in UNRRA.[37]

Chennault and Willauer immediately went to work to obtain the necessary sanction of the Chinese government. The resulting negotiations, Willauer wrote, proved "a difficult and wearing operation." Chennault, at one point, wanted to give up and go home. Willauer often considered "throwing in the sponge." Finally, progress was made. Willauer forced CNAC to admit that it could fill only a fraction of China's relief needs. He countered Young's objections by pointing out that foreign exchange would be supplied by UNRRA; there would be no additional drain on China's dwindling reserves. Emphasis on the relief character of the enterprise also helped to undermine opposition on nationalistic grounds. Following a series of deft maneuvers, and with crucial support from T. V. Soong, the Chinese government in late April gave tentative approval for operation of the relief airline.[38]

UNRRA's consent proved an even thornier problem when the airline project became the focal point in a continuing dispute between UNRRA and CNRRA over the conduct of relief operations in China. Some three weeks after securing approval for the airline from the Chinese government, Willauer reported in despair: "As of today the whole show seems to be lost."[39]

In early May a long-simmering dispute between T. V. Soong and T. F. Tsiang (Chiang Ting-fu), director of CNRRA, came to a head when two senior UNRRA officials arrived in China to lend support to Tsiang and work for Olmstead's removal. Willauer, rightly or wrongly, viewed the dispute primarily as a battle by Soong and Olmstead against corrupt practices. "CNRRA is the biggest piece of political patronage in China today," he explained to his wife. "The way the racket works is that by the basic UNRRA agreement with China, CNRRA has the right of distribution of materials imported by UNRRA. Since the total is $600,000,000, and much is bought at big discounts through surplus, the racket is worth a billion or more. There can be little doubt that it is being used as a racket, and that the goods are coming on the market at high prices. The evidence is scandalously clear." Olmstead, supported by Soong, was trying to deliver supplies directly into the interior of China, bypassing Shanghai. "Shanghai," Willauer continued, "is the place where the corrupt ones in CNRRA want most of the things, and since there is a tremendous amount of money in it for CNRRA if they control the transport of such of them as they ship out of Shanghai, R's [Olmstead] policy ran squarely into their racket." Determined to control distribution, CNRRA wanted to operate the proposed relief airline "as their own little racket, if it is run at all."[40]

Olmstead was convinced that opposition to the program was politically inspired by Communist influences. Willauer claimed to have "positive proof" that a senior official of UNRRA "was a Communist who was trying to sabotage Olmstead from creating UNRRA into an effective agency." His proof apparently consisted of an overheard conversation, an intercepted letter by the senior UNRRA official to a prominent Communist in the United States, and the fact that the mistress of an associate of the senior official had held an important post with the Institute of Pacific Relations.[41]

The Communist threat to the airline, Willauer believed, was part of a larger effort to wreck all relief activity in China and undermine the National- ist government and was related to the worldwide Communist conspiracy, directed from Moscow. Russian policy, Willauer wrote to Henry R. Luce, influential publisher of *Time* and *Life* and Willauer's longtime friend, was aimed at "communizing the world, sometime, somehow." Moscow's tech- nique was to "proceed simultaneously on all fronts which *might* somehow, somewhere, become advantageous. One thing she has in great abundance is a stable of thoroughly trained political organizers of almost all races and creeds, and the product of decades of training in her superlative political schools. Therefore unless she fears, or can be brought to fear, a serious world reaction against political infiltration, she is bound to continue to use these men throughout the world, for a variety of purposes ranging from mere observers to fomenters of open strife."

Willauer rejected the popular view of China as "a nation of property- loving farmers who would never fall for communism because of their love of property and their natural independence toward regimentation." The Com- munists regularly adopted popular objectives as a way to gain power, hence the present emphasis on agrarian reform rather than collectivism. "But," Willauer warned, "Lord help those objectives once control is established."

The United States should develop "a positive, long range policy of moral and material support to China, which is publicly announced, and which will be given almost the dignity of a treaty." Such a policy would not be easy to implement because there existed considerable American distrust of Nationalist officials — "some of which [is] justified." The bureaucracy was characterized by inefficiency, and some "downright stealing" had taken place. But Willauer optimistically argued that "with proper technical and financial help the best leaders of China would today gladly embark on any reasonable reform measure."

Willauer admitted that his views of Communist intentions lacked solid evidence, "but what else could or should we do here than to take something on a bit of faith? If everything I fear about Russian policy proves to be wrong, and she would like to see a peaceful, prosperous, and reasonably democratic China, she can hardly take offense. But if I am right in holding the other view, we have then tried to buy the only existing insurance policy against chaos among a quarter of the world's population."[42]

While Willauer and Olmstead struggled in China against efforts to undermine the airline project, the major battle for UNRRA's approval was being fought in the United States. It was at this juncture that Thomas Corcoran, a veteran Washington lobbyist, brought to bear his considerable political talents. The details of his activities are unclear. A cautious man by nature, even when communicating with close associates, Corcoran mentioned only the "hard fight" in gaining approval from UNRRA and the State Department for the airline and alluded to the machinations of "the old opposition." Corcoran's efforts proved successful, although only after the personal intervention of Fiorello LaGuardia, director-general of UNRRA, was final clearance granted.[43]

On October 25, 1946, Chennault and Willauer signed the contract with CNRRA creating CNRRA Air Transport (CAT). The agreement stipulated that UNRRA would allocate $2 million to CNRRA for purchase of aircraft and equipment, and would provide an additional $1.8 million in foreign exchange for payment of wages to foreign personnel, and purchase of fuel and other imports.[44] CAT would operate the aircraft primarily to carry relief supplies from coastal ports into the interior of China. Although CNRRA cargo would have first priority, CAT could sell unused return space to the general public at prevailing commercial rates. CNRRA would pay CAT forty-six cents per ton-mile for the first 10 percent of relief cargo flown each month and ninety cents per ton-mile for the remainder. Chennault and Willauer were obligated to furnish $1 million for working capital and to absorb any losses in the conduct of

Claire L. Chennault (Courtesy Felix Smith)

operations. Most important, they were granted an option to purchase the aircraft at cost plus 10 percent interest, compounded annually.[45]

Criticism of CAT appeared before the ink had dried on the contract. A group of disgruntled Chinese businessmen who had failed in their efforts to enter the commercial aviation field attacked the proposal as a thinly disguised scheme to establish a private American airline in China. The *China Press* cited the generous provisions for purchase of the aircraft and agreed that the original humanitarian purposes of the operation had been steadily diluted by self-interest. "One may of course argue," it continued, "that Chennault's airline will be aiding the distribution of supplies, that is true. But it will be a minor operation, the major operation being to earn profits as a purely commercial airline."[46]

Stung by this public criticism (which hit a bit too close to home), Willauer promptly responded in a letter to the editor of the *China Press*. He defended the sincerity of Chennault's desire to assist the Chinese people in time of need, and he denied the insinuation that the general was "a profit seeking commercialist." Furthermore, the contract with CNRRA guaranteed that priority would be given to relief cargo. CAT's rates would be reasonable, and there was no guarantee of profit. "It is true," he acknowledged, "because of his long experience in operating air transports in China on a minimum of supplies General Chennault believes that he can repay all funds advanced to equip and operate the airline, but he greatly fears the possibility of some deficit at the end of the operation." Complaints of unfair practices were not new, Willauer concluded; they had all been raised previously "by representatives of certain interests who are anxious to perpetuate themselves in a monopoly position in China." They were completely without foundation, then or now.[47]

Near disaster came more quickly than Willauer could have imagined. Just as months of difficult labor had come to happy fruition with conclusion of an operating agreement, the entire project threatened to collapse because of the lack of essential operating funds. "I don't think either the General or I will ever forget the shock when we received the cable [from Corcoran] that the much-needed financial support had been withdrawn," Willauer recalled. "We were left with an airline franchise and airline equipment, but only enough money between us to carry on as we were and to pay our loyal employees for about a month and a half longer. At the end of that time all would have been wasted."[48]

During the early stages of negotiations, Pennsylvania Central Airlines, original backer of the project, appeared ready to supply the necessary funds to begin the operation. These plans fell through, however, and Chennault had to return to the United States to assist Corcoran in search of financial support. Sometime during summer 1946, Chennault concluded an agree-

Whiting Willauer

ment with Robert Prescott, former member of the American Volunteer Group and now head of Flying Tiger Line, a pioneer air freight operation, whereby Prescott would lend CAT the necessary operating capital in return for an equity of 24 percent in the airline. Following a personal survey of the situation in China, Prescott advanced an initial $20,000 to CAT and sent out his brother, George Lewis Prescott, an accountant, to control expenses.[49]

Unfortunately an accident destroyed these carefully laid plans. George Prescott was quietly sitting on a couch in the Hotel Manila on October 5, having come to the Philippines to check on the purchase of surplus C-47s, when he was caught in the middle of a gun battle between rival Filipino gangster factions. Struck in the head by a stray .45 caliber slug, he died instantly. Robert Prescott, who apparently had reservations about the scheme, pulled out of the China venture in the wake of his brother's untimely death.[50]

At the same time that arrangements with Prescott fell apart, Willauer received depressing news from Corcoran. "I have . . . been impressed from our experience with the airline," he wrote to Willauer in early October, "that the romance of China has about worn out in the American securities market due to the amount of finagling done by all kinds of people representing themselves as important Chinese interests — and that any substantial capital coming from American bankers — which as I told you in an early letter is ultimately the American securities market — has got to show profits or profit-making capacity on the basis of real earnings or well-documented figures and contracts — not on the lovely kind of boloney off-paper stuff on which we tried to sell this airline." Terming the venture "a nightmare for a Cotton-Franklin trained banker like me," Corcoran said that he intended to concentrate on more lucrative projects in South America.[51]

With CAT's meager funds being rapidly depleted and lacking prospects — and time — for American financing, Willauer turned in desperation to Chinese businessmen. L. K. Taylor, a wartime associate, and Wang Wen-san, manager of the Kincheng Bank, a large Chinese commercial institution, put together a syndicate of financial backers, headed by Wang Yuan-ling, that offered a loan of $250,000 (in Chinese currency). The terms, as Willauer had expected, were stiff. The loan, which represented only one-quarter of the originally desired operating capital, would run for eighteen months at interest. In return, the Chinese financiers would obtain an equity of 42 percent in the airline. Willauer had no choice but to agree. The working capital was paid in on November 30, 1946.[52]

Although Willauer had saved CAT from an early demise, he received little thanks from backers in the United States. In a sharp letter, Corcoran argued that Willauer should have held out for a better agreement. Furthermore, Corcoran continued, American capital was still a possibility. He pointedly reminded Willauer that his associates had expended $120,000 on the airline project over the past fifteen months, as well as enormous effort to secure UNRRA's blessing. During negotiations with Prescott, Chennault had agreed that Prescott would receive an equity of only 24 percent in the airline, with Chennault and Willauer obtaining 38.5 percent, and 37.5 percent going to Corcoran and his associates. The new arrangement, with greater Chinese equity, meant that Corcoran would receive only 28.5 percent. "To be frank with you, Whitey," Corcoran concluded, "the commitments I made here to help get the Chennault airline going as far as it has make it essential that this side get the percentage of stock on which I agreed with the General."[53]

Willauer may not have fully understood the problems in the United States, but Corcoran failed to appreciate the situation in China. Money had been needed immediately or everything would have been lost. Moreover, as Willauer pointed out to Corcoran, Chinese participation was proving essential to the success of the enterprise. "If today we had to bear the burden of being U.S. financed," Willauer told Corcoran, "we would not have a chance of either temporary or permanent survival in China."

Most disturbing to Willauer was an apparent lack of concern for Chennault's contribution to the scheme. Chennault had taken "a hell of a beating" in carrying out the project, Willauer argued. "He would have abandoned it in April 1946 unless I had persuaded him to stick it out. In the process of these negotiations he has lost one hell of a lot of face and has seriously impaired his health." Chennault's association with the project was the key to raising the necessary capital, and "that was always the crux of the deal." Willauer concluded: "I am sick and tired of what appears to be a failure to appreciate General Chennault's position with reference to the job which has been accomplished in establishing CNRRA Air Transport as a going concern. I insist that he be given a one-third (1/3) share of the American interest in CNRRA Air Transport or any successor, without any reservations of any kind whatsoever." In a quixotic gesture, Willauer enclosed a deed of trust and gave Corcoran the power to make any necessary adjustment to guarantee Chennault's proper share of the enterprise. "From my point of view," Willauer emphasized, "I do not give a damn what I get out of this thing so long as I have made a success of getting the thing going and operating it."[54]

Early one morning in November, at a time when the entire project teetered on the brink of disaster, Willauer woke from a troubled sleep and muttered to his wife, "If I ever do put this thing over everyone will say, 'Yes, but it was easy for General Chennault and Willauer to get things done in China.'"[55]

It had of course been anything but easy to breathe life into the airline scheme that had been conceived in Washington in fall 1945. Chennault may have been a national hero in China with excellent connections to the generalissimo, but this did not guarantee success for the enterprise — it only made success a possibility. Chiang Kai-shek governed by maintaining a careful balance among competing interests. Chennault and his airline were only minor factors in a greater political game. If he could bring the project to the point where Chiang could approve it without significant political damage, well and good, but there never was the slightest prospect of direct intervention from the top against the powerful Chinese factions that opposed the airline.

Chennault and Willauer had superbly navigated the treacherous crosscurrents of Chinese politics. Chennault opened key doors, leaving the energetic Willauer to shoulder the burden of negotiation. Willauer performed with consummate skill, in large part because of his positive attitude. Unlike many prewar businessmen who found it difficult to adjust to a China without the privileges of extraterritoriality, Willauer had no problem with the new realities. "I have struggled with the vagaries of Chinese government for four years," Willauer noted shortly after arriving in Shanghai, "and I do not expect it to be a government in our sense of the word. So when something does happen, as it sometimes does, I feel pleased. With the others, there is a constant state of resentment that more does not happen. The net result is more cussing than analysis."[56]

Credit should also go to Corcoran, who guided the scheme through the tricky and, at times, Byzantine world of American politics. Although the details of his activities are lacking, it is not hard to imagine the pixieish lobbyist at work, exploiting his friendships with the movers and shakers in Washington, manipulating the smoke and mirrors that transform the illusion of power into reality.[57]

The talents of Chennault, Willauer, and Corcoran were equally crucial to the initial success of the project. They had brought the idea of an airline to the reality of aircraft, pilots, and routes. With great difficulty and after considerable frustration, they had secured a temporary franchise from the Nationalist government. The contract with CNRRA involved some risk, but it offered attractive possibilities for profit. And operating capital had been raised, even if not on the most favorable terms.

But there had been a cost. As Willauer noted earlier, Chennault's public stature in China had been tarnished: the heroic military figure had been forced to dirty his hands in the rough-and-tumble world of commercial competition. Also, the search for working capital had damaged the relationship between Corcoran and Willauer. As his wife remarked, "I have never seen Whitey so thoroughly kicked in the teeth by people he thought were his friends, and I'm not talking about Chinese people." Much of this damage would be repaired, but a residue of bitterness and misunderstanding would remain.[58]

Ahead lay the challenging task of making an airline, which so far had existed only on paper, into a going concern. As events during the winter of 1946–47 made clear, operating aircraft in China was a hazardous undertaking.

2 CNRRA Air Transport

Christmas Day 1946 dawned damp and bleak in Shanghai, further depressing the spirits of Westerners forced to spend the holidays far from home. Heavy fog blanketed the city throughout the morning. The afternoon brought drizzle and fog so dense that visibility was restricted to a few feet. Despite the terrible flying weather, four aircraft approached Shanghai for landing as night fell. Perhaps the pilots, eager to reach their home base for Christmas, had been seduced by forecasts promising a break in the weather; perhaps they had placed undue confidence in their alternate landing areas. For whatever reason, four young fliers soon found themselves in deep trouble.

The tragedy of what became known as "Black Christmas" began shortly after 6:00 P.M. A CATC transport, attempting to land at Kiangwan field, one of Shanghai's three airports, hit a house short of the runway, exploded, and burned.

Captain William Greenwood, flying a CNAC DC-3, also arrived over Shanghai to find all airports closed by fog, as were nearby alternatives. The weather was better at Tsingtao, 350 miles away, but Greenwood decided against it because there were no runway lights. Kiangwan, used by the American Army Air Force's Air Transport Command, had long, well-lighted runways and radar landing facilities (ground controlled approach or GCA). As Greenwood made his approach to the field, he lost radio contact with Kiangwan's GCA unit. He then decided to try an automatic direction finding (ADF) landing at Lunghwa field, CNAC's main base. Although ADF was less precise than radar, Greenwood was thoroughly familiar with the procedure, having used it at Lunghwa many times in the past.

Greenwood went through the ritual heading-time-distance of ADF procedure several times, but he could not find the field. Nearly out of fuel, he had no option but to continue attempts to penetrate the dense fog. On the ground, anxious spectators heard the aircraft approach from the southwest.

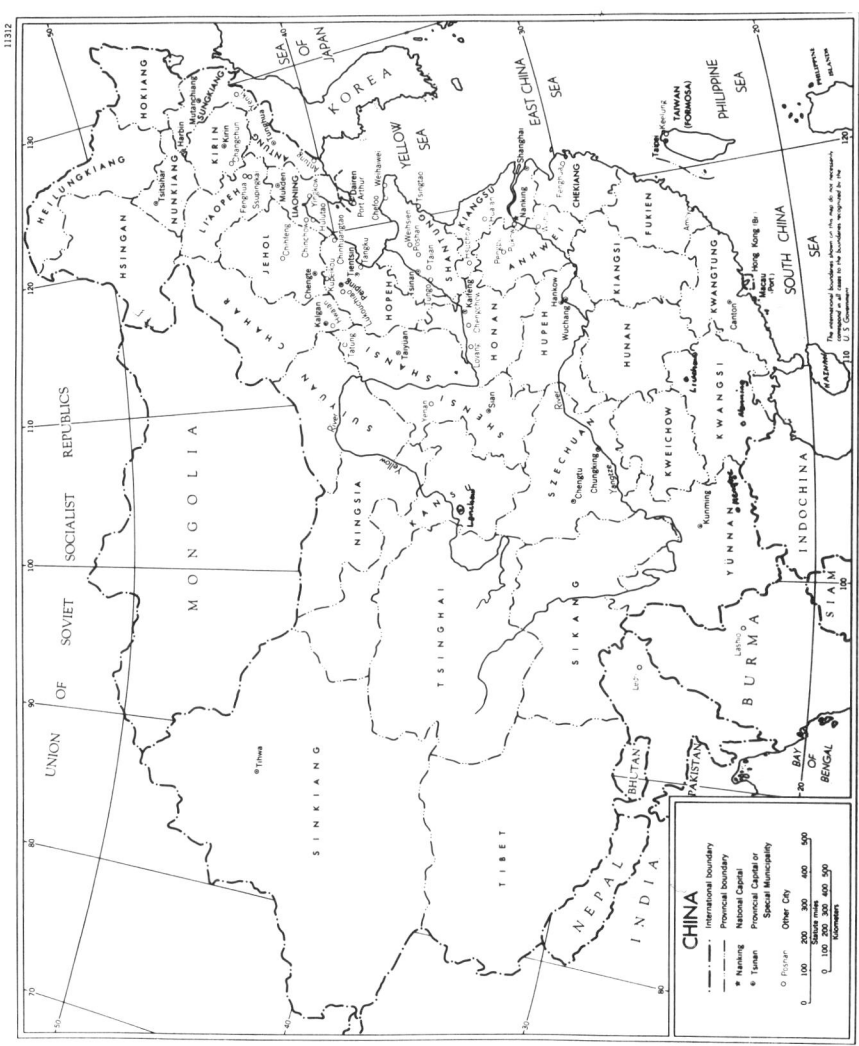

Map A: China, 1947

The engines gradually grew to a roar, the whistling of the airfoils clearly audible. Suddenly, a dull red cone appeared in the fog some two hundred yards from the control tower; a muffled boom followed in an instant. Then, except for a hushed, "God! oh God!" from one of the stunned onlookers, the silence was complete.

While a ground party searched for the wreckage, a second CNAC aircraft, assisted by GCA, landed successfully at Kiangwan. But Captain Rolf Preus, in command of a CNAC C-46 that lacked the VHF radio equipment necessary to establish contact with GCA, remained overhead. Unaware that Greenwood had crashed a short time earlier, Preus also elected to try an ADF approach to Lunghwa. With a ceiling of fifty feet at best, visibility less than a quarter-mile, and the runway lighted only by smudge pots, an ADF approach was hopelessly inadequate to the precision required to find the field. Under such conditions, Preus would have needed a miracle. Two miles short of the runway, he slammed into a Chinese school. Fortunately, it was empty.

The worst day in Chinese commercial aviation finally came to an end after seventy-two lives had been lost.[1]

The search for scapegoats began immediately. Investigations were launched by the Ministry of Communications, the Control Yuan, the People's Political Council, local Chinese courts, and, of course, the press. It was rumored that CNAC's operations manager would be jailed and the managing director shot. A group of CNAC and CATC pilots, decrying the grossly inadequate airport facilities and radio aids to navigation, set forth the "minimum requirements" for safe airline operation in a petition to Chiang Kai-shek.[2]

The new year failed to ease growing public anxiety about the safety of China's skies. On January 5 a CNAC C-46 with forty-six people on board slammed into the side of a mountain near Tsingtao. The newly organized Civil Aeronautics Administration (CAA) suspended all commercial service for one week. No sooner had flying resumed when two more CNAC transports crashed. With 146 people killed in seven weeks, the CAA halted indefinitely all passenger operations.[3]

Among the welter of post-mortems, a report by Brigadier General John P. McConnell, director of the Air Division of the U.S. Army Advisory Group, is the most persuasive. McConnell had been asked by General George C. Marshall, head of what turned out to be an abortive peace mission to China, to prepare a confidential study of civil aviation, which Marshall intended to present to the generalissimo.

McConnell pulled no punches in his comprehensive inquiry into the causes of China's air disasters. The recent loss of commercial aircraft, he stressed, was "more than mere accident." Rather, it revealed glaring deficiencies in all areas of aeronautics. China lacked suitable airfields; point-to-point and air-to-ground communications were inadequate; few modern radio aids to navigations existed; and weather reports were sparse and unreliable. Maintenance standards at CNAC and CATC left a good deal to be desired, and both airlines lacked a continuing training program for pilots. The government had failed to set standards or exercise proper regulatory authority in all areas. McConnell concluded: "Commercial aviation in China is not satisfactorily organized, is improperly operated, is not adequately supervised or regulated, is not soundly backed financially, is not equipped with the necessary facilities to provide for safe and efficient operations, is undesirably entangled with military aviation, does not receive support and cooperation of military aviation and is attempting a 1946 type of operation with 1926 type of facilities." McConnell offered a series of recommendations but acknowledged that it would take years to correct many of the problems. In the meantime, China would continue to be a hazardous environment for aviation.[4]

It was in this context of public apprehension about air safety that CNRRA Air Transport prepared to commence operations.

Chennault had been working for months to bring together the necessary men and equipment to get CAT off the ground and into the air. Colonel Richard W. Wise, a career officer (West Point, 1931) who had served under Chennault in the Fourteenth Air Force, arranged detached service through Secretary of War Robert P. Patterson and joined the airline as operations manager. Wise supervised establishment of airfield facilities and played a major role in recruitment and organization of air and ground personnel. He was assisted by old China hand Charles W. Hunter, who would take over operations when Wise returned to military duty in mid-1947. Major Kenneth W. Buchanan, air inspector for the Air Transport Command at Shanghai and veteran of the Hump, became chief pilot. H. L. Richardson and Mervyn A. Garrold were hired to set up maintenance facilities, while John M. Williams and Roger Shreffler organized communications. Great China Aviation Corporation, on the verge of bankruptcy after several months of sporadic operations, provided former navy pilots Willis P. Hobbs and Weldon D. Bigony. The Marine Corps Air Wing at Tsingtao contributed several young aviators who were destined to play an important role in CAT's future, including A. Lewis Burridge, Var M. Green, and Lawrence R. Buol. Robert E. Rousselot, a marine stationed at Peking, also took his discharge and joined the airline. From the Peking-based 332d Troop Carrier Squadron, Wise recruited Army Air Force pilots Harry B. Cockrell, Stuart E. Dew, Paul R. Holden, and Frank L. Hughes. Doreen Lonberg, Chennault's wartime secretary, established an office in Washington and began to recruit American personnel, arrange purchases in the United States, and set up a system of home pay allotments.[5]

CAT's contract with CNRRA called for the continuous operation of twelve aircraft. To maintain this level, Chennault decided to acquire five C-47s and fourteen C-46s for flight and three C-46s for spare parts. Suitable C-46s were located among surplus stocks in Honolulu, but some time would be needed before they could be flown to China. The five C-47s, however, were available immediately in the Philippines. In early November, while Willauer negotiated with Chinese bankers and working capital was at an absolute minimum, Chennault gave Burridge and Green a certified check for $500 and sent them to the Philippines with orders to get the C-47s to Shanghai as soon as possible.[6]

The former marines found a depressing sight when they arrived at Clark Field. The aircraft had been in dead storage for over a year, and decay had taken a heavy toll. Preparing the rusting "gooney-birds" for flight seemed an impossible task. "We were so short of cash," Burridge recalled, "that we stayed in uniform so we could eat at the Clark Field mess for less money. But even with short cuts our $500 was dwindling fast." They hired two Filipino mechanics, "partly because they said they were good mechanics but most because they had a jeep. We couldn't afford transportation." With everyone working long hours and with liberal "borrowing" of parts and equipment from sympathetic Army Air Force former comrades-in-arms, the men worked a minor miracle. By mid-January the first three C-47s were ready for flight. There even was enough money remaining to paint #404 with airline colors.[7]

Meanwhile, CAT's staff at Shanghai accelerated preparations for arrival of the first aircraft. The new boy on the block of Chinese aviation, CAT had to settle for two shantylike buildings on Hungjao airfield, the least desirable of Shanghai's three airports. As they picked up rocks and filled in chuckholes preparing the landing area for operations, CAT personnel could only look with envy at the superior facilities at Kiangwa, used by the Army Air Force, and at Lunghwa, CNAC's main base. Hungjao even lacked a windsock. But Merv Garrold, demonstrating the "CAT spirit," solved the problem by designing one himself, purchasing several yards of silk, and arranging with a Russian dressmaker to stitch together the most elegant landing aid in China.[8]

The three C-47s, flown by Burridge, Green, Cockrell, Dew, Holden, and Hughes, left the Philippines on January 24. Delayed at Canton because of low ceiling and poor visibility at Shanghai, the aircraft did not reach Lunghwa, the designated port of entry, until the afternoon of January 27. "It was the coldest day we have had yet," Louise Willauer reported, "and waiting on the airport was agony." But discomfort was forgotten when the

C-47s taxied up the ramp. All eyes turned to #404. Painted in silver trimmed with blue, with C A T in bold red letters on the side of the fuselage and the company insignia on the nose, the transport produced an excitement and pride that would remain vivid through the years. Following customs formalities and picture-taking, the aircraft were flown to Hungjao. Louise Willauer drove over by car, while her husband and six-year-old son, Tommy, rode in #404. "Tommy was quite pleased to be [CAT's] first passenger," Louise wrote, "and is more excited about the airline than all the rest of us put together."[9]

The "official" start of the airline came — almost — on January 29, when #404 left Shanghai for Canton with General Chennault, twelve company and CNRRA employees, a jeep, and office equipment. Seventy-five miles out of Shanghai, however, the aircraft ran into severe icing. Because #404 lacked deicing boots, Captain Hughes had no choice but to return. With bad weather forecast for the next day (it turned out to be the nicest day in months), the flight was rescheduled for January 31.

Although the weather finally cooperated on January 31, CAT's problems were not over. When Captain Hughes hopped over to Lunghwa for fuel on the morning of the flight, Chinese customs agents impounded the aircraft on the grounds that the cargo had not been inspected. Everything would have to be unloaded and approved, they demanded, before the aircraft could depart. Frustrated CAT officials estimated that this procedure would entail at least another twenty-four-hour delay. After considerable conversation, customs relented and permitted #404 to leave in the early afternoon. CAT personnel no doubt burned more than one joss stick to the appropriate Chinese gods, praying that the difficulties encountered in sending this first flight from Shanghai to Canton were not omens of future troubles.[10]

Canton, designated by CNRRA as the main base for airlift of supplies into the interior, became the focal point of activity in early February, as CAT personnel worked to set up permanent maintenance facilities at the Tien Ho military airport. Two C-47s inaugurated relief operations on February 2 when they left for Liuchow with nine thousand pounds of medical supplies. Earmarked for distribution throughout Kwangsi Province, the supplies had been sitting in Canton godowns for three months, awaiting shipment inland. Even had a junk been available, the journey to Liuchow would have taken three weeks. CAT delivered the cargo in two hours.[11]

Two additional C-47s arrived from the Philippines by mid-February, and the pace of operations quickened. "Daddy is working harder than ever," Louise Willauer wrote to her two children in the United States. Employees were added to the payroll at a rapid rate, reaching a total of 158 by the end of the month. Despite a plague of icing, low ceilings, and poor visibility, CAT

CAT's first C-47s, January 1947 (Courtesy R. E. Rousselot)

First CAT C-47s arrive Shanghai, January 27, 1947. Left to right: Whiting Willauer, Paul R. Holden, Frank L. Hughes, Claire L. Chennault, Harry B. Cockrell, Stuart E. Dew, Alvin L. Burridge, and Var M. Green. (Courtesy A. L. Burridge)

crews continued to pile up flight hours. The airline flew 40,117 ton-miles in February, a modest but respectable beginning.[12]

Early March brought the arrival of the first three of seventeen C-46s, aircraft destined to form the backbone of CAT's fleet over the next decade. After hearing reports about surplus C-46s in Hawaiian depots, Chennault had asked his son-in-law, Robert Lee, to inspect the large twin-engine transports. Lee reported that the aircraft were in mint condition, with a bare 165 hours the highest time on any one. Chennault snapped them up. Based on initial reports he hoped to have the seventeen airplanes ready for delivery in two weeks. Unfortunately, the C-46s had been thoroughly "pickled." The preservatives had to be removed, engines and flight instruments cleaned and checked, overwater navigation equipment installed, and test flights conducted. CAT's staff in Honolulu grew from half a dozen to fifty, and the weeks stretched into months.[13]

The detached personnel, especially pilots, later recalled this period with great fondness. Newly available operating capital eased the financial crisis, and there was no longer the need for the penny-pitching that Burridge had had to do in the Philippines. The ground staff worked hard to get the airplanes ready for flight, although the previous sense of urgency seemed lacking. The pilots drew their salary, $10 per diem, and had their bill paid at the Niumalu Hotel. With little to do, they rented cars and enjoyed the Hawaiian social scene. William J. Wingfield, an island resident and new employee, hosted numerous luaus, featuring Mae Wingfield's barbecued beef marinated in soya sauce.[14]

The first four aircraft, flown by John R. Rossi, C. Joseph Rosbert, Robert Conrath, and Ozzie Young, left Honolulu in late February. Young was grounded on Johnson Island with engine trouble, but the remaining three fliers continued the island-hopping route to Manila. Following a brief layover in the Philippines they flew in formation to Canton, completing the four-thousand-mile trip on March 2. Additional aircraft kept coming for several months, with William A. Dudding bringing in the last C-46 at the end of May.[15]

March and April 1947 saw CAT make steady progress, amassing ton-miles of 91,343 and 109,426, both figures more than double February's total. UNRRA/CNRRA cargo included 100 tons of medical supplies for a leper hospital at Nanchang, 150 tons of seeds needed for early spring planting, more than 1,300 displaced persons, and thousands of tons of miscellaneous relief items.[16]

The most challenging operation came in early March, when UNRRA asked CAT to transport several hundred sheep into the far northwestern province of Kansu. Colonel Wise argued that CAT should refuse the cargo because the aircraft would be left smelling so badly that they could never be used for anything else. Louise Willauer suggested diapers. To Wise's chagrin, Chennault sided with Louise. Instead of diapers, however, he ordered the floors covered with canvas and the aircraft disinfected afterward.[17]

Operation "Bo-peep" began on March 22. Captain Robert E. Rousselot, who had grown up on a farm that had a few sheep, took charge of twenty-five pedigreed New Zealand rams and ewes, a gift of Corridale breeders, for the twelve-hundred-mile journey from Shanghai to Lanchow. Seventeen bales of hay divided the aircraft into four pens. The sheep could nibble the hay en route; after arrival, it would be used for feed during the three-day truck ride to a final destination in the interior of the province. The flight went off without a hitch. "Bo-peep" continued until May 22. Altogether, CAT carried 425 sheep from Shanghai to Lanchow and 200 from Shanghai to Peking. The success of the operation added to the airline's growing reputation that it would transport anything anywhere anytime.[18]

Despite the shipment of tons of medical supplies and seeds, hundreds of sheep, and thousands of displaced persons, it was clear by early April that there was not enough priority relief cargo to keep the airline operating at full capacity. Unless additional cargo could be found, CAT would be in deep financial trouble. Chennault and Willauer flew to Nanking, met with Chiang Kai-shek, and asked for an amendment to their contract with CNRRA that would permit carriage of any cargo on China's approved import list. They argued that the import list represented the government's choice of items needed for relief and rehabilitation. Chiang readily agreed to this crucial contract revision, and CAT's owners breathed a sigh of relief.[19]

The new policy on inbound cargo, plus a contract with the Chinese Post Office to carry mail, contributed to a sharp increase in ton-miles during May (286,343) and June (322,820). UNRRA/CNRRA cargo, which continued to have priority, now represented only 40 percent of ton-miles flown. The increased totals also reflected progress in solving the continuing problem of locating return loads for the airline's growing fleet of transports.[20]

Filling return cargo space, available to the public at prevailing commercial rates, had been left for the most part to the pilots, who handled this responsibility well on occasion. Rousselot, for example, made a double success of the first "Bo-peep" flight by arranging in Lanchow for a return load of bristles. A valuable export commodity, the bristles brought the government $18,000 in precious foreign exchange. But all too often CAT's airplanes flew empty. Willauer managed a partial solution to this vexing problem by filling an empty leg in the Canton-Liuchow-Kunming route.[21]

CNRRA had abundant cargo at Canton for Liuchow, but CAT had to fly to Kunming, nearly four hundred miles away, to locate a return load for Canton. In April Willauer signed a contract with Standard Oil to carry one thousand tons of petroleum products from Liuchow to Kunming. In return

Willauer agreed to give CAT's fuel contract to Standard when UNRRA supplies came to an end on June 30. Not only did the agreement mean profits for the Liuchow-Kunming route, but Standard also made a down payment of CN$1.5 billion (US$130,000 at CN$12,000 = US$1). These funds came at a crucial time. CAT's working capital had been used up, and the large outstanding balance for freight carried to date had not yet been paid. As Willauer reported, "The Standard Oil deal is our real backlog of security." The problem of return cargo, however, remained a source of concern throughout the year.[22]

Another potential trouble spot was the dwindling reserves of spare parts for CAT's fifteen operational C-46s. By early April the airline had an estimated six-week supply of parts. Fortunately, twenty-five surplus C-46s were located in the Philippines. UNRRA, after some foot-dragging, agreed to provide $183,000 to purchase the aircraft. Chief Engineer Richardson had the C-46s in China by late June, thus giving CAT an assured source of spares and a reserve for possible later expansion of its fleet.[23]

Chennault and Willauer were less successful in ongoing dealings with the Chinese Air Force, which required CAT to clear all flights with the Civil Aeronautics Administration. Although CAT's landing permits were routinely granted by the CAA, they were not always honored by the Air Force. All too often, the CAF would allow an aircraft to land, then impound it. Kunming, where the airport was named after General Chennault, had an especially unsavory reputation. As Lincoln Au, CAT's station manager, observed, "Our hard-flying pilots used to think of Kunming as a forced rest camp because CAT planes have been impounded on Chennault Field for periods as long as two weeks — not just once or twice, but many times." The problem, Willauer noted, arose because the CAF's Troop Carrier Command "is in fact in the airline business." The CAF, which did not appreciate competition, earlier had used the same technique to crush the Great China Aviation Corporation, and it now seemed intent on undermining CAT. Although Chennault spoke to Chiang Kai-shek about the problem and received assurances of cooperation, the CAF remained a law unto itself.[24]

"UNRRA over here stinks," one of Corcoran's partners had advised Willauer from Washington during the final stage of contract negotiation, "but I don't see how they can get out of the airline although they will undoubtedly be guilty of all kinds of inefficiencies and delays."[25] The prediction of trouble proved accurate. Although relations with CNRRA had improved steadily, especially after P. H. Ho replaced T. F. Tsiang as director-general, UNRRA seemed intent on making life difficult for the fledgling airline. Tardy payment of foreign exchange caused continuing crisis. On more than one occasion, Chennault and Willauer had to soothe disgruntled pilots and mechanics who were threatening to strike because home allotments had not been paid. During such times, Willauer thought of the airline "as a tarpaulin, lying on the lawn with a high wind blowing, four corners, and me with only two rocks to place on the corners in the face of a shifting wind."[26]

Despite the many problems, business remained good. "Right now the airline is going great guns," Willauer wrote to his wife in mid-July. "In the first ten days of July we flew 300,000 revenue ton miles which equals the entire month of June." And the pace continued throughout the summer. CAT flew 617,693 ton-miles in July, followed by 762,251 in August, and 690,948 in September.[27]

A rapid growth of traffic north of the Yangtze River caused Shanghai to become the airline's main operational base by summer, with Canton remaining the center for maintenance. CAT acquired additional facilities at Hungjao, invested CN$300 million (US$250,000) in runway improvement, installed runway lights, arranged housing for newly assigned flight crews, and consolidated its head offices on the seventh floor of number 17, The Bund.[28]

CAT's management stressed safety in flight operations, a vital consideration in light of the many accidents suffered earlier in the year by China's commercial airlines. Thanks to this policy—and to fate—CAT managed to escape serious accidents during a summer of rapid expansion, but there were at least two close calls.

The first came in August, when Captain Rousselot lost an engine over mountainous terrain between Liuchow and Chungking. Gradually losing altitude in clouds, Rousselot ordered part of his cargo jettisoned. He broke out in a valley between high mountains and returned safely to Liuchow. As it happened, his cargo consisted of five-gallon-size rectangular canisters filled with the government's new CN$10,000 notes. For a time CAT faced the threat of a claim for US$1 million, the value of the bank notes, but nothing came of it. "Some of the notes have been recovered," Willauer told his wife, "but I think that on the whole there will be a bunch of pretty rich peasants in that remote part of the world who will be wondering what it is all about."[29]

The following month brought a serious incident in the Northwest. CAT was required by the CAA to use CNAC radio aids to navigation. CNAC, CAT's major competitor, charged what Willauer and Chennault considered to be exorbitant fees for the service. When CAT refused to pay, CNAC cut off service without warning, endangering an airplane en route to Lanchow. "The General and I were so damned mad," Willauer told his wife, "that we were ready to go down and beat up the whole outfit. We finally wrote them a letter telling them if anything like that happened with a crash resulting we would prosecute them for murder."[30]

The Chinese economy took a sharp turn for the worse during the summer of 1947. Commodity prices skyrocketed, and attempts to stabilize the currency proved fruitless. In August, under great pressure, the government retreated from the increasingly unrealistic official exchange rate of CN\$12,000 to US\$1 and added an open market rate of CN\$40,000 to US\$1. Although the accelerating inflationary spiral forecast the ultimate doom of CAT and all other economic enterprises in Nationalist China, the immediate effects were mixed. CAT had to use the open market and, on occasion, black market rate to purchase dollars for home allotments, fuel, and other imported items. Because changes in prevailing commercial rates for air freight, set by the government, lagged behind inflation, CAT's operational costs climbed steadily. Also, CNRRA continued to pay for transportation at CN\$12,000 to US\$1. But these difficulties were more than offset by CAT's ability to use the official rate in repaying its loan to CNRRA. The financial picture changed so quickly, Willauer reported on September 1, "that we don't know whether we are afoot or horseback, except we still seem to be able to pay our bills and are paying off for the equipment at a fairly good rate."[31]

CAT's owners wisely plowed back as much as possible to pay off the loan. A crucial breakthrough came in late September, when the Yunnan People's Development Corporation agreed to purchase a 7 percent equity in CAT, based on a valuation of \$3 million. This transaction not only brought powerful provincial interests into the company, but also established the airline's worth. "Since the equipment only cost a little over a million," Willauer explained, "and since the purchaser is willing to buy at three, we think that we have a pretty good yardstick that the show is worth five million if we get a permanent charter."[32]

The sale of stock, Willauer pointed out, had gone far in assuring CAT's future. The Yunnan interests paid \$210,000 for the 7 percent equity at an open market rate of CN\$46,000 to US\$1, or CN\$9.66 billion. CAT's stockholders promptly loaned the money back to the company to pay off CNRRA's loan at the official rate. Using CN\$12,000 to US\$1, CAT paid CNRRA the equivalent of US\$805,000, or nearly half the total amount of the original loan. Added to prior payments, this meant that Chennault, Willauer, and associates owned nearly 90 percent of the airline. On this basis, Willauer concluded, the government "will either have to make us permanent or buy us out at a decent price."[33]

CAT finished 1947 with a flourish, flying more ton-miles in the last three months of the year (3,414,996) than it had during the first eight months of operations. CAT carried 300 tons of wolfram ore from Kunming to Liuchow for the National Resources Commission; 138 baskets of silkworm eggs from Kunming to Shanghai, which when hatched would supply one-quarter of China's silk export; 3,000 tons of cotton and tobacco from Peking to Taiyuan; tons of high-denomination bank notes to cities throughout the country; 748

Japanese repatriates from Taiyuan to Peking; 220 orphans, 19 Sisters of Charity, 67 Trappist monks and mission staff, and 8 cows from Shihchianchuang to Peking; and 55 Russian refugees from Lanchow to Shanghai. Requests for air transportation far exceeded supply. Ma Kuo-yi, chairman of the Sinkiang Moslem Cultural Association, implored CAT to fly 500 tons of critically needed cargo to Sian for delivery to Sinkiang by truck. The goods—paper, movie projectors, printing machines, well drillers, water pumps, and cotton—had been sitting in Shanghai for months. Without these items, Ma wrote, "the sufferings of the Sinkiang people will be greatly increased." Ma was only one of many who begged CAT for assistance during the year.[34]

Shantung Province registered the most dramatic increase in business. In April 1947 Chennault had assigned A. Lewis Burridge, an able young pilot, to shuttle medical supplies between the port city of Tsingtao and the provincial capital of Tsinan. The mission was supposed to last four days; however, because of red tape it took nearly a month to accumulate fifteen hours of flying. The energetic Burridge used the enforced free time to explore the province's transportation needs. The Communists, he found, controlled 80 percent of Shantung. As was usually the case, Nationalist elements held the large urban areas, while the Communists ruled the countryside. Railroads, the lifelines that connected government-held centers, were coming under heavy attack as the Communists stepped up their efforts to interdict traffic. Increasingly, the cities were becoming Nationalist islands in a Communist sea, with air the only means of transportation.[35]

Largely through Burridge's efforts, CAT's activities in Shantung grew appreciably during summer and fall. The airline carried a variety of goods, ranging from cows for missionary dairy farms to hospital supplies. The main cargo, however, was raw cotton, airlifted two hundred miles from Tsinan to the government's China Textile Corporation at Tsingtao. The corporation, one of the country's largest cotton mills, employed 19,000 workers, used 332,468 spindles, and produced each month 13,000 bales and 30,000 bolts of cotton cloth. Use of aircraft to haul raw cotton, which normally would move by rail, obviously made sense only because of the exigencies of war. But the giant Tsingtao mill would have stood idle without CAT.[36]

CAT extended service to Tientsin in early November, agreeing to carry one hundred tons of Tsinan cotton to the old treaty port on the Hai River and return with six hundred drums of badly needed kerosene. Burridge also opened a route to Lini, a Communist-isolated city in southern Shantung. December brought a contract with the Tobacco Development Company, a provincial concern, to airlift five hundred tons of tobacco from Tsinan to Tsingtao.[37]

Flying in Shantung, an increasingly active war zone, was not without hazard. CAT aircraft often were fired on and sometimes hit. Captain Hughes took a bullet through the "tiger-cat" insignia on the nose of his C-46 while en route to Tsinan from Tsingtao. Captain Green found four bullet holes in the tail section of his airplane following an instrument letdown at Tsinan. These incidents turned out to be only a modest taste of what CAT pilots would face in the near future.[38]

The approach of winter brought late sunrises and early sunsets to northern China, sharply cutting into available flight time. Undaunted, Burridge devised a system of runway lighting to permit limited night operations at Tsingtao. Mixing gasoline, oil, cotton, and sand in a specially cut GI vegetable tin, he improvised flares that would burn for four hours. The system worked extremely well.[39]

The jerry-built lighting system represented only one of Burridge's many contributions to the success of CAT's operations in Shantung. Dr. Frank Herrington, in charge of UNRRA operations in Tsingtao, wrote to Chennault that Burridge was the "main sparkplug" of CAT's "excellent organization" in the province. Robert C. Strong, American consul at Tsingtao, remembered the young, curly-headed former marine as a "gung-ho, can-do type, always full of ideas and plans, with great nervous energy, apparently thriving on pressure and confusion. Almost every time I was in the CAT offices in Tsingtao the place was a bedlam; Burridge was part of it, making instant decisions on myriads of problems put to him rapid-fire by his mostly Chinese staff. He had good human instincts, never lost his 'cool' and had the loyalty of his personnel." A fellow pilot stressed Burridge's buoyant optimism and *joi de vivre* when he wrote that "working for him was sheer joy, like flying through space with a masculine Tinker-Bell."[40]

Evidence of the spirit that Burridge brought to the Tsingtao operation came once again on December 22. That day began long before sunrise when the call "Chow Be Ready!" sounded at 4:30 A.M. in the CAT "Castle." Sleepy flight crews hurried through breakfast, then left for the airfield at 5:00 A.M. Four aircraft stood ready on the flight line; cargo had been loaded and manifested during the night. Burridge's improvised flares lighted the runway for takeoff at 5:45 A.M., some two hours before the rising sun touched the red-tiled roofs of the city. While the twin-engine transports made the four-hundred-mile round trip to Tsinan, coolies staged the next load on the ramp. When an airplane returned, a Standard Vacuum Oil Company gasoline truck appeared for refueling even before the transport's propellers had stopped turning. Well-trained coolies offloaded and reloaded, a mechanic checked for problems, and the crew grabbed a quick sandwich. Everything was done in twenty minutes, and the fat-bellied C-46 was on its way again. The scene was repeated throughout the day until the last flight returned to Tsingtao long after dark. A weary but proud staff finally made their way back into town, content in the knowledge that they had set another record: 219.43 tons carried and 29,108 ton-miles flown in one day.[41]

Chennault and Willauer also experienced the deep sense of satisfaction that comes when a long and tiring effort ends in success. December brought long-awaited news: the airline's franchise would be renewed.

CAT's original agreement permitted operations only during the lifetime of CNRRA. With the relief agency scheduled to go out of business at the end of 1947, Chennault and Willauer quickly began work establishing the airline on a more permanent basis. In early July they toured the provinces, hoping to drum up support for a reorganized and recapitalized company. "We got a very good reception," Willauer reported, "but as yet no firm commitment." The missionary work finally paid off in September, when Yunnan provincial interests purchased 7 percent of CAT. Use of these funds to push amortization beyond 80 percent went far toward assuring the airline's continued operation; the agreement also brought a powerful provincial voice to CAT's side during negotiations of franchise renewal.[42]

Clyde A. Farnsworth, the airline's talented public relations officer, orchestrated an impressive publicity campaign, designed to fend off criticism and create a favorable climate of opinion for continued operations. He cultivated Shanghai newspapermen and kept them well supplied with stories about CAT's activities. The pieces stressed China's great need for air transportation and CAT's contribution to the relief and rehabilitation program. The climax of Farnsworth's efforts came in October with publication of an "Anniversary Supplement" to the *CAT Bulletin*. CAT printed and widely distributed some fifteen hundred copies of this sixty-seven-page bilingual recitation of the airline's many services to China.[43]

Intense lobbying in Nanking by CAT's Chinese stockholders, led by Wang Wen-san, added a key element to the fight for renewal. "Wang Wen-san," Willauer later wrote, "in his own way is to Nanking what Tom [Corcoran] and Bill [Youngman] are to Washington. He knows everyone. There are few people who in some way or other are not either his friends or under some obligation to him and he has an unbeatable way of getting things done. I give him at least fifty percent of the credit for the extension of life of CAT."[44]

On January 2, 1948, months of intense effort reached fruition when Chennault and Willauer signed a draft agreement for continued operations of the airline; Colonel Tai An-kuo, director of the Civil Aeronautics Administration, signed for the government. Under terms of the draft, confirmed in the final contract on May 28, 1948, the government granted Chennault and Willauer, personally, the right to operate an airline in China under the direct control of the Ministry of Communications. "Civil Air Transport of the Civil Aeronautics Administration, Ministry of Communications," the authorized name under which the partnership would function, was granted the right to conduct nonscheduled air service in all areas of the country for one year.[45]

The government insisted on this partnership arrangement, Willauer explained, "in order to make our operation a special case. They are under tremendous pressure to permit private airplane companies and they have felt that they could avoid some criticism as to us by not going whole hog and allowing us to be a company as yet." Also, the Ministry of Communications later explained, the civil aviation law of China, which had been promulgated but not yet put into effect, prohibited foreign ownership of aviation companies. As a partnership (not a company) operating within the ministry, CAT would not be in violation of the law. Although this special status would cause bitter controversy in the future, it seemed at the time a reasonable way of resolving a difficult problem. Moreover, it was the only way for the airline to continue operations in China.[46]

Despite some reservations about the arrangement with the Chinese government, Corcoran was pleased with this outcome. "As I was going over certain affairs which you had the General write to me about the other day," he advised Willauer, "I couldn't help remembering how far behind I was in congratulating you for the job you and the General had done the last year in getting the airline extended. You're wild and wooly and full of fleas and mighty hard to curry up around the knees but you're a first class promoter."[47]

Looking back on the year's activities, Chennault and Willauer had every right to take pride in their accomplishments. CAT had flown nearly two million miles in fifteen thousand hours and had carried almost seven million ton-miles of cargo. The airline had transported tons of needed relief supplies to the interior and had brought out exports valued at over $6 million. More than twenty-seven thousand passengers had been airlifted without fatality or serious injury, a remarkable safety record in light of the primitive operating conditions in China. Indeed, Corcoran later stressed, CAT's reputation for safety had been one of the keys to continued operations.[48]

Chennault and Willauer had paid off the funds advanced by UNRRA. They and their partners owned an airline with eighteen operational aircraft, 822 enthusiastic employees, and a reputation for efficiency and flexibility. The transition had been made from CNRRA Air Transport to Civil Air Transport, and future profits seemed assured.

But all was not well in China. The new year brought heavy fighting in Manchuria between Nationalist and Communist forces. The civil war had taken a turn for the worse, and CAT soon was caught up in the growing conflict.

CAT and Civil War

The long-simmering civil war in China entered a new phase during the winter of 1947–48. Ignoring sound military advice, Chiang Kai-shek had concentrated his best troops in Manchuria. Led by the American-trained New First and New Sixth armies, Nationalist forces had seized control of the major cities in the province but never were able to extend their authority very far into the countryside. The generalissimo watched with growing apprehension as Communist forces tightened the noose around his isolated garrisons. November–December 1947 brought a series of Red offensives that threatened Mukden and caused panic among the civil population. To reinforce the provincial capital, the government stripped Kirin and Changchun of troops, increasing Mukden's strength to some 175,000 men. When Communist units destroyed the Alingho bridge near Chinchow, severing the vital rail line to Peking, air provided the sole link to the outside for the city's beleaguered inhabitants.[1]

The deteriorating military situation in the North was the most compelling reason for the government's decision to continue CAT's franchise. Nationalist officials made clear at the time of renewal that they expected the airline to support military operations in Manchuria by transporting food and personnel. Accordingly, CAT signed a contract in early January 1948—the first of many—to airlift seven thousand government technicians and their families from Mukden to Peking. This exodus did not portend a total evacuation of Mukden, the airline hastened to reassure the press. "Correspondents in that frozen city," an airline spokesman said, "state emphatically that Nationalist defenses there have never been stronger."[2]

Operation Mukden began on January 18. Captain Richard L. Bushbaum led the way, carrying five tons of flour from Peking to the besieged city and returning with a load of evacuees. CAT personnel, headed by operations agent David H. Stauffer, arrived the following day to set up control procedures at Mukden's Hun Ho airfield. Facilities were meager. There was no control tower, a bare half-mile of runway, a parking area, and a few abandoned, wind-swept hangars. Stauffer installed a VHF transmitter-receiver in a dilapidated bus and established air-to-ground communications at the airport. At the end of each day, the bus carried CAT personnel back to the warmth of the Railway Hotel.

Operations quickly settled into a routine. An aircraft would arrive from Peking, the crew covered in white flour dust that had sifted from the thin sacks. Coolies unloaded the transport while waiting passengers shivered in buses, unable to keep warm in the biting, subzero temperatures. Then fifty-odd men, women, and children would board the pot-bellied C-46 for the four-hundred-mile flight to comparative warmth and safety.

To avoid being hit by Communist ground fire, aircraft would circle the field after takeoff, climbing to five thousand feet before heading on course for Peking. Arriving aircraft would hold over the city at high altitudes, then make a rapid, circling descent to land. The wreckage of a CNAC C-46, which had crashed on January 20 while attempting to take off from Hun Ho, served as a constant reminder of the "ordinary" hazards of flight.[3]

CAT completed its contract with the National Resources Commission in late February, ahead of schedule and without incident. Business continued to increase, however, as the military picture grew bleaker for the Nationalists. Working under a series of contracts with various government agencies, by May 25 CAT had flown 2,210 tons of flour into Mukden and brought out 22,173 passengers, including 4,571 wounded soldiers.[4]

Mukden was only one point of Communist pressure. Nanking's forces, American diplomats noted, were "hard pressed and on the defensive in practically every theater"; the government, in fact, controlled no more than 15 percent of China north of the Yellow River. CAT, CNAC, and CATC joined the Chinese Air Force in providing crucial logistical support for isolated government outposts. The dangers of these paramilitary operations — and the growing extent of CAT's involvement in the civil war — became apparent in March and April 1948.[5]

Linfen, a pocket of anti-Communist resistance in southern Shansi Province, came under heavy attack in early March. Red troops seized the outlying airfield, trapping CAT's James R. Stewart and several Chinese employees inside the walled city. Aware that military assistance for Linfen's defenders would not be forthcoming, Willauer ordered Stewart to prepare a landing area for a light plane. After flying to the provincial capital of Taiyuan and securing permission from Governor Yen Hsi-shan to attempt a rescue mission, Willauer went to Peking and tried to persuade the Chinese Air Force to furnish air cover.

The CAF, as usual, was evasive. Nationalist aviators knew all too well the dangers of being forced down in Communist territory. They had no desire to share the fate of two comrades who had fallen into enemy hands the previous June. The Communists had returned the pilots — with their hands cut off and eyes put out. As diplomat John Melby noted, Mao's forces resorted to such atrocities "to dampen the enthusiasm of the Nationalist Air Force. It works rather well."[6]

By March 18 desperate fighting around Linfen's perimeter made an immediate rescue effort imperative, with or without CAF assistance. Eric Shilling, CAT's chief pilot and AVG veteran, volunteered to take a single-engine L-5 into Linfen. With CAF air support unlikely, James Bledsoe offered to fly cover in a C-46 and attempt to distract Communist troops by tossing out small bombs provided by Governor Yen.

Shilling and Bledsoe arrived over Linfen and were relieved to find a CAF fighter-bomber on station. The Chinese pilot, however, refused to fly lower than five thousand feet; his efforts to harass the ground troops were futile. Bledsoe, perhaps recalling his younger days as a fighter pilot, attacked. Not surprisingly, the sight of a lumbering C-46 making a low-level bomb run had the desired effect. Shilling slipped in unnoticed and evacuated the employees. While vehemently denying Communist reports about a "CAT bomber," airline executives breathed a sigh of relief. But their respite was brief. Linfen turned out to be only a prologue for the great drama of Weihsien.[7]

An important halfway station on the rail line between Tsingtao and Tsinan, Weihsien lay in the heart of what had been the Kingdom of Wei thirty centuries before. A sandy-bedded river separated Weihsien into two distinct cities, the east city and the west city, each surrounded by massive stone walls. Just outside the walls Catholic missionaries had built an imposing church; farther out lay an American Presbyterian mission school.

Weihsien had been isolated by the Communists since mid-1947. The Chinese Air Force made occasional landings with munitions and food, but civilian airlines refused to serve the city. Weihsien had no ground radio facilities or weather information, and the runway was in poor condition. To the dismay of local residents, the Japanese had built an airstrip just outside the city on a piece of flat land that had been used for centuries as a graveyard; heavy aircraft tended to break through the surface, and nothing larger than a C-47 could risk a landing. Undaunted, the aggressive Burridge brought the first CAT airplane into Weihsien on June 12, 1947, in search of business. Burridge immediately ran into numerous problems, but at a conference on July 30 with local officials and the Chinese Air Force, District Commissioner Chang Tien-tso pledged full cooperation, enabling service to begin in earnest.

CAT assigned two C-47s to the hundred-mile run between Tsingtao and Weihsien. Inbound cargo included medical supplies, iron rails, water pumps, mail, and a variety of other daily needs. CAT brought out hog bristles for export and tobacco for Tsingtao and Shanghai factories. Citizens of Weihsien petitioned for increased air service. "Since the arrival of your planes," three community leaders explained to Chennault in September 1947, "the supplies have been regulated, prices lowered, gradually in line with those of Tsingtao. Moreover, the prices of food locally produced are also getting lower by 50% due to the stability of financial conditions."[8]

Conditions deteriorated as Communist forces in Shantung prepared to launch a major offensive against Nationalist outposts in the province. By early April 1948 CAT's Chinese staff in Weihsien was filling the air to Tsingtao with frantic radio messages, begging to be evacuated. Burridge was not impressed. He had heard such cries before; the fears always had proved groundless. Chinese military authorities in Tsingtao gave firm assurances that Weihsien was not in any immediate danger. Together with assistant manager John R. Plank, Burridge flew into the city with a scheduled run on the afternoon of April 11 to calm the jittery employees. To demonstrate their confidence in Weihsien's security, the two Americans decided to stay overnight. Early the next morning, Communist forces attacked. Supported for the first time by heavy artillery, the Reds quickly captured the Japanese-built airstrip and threatened to breach the city's walls.[9]

Three Nationalist divisions garrisoned Weihsien, but their willingness to fight was questionable. Commissioner Chang had much more confidence in local militia he had trained and commanded, but the situation was perilous. American diplomat Robert C. Strong telegraphed to Washington on April 12: "Morale of Nationalist soldiers and population now low ebb and fall of city likely in next few days."[10]

Burridge and Plank, hoping to repeat the success of Linfen, cleared a landing strip on a school playground in the west city, even though CAT's L-5 would not arrive from Shanghai for twenty-four hours and by then it might be too late.

Spurred on by Communist radio broadcasts warning that all CAT employees in Weihsien would be shot after the city had been captured, Burridge's assistants in Tsingtao asked Vice Admiral Oscar C. Badger, senior American military commander, for the loan of a Marine Corps reconnaissance aircraft. Although the fiesty admiral wanted to help, he was under strict orders to avoid actions that could be construed as intervening in the civil war.

Looking for a loophole in his instructions, Badger sought the advice of Consul Strong. Burridge was not engaged in combat and had a right to protection as an American citizen, the young diplomat reasoned. Because the aircraft would be used solely for the peaceful purpose of a rescue mission, the action should not constitute improper conduct. "As for the problems in case of loss of the plane," Strong recalled, "I was prepared to share the blame by confirming that I had recommended the loan of the plane in the interest of trying to save the life of a private American citizen employed by an American-led organization famous in the United States." Badger was convinced. He ordered Marine Corps markings obliterated and the aircraft turned over to CAT.

Richard B. Kruske arrived over Weihsien in the borrowed light airplane on the afternoon of the twelfth. He did not like what he saw. The landing strip, surrounded by buildings, was only four hundred feet long with a dogleg at one end. Demonstrating more courage than sense, Kruske decided to land. He touched down on the end of the strip, swerved to follow the dogleg, and stood on the brakes. To everyone's intense relief, the airplane stopped just short of a nearby house. But Kruske had used up his quota of luck for the day. Attempting to leave with Burridge, he clipped a wing on takeoff and demolished the aircraft. Fortunately, both occupants escaped injury.

As darkness fell, the Communists launched a series of sharp attacks. The Nationalist divisions fired a few shots to save face, then abandoned the west city. General Chang, however, rallied his militia to defend the east city. Dressed in a black uniform topped by a large black hat and smoking a long black cigar, he walked slowly along the top of the wall and defied Communist gunners to hit him. His soldiers cheered and fought with renewed spirit.

Chang had counted on the Chinese Air Force to drop flares and illuminate the attackers. When the promised air support failed to appear, CAT joined the fight. Burridge removed the landing lights from the now useless USMC aircraft, slung them over the shoulders of a soldier, and connected them to a battery on his back. The human searchlight prowled the walls of the city, turning himself on to pinpoint Communist attackers, then moving away to new targets after Chang's soldiers had eliminated the threat. At the same time, Captain Rousselot circled overhead in a C-47, dropping flares and beer bottles that fell with a whistling noise, causing Red soldiers to interrupt their assault and take cover.

Early the following morning Willauer flew over Weihsien to assess the situation. He observed the Nationalist divisions marching to the southeast, on their way to surrender. Burridge, Plank, and Kruske had moved to the east city and were smoothing a parade ground for a landing area. Returning to Tsingtao, Willauer began to put together a rescue fleet of small aircraft. CAT's disassembled L-5 arrived by C-46 from Shanghai; Willauer arranged to borrow a Piper Cub from L. K. Taylor, who had the Piper agency in China; and a local intelligence unit volunteered a small airplane. No one had the courage to ask Admiral Badger for another USMC aircraft.

Operations got off to a good start on April 13. By mid-afternoon Burridge and Kruske had been flown out by Roger Fay, leaving behind only Plank. But the tide of fortune turned when CAT's L-5, piloted by Edwin L. Trout, nosed over on landing and broke a propeller. Marshall J. Stayner, newly

Felix Smith in Lanchow with Governor Ma Pu-fang, who is accepting the first airmail from Hsining (Courtesy Felix Smith)

hired from the Marine Corps and with limited light plane experience, followed with the Piper Cub. He set down too hard, bounced thirty feet, and cracked up the landing gear. As the three pilots spent an anxious night in Weihsien, two CAT transports circled the city, unloading flares, beer bottles, and an occasional bomb.

April 14 saw repairs completed on the damaged Cub, enabling Stayner and Trout to leave. Rousselot, eager to participate in the action despite his nearly two hundred pounds (a less than ideal weight for operating light planes off short runways), landed with an L-5 to pick up Plank. Belatedly, Rousselot realized he could not clear the surrounding buildings with Plank on board, so rather than waste the day's effort he decided to carry one of CAT's slightly built Chinese radio operators.

Spectators packed the parade ground, as they had since the beginning of the rescue drama, standing on every wall and rooftop. The crowd had sighed and moaned when an airplane made a pass at the field, missed, and went around for another try. A successful landing had brought loud cheers. Now they waited for Rousselot. The tough former marine pushed the throttle forward, waited until the engine reached maximum revolutions, then released the brakes. The L-5 slowly gathered speed across the parade ground, then staggered into the air as nearby houses and buildings loomed close ahead. But, hopelessly overweight, the plane smashed into a telephone pole, killing one spectator. The crowd, in Chinese fashion, gave the uninjured pilot a hearty round of applause for the marvelous show.

Later in the day, Stayner—who had flown out only hours earlier—brought in the Cub. Plank used it to leave Weihsien for the first time. Kruske arrived with another light plane and picked up Stayner. Only Rousselot remained as darkness brought operations to an end for the day.

CAT personnel, including Louise Willauer, went out to the Tsingtao airport that evening to load the aircraft assigned to the night's cover mission over Weihsien. Louise held a flashlight as the men lashed down the flares and bombs. "I tried very hard to find a moment when no one was watching to hide in the lavatory, as I wildly desired to go along on a bombing raid," she wrote to her family, "but they all knew what I had in mind and kept a close watch on me." CAT's "bomber"—without Louise—arrived over Weihsien to find the Chinese Air Force in action, for once. Communist attackers remained in their trenches during the night.

April 15 began poorly when Stayner, trying to pick up Rousselot and end the lengthy drama, damaged his aircraft upon landing. Kruske, next in line, added to the growing frustration by rolling over his L-5. To put a capstone of misery on an already depressing day, the pilots learned that the city's defenders were running out of ammunition and might not be able to hold out for another night.

Efforts to rescue two Americans had started on the twelfth. Three days later, after ten attempts that resulted in six crashes and one fatality, three Americans needed to be rescued. Lack of familiarity with light aircraft had taken its toll, but more than anything else the results mirrored the almost impossible operating conditions. A military commander, looking at the situation with a cold, hard eye, might have decided to cut his losses and abandon the operation at this point. But not CAT.

While the trapped aviators hastened repairs on the damaged aircraft, Willauer flew to Tientsin in a C-47 and obtained a load of hand grenades and rifle ammunition for airdrop at Weihsien. The mission nearly ended in disaster. As Willauer later recalled:

> We did not have any parachutes for cargo dropping but the Chinese had some small ones that they made up out of cotton cloth. Var Green was the pilot and I was the co-pilot and Lou [*sic*] Burridge was in the rear handling the kicking out of the load which was tied to these parachutes. Var asked me to do the flying so that he could watch very carefully on his side as to when to ring the bell to kick out the load. He rang the bell and all of a sudden the plane went

out of control and started to climb almost vertically. Var and I pushed her forward just as hard as we could and did everything we could think of. Just as we were about to spin in she suddenly leveled off and we were certainly two scared people. When we finally got squared away Lou came up and told us what had happened. The rip cord on these parachutes had been just the wrong length and the first load of about 100 pounds of hand grenades had caught its parachute on our tail and this was of course dragging against us and causing us to climb into a stalling position. Fortunately it shook loose just in time. We beat it back to Tsingtao to see if it had done any damage and believe you me we were really shaking. Anyhow we straightened out the ripcord situation and went back and dropped our load, most of which we saw land within the city and which our trapped pilots told us was very useful.[11]

CAT's persistence finally paid off. Stayner and Kruske flew out in one repaired aircraft before nightfall on the fifteenth. Rousselot spent another restless night in a dugout, bothered more by the snoring of two Chinese generals than by Communist artillery, before Stayner picked him up on the morning of April 16. The airline's Chinese staff members were left to slip through enemy lines, if possible.

Weihsien fought on, and CAT continued to support General Chang with airdrops of ammunition. But repeated Communist assaults wore down the stubborn defenders. Angered by the timidity of the Chinese Air Force, Burridge cabled Willauer on April 25: "Wish to add that CAF air support failure responsible for effectiveness Communist big guns. CAF failure to fly continuous night bombing responsible for thousands Nationalist night casualties. This is a disgraceful exhibition of Chinese air power."[12]

Weihsien fell two days later. General Chang died fighting.[13]

Reports of CAT's growing participation in the civil war sent ripples of concern through the Far Eastern division of the State Department. William McAfee spoke for a sizable group in the division when he recommended that strong action be taken against the airline's American pilots. McAfee drafted a cable for Nanking, directing the embassy "to express informally and orally to American CAT pilots this Govt's concern over activities such as those participated in around Weihsien involving dropping of flares and bombs in support military operations." The fliers should be warned that "future participation in such acts will result recall of passports which will not be returned until US national concerned leaves China."[14]

W. Walton Butterworth, head of the division, rejected McAfee's draft. In a memorandum to the secretary of state on May 10, he reaffirmed the department's disapproval of participation by American nationals in the political affairs of foreign states. With regard to the CAT pilots, however, he wrote: "We are of the opinion that the situation should be followed closely but that, in the light of existing conditions, the Department should take no action for the present."[15]

The State Department's ambiguous attitude toward CAT mirrored American policy in China during the final stages of the civil war. John Moors Cabot, a perceptive observer who had served most recently in Yugoslavia, arrived in China for the first time early in 1948 to take up the position of consul-general in Shanghai. He was appalled by conditions. The economy was in shambles, and the army lacked the will to fight. "The National Government," he wrote to Butterworth, "appears to be so steeped in reaction and corruption, so split in factions, and so generally inefficient despite outstanding exceptions, that it cannot assume effective leadership." But Cabot did not see communism as the answer. He rejected the views of those who saw the Communists "as coming with gilded halos and wings to save and modernize China." He had heard Communist promises in Yugoslavia, then experienced the reality of a Communist regime. "Communism," he concluded, "would be a terrible alternative even to the rottenness of the present regime, quite apart from its implications in the world picture."

The United States, he conceded, faced a terrible dilemma. Should aid be granted to the present government? If so, how much? A moderate amount of assistance would not be effective and would provide an excuse, if one was needed, for the Communists to harass American citizens and property. But the Nationalists were so corrupt and inefficient that they would not be able to use massive aid with any effect, even should strict controls be applied. "We do not wish to get our prestige irrevocably involved," Cabot warned, "unless we are quite certain that it will be effective, that it will be supported by the American people, and that it will not merely be used by the Chinese to saddle us with an impossible burden." The United States, he pointed out with resignation, was "damned if we do and damned if we don't."[16]

The American government continued to follow a general policy of moderate aid to the Nationalists: enough to antagonize the Communists but not enough to make any real difference in the war. For example, the Nationalists had a pressing need for air transport in spring 1948, especially to increase the Mukden airlift. Washington responded in late April by declaring surplus thirteen flyable C-46s and authorizing Air Force personnel to deliver them to Shanghai. In typical fashion, the American government attempted to maintain a low profile. Air Force markings on the aircraft were obliterated before delivery, and no more than three C-46s were to arrive in Shanghai at the same time. In equally typical fashion, the Shanghai press gave the transfer wide publicity.[17]

Rather than give the C-46s to the Chinese Air Force, which had been using its transport to smuggle cigarettes and other salable items into Mukden, Nanking leased seven planes to CNAC and six to CAT. Chennault and Willauer could use the additional aircraft. Demand for cargo space far exceeded supply as the Nationalist military position deteriorated.[18]

The expanding civil war was at least temporarily good for the airline business. CAT averaged three million ton-miles a month by mid-1948 and ranked third among the world's airlines in this important category. But it was not easy to translate increased flying into profits when in a single month (June) the exchange rate on the black market soared from CN$1 million = US$1 to CN$4 million = US$1. With such rampant inflation, Willauer noted, "it is practically impossible to tell how you stand other than to measure up from month to month what you have left in the bank or have been able to invest in one form or another."[19]

Chennault and Willauer, awash in rapidly depreciating Chinese currency, easily paid back the $250,000 loan for working capital. They also funneled through Hong Kong $225,000 in dollars and gold for transfer to the United States. Surplus Chinese currency was used to buy "everything in sight" — stocks, bonds, real estate — for later liquidation.[20]

Willauer concluded arrangements in June for a 20 percent participation by CAT's American partners in the Jardine Aircraft Maintenance Company, (JAMCO) of Hong Kong, an investment that would prove highly profitable. JAMCO had been organized in 1947, primarily to provide maintenance facilities for Hong Kong Airways and BOAC. In 1948, when the company decided to expand its facilities to include engine overhaul, Willauer leaped at the opportunity to become a financial backer. CAT engines no longer would have to be crated and shipped to the United States for major overhaul, a lengthy and costly ($4,000 to $5,000 each) procedure. Maintenance would be done expeditiously in Hong Kong at a savings of $400 to $500 an engine. The investment in JAMCO, however, turned out to be even more important than envisioned: in 1949–50 the shops in Hong Kong would be crucial for CAT's survival when Communist advances caused major dislocation of the airline's vital base maintenance facilities.[21]

In an effort to cope with the never-ending search for foreign exchange, Chennault and Willauer got together with L. K. Taylor and the Kincheng Banking Corporation to organize International Suppliers' Corporation. ISC was an expanded version of an earlier scheme to stimulate return cargo from the interior and transfer dollars out of the country. For example, CAT would purchase weasel skins in Kunming worth approximately $5 a pair in New York. "In order to export the weasel skins," Willauer explained, "the exporter must sell his foreign exchange to the Central Bank at the open market rate. However, in order to encourage exports the Central Bank permits a valuation of say $3.00 per pair." On a $25,000 transaction, CAT would obtain $10,000 in American currency and the equivalent of $15,000 in Chinese money. The airline had made a small profit in Chinese currency, the value of air transport had been demonstrated to upcountry merchants, and, best of all, precious American dollars had been obtained.

In mid-1948, when the Chinese government responded to inflationary pressure and dwindling reserves of foreign currency by linking exports and imports, ISC became a necessity. Under the new arrangement, CAT had to produce certificates showing the foreign exchange value of goods taken out of the country in order to import the equivalent value in parts and supplies. ISC provided the necessary export documents.[22]

While Chennault and Willauer juggled currencies and commodities, trying to turn a profit in the midst of financial chaos, the government's military situation continued to decline. Shantung Province remained the scene of heaviest fighting. As Consul Strong and Admiral Badger pointed out following the fall of Weihsien, Communist use of heavy artillery and willingness to suffer severe casualties doomed Tsinan and other government strong points in the region. Major General David Barr, commander of the United States Advisory Group, agreed that an isolated defensive position could no longer be maintained. "Having no confidence in the will to fight of the Tsinan garrison . . . and having heard reports of the questionable loyalty of some of the senior commanders," Barr recalled, "I recommended that the city be evacuated, and the troops withdrawn to Hsuchow." Chiang Kai-shek, however, rejected this sage advice. Tsinan, provincial economic and administrative center, had to be defended "because of political reasons."[23]

CAT suffered its first fatalities while supporting Nationalist forces in Tsinan. On July 29 Captain Clyde T. Tarbet, copilot Har Yung-shing, and radio operator Chan Wing-king were assigned to the shuttle run between Tsingtao and Tsinan. They had made two four-hour round trips, carrying rice, ammunition, and troops belonging to a division that Chiang had ordered airlifted into the beleaguered city. Shortly after 5:00 P.M., Tarbet's ungainly C-46 took to the runway for the day's final flight. Everything appeared normal as the airplane lifted off the ground and began to climb. Suddenly, at about one hundred feet, the C-46 nosed up sharply, stalled, spun into the ground, and burst into flame. The crew and sixteen soldiers perished.[24]

An investigation revealed that the accident never should have happened. The ground staff had failed to remove the gust locks from the control surfaces of the aircraft, a not uncommon oversight. The final item on the predeparture check list was designed to deal with this problem. Pilots were taught to roll all directional controls "free and clear" before takeoff. Tarbet, normally a cautious pilot, had failed to follow this basic dictum.[25]

The airlift continued. Although CAT flew more than 1,250 trips into Tsinan between mid-March and mid-September, the effort came to naught. On September 17 Burridge learned that the airfield was in danger of capture. Fearing another Weihsien, he ordered the immediate evacuation of CAT's staff. Captain Shilling arrived early the next morning only to learn that many employees had run into trouble with their passes while trying to reach the airfield. Shilling waited three hours before leaving with only half the staff, spurred by the control tower's advice that Communist forces were approaching.

Burridge flew to Tsinan later in the day to see if the remaining staff, who finally had reached the airport, could be safely evacuated. He circled the area and saw heavy fighting to the east and north, a mile or two from the field, but everything below seemed quiet. He decided to go in. Besides the anxious CAT personnel, only a lonely army private remained to guard the control tower. "About that time," Burridge recalled, "a group of field guards came running around the corner of the tower, yelling: 'The Reds are here!' Their shouts were punctuated by the whine of bullets coming from the direction the guards were rapidly leaving." Everyone piled aboard the transport. Captain Raymond E. Carleton started up the engines and began taxiing toward the runway. "The rest of us," Burridge continued, "stood in the back with both doors open, shoving off rice and hauling in the assorted citizens still clinging to the outside of the ship." As the C-46 lifted off the rice-strewn runway, Burridge made a hasty head count: all airline personnel were safe.[26]

CAT continued to airdrop rice for the city's garrison. Although a long siege of the heavily defended Nationalist bastion was anticipated, resistance collapsed when a division guarding the western approaches to the walled city went over en masse to the Communists.[27]

Mukden came next. Since January 1948, when the airlift began, CAT, CNAC, and CATC had flown thousands of missions in support of the government's futile effort to hold the strategic northern city. During the first nine months of the year, CAT alone had carried 17,200 tons of cargo into Mukden and evacuated more than one hundred thousand people. As the Communist vise tightened in October, the airlift became frantic. CAT launched a maximum effort, flying in 1,289 tons of food and bringing out ten thousand people in twenty days. But on October 15, the fall of Chinchow, a key supply base, signaled the end. CAT abandoned Mukden on October 29, the last airline to leave the city. Two days later the Nationalist garrison surrendered.[28]

The Manchurian debacle sent shock waves throughout China. "It spelled the beginning of the end," General Barr observed. Mao Tse-tung announced that the military situation had reached "a new turning point": victory for the revolution was at hand. Ambassador J. Leighton Stuart consulted with senior American military personnel, then warned Washington that "early fall present Nationalist Government is inevitable."[29]

As if Nanking did not have enough to worry about, the country's economy took a sharp turn for the worse. In mid-August, the government had nationalized gold, silver, and foreign currency. A new gold yuan, backed by reserves of precious metal and foreign currency, became the only circulating medium, with CN$ exchanged for the new notes at the rate of CN$3 million for GY1. At the same time, the government froze commodity prices. But despite harsh measures to enforce the law, Nanking's fiat could not alter economic realities. Black markets sprang up as the new currency slipped in value. On November 1, the day after Mukden surrendered, the government admitted failure of currency reform and lifted price ceilings. Mayor K. C. Wu of Shanghai asked his fellow citizens to "abide by your conscience" in dealing with the free market. Prices promptly skyrocketed. Within a few days, business had ground to a halt.[30]

As the Kuomintang's senior bureaucrats began to gaze with longing at Hong Kong, Taiwan, and more distant friendly shores, General Chu Teh of the People's Liberation Army massed six hundred thousand troops for an assault on Nanking. Chiang Kai-shek, in personal command of an equal number of soldiers, chose to give battle on the plains around Hsuchow, where the terrain favored the mechanized Nationalist army.[31]

A city of three hundred thousand about 175 miles north of Nanking, Hsuchow stood at the juncture of the Tientsin-Nanking railroad and the Lunghai line that ran from Kaiteng to the East China Sea. General Liu Chih, Chiang's field commander and an officer of limited ability, deployed his four group armies in and around the city. Liu had reason for confidence as he faced what promised to be the civil war's greatest clash of arms. Although the opposing forces were equal in number, the government boasted superiority in artillery and tanks, and its air force flew unopposed. "But," as General Lionel Chassin, French military historian, later observed, "poor morale, inept command, and a fixedly defensive frame of mind were to bring the Nationalists to another terrible disaster."[32]

The Communists struck on November 8, attacking General Huang Po-tao's Seventh Group Army. Huang, with ninety thousand men and a thousand artillery pieces, held strong defensive lines east of Hsuchow. In the midst of battle, however, two Nationalist generals and twenty-three thousand troops went over to the enemy. His position undermined by the defection, Huang fled westward, trying to reach the shelter of Hsuchow. Communist forces trapped the Nationalist general some fifty miles short of his objective. By November 22 the Seventh Group Army had ceased to exist.

Responding to Communist pressure, General Liu Chih concentrated his three remaining group armies in Hsuchow and turned over tactical command of the battle to his deputy, General Tu Yu-ming. This decision was unfortunate. Described by General Barr as "an officer of little worth," Tu had proved inept during the fighting in Manchuria. His dismal record would continue.[33]

During the battle, CAT, together with CNAC and CATC, operated as a paramilitary adjunct of the Nationalist Air Force. As the fighting intensified around Hsuchow, the airlines began flying around the clock, carrying rice and ammunition to the garrison and evacuating wounded soldiers. Many of the casualties, jammed into the aircraft, were in critical condition; the flight crews could offer only a drink of water. Those who survived the trip found little aid and comfort in Shanghai. Hospital facilities, inadequate to begin with, could not cope with the thousands of wounded who poured into the city. Willauer recalled:

> I personally was directly in charge of the evacuation . . . and the sights I saw were indeed pitiful. Most of these men had lain wounded without antiseptics or morphine or bandages on the battlefield three or four days before they had been picked up and brought in, and the stench of gangrene and the suffering of these Chinese boys was horrible. . . . We ran a base hospital and dispersal station at our own warehouses at our airport at Hungjao in Shanghai and used our own trucks to assist the Chinese Nationalists in further dispersing these people to the hospital. Our flight surgeon, Tom Gentry, performed miracles of first aid but with many of these poor chaps there was nothing more that could be done. A truly horrible sight it was and it shall remain forever indelible in my mind.[34]

In late November Chiang Kai-shek ordered General Tu to march south-westward and link up with a relief column from Nanking. As Tu moved out of Hsuchow, the situation at the airfield turned ugly. By November 30 all semblance of order had disappeared. Officers and heavily armed soldiers pushed the wounded aside and scrambled onto the aircraft. One soldier, dazed by panic, ran into a whirling propeller. Captain Stuart E. Dew found himself in a desperate situation as troops swarmed over his C-46. He stood in the doorway and tried to beat off the fear-crazed soldiers with a cargo tie-down stick. His copilot ran to the cockpit, started the left engine, and ran it up to full power, blowing people away from the doorway and against the tail surface. "It was something we had to do to get out," Dew recalled. "We were overloaded and otherwise couldn't have taken off." Once in the air, he radioed Shanghai: "Situation Hsuchow very bad. Hundreds of troops swarming our ships. Have 60 or 80 onboard. No stopping them." CAT abandoned the airlift. Hsuchow fell on December 1.[35]

"Nanking begins to look like a city that was," diplomat John Melby wrote in his diary, "and night after night the trucks rumble down to the barges on the river as the Government continues its move to the south." CAT joined the exodus. Several months earlier, against Willauer's advice, Chennault had ordered the airline's base maintenance facilities transferred from Canton to Shanghai. Following Mukden's surrender, both men agreed that the shops had to be moved back to Canton. Although planned as a gradual, orderly relocation, with most heavy equipment going by sea, the move was hastened by the calamitous Nationalist defeat at Hsuchow.[36]

"I am working like hell," Willauer wrote on December 2 to his wife, who had gone ahead to Canton, "am not down-hearted, see my way thru most of the problems and love you more than ever. Sorry you are having to see this type of chaos, but it is not a new thing to China. We will worry through somehow or other, and anyhow if worst comes, you and Sally [his daughter] can collaborate on a book to support me in old age, which is fast creeping up on me. . . . I never knew so many people have decided that I am their best friend—and own an airline."[37]

By early December Hsuchow's two hundred thousand surviving defenders, harassed by Communist attacks, drew up in defensive positions about sixty miles southwest of the city. CAT began airdrops with ten aircraft based at Nanking. On Christmas Day a desperate General Tu radioed a plea for help to the Chinese Air Force, with a copy to CAT:

> Our troops have been surrounded for more than ten days without any air drops. The officers and soldiers are so hungry and cold that they have killed the horses and cows, ate the bark and roots of grasses, and burned the houses, furniture and clothes for fuel use. Under such hungry-stricken conditions, there is no way to encourage the esprit-de-corps of the troops. In recent days, the soldiers are gradually deserting, and there is no means to get hold of the main force. In case such continue to last for some days, we shall be fallen to the Communists' trick of besieged to death. This is lamentable. It is therefore requested that the CAF will courageously run the risk of effecting air drops both in day and night (because it is necessary to seize opportunity before the snow days as we have previously by wire), in order to strengthen the spirit of the troops.[38]

Despite heavy antiaircraft fire that began to find its mark, CAT made every effort to assist the Nationalist troops. But, as Seymour Topping has noted in his moving account of the battle, "The airdrops made from about two thousand feet could not supply the garrison adequately. Many of the parachutes caught in the stiff plains winds drifted into the Communist camp."[39]

Red gunners opened a final artillery barrage on January 6, causing demoralized Nationalist soldiers to surrender in droves. David Tseng, CAT liaison to the government in Nanking, advised Shanghai on January 11 to cancel all airdrops over the area "because there is no longer such need now."[40]

CAT had performed admirably during the battle of Hsuchow. Between November 23, 1948, and January 11, 1949, the airline had transported 37,136 troops, 135 tons of ammunition, and 1,501 tons of rice, cakes, and biscuits. The effort came in a losing cause. As Willauer pointed out, Hsuchow "broke the back of the Chinese Nationalist resistance."[41]

Chiang Kai-shek relinquished office — but not power — on January 21, 1949, a sure sign that the end was approaching. The generalissimo began to move key personnel and the government's treasury to Taiwan, leaving acting President Li Tsung-jen to salvage something from the looming disaster. But as the Year of the Rat gave way to the Year of the Ox, most observers agreed that Nationalist China was finished.

CAT flourished in the adversity of China's civil war. Air transportation was at a premium in troubled times. During 1948 the airline carried 223,700 passengers and 88,238 tons of cargo and flew more than 34 million ton-miles. Profits sometimes proved elusive because of chaotic financial conditions, but Chennault and Willauer managed to wheel and deal with aplomb. Although a number of high officials in the State Department had grave reservations about CAT's paramilitary activities, the ambiguity of American policy worked against any attempt to restrain the airline's owners.[42]

It was during these bittersweet days that the "CAT spirit" emerged, a Hemingway insouciance in the face of danger, a determination to get the job done no matter the odds. Linfen, Weihsien, and Tsinan became legends. The exploits of Burridge, Shilling, Rousselot, Stayner, and other pilots who put their lives at hazard with a shrug of shoulders assumed mythic proportions. But the greatest adventure lay ahead: CAT would be tested to the limit during the siege of Taiyuan.

# Siege of Taiyuan

Shansi Province, about the size of Kansas, stands on a great loess plateau in northern China. Protected by river and mountain barriers from the neighboring provinces of Shensi, Hopeh, and Honan, Shansi retained a high degree of cultural and political autonomy during the first half of the twentieth century. Its people were reputed to be shrewd, diligent, persistent, frugal, and acquisitive. Proud in their isolation and independence, they gave the province a defiant motto: "Shansi Over All!"

Yen Hsi-shan shared in full measure the diverse qualities of his provincial countrymen. Born in 1883 in a small village in northeastern Shansi, Yen came from a family of minor bankers and merchants. He attended National Military College in Taiyuan, followed by five years at the Imperial Military Academy in Japan. Returning home in time to lead a revolt in 1911 against Manchu rule, Yen emerged as military governor and unchallenged leader of Shansi.

A reformer and modernizer, Yen reorganized provincial administration, campaigned against the queue and footbinding, sponsored irrigation and other agricultural improvements, and emphasized school and road development. Exploiting local resources of coal and iron, he built the great Taiyuan Arsenal, among the largest facilities of its kind in China and centerpiece for an ambitious program of industrialization.

Yen was adept at making opportunistic alliances, and his mastery of the political game, coupled with Shansi's geographic isolation, produced relative tranquillity for the province during the turbulent warlord era of the 1920s. Nominally loyal to the Nationalist government during the 1930s, Yen and Shansi retained a good measure of autonomy. In 1936 he sought Chiang Kai-shek's assistance to crush a Communist uprising in the province. Later he turned to the Communists for help against the Japanese. At the end of World War II, Yen retained Japanese technicians to assist economic recovery and incorporated Japanese troops into his army to fight the Communists.[1]

Despite Japanese assistance, Yen made little progress against the Communists. A. Doak Barnett, peripatetic scholar and keen observer of postwar China, visited the province in March 1948 and reported that Yen's prospects were not bright. The marshal held only three isolated areas at that time: Tatung in the north, Linfen in the south, and Taiyuan. Eleven million people lived under Communist rule; Yen governed four million. Although the military situation was relatively quiet, except for Linfen, Taiyuan faced a critical food shortage.

Commercial, industrial, and political center of the province, Taiyuan lay on the east bank of the Fen River in the middle of the fertile central plain. It was heavily defended. Touring the area, Barnett noted some nine thousand stone pillboxes surrounding the city. These tall, awkward, imposing structures, however, seemed to have been placed without regard to field of fire. An armored train made a daily run around Taiyuan on a special military railroad. More than seven hundred pieces of artillery ringed Yen's bastion.

"It is almost unbelievable," Barnett wrote, "in an area surrounded by mountains and Communists, to see large factories going full blast and huge shops, containing hundreds of machine tools, turning out complicated metal products." He reported that "a fantastic import-export trade" was going on by air between Taiyuan and other Nationalist areas of China. CAT, CNAC, and CATC were bringing in cotton, tobacco, oil, steel alloys, and dyes; they were taking out chemicals, steel products, and cement.

Although Yen advocated a progressive reform program, Barnett saw a considerable gap between words and deeds. Shansi, he contended, was in practice "a police state, ruled with an iron hand, and a place of near-starvation, fear, and despair." But the flood of refugees into Taiyuan suggested a lack of enthusiasm for the Communists. The people of the province seemed caught in the middle. Yen was an enigma. Though he was witty, charming, and a delightful host, the marshal's complex character defied analysis. Barnett concluded, "He is an extremely shrewd old man."[2]

The Communists sent 150,000 troops against Taiyuan in July 1948. In a series of fierce battles, the attackers neared the city's forty-foot-thick walls but were thrown back. Yen seized the initiative and forced the Communists to retreat into the surrounding mountains. October brought renewed action. Again Yen held out, but the rest of the province fell to the enemy. Taiyuan now stood alone.[3]

Robert Doyle of *Time* magazine visited Yen in early November and sent back to the United States a story that generated considerable public interest and sympathy for the beleaguered defenders. Doyle wrote:

Marshal Yen Hsi-shan received us in one of the small visiting rooms in his huge compound. The room was stocked with overstuffed chairs and handsomely carved table bearing cloisonné boxes full of Philip Morris cigarettes. . . . At 65 the Marshal is a tired old man suffering from diabetes. His grey-green unadorned uniform hangs baggily below a long face with sagging jowls and a scraggly grey mustache (his doctors report he has lost 25 pounds since summer). . . .

The unhappy Marshal sat at a modest desk adorned with a big color photograph of General Chennault and a smaller one of General George C. Marshall. Would he fight to the last? Yen bobbed his close-cropped head and smiled: "*Yi-ting, yi-ting*" (certainly, certainly). "But if the Communists smash into the city?" The Marshal sent an orderly who reappeared with a small cardboard box. He opened the box and displayed 500 tiny vials of potassium cyanide prepared for him by a German doctor. He picked out three. "These are for myself and my family." The rest were for his staff. Marshal Yen will not only prevent the Communists from capturing him alive—he will not even let them find his body. There are bottles of gasoline stored in his closet, ready to set fire to his room after his suicide.

But perhaps—just perhaps—this tragedy could be avoided. Yen outlined for Doyle a plan to save North China from the Communists. The United States, he said, should fund a hundred-thousand-man army of Japanese mercenaries, supported by a two-hundred-plane air force under the command of General Chennault. Although contrary to existing American policy, Yen acknowledged, "it is the only hope to stop the Communists."[4]

Chennault was eager to do his part. He had been calling for increased American aid since the beginning of the year. The United States must provide immediate and substantial assistance to anti-Communist forces in China, he had told a House committee in March 1948, or else face "the greatest failure of American foreign policy in all of our history and . . . inevitably set the stage for World War III."[5]

In early November 1948 Chennault raised with Chinese military leaders the possibility of forming a new American Volunteer Group, patterned after the organization that had flown so effectively against the Japanese in 1941–42. Airmen from CAT and former personnel of the Fourteenth Air Force with fighter pilot experience could be brought together quickly. Given such a unit, Chennault predicted with an overstatement typical of those that had caused him so much trouble during the war, he could halt the Communist offensive in a fortnight.[6]

Rumors that a new AVG was to be formed surfaced in Washington in mid-November. In response to a query from the State Department, Nanking cabled on November 18 that available evidence suggested "something of the sort [is] being considered and plans may be fairly well advanced." The following week, Secretary of Defense James Forrestal, who believed that the United States should take a more active role in China, suggested to Undersecretary of State James A. Lovett and Secretary Marshall that they explore reactivation of the AVG. Marshall withheld comment, but he clearly was not enthusiastic.[7]

Alarm bells began to clang in Foggy Bottom following the Forrestal-Marshall encounter. Assistant Secretary Butterworth hastened to prepare a memorandum that set forth State's objections to an American volunteer air force for China. "The formation of an AVG," he wrote on November 29, "with or without U.S. Government support or tacit approval, would have serious implications for our policy in China, the position of U.S. nationals there and our relations vis-a-vis the USSR." Such an organization would be viewed by people around the world as direct American intervention in the civil war, a policy "which we have consistently and scrupulously avoided." It could also have adverse effects on American nationals residing in areas that were or might later fall under Communist control. Further, Butterworth raised the specter of Russian backing for a "Soviet Volunteer Group," leading to aerial combat between American and Soviet fliers over Chinese territory. "It would therefore appear," the assistant secretary concluded, "that the formation at this time of an AVG in China would carry with it all the disadvantages of open American intervention in China's civil war and none of the possible advantages. For it is obvious that, while such a group could provide considerable annoyance for the Communists, it could not turn the tide in favor of the Nationalist forces."[8]

Later in the week, Brigadier General Marshall S. Carter, special assistant to Secretary Marshall, asked Butterworth "what the Department is doing to stop the formation of a revived AVG." Nothing, Butterworth replied. The subject had never been raised, formally or informally, so it seemed best to ignore the "rumors." "It is extremely unlikely," he reassured Carter, "that General Chennault would attempt to take unilateral action in the matter without first obtaining at least the tacit consent of the Government, for without such consent he could not be assured of receiving continuing supplies and material for the operation."[9]

The Chinese, as it turned out, were no more enthusiastic than the State Department. When Chennault spoke to Chiang Kai-shek about the idea, the generalissimo replied that China could not fund the project. Any new AVG, he said, would have to be underwritten by the United States. The demise of the scheme became apparent a few days later when Consul Strong in Tsingtao spoke to Burridge, staunch advocate of a volunteer force. Burridge, Strong reported to Ambassador Stuart on December 10, "was positive in his assertion that the reestablishment of an American Volunteer Group was now a dead issue."[10]

As plans for an AVG fizzled out, conditions at Taiyuan worsened. Following the Communist offensive in October, CAT had reorganized its operations in North China so as to support Yen more effectively. Tsingtao remained the airline's major base, while Tientsin (280 miles from Taiyuan) and Peking (250 miles away) became primary staging areas for the transport of food into the besieged city. Burridge, area manager at Tsingtao, was in overall command of the airlift, assisted by John R. Plank at Tientsin and William J. Wingfield at Peking.[11]

Taiyuan needed two hundred tons of food a day to survive. CAT, together with CNAC and CATC, kept supplies above this critical level until the airfields at Tientsin and Peking fell to Communist forces in mid-December, causing the airlift to falter. CAT delivered only twenty-two tons of rice on December 26 and forty-five tons the next day. Marshal Yen radioed a plea to CAT two days later, urging the airline "to overcome any difficulty" and deliver the daily minimum of two hundred tons. "For months," Yen later recalled with emotion, "we lived from day to day for the song of American planes over Taiyuan. I wasn't bothered so much about the sound of Communist shells or rifle fire — I was sure we could hold our own; but if I couldn't hear the planes, then I really worried. Planes meant rice. Rice meant the survival of the city."[12]

With the airlift going badly, Chennault took steps to implement a desperate scheme to help Yen. When *Time* correspondent Doyle had interviewed the marshal in November, Yen had commented: "One American told me that five U.S.-piloted planes with Napalm fire bombs could clear out the Communists around Taiyuan in three days. I believe this to be true." No doubt Chennault was the American who had raised Yen's hopes about the effectiveness of a napalm drop around Taiyuan. On December 28 and 29 Chennault and Willauer conferred with Minister of Communications Yu Ta-wei about Project Demonstration. Discussions continued after the first of the year with General Chou Chih-jou, CAF commander. After some initial reluctance on Chou's part, the two Americans received word on January 8 that the Chinese Air Force "wants us to go to work."[13]

Chennault, assisted by Operations Manager C. Joseph Rosbert and Chief Pilot Rousselot, prepared "in utmost security and secrecy" the operational plan for Project Demonstration. Ten P-47N fighter-bombers would be staged at Sian, a Nationalist base 330 miles southwest of Taiyuan where tight security could be maintained. There a detachment of CAT volunteers with fighter experience, temporarily employed by the Chinese government, would fly three or four hours of practice, including one napalm drop. Two six-plane missions would be launched on D-Day, followed by additional sorties on D + 1 and D + 2. As Communist units were cleared from the area, the detachment would operate from fields at Taiyuan. Project Demonstration not only would relieve the close siege of the city but would also impress the

Chinese Air Force with the value of napalm drops. The CAF could then expand the scheme into "a full scale operation."[14]

Rousselot had the pilots lined up and ready to go, but at the last minute Chennault began to have second thoughts about conducting such an enterprise without at least tacit approval from the American government. On January 12 he sent Willauer to brief Consul General Cabot in Shanghai. Although disagreeing with Washington's stand about noninvolvement in the war, Willauer assured Cabot that he and Chennault were loyal American citizens and would not defy official policy. Would there be any objections to activities by private American citizens to support the Nationalists? Cabot's reply is not recorded, but the next day Willauer jotted in his pocket diary: "No demonstration."[15]

Deep gloom settled over CAT's headquarters on The Bund. The Nationalists reeled southward following the bloody defeat at Hsuchow, while Washington seemed ready simply to watch the dust settle; the Chinese government owed the airline GY100 million for airdrops, causing a financial crisis for the airline; and disgruntled foreign personnel were three months behind in dollar allotments.

Chennault wanted to sell out and go home. "We have decided," Willauer wrote to his wife following a meeting of the airline's policy board, "against the General's first idea of just folding up CAT. If we did that, we might get out with [U.S.]$5,000,000 plus a slow liquidation of trucks, spares, etc. for an uncertain value. Please of course do not even intimate to anyone that the question of liquidation was even under consideration." Although he predicted that Nanking would fall by mid-February, followed by Shanghai in mid-March, Willauer remained optimistic about prospects for reduced operations in the Northwest and Southwest. "Many projects in these areas are well advanced," he reported, "and in some limited way at first, perhaps growing later, I think we can survive another year. With easy black markets following in the wake of chaos, I feel sure that we have a chance such as we never had before to get a bit of a nest egg out of the country if we survive at all. Anyhow in times of chaos air transport commands quite a price, if you have the means to operate it."[16]

Taiyuan remained defiant into the new year. "Our job right now," Burridge wrote to his parents in early January 1949, "is to get 200 tons of food flown in there each day, rain or shine." CAT carried about four tons per aircraft, so at least fifty flights per day had to make the long round trip from Tsingtao, the major supply base since the loss of Tientsin and Peking. A mission to Taiyuan meant six hours over enemy territory, without alternate landing areas or en route navigational aids, and because cargo doors were removed for airdrops, temperatures reached well below zero.[17]

To support the airlift, Marshal Yen completed two airfields, numbers 7 and 8, hard against the Communist-controlled mountains on the west bank of the Fen River. The fields were primitive dirt strips with steep gradients, well within range of enemy mortars. Communist gunners needed a few minutes to adjust fire, however, so it was possible to land, drop rice, and take off without getting trapped.[18]

On January 8 Yen urged CAT to use the new fields "so as to avoid difficulties and great losses sustained in making air drops." A few days later, Yen tried to make landing more attractive by offering a bonus of $100, payable immediately upon arrival, to those pilots willing to take the risk. "Most of the crews," Burridge recalled, "after a few firsthand experiences watching thousands of people scrambling for spilled rice, didn't have the heart to take the Marshal's money."[19]

Pilots who landed at Taiyuan usually found the experience memorable. Captain Roy Watts still recalls the day — January 14 — when three mortar shells fell within 150 yards of his aircraft on number 7 field. "We managed a hasty departure between mortar rounds," he explained. "I made no further daylight landings." Two days later Ernest W. Loane ran into trouble on number 8. Two mortar shells bracketed his aircraft, then a third shell landed less than 200 feet behind the C-46, spraying shrapnel around the aircraft. "Did not wait for fourth shell," he radioed Shanghai.[20]

Despite the hazards, Willauer planned to visit Taiyuan and discuss two important matters with Marshal Yen. The first related to "our postponement of combat work [Project Demonstration], and the hopes the General had stirred up in him [Yen] about that. Sort of an unbailing problem." He also hoped to persuade Yen to leave Taiyuan before the city fell to the Communists.[21]

Willauer tried to land on January 21, but constant shelling put both airstrips out of action. An attempt to sneak in at night failed when the pilot could not pick up the unlighted runway. Louise Willauer was not pleased. "You won't do any good to Marshal Yen if you kill yourself trying to help him," she scolded, "and you certainly will let your shareholders down, not to mention all the airline employees and omitting your wife and kids. Cut out the heroics, you damn fool!"[22]

Ignoring his wife's pleas, Willauer showed the level of his determination to see Yen by accompanying Chief Pilot Rousselot with a vital cargo of TNT and detonators into Taiyuan on January 26. "Incidentally," Willauer later pointed out, "about the easiest way to commit suicide is to carry TNT together with detonating caps. Either one or the other is okay. In this case we had to take the chance." Immediately after landing at Taiyuan, the aircraft came under mortar fire. Rousselot managed to park the shrapnel-punctured C-46 under the protection of a cliff. Willauer and Eva Wong (Yen's Eurasian secretary, who also had flown in on the C-46) dashed across the field between mortar rounds to a waiting station wagon. As they drove off, a shell exploded behind the car. "Just at the moment," Willauer recalled, "we were descending into a sunken road which ran along side the airport. The net result was that the other CAT men who were behind the plane, having seen the mortar shell hit and then the station wagon disappear, thought that we had been blown to smitherines."[23]

Willauer drove into the city, met Yen, and apologized for the failure of Project Demonstration. He urged Yen to leave the doomed citadel. The marshal should blow up Taiyuan's factories, then break out of the Communist encirclement with picked troops and head toward Paotow, 250 miles to the northwest. CAT would drop rice along the way and provide airlift from Paotow. Willauer alluded to a "popular movement" in the United States supporting Yen, led by such prominent figures as Senator Arthur H. Vandenberg, Representative Walter Judd, former ambassador William C. Bullitt, and Paul G. Hoffman, director of the Economic Cooperation Administration. Aid to China, Willauer stressed, required a demonstration of the country's ability to resist; Yen could provide such an example. The marshal remained noncommittal.[24]

Willauer returned to the airport and took off through heavy mortar fire. Climbing out of the valley, Rousselot radioed Shanghai: "You just about lost an aircraft, executive vice president, chief pilot, etc. About heaviest and most accurate shelling number seven field for two and a half hours. Suggest no more hazardous cargo flights [next] few days." The chief pilot counted more than seventy shrapnel holes in the C-46 after landing at Tsingtao.[25]

Between the middle of December and the end of January, CAT averaged twenty-eight flights daily between Tsingtao and Taiyuan and airdropped or landed 1,869 tons of food and fourteen tons of miscellaneous cargo. CNAC and CATC shared the burden of keeping Marshal Yen supplied. In January CAT had fourteen aircraft assigned to the Tsingtao-Taiyuan route, CNAC had twelve, and CATC had ten. The risks were also shared. A CNAC C-46 was hit by antiaircraft fire while airdropping at Taiyuan in mid-January and crash-landed. Another CNAC aircraft landed the next day under hazardous conditions and rescued the crew. CNAC, the airline's chief executive wrote, "can be credited with contributing effectively and substantially to the prolonged stand there by Marshal Yen."[26]

February brought a crisis. Funds to operate the airlift were GY100 million in arrears, but officials in Nanking were more inclined to complain than to make good on the deficit. "I suppose we will finally bail something out of this affair," Willauer told Chennault, "but I swear I would have told them all off if it had not been for the Marshal." Additionally, Chinese ground crews at Tsingtao threatened to strike; Nationalist forces guarding the city grew ner-

C-46 taking off from Shanghai's Hungjao airfield (CAT Operations, Engineering, and Supply buildings in background), 1949

vous as Communist pressure increased; and the weather was atrocious. "I had three planes in the air all at once with engines cutting out due to carburetor icing," Burridge recalled. Still, there was no lack of spirit among the pilots. As Burridge pointed out, "The guys took flights for Marshal Yen they wouldn't have taken for anyone else in China." But enthusiasm alone could not keep planes in the air. On February 10 operations came to a halt when Tsingtao ran out of gasoline.[27]

A string of frantic radio messages poured out of Taiyuan protesting the shutdown. His people had not had any food for three days, Yen cried; they were starving. He implored Burridge to get the airlift going again. CAT's area manager could do nothing. Finally, Yen came out of Taiyuan to put pressure on officials in Tsingtao, Nanking, and Shanghai. He promised his troops he would get food for them or return to die.[28]

Yen first met with Burridge and Admiral Badger in Tsingtao. He told Burridge that his life depended on CAT and asked for a frank discussion of problems. "I told him," Burridge reported to Willauer, "that they [the problems] were basically lack of gasoline and failure to pay freight money which caused strikes and other problems due to delay in payment of CAT personnel." The American naval commander promised to do what he could to help. He would be happy to assist with the gasoline shortage if anyone could show him how to do so. In the meantime, Badger ordered marines ashore on a "training exercise" to bolster local morale.[29]

Yen continued to Nanking and called on Ambassador Stuart. The marshal wanted the Economic Cooperation Administration to assist in the airlift. "I felt unable to give him any encouragement," Stuart cabled to Washington, "believing this operation one for Chinese Government and not ECA."[30]

Chinese officials proved more responsive. Yen arranged to borrow seven hundred thousand gallons of fuel from the Chinese Air Force at Shanghai. Nearly five hundred thousand gallons would be shipped to Tsingtao, arriving by February 26. At the rate of seventy flights a day, this fuel should permit operations until early March. The government also promised US$450,000 in foreign exchange to purchase an additional month's supply of gasoline. Arrears in freight charges would be paid to anxious airlines and a system of prompt reimbursement established.[31]

Although frustrated with Chinese officialdom, Willauer continued to support Yen's heroic struggle. As he explained to his wife on February 20:

> I believe the Old Marshal is sincere when he told President Li Tsung-jen that his personal life depended on the supply by airdrop of the three airlines. He came out for the sole purpose of getting that set up again after all but CAT had given up, and it looked very much as if we would have to because we were in serious arrears on payments, and it seemed that Tsingtao was about to fall. Now it looks as though all of those problems have a chance of coming out okay, and in the meantime the Marshal is using me as sort of a brain trust to steer him along. . . .
>
> Hard-boiled as I may sometimes seem, I am caught with the real sense of the dramatic by that old Marshal flying out to do battle with all the vagaries of the present chaos of the Chinese government in order to hold onto his world and the people he rules. There is a story for you to write sometime — maybe now. It's Horatio at the bridge and the Berlin airlift rolled in one. Complete with Hairbreadth Harry in the [person] of our pilots, and even your crazy husband.[32]

The airlift began again in earnest when gasoline reached Tsingtao in late February, and CAT pilots once more flew long hours under difficult conditions to keep Taiyuan supplied. Randall S. Richardson probably set the record when he logged twenty-one hours and forty-five minutes of flight time on March 3. Bernard Hickley, correspondent for the *London Daily Telegraph*, spent a week with CAT at Tsingtao and came away impressed. "Quite often the crews were flying 18 hours a day," he reported, "but it doesn't seem to worry them, and I found more of a wartime combat team spirit among them than among any group I've met since the end of hostilities."[33]

Dramatic incidents became commonplace. James B. McGovern initiated one on March 8 when he made an emergency landing at Taiyuan after an engine froze up. A short time later, John Plank arrived over the city for a rice drop, heard about McGovern's plight, and landed on the same airstrip. Plank ordered McGovern to collect both crews and take off with the operable aircraft. The assistant area manager then spent an uneasy night under Communist gunfire as ground crews in Shanghai worked to remove a good engine from another aircraft. Norman A. Schwartz arrived from Shanghai early the next morning with rice, a new engine, and four mechanics. He unloaded, picked up a full load of passengers, mail, and empty rice sacks, and made a hasty departure. As Yen's artillery kept up a massive counterbattery fire, the mechanics changed engines in record time. At 8:00 P.M. Plank and his tired colleagues flew out of the doomed but still defiant city.[34]

Despite the heroism of the pilots, the courage of the defenders, and the indomitable will of Marshal Yen, Taiyuan could not stand against the Communist spring offensive. On April 16 the city's outer defenses came under fierce attack. Yen, who had been summoned to Nanking for a conference, tried to return to his post, but the Chinese Air Force would not furnish an aircraft. He pleaded with Burridge for CAT's assistance. Burridge said that it was too risky. Yen offered to buy an aircraft. Burridge replied that he could not hazard the lives of the crew. Desperate, the sixty-six-year-old marshal wanted to parachute in. Burridge demurred.[35]

The enemy breached the city's massive walls on April 20, and house-to-house fighting ensued. A series of faded radio flimsies record the end:[36]

April 20
   Burridge to Rosbert: Suspend airdrops temporarily because the troops are unable to reach the parcels.

April 21
   David G. Davenport to Operations: "Over Taiyuan 11,500 feet. Flack so thick you can walk on it. Am returning with full load. Would not advise any ships to drop. Flack had Bushbaum bracketed for sixteen bursts, no hits, over east side of city."

   Tsingtao to Shanghai: Only two planes completed airdrops this morning. All pilots reported heavy concentrations of flak up to eleven thousand feet. No planes hit. Unable to get any information from local authorities about Taiyuan.

April 22
   William D. Gaddie to Operations: "Made passes over Taiyuan 11,000–14,500 feet. Each time they had my range close enough to hear the burst. Estimate gun range up to 15,000 feet. Advise airdrop not safe."

April 23

> Burridge to Rosbert: All Taiyuan airdrop planes are carrying oxygen. So far, no antiaircraft fire observed over fifteen thousand feet.

> Rosbert to Burridge: "Do not believe Taiyuan airdrop can last indefinitely and still do not think it advisable to make drops in face of antiaircraft fire. Commies will hold fire occasionally just to draw in more planes."

On April 24, after bitter fighting in the streets, Taiyuan fell.[37]

Yen's followers kept their vows. Five hundred close associates, led by Acting Governor Liang Hua-chih, swallowed vials of poison and had their bodies burned. The old marshal survived to serve as premier of the dying Nationalist government and to live in exile on Taiwan—but everyone knew that his spirit had died in Taiyuan.[38]

As the end grew near for Taiyuan, President Li Tsung-jen in Nanking watched as Mao's legions poured across the undefended Yangtze River. Chiang Kai-shek already had ordered the government's treasury—gold and silver valued at US$335 million—and selected air and naval units moved to Taiwan. Li, who held title but no power, called on his associates for plans to defend Southwest China. His advisers, Li wrote, "could only sigh." Communist troops entered Nanking on April 24, the same day Taiyuan surrendered.[39]

Chennault, who was preparing to leave for the United States in a last-ditch effort to drum up support for continued resistance on the mainland, left instructions to guide Willauer during the days ahead. Following the fall of Shanghai, probably in early May, Chennault expected the Communists to drive toward Canton via Changsha or Suichwan. If Mao's forces took either city, the airline should evacuate Canton. "In fact," Chennault told Willauer, "this might be considered the signal for the liquidation of CAT."[40]

The siege of Taiyuan produced one of the most heroic—and least known—airlifts in history.

The great drama of the Berlin airlift, mounted in June 1948, took place before an audience of millions. The eyes and hearts of people on both sides of the Atlantic turned toward that beleaguered city as hundreds of planes from many nations streamed along the three Berlin air corridors with military precision, evenly spaced, carefully guided to landings at the American, British, and French airports. Turnaround crews unloaded the aircraft while engines were still running; in minutes the transports were again airborne. Reports of the massive airlift filled newspapers and magazines. People were mesmerized, their hearts gladdened by pictures of Berlin children scrambling for candy that pilots had dropped in miniature parachutes.

The only people mesmerized by the tiny fleet of aging aircraft that rattled between Tsingtao and Taiyuan for six bone-chilling hours (nine from Shanghai) were the starving populace of Taiyuan. They waited patiently in the bitter cold as pilots picked their way across enemy territory, substituting skill and intuition for nonexistent navigational aids. Arrivals were announced by Communist antiaircraft fire. Ringed by flak bursts, crews worked feverishly to kick out their precious cargo of rice. The "song of American planes over Taiyuan" meant survival.

When Taiyuan fell in April 1949, the Berlin airlift was at its height. The following month, the Western allies celebrated a victory: the Berlin airlift had prevailed, a magnificent triumph of organization.

But Taiyuan, in defeat, was an even greater triumph—one of spirit.

5

The Chennault Plan

"The United States is losing the Pacific war."

This dramatic opening sentence leaped out at readers of Chennault's auto-biography, *Way of a Fighter*, published early in 1949. CAT's president went on to paint a bleak picture of events in China. The Communists had won in Manchuria and were preparing to cross the Yangtze River. The entire main-land stood in imminent danger of collapse, an event that would cause a chain reaction throughout the Far East. Chennault envisioned "a ring of Red bases," stretching "from Siberia to Saigon." With its vital eastern flank se-cured by Chinese subordinates, the Soviet Union would be in position to threaten the United States with destruction. "I can hear the time fuse of a third world war sputtering in China as it burns toward the final powder keg," he wrote, "and I cannot stand idly by without making every effort in my power to snuff it out."[1]

Publication of *Way of a Fighter* marked the start of Chennault's effort to mobilize American support for a plan to stop communism on the periphery of China. Assisted by Corcoran, Washington lobbyist par excellence, Chen-nault mounted a full-scale publicity campaign, making speeches, giving in-terviews, testifying before congressional committees, writing articles and letters, and importuning public officials.[2]

Chennault set forth the main theme of his program during an appearance before the Senate's Armed Services Committee on May 3, 1949, shortly after his arrival from Shanghai. The craggy-faced aviator began by developing at length his "domino theory" of events in Asia. Mao's victory, he argued, would result in massive Communist support for Ho Chi Minh in Indochina. After the Vietminh defeated the French, as they surely would with Chinese material assistance, an encircled Thailand would fall next. In turn, Burma and an already troubled Malaya would collapse. These losses would mark only the beginning: Chennault spoke about pressure on India and a Soviet move toward the Middle East. Japan and the Philippine Islands would be endangered. A new East Asia Co-prosperity Sphere, "from the Bering Sea to Bali," would grow up under the direction of the Soviet Union. With the Pacific a Russian lake, a threatened United States would have to strike back with nuclear weapons.

It was not too late, however, to avert "the ultimate catastrophe" of World War III. Chennault pointed out that an extensive anti-Communist area remained in China, extending from the Mohammedan-dominated provinces of the Northwest, through Szechwan and Hunan, to Yunnan in the Southwest. These regions had a strong tradition of local autonomy and were led by men determined to resist the Communists. Protected by shifting deserts and impassable mountains, they could easily be defended. Chennault knew this territory well: it encompassed much of what had been Free China during the recent war against Japan.[3]

In his testimony before the committee and elsewhere, CAT's president advanced the "Chennault Plan" to preserve this area from Communist rule and contain Mao's forces. The United States, he said, should send a military mission to China, charged with procurement and distribution of supplies to regional armies in this "sanitary zone." American advisers would train and plan, serving in Chinese units down to the company level. The emphasis, naturally, would be on air power, with a Sino-American unit as the major combat arm. CAT and other civilian airlines would provide essential logistical support. The scheme, he estimated, should cost about $150 to $200 million a year. "With the proper kind of aid and support from the United States," Chennault predicted, "and the kind of communication and strategy that can be given them by air, these peripheral areas can be welded into an effective union of Chinese resistance."

Although Chennault's dramatic plan to halt communism in the Far East impressed most listeners, several congressmen voiced concern about his motives. Was the plan simply a device for advancing his own economic purposes? Questioned about a possible conflict of interest should an assistance program be implemented, Chennault replied: "I am not advocating any aid here to the benefit of my airline. I have offered to give up all my interests in the airline, resign my position with it, if my recommendations for aid are carried out and if I can be used personally in the program."[4]

Chennault took his plan to a skeptical State Department. Secretary Dean Acheson, an "Atlanticist," considered Europe to be most vital to American interests. When he did look across the Pacific, the corruption and venality of the Nationalists filled him with disgust. Because the United States had neither the will nor the power to affect the course of the civil war, he felt he had no choice but to sit back and maintain a broad historical perspective on events.[5]

W. Walton Butterworth, director of the Division of Far Eastern Affairs, agreed with Acheson. A Princeton graduate, conservative, and staunchly anti-Communist, Butterworth liked to consider himself an unsentimental realist. Lacking any illusions that a special relationship existed between China and America, he saw no hope for the Nationalist government. Chinese leaders, he believed, were more concerned with lining their pockets than fighting Communists. Like Acheson, Butterworth was prepared to accept the inevitable and make the best of the new situation.[6]

Dean Rusk, deputy undersecretary of state and important in the formulation of Far Eastern policy, was one of a number of individuals in the department who were bothered by the relative neglect of China. But he was no admirer of the Nationalist government or of Chennault. A staff officer under General Stilwell during the war, Rusk questioned Chennault's ties to the Chiang-Soong coterie and had deep doubts about the general's personal honesty. If there was hope of salvaging something from the China mess, it would not be through the Nationalists — or Chennault.[7]

Chennault visited the State Department on May 11, met briefly with Undersecretary James E. Webb, then presented this plan at length to Rusk. "What individuals could carry the plan at the top?" Rusk asked. "Only one man," Chennault responded, "Chiang Kai-shek." The diplomat remained inscrutable as he escorted the general to the door.[8]

The State Department sent the Chennault Plan to the embassy in China for comment. Ambassador Stuart discussed the proposal with his military attachés and reported: "Our feeling is that, while plan may have validity in some of its aspects, as a whole it is impractical and of doubtful value to furtherance US national interests." The situation in China, Stuart emphasized, "has gone too far to be retrieved."[9]

Minister-Counselor Lewis Clark took a stronger position. The Chennault Plan, he advised Washington, was ill-conceived, unrealistic, and would benefit only the commercial interests of CAT. Chennault's vaunted "sanitary zone" of anti-Communist resistance did not exist. Although the Mohammedan leaders of the Northwest would fight with or without American assistance, they lacked popular support and were doomed. Szechuan officials were distraught by the prospect of a Nationalist move to Chungking, fearing that it would invite early Communist attack; they wanted only accommodation. Yunnan's government likewise hoped to make the best terms possible with the Communists, not fight. "In other words," Clark concluded, "disintegration is so far advanced, morale so low and the desire of the people for peace so strong that any effort [to] support continued resistance in West or Southwest China seems doomed in advance to failure."[10]

Secretary Acheson, testifying during a closed session of the House Committee on Foreign Affairs in June, seemed to shut the door on the Chennault

Plan. Questioned by Representative Walter Judd, one of Chennault's supporters, Acheson replied: "We are of course familiar with General Chennault's view. Military authorities did not consider them to be soundly taken. We are not closing our minds to any of these things. If some developments take place that warrant, we will be eager to follow them. I am not in a position to come to Congress and ask Congress for money at this time to do something which we do not believe can possibly be effective."[11]

According to the public record, which has been maintained for more than three decades, Washington's interest in the Chennault Plan died when Acheson dismissed the proposal. But the public record is not complete. Chennault found another organization in Washington more sympathetic toward his ideas, one that shunned the light of publicity: the Central Intelligence Agency (CIA).

In early May Corcoran had arranged a meeting between Chennault and Rear Admiral Roscoe H. Hillenkoetter, director of the CIA. Their discussions proved inconclusive, but Chennault's views sparked the interest of Paul L. E. Helliwell, a CIA official and former chief of the Office of Strategic Services' (OSS) Intelligence Division in Kunming. Helliwell had worked closely with Chennault during the war, and he had a higher opinion of him than did Rusk. Helliwell recommended to Frank G. Wisner, head of the Office of Policy Coordination (an intentionally vague designation that masked the government's covert action arm) that contact be established with Chennault, looking toward the possible use of his airline for clandestine operations in China. Thus was set in motion a train of events that would have far-reaching consequences for CAT.[12]

Before tracing these developments, however, the Office of Policy Coordination (OPC) and its dynamic head require an introduction.

American capability for covert activities had ended with the disbandment of OSS at the end of World War II. By fall 1947, however, mounting problems with the Soviet Union made the need for a clandestine option painfully clear. The responsibility for covert psychological warfare was initially assigned to the State Department, but Secretary Marshall soon raised powerful objections. He believed that clandestine operations, if exposed, could embarrass the department and discredit American foreign policy, a view that many foreign service officers came to share over the years. The secretary slammed his VMI-ringed fist on the desk and the waters parted: on December 14, 1947, the National Security Council (NSC) transferred to the CIA— established by the National Security Act of July 1947 to coordinate intelligence activities—responsibility for covert psychological operations. Thus, by default, the CIA first acquired a limited covert capability.[13]

As the situation in Europe grew worse—the Czech coup of February 1948 had a major impact on Washington—sentiment increased for expansion of clandestine activities to meet the Russian challenge. George F. Kennan, director of the department's Policy Planning Staff and a persuasive spokesman for containment, advocated in May 1948 that a covert political action capability be developed to supplement psychological warfare. In response, the National Security Council adopted directive 10/2 in June 1948, authorizing a dramatic increase in covert operations against the Soviet Union. NSC 10/2 assigned responsibility for the conduct of these operations to the newly created Office of Policy Coordination.

OPC occupied a peculiar position in the bureaucracy. Its budget and personnel were appropriated within the CIA's allocations, but the secretary of state appointed its director. Policy guidance came from a committee composed of representatives of the State and Defense departments. Originally perceived as a small contingency unit to mount limited operations, OPC quickly established itself as a significant, permanent force. Its rise was in part a result of the worsening world situation; however, Frank G. Wisner played a key role in shaping and expanding the organization.

Appointed head of OPC on September 1, 1948, Wisner brought to the job intelligence, ambition, and energy. A southerner, he had attended the University of Virginia as an undergraduate and law student, then had practiced corporate law with a prominent New York firm. He served briefly in the navy during World War II before joining OSS. Wisner quickly rose to a responsible position, gaining experience in clandestine activities that he later would put to good use. In 1947, after a brief return to legal practice, he became deputy to the assistant secretary of state for occupied areas before moving to OPC.

The new director flourished at OPC. "Wisner landed like a dynamo," William Colby recalled, "read all the intelligence and set out to form a clandestine force worldwide. By hard work and brilliance, and by reaching widely for similarly activist OSS alumni, he started it operating in the atmosphere of an order of Knights Templars, to save Western freedom from Communist darkness — and from war."[14]

Circumstances favored Wisner's ambitions for OPC. Rear Admiral Hillenkoetter, CIA director from May 1947 to October 1950 and potential rival for power, offered little interference. Only recently promoted to flag rank, he lacked the leverage and bureaucratic expertise to deal effectively with senior policy makers in State and Defense. "He remained a sea captain in mind and heart," one knowledgeable writer has observed. On the other hand, Wisner, a man of independent wealth, had the professional and social contacts to thrive in the Washington milieu. Although he met approximately once a week with the designated representatives from State (George Kennan, 1948–50) and Defense, they did not attempt close supervision. As noted in Anne Karalekas's history of the CIA, "The guidance that State and

Defense provided OPC became very general and allowed maximum opportunity for project development."[15] During the winter of 1948–49, Wisner built up OPC's staff, relying on OSS veterans to fill the ranks. The organization also undertook a limited number of covert operations in Europe. By the time Chennault came to Washington in May 1949, Wisner had begun to consider plans for anti-Communist resistance in the Far East. He therefore was pleased to learn that Chennault had a concrete proposal — and the necessary air transport to implement it.

Acting on Helliwell's recommendation, Wisner and several associates (including Franklin A. Lindsay, Carmel Offie, and Joseph A. Frank) met with Chennault at the Hotel Washington on May 9. The general outlined his plan to contain communism in Asia, emphasizing CAT's role in providing essential logistical support. Wisner came away impressed by Chennault's forceful presentation. Here was a man of action! Wisner had Alfred A. Hussy draft a memorandum for the State Department to express OPC's interest in the project. Because OPC planned to contract with CAT to carry supplies to anti-Communist elements in China, Wisner hoped to ensure the airline's financial stability through a grant from the Economic Cooperation Administration.[16]

Wisner found little sympathy at the State Department, and ECA officials, who earlier in the year had rejected a similar proposal to assist airlines in China, continued to resist helping CAT. Undaunted, Wisner asked Helliwell to consider means of direct or indirect subsidy to CAT in order "to preserve its operations, facilities and personnel for ultimate OPC use in China."[17]

Helliwell had a "preliminary and *unofficial*" discussion with Corcoran on June 27. Chennault had indicated to Wisner that CAT's financial problems were severe; Corcoran portrayed the situation as desperate. "The primary trouble," Helliwell reported to Wisner, "is acute 'dollaritis.'" The airline needed foreign exchange to purchase gasoline and spare parts and to pay allowances to American personnel. Helliwell estimated that OPC would have to provide a minimum of $1 million a year to hold the airline together. Would any possible gain be worth the cost? Helliwell concluded with a strong recommendation, which later would provide the rationale for OPC's acquisition of the airline:

> It is the opinion of this writer that if at all possible action must be taken to hold C.A.T. intact. The "face" of the C.A.T. operation, coupled with its communications and operation, cannot be established by a new operation without the expenditure of many millions of dollars. The operation is so set up that it can be militarized, if that should become necessary, and unquestionably OPC flying and other personnel can be gradually introduced into the operation to ensure continuity and proper function. It is strongly urged that

favorable policy decisions be taken promptly and that thereafter the necessary contacts and representations be made looking toward ultimate operational subsidy sufficient to maintain C.A.T. as an American-owned airline
with complete facilities in non-Communist China.[18]

While heavy decisions were being weighed in Washington, events in
China—especially in the Northwest—were casting doubt on the viability of
the border areas that Chennault hoped to bring together as an effective anti-
Communist force.

CAT's plans for extensive operations in the northwestern provinces of
Kansu, Ninghsia, and Chinghai had begun in 1948. Lanchow, ancient walled
city on the south bank of the Yellow River and capital of Kansu, was seen as
the hub for a network of feeder routes, operated by light aircraft, that would
extend several hundred miles into adjacent areas. Savings in transportation
time would be dramatic. A truck took a week to cover 225 miles of poor road
that linked Lanchow with Ninghsia; a light aircraft could make the round trip
in a morning. Light planes would funnel into Lanchow personnel, mail, vital
parts for machinery, and other lightweight—high-value cargo. C-46s would
carry drummed gasoline into Lanchow, then pick up passengers, wool, and
accumulated cargo for the thousand-mile trip to coastal points. In November
1948 CAT moved to implement this scheme and ordered—at a cost of
$15,000 each—six single-engine Cessna 195s, designed to haul five pas-
sengers or one thousand pounds of cargo over a distance of six hundred to
nine hundred miles.[19]

As the military fortunes of the Nationalists plummeted during the early
months of 1949, Chennault raised the possibility of liquidating CAT. Willauer
argued in opposition that liquidation would not only be difficult under existing circumstances but that operations in the Northwest and Southwest offered reasonable prospects for profit. If the Taiyuan airdrop continued into
mid-February and if—a big if—CAT was paid, there would be "a good
enough cushion" to begin full-scale operations in the border areas. In the
meantime, Willauer worked with Operations Director Rosbert to streamline
CAT for "what I fear may be some pretty slim times in the next few months."
He also sent Judge Norman F. Allman—old China hand, editor of the *China
Press*, and CAT intimate—to discuss with northwestern leaders the prospects for American arms assistance.[20]

In late February, as the first four Cessnas arrived for assembly in Hong
Kong, CAT received final permission from the Ministry of Communications
to go ahead with the project. Chennault visited the area during the first week
of April, hoping to cement trade relations and gather material for the resistance plan that he soon would present in the United States. As the large

Cessna 195s in China's northwestern provinces, 1949

The first Civil Air Tranport C-46s from Hawai arrive over Shanghai (Courtesy Felix Smith)

transport reached cruising altitude and passengers and crew settled in for the tedious flight to Lanchow, Chennault no doubt pulled from his briefcase the lengthy memorandum that Willauer and others had put together for him. It contained CAT's confidential view of the situation in the Northwest.[21]

CAT placed high hopes in General Ma Pu-fang, governor of Chinghai province and leader of Moslems throughout the Northwest. "Fair dealing and sincere," Ma Pu-fang had an army of fifty-thousand well-armed soldiers and the same number of partially armed men; in reserve he had two hundred thousand trained but unarmed troops. The memorandum stated: "It is likely that, if this man were armed with sufficient weapons of the lighter type such as rifles, machine guns, tommy guns, mortars, bazookas and mountain (pack) artillery, he would prove to be impossible to drive out of his province, and he would very possibly become a strong rallying point for Chinese anti-Communists. It is entirely possible that he could become a spearhead for a real drive against the Communists owing to the fighting qualities of his troops and his aggressive policy."[22]

General Ma Hung-k'uei, leader of Ninghsia province, possessed neither Ma Pu-fang's "political stature nor his broad concept of political and industrial development in the north west." He had an army of fifty thousand men, well trained and partially equipped, and an equal number of unarmed reserves. "Acquisitive and petty" in business, Ma Hung-k'uei should be treated with great care.[23]

General Kuo Chih-hsiao, governor of Kansu, was serious, pleasant, fairly capable, and honest but could not be considered a major factor in the Northwest. A Nationalist functionary, Kuo had no troops of his own. The more aggressive Mohammedan leaders "make no secret of the fact that if he does not go along with them, he is out."[24]

CAT had an agreement with Ma Pu-fang to buy and ship without interference all Sining wool — by far the best in China. Discussions for a similar arrangement were under way with Ma Hung-k'uei. The memorandum estimated that 25 percent of CAT's flying capacity of three thousand hours a month "can be occupied on wool alone if in-bound cargoes can be found."[25]

Chennault reached Lanchow on April 3, sipped grape wine with Governor Kuo, and danced with his wife to "real American jazz music." He went on the next day to Ninghsia, where Ma Hung-k'uei put on a military exhibition. Although overweight and suffering from diabetes, the governor personally led his men in sword exercises. "As long as I live," he assured Chennault, "there will be no surrender to the Communists. If I die, my son will rise up in my place, and — if he dies — his son. We will never quit."[26]

Sining, ancient center of trade high on the Tibetan plateau, was the final stop on the trip. A sand-filled wind blew constantly, covering everything with gray-white dust while Chennault met with the man whom he considered "one of the most liberal and progressive officials in China." Chennault toured Ma Pu-fang's reforestation projects, dined on mutton and lotus-seed soup, and assured the governor of CAT's continued support.

Impressed by what he had seen, Chennault returned to the United States and told Congress that "these people are willing, indeed anxious, to fight if provided with the minimum of aid."[27]

While Chennault lobbied in Washington, Willauer struggled to keep CAT in business. After reaching an all-time high in March of 4,508 hours and 5,194,825 ton-miles, flying declined in April to 3,485 hours and 3,198,745 ton-miles. The bottom fell out in May,[28] although there were a few bright spots. Operations in the Northwest got off to a promising start. After CAT established a radio station, homer beacon, and crew hostel at Lanchow, service to Sining began on May 9, when Felix T. Smith delivered a sack of mail to Ma Pu-fang. Sterling Bemis inaugurated the route to Ninghsia on May 15, carrying as first passenger Ma Hung-k'uei's attractive wife. CAT flew two hundred tons of medical supplies from Canton to Chungking for ECA. The airline contracted with the Chinese army for thirty flights a month from Amoy to Lanchow, Chungking, and Hengyang, carrying silver dollars — Operation Payroll. Willauer, however, reported to Chennault, "For the first time in CAT's history, as far as I know, we have had to pay squeeze to get a contract. . . . It probably was the only way the contract could have been gotten . . . but still I do not like it."[29]

But kickbacks to the Chinese army were the least of CAT's problems. Large contracts had ended with the fall of Taiyuan and evacuation of Nanking. Adding up the totals for May, Willauer found that CAT had flown only 1,705 hours and 249,906 ton-miles. The prospects for June seemed even bleaker. CAT, he estimated, would be lucky to fly 1,000 hours.[30]

Willauer worked long and hard to drum up business. He sent men to scour the interior and coastal areas for cargo, he appealed to the government for contracts, and he increased scheduled flights in an attempt to attract small shippers. These efforts paid off, at least to the extent that the situation did not deteriorate in June. Light plane operations continued to expand. CAT stationed Cessnas at Taipei (Taiwan) and Amoy, hoping to promote business in portions of the Southeast that had not fallen to the Communists. Using four Cessnas based at Lanchow, the airline extended service in the Northwest to include Pingliang, Wuwei, Siaho, Shantan, Tienshui, Dinyuanning, and Shansah.[31]

On June 19 Edward R. Norwich and two Chinese passengers became the first — and only — fatalities in CAT's light plane operation. Caught in a sudden sandstorm, the twenty-seven-year-old former Marine Corps navigator turned pilot crashed while attempting to land in rugged terrain outside Lanchow.[32]

June's most promising development came in the Southwest with the start of an airlift of tin from Yunnan to French Indochina, the culmination of eighteen months of hard work. Yunnan had been one of the world's leading tin producers before World War II, exporting ten thousand metric tons a year. More than one hundred thousand people worked in the mines, while another million, or 10 percent of the province's population, depended on the industry for a living. After the war, however, production slumped to thirteen hundred metric tons a year. Lack of mining machinery and spare parts caused part of the decline, but inadequate transportation was the main problem. Tin reached the outside world on the backs of coolies, via sampans, and on ancient trucks that traveled on terrible roads from Kunming to Rangoon and Canton. In June 1948 CAT had offered to airlift eight hundred metric tons a month from the mining center of Mengtze in southern Yunnan to the port of Haiphong in French Indochina. The trip would take two hours at a cost of six cents a pound.[33]

CAT's proposal had manifest advantages. It would restore the depressed economy of Southwest China, channel tin to the United States and other world markets, reduce the world price of tin by an estimated 25 percent, and provide China with sorely needed exchange. These rosy prospects were darkened by the difficulties of implementing the scheme. The French had to permit landings by Chinese-registered aircraft, and the Chinese had to grant reciprocal rights to French airlines; the United States had to agree to buy the tin, and the producers had to agree on price, methods of payment, and other arrangements; oceangoing shipping had to call at Haiphong, and oil companies had to expand service facilities for aviation gasoline at the French port; the Ministry of Communications had to designate Mengtze as an international airport, and Chinese customs had to set up clearance procedures; finally, CAT had to establish communications, make billeting arrangements, and handle the myriad details connected with such an operation. The task would be challenging.[34]

After months of frustrating negotiations, all the pieces began to fall into place. In January 1949 the Reconstruction Finance Corporation signed an agreement to purchase tin from the Yunnan Tin Producers' Association. In April the French gave permission for a limited number of flights into Haiphong, and Standard Vacuum Oil Company built storage tanks and feeder lines for aviation gasoline at the port. CAT contracted with Descours & Cabaud, a leading import-export firm, to act as agent in French Indochina and installed communications apparatus on the roof of its office building in Haiphong. Frank L. Guberlet, one of the airline's two French-speaking employees, took over as operations manager.[35]

The airlift began on June 25. Over a three-day period, CAT flew thirty-three trips and airlifted 165 tons of tin from Mengtze to Haiphong. Waiting at the French port was the U.S. Lines' *Pioneer Lake*, the first oceangoing freighter to call at Haiphong since the end of World War II. "At long last we have started the Haiphong tin deal," Willauer wrote. "And vistas of Indo-China are opening up, at least in my mind."[36]

One day in early July, Willauer stood by the open window of an apartment on Victoria Peak in Hong Kong and watched the fog begin to roll in. He became homesick for Nantucket and his family. Reflecting on what had happened since April, he wrote to his wife:

> I . . . generally feel fine and quite relaxed now that I have been able to see the airline through two months of drastically reduced operations without losing any real money, and maybe with making modest sums. I do not personally care too much about the money end, except insofar as it will be used by others as an index of my running of things. When you left, the bugaboo that was haunting me was that in two or three months everything which had been built up would be wiped out, and I was far from sure that I could either do anything about it, or if there were things which could be done, that I had the temperament to carry through on that score. I have had many searchings of heart and mind since then, and have felt easy in both since I finally decided to put as much of my heart into a reduction program as I once did in a building up. I was only able to get to this point after, or rather during, some of the trips which I have been taking [to the Northwest] when I got away from the day-to-day details. I could sit at the controls of a C-46 and get some of those thoughts in focus, and also seeing some of the country which I had never seen before, and realizing the important part we were playing in their picture, it suddenly became worth while to me to do whatever it takes to keep up whatever service we can render.[37]

It was just as well that Willauer had a moment to pause. Floods in late May had severed Communist lines of communications and caused Mao to break off offensive operations following the fall of Shanghai. Now the Red armies were on the move again. Minister-Counselor Clark advised Washington in July that no real resistance could be expected; Canton, he predicted, would fall in mid-August.[38]

Willauer put into action longstanding plans to ensure CAT's mobility. A converted LST carrying the airline's machine shops and a barge loaded with spare parts and supplies moved alongside the Standard Vacuum installation in Hong Kong. At the same time, engineering personnel were shifted to the JAMCO facilities in the British colony. While the head office remained at Canton, ready to evacuate on a moment's notice, operations and line maintenance relocated to Kunming.[39]

As Communist units advanced toward Canton, the situation in the Northwest took a turn for the worse. In May a 150,000-man Communist army under General P'eng Te-huai had occupied Sian, strategic capital of Shensi Province, and began to drive toward Lanchow. General Hu Tsung-nan, old Whampoa favorite of Chiang Kai-shek and in command of government forces in Shensi, withdrew toward Pinglian and called upon Ma Pu-fang for assistance. The Mohammedan leader responded by engaging P'eng about seventy miles outside Sian. A frontal assault halted the Communist column while Ma's twenty-nine-year-old son, General Ma Chi-yuan, attacked from the flank with twenty-five thousand cavalrymen. The Communists reeled back toward Sian, having suffered an estimated ten thousand casualties. An exultant Ma Pu-fang told a *Time* correspondent: "Without aid from the Nationalist government or the U.S. we can hold this area indefinitely and even get back Sian. With aid, I could mount an offensive that would take back Peiping."[40]

But Ma's triumph proved short-lived. Two Communist armies, the Sixty-second and Sixty-third, rushed to P'eng's assistance. The Red forces, now two hundred thousand strong, renewed their offensive in early August, advancing on Lanchow in three columns. Ma Pu-fang planned a countermove. He would strike eastward from Lanchow, driving wedges between the Communist columns, while Ma Hung-k'uei attacked from the north and Hu Tsung-nan moved in from the south. The enemy, outnumbered by one hundred thousand men, would be chopped up and destroyed. The scheme, however, depended upon adequate stocks of ammunition and the cooperation of Hu Tsung-nan.[41]

Ma Pu-fang flew to Canton and Taipei in mid-August to plead for support. Results were disappointing. His mission, he told Minister-Counselor Clark, had been a "complete flop." The Canton government was "a totally worthless, hopeless organization, expert only in passing [the] bureaucratic buck." Any assistance from the United States should go directly to regional leaders and not to the central authorities. Clark asked about Hu Tsung-nan, who had accompanied Ma to see the generalissimo. Although Hu lacked a cooperative spirit, Ma admitted, the Nationalist general "must fight—or else."[42]

Willauer echoed Ma's frustration, but his target was the American government. Predicting that the Mohammedan leader, who was staying at Willauer's apartment in Canton while he called on President Li Tsung-jen, would be forced to surrender Lanchow because of lack of ammunition, the CAT executive wrote in anger to his wife: "I do wish the US would get a move on. There are lots of these people who will still fight if we can get to them before the last vestige of their morale is gone. Everywhere you go there is this awful depression. It is killing the spirit of the boys in the airline, of our servants, of everyone. The God damned State Department ought to be taken out one by one and hung."[43]

CAT began to airlift from Chungking to Lanchow small quantities of ammunition supplied by the central government, but most turned out to be the wrong kind. Nevertheless, on August 18 Ma Pu-fang attempted to launch a coordinated attack on the Communists. It broke down when Hu Tsung-nan failed to move and the Chinese Air Force refused to fly promised support missions. According to President Li Tsung-jen, Chiang Kai-shek had issued secret orders to Hu and the Air Force not to assist Ma Pu-fang and was glad to see the Mohammedan armies destroyed.[44]

Ma Pu-fang's troops fought hard until they ran out of ammunition. Forced to give up Lanchow, Ma retreated toward Sining. On August 28 CAT evacuated the Mohammedan leader and $1.5 million in gold bars. Ma Pu-fang stopped in Canton, called on President Li and asked his forgiveness, then continued on to Mecca. A short time later CAT brought out Ma Hung-k'uei and his treasury. The Ninghsia governor did not stop at Canton but went directly to southern California to raise horses. His cousin surrendered the province to the Communists and became vice-governor under the new regime.[45]

Just as the Northwest collapsed, affairs in Yunnan reached a crisis. In mid-August rumors began to circulate that Governor Lu Han, known as an opportunist, would deliver the province to the Communists. At 5:30 P.M. on September 2 the Ministry of Communications issued secret orders to CAT to evacuate Kunming within forty-eight hours. The airline no sooner had complied than the central government resolved its problems with Lu Han, at least temporarily. On September 5 CAT received instructions to return. "It cost us $250,000 worth of useless flying!" Willauer complained. Nor did it encourage optimism about the stability of the Southwest.[46]

Prospects for anti-Communist resistance in China appeared dismal as the summer wore on. Nationalist forces everywhere were in retreat, and Chennault's impenetrable "sanitary zone" looked like a piece of Swiss cheese. Paradoxically, the atmosphere in Washington seemed to improve as the situation in China got worse. On the surface, the policy of noninterference remained fixed. Ignoring congressional critics, the State Department on August 5 issued what some considered an exercise in handwashing, *United States Relations with China, with Special Reference to the Period 1944 – 1949*, and gave every indication of settling back to watch the inevitable course of events on the mainland. But beyond public view, voices of concern could be heard with increasing frequency and urgency in the corridors of power.

As recent documentation has revealed, American policy makers were coming to see China as part of the worldwide Communist problem. Chennault was not the only one to detect a Russian presence in Asia and to advance a domino theory of events. NSC 48/1, drawn up in June 1949, took a similar view. Termed by some the "key document" in framing the domino theory, NSC 48/1 labeled the Soviet Union, not China, the principal threat to peace and stability in Asia. The United States, it argued, had to formulate a policy to "contain" Soviet power and influence in the Far East.[47]

There were other straws in the wind. Dean Rusk wrote to Secretary Acheson on July 16 calling for an "action program" that would include aid to non-Communist groups in China. George Kennan, foremost advocate of containment in Europe, and John P. Davies, Jr., China expert on the Policy Planning Staff, showed similar concern. Davies even contemplated the "selective use of air power" against the Chinese Communists "to compel them to respect the United States and moderate their behavior." Most important, President Harry Truman was coming to see China as part of the "Communist problem."[48]

It was in this context of growing concern in Washington that OPC's plans for China, including the use of CAT, matured. On August 24 and 25, as Ma Pu-fang retreated in anger and sorrow from Lanchow to Sining, Chennault met in Washington with Colonel Richard G. Stilwell, head of OPC's Far East Division. Although a record of these discussions is not available, indirect evidence makes clear their purport. Following a trans-Pacific telephone conversation with Corcoran on August 28, Willauer informed his wife that the "situation at the moment appears to be that aid of some sort to China is 90% sure, and that some of our people are counting on us heavily if there is such aid. I have suggested an operational plan covering Japan, China & Indo China which seems to be meeting with some favor."[49]

"Aid of some sort" came a giant step closer two days after the Corcoran-Willauer telephone call when Assistant Secretary of State Ernest A. Gross appeared before an executive session of the Senate's committees on Foreign Relations and Armed Services. The committees were considering appropriations for military assistance, and a group of administration critics, led by Republican Senator William F. Knowland, wanted to include $100 million for China in the Europe-oriented program. State, Gross testified, "flatly opposed" the Knowland amendment. But the department, through Senator Tom Connally, offered an alternative that would give the president broad discretionary authority to spend the money in the Far East as he saw fit. Senator Arthur H. Vandenberg raised a constitutional problem about such an open-ended grant of power to the executive. No doubt, he said, the president "could by intrigue and manipulation raise unshirted hell in the Far East and do $15 billion worth of damage to the cause of communism, and that is what I would like to do, but I do not know how you would do it under our form of government." Gross assured Vandenberg that ample precedent existed, pointing to the wartime financing of OSS.

As it finally emerged, Section 303 appropriated an emergency fund of $75 million to be used in the "general area" of China. The president had to specify the fact but not the nature of expenditures. Although inclusion of the Far East in the Mutual Defense Assistance Act of 1949, signed into law in October, was in large part a nod in the direction of the China bloc in Congress, President Truman now had both funds and wide discretion to implement security programs in Asia beyond public — and congressional — scrutiny.[50]

CIA Director Hillenkoetter called at the State Department on September 1 and spoke to Secretary Acheson, Kennan, and Ambassador Philip C. Jessup about OPC's plan to subsidize CAT. Three weeks later the department gave informal approval to the scheme at a meeting between Hillenkoetter, Undersecretary James E. Webb, and Assistant Secretary Butterworth. Although not enthusiastic, Butterworth explained, the department would not object to minimal covert financial support to the airline if it would facilitate CIA secret operations.[51]

The final element of the plan fell into place on October 4. George Kennan, the department's representative on the OPC oversight committee, sent a memorandum to Wisner about plans for covert assistance to anti-Communist elements in China. Although the document neither approved nor disapproved of the project, Wisner interpreted the ambiguity in OPC's favor and ordered prompt implementation of the scheme.[52]

CAT began to fly for OPC on October 10, 1949, China's national day. A formal agreement came on November 1, Corcoran signing for CAT and Emmett D. Echols of the CIA's Office of Finance representing the government. The CIA pledged up to $500,000 to finance a CAT base and underwrite deficits that might occur in hazardous flying on agency missions. In return, CAT would give priority to agency cargo and personnel for one year at rates to be negotiated. An advance of $200,000 confirmed the engagement between the CIA and CAT.[53]

Chennault and Willauer labored long and hard in their respective vineyards between May and October 1949. In China, Willauer turned his considerable managerial talents to the survival of CAT. As monthly aircraft hours plummeted from over four thousand to less than two thousand, he streamlined operations, executed complex schemes to expand business in border areas, supervised evacuations, wrestled with all manner of financial and personnel problems, and generally kept his head in the midst of continuing crisis. In Washington, Chennault, guided by Corcoran, made a strenuous effort to mobilize support behind his plan—one of many floating around Capitol Hill at the time—to assist anti-Communist forces in China. In a series of public appearances and private meetings, the general sounded a clarion call of alarm, predicting dire consequences for the United States in the wake of a Communist victory on the mainland.

While Willauer watched conditions in China grow worse, Chennault saw glimmers of hope. To be sure, Chiang Kai-shek and his Nationalist cohorts remained anathema in the highest councils of government, but many officials registered increasing concern about the spread of communism in the Far East. Talk about domino theories and containment became common. A dramatic shift in policy did not occur during the summer of 1949; there would be no massive American assistance or advisers. But sufficient changes did take place to permit OPC's talented and ambitious director to go forward with a project of covert aid to anti-Communist groups in China. This scheme required secure air transport. CAT seemed ideal for the purpose. As the end approached in China, CAT and the CIA entered into what would prove a lengthy and intimate relationship.

OPC and CAT

Alfred T. Cox left Washington in haste. Selected at the last minute to head OPC's projects in China, the OSS veteran spent a frantic weekend in a round of farewells and briefings, climaxed by a reception hosted by Colonel Stilwell. After an all-night flight across the country, Cox arrived in San Francisco on October 4 and checked into the St. Francis Hotel. He spent the day shopping for clothes and a suitcase and having passport photos taken. In the evening, he wrote to his wife about household arrangements and enclosed one of the photos. "Remember," he warned, "not to in any way indicate that I am connected with anything other than my job with Civil Air Transport."[1]

Early the next morning, Cox departed on Philippine Airlines for Hong Kong, a tedious three-day trip via Honolulu, Wake Island, Guam, and Manila (where he stayed overnight and changed planes.) As the four-engine transport droned across the broad Pacific, Cox had ample time between eating, reading, and fitful naps to let his thoughts drift back over the events that had brought him from Lehigh University to the CIA.[2]

Raised in the New York City area, where his Christian Scientist father was a private chauffeur for Helen O. Brice, daughter of a wealthy Ohio businessman and politician, Cox seemed drawn to a military career from an early age. He tried to get into West Point after graduating from DeWitt Clinton High School but failed the stiff physical examination because of missing teeth (small monuments to his love of sports). Disappointed, Cox enlisted in the army for three years. Heeding the advice of a sympathetic officer who saw promise in the enthusiastic young soldier, he accepted his discharge in 1936 and enrolled in Lehigh University.[3]

Cox took Lehigh by storm. He was a talented athlete and natural leader as quarterback and captain of the football team, co-captain of the baseball team, and basketball star. Interested in student politics and popular with colleagues, Cox served as president of the junior and senior classes. He commanded the ROTC regiment and won the John J. Pershing medal as most distinguished student officer in the Middle Atlantic states. He took honors in civil engineering, received the Wilbur award in English, and earned the prized Phi Beta Kappa key for superior intellectual achievement. "Voting [alone] has not made Al Cox the man who *Did the Most for Lehigh*," the school's yearbook pointed out. "During four years he has done that as our leader in sports, politics, and student government"[4]

Employed after graduation by the Dravo Corporation, a Pittsburgh-based construction company, Cox was working as an engineer on the construction of huge submerged shipways at Newport News, Virginia, when the Japanese attacked Pearl Harbor. A reserve officer, he went on active duty early in 1942, took paratrooper training, and volunteered for OSS. Cox became a pioneer in developing Operational Groups (OG), a pet project of OSS chief William J. Donovan that called for small groups of highly trained men to drop behind enemy lines, contact local resistance groups, and cause as much trouble as possible.[5]

Cox commanded Company "B", 2671st Special Reconnaissance Battalion, Separate (Provisonal), the long-winded and deliberately obscure designation for fourteen OG units of two officers and thirteen enlisted men each. Trained to a fine edge in North Africa, Company "B" parachuted into southern France in advance of Allied invasion forces. Personally leading OG "Lehigh," Cox jumped into a meadow in the Rhone Valley shortly after midnight, August 25, 1944. His units destroyed bridges and power lines, set up roadblocks, and ambushed enemy columns. Combined OG-Maquis forces killed 461 Germans and captured 10,021 at a cost of five American dead and twenty-three injured or wounded. As Major Cox noted in his final report, this was "the first real use by the American Army of Organized Guerillas, of highly trained, bilingual Officers and Soldiers who operated in small hard hitting guerilla bands behind enemy lines."[6]

Back from Europe in January 1945, Cox met Dorothy Branson through a mutual friend. An attractive, charming, and exciting young woman with a soft, southern accent, Dorothy was working in New York as a fashion illustrator. "The very first time I met Al," she recalled, "on his birthday — Jan. 6, 1945, one of his officers told me 'if Colonel Cox ordered me to walk out a ten story window I would do it without a second's hesitation' and I knew I had just met an extraordinary man — one I wouldn't forget." They were married a year later.[7]

General Donovan sent Cox to China in March 1945 on an experimental project to organize Chinese commando units. Under his direction, a training mission of 350 officers and men set up a weapons school, parachute facility, and tactical training area near Kunming. The aim was to produce twenty commando units of 200 men each. With limited personnel and constant delays in receipt of supplies, Cox faced a challenging task. "Sometimes I think we're just butting our heads against a stone wall here," he wrote to his future wife, "progress is so damned slow — but I hope we wind up with something to show for our effort."[8]

The First Commando, one of six units that completed the program before the war's end, went into action on July 12, 1945. Operation APPLE — "the first airborne movement in the history of the Chinese Army"—proved a great success, as did similar missions in the waning days of the war. Lieutenant Colonel Cox's commendation for "exceptionally meritorious service" noted that "the fighting spirit of the Commandos" served as a tribute to his ability.[9]

Discharged in 1946, Cox married the vivacious Dorothy, started a family, and tried to settle down in a managerial job with the Atlantic Coal Company in Providence, Rhode Island. Restless and drinking too much, he left Providence in 1947 and joined the Alpine and, later, Avin corporations, related companies that sold aeronautical products worldwide. Detesting the nine-to-five routine of desk work, Cox spent as much time as possible in the field. He seemed happiest when he could get together with old comrades to drink and reminisce.[10]

"The war," one friend recalled, "was the perfect setting for Al." He had flourished in the heady excitement and adventure of OSS, and everything that followed paled in comparison. Approached by Wisner in spring 1949, Cox jumped at the invitation to join OPC. As another new recruit pointed out, enlisting in the government's covert army in the midst of the Cold War was "a highly esteemed, indeed rather glamorous and fashionable and certainly most patriotic thing to do."[11]

Cox reached Hong Kong just in time for a unique operational briefing. Swept up in a CAT evacuation, he quickly learned about the airline's agility, ingenuity, determination, and daily operational dangers. CAT had been asked by the government to remain in Canton until the last minute, which airline officials judged would come in the week of October 17. But on October 9 Nationalist troops withdrew from Kukong, a key defensive point ninety miles to the north, signaling the beginning of the end for the city. With the sound of Communist artillery echoing in downtown Canton, Willauer sent word from Hong Kong on October 9 to evacuate key office personnel and communications equipment. As news of the exodus spread, CAT field-coolies and security guards at White Cloud airport in Canton seized assistant personnel director Reese T. Bradburn and traffic manager Arthur Fung and demanded "termination pay."

Willauer boarded a C-47, flew to Canton, and circled overhead to assess the situation. After lengthy radio conversations, he agreed to terms and returned to Hong Kong to raise ransom money. While financial expert James J. Brennan scoured the colony for the large quantity of Hong Kong dollars

Whiting Willauer and Alfred T. Cox, 1950

needed, Willauer prudently sought permission for a night landing on the return trip at Hong Kong's Kai Tak airport. British airport authorities at first agreed, but at 5:00 P.M. Willauer learned that Kai Tak would close at the usual curfew of 7:15 P.M.

Pistols strapped to their hips and carrying bushel baskets of Hong Kong dollars, Willauer and Brennan hurried to the airport and in threatening weather took off at 5:30 P.M. Chief Pilot Rousselot kept the airplane below the clouds, made a shuddering turn after takeoff, found the mouth of the Pearl River, and at about one hundred feet followed the "wet compass" to Canton.

The money was unloaded at one end of the field at Canton, then Rousselot taxied to the takeoff end lest they also be taken hostage. Loyal CAT employees paid off the coolies and guards, "buying" their guns. Some eighty people then crammed into the aircraft for the short flight to Hong Kong. After coaxing the overloaded C-47 off the ground and snaking his way back down the Pearl River, Rousselot touched down at 7:13 P.M. Hong Kong police inspectors took three hours to check in all the purchased weapons.[12]

Viewing this dangerous and chaotic scene, the restless Cox, who had found no peace in peacetime, must have felt he had come home.

For CAT, operating a head office in the British colony became an exercise in improvisation. Some three thousand employees and their families needed housing in the refugee-crowded city, creating a problem more challenging, if less dangerous, than the evacuation. Willauer finally decided to charter a riverboat. The moored steamer provided housing for most people, and Brennan found apartments for the remainder. Top executives worked out of a dress sample room in the Gloucester Hotel, while subsidiary officers were scattered all over town. Because telephones were unobtainable, department heads had to meet daily in a room ("the Goldfish Bowl") on the mezzanine of the Gloucester. There, according to Willauer, they would sit and "fish in troubled waters."[13]

Communications — the heart of the airline — posed the major difficulty. Because the British did not permit private radio facilities, CAT had to make do with a radio station in nearby Macao, an awkward arrangement. The various currencies required for operations also caused headaches. Willauer, Brennan, and a handful of trusted employees juggled gold bars, silver dollars, francs, pounds, and Hong Kong and American currency. "There were times," Willauer recalled, "when Jim [Brennan] and I literally did not take off our clothes for 24–48 hours on a stretch."[14]

While CAT executives searched for telephones in Hong Kong, Cox began work on OPC's project to assist anti-Communist groups on the mainland. Details of the covert scheme remain locked in the CIA's archives, but the main outlines are clear. By the time Cox reached China, General Pai Ch'ung-hsi commanded the only viable military force left to oppose the Communists. Pai, a close associate of President Li Tsung-jen and member of the Kwangsi clique, had been an important regional figure during the interwar years. A capable administrator and organizer in Kwangsi Province, he had very reluctantly accepted Chiang Kai-shek's authority. Although Pai remained outside the centers of power in the Nationalist government, he had gained prominence as a successful field commander against the Japanese. Later most observers considered him one of the best Nationalist strategists during the civil war, although his advice was rarely heeded.[15]

In early October 1949 Pai again demonstrated his ability by handing Communist General Lin Piao a rare setback. Retreating from Changsha to Hengyang in the face of a strong enemy force, Pai abruptly turned and counterattacked. He trapped and savaged a column of fifty thousand men at Tsin-shu-ping and sent Lin Piao reeling back to Changsha. Pai pleaded for supplies. Chiang Kai-shek turned a deaf ear. President Li, who had nothing to give, could only note in sorrow that Pai "was an extraordinary fighter, but as a Chinese saying points out, 'A gifted housewife cannot produce a meal without rice.'"[16]

Cox visited Pai in Kweilin on October 14. During the course of a two-day stay, he no doubt learned of Pai's plans to defend Kwangsi on a line running southwest from Kweilin to Nanning, then bending southeast in Kwantung Province to the Liuchow peninsula and nearby Hainan Island. To implement this strategy, Pai had two hundred thousand tired and hungry troops. Paid one silver dollar a month, the men subsisted on a meager rice ration. They lacked winter uniforms. Pai could not pay replacements and had no reserve supplies. He estimated that his army could fight one, perhaps two, major battles before losing combat effectiveness. He needed weapons and ammunition; specifically, he wanted ten thousand light machine guns and five thousand 60mm mortars.[17]

Cox returned briefly to Hong Kong, then flew to Taipei for discussions with Nationalist leaders. Later he visited Chungking and Kunming, trying to assess prospects for resistance. Although arranging for a shipment of arms to Pai, he was not optimistic about the siutuation. "Things are certainly going badly out here," Cox wrote to his wife. "Our air bases are falling one after the other, and pretty soon we'll have to buy an aircraft carrier to have a place to land. Time is running out."[18]

As Cox shuttled among the few remaining Nationalist pockets on the mainland, two fast-moving Communist columns converged on Pai's army. In mid-November President Li went to Nanning to review the situation with Pai. "Now the war was desperate," Li recalled, "all of southwestern China was doomed, but it was possible that the island of Hainan might be held as a future base." After Kweilin fell on November 22, Pai moved toward the Liuchow peninsula and Hainan. CAT established a base at Sanya on Hainan and began to transfer personnel and equipment from Kunming.[19]

Chungking, last mainland capital of the Republic of China, surrendered on November 30. Operating from Peishiyi, a wartime Fourteenth Air Force field that was located across a range of hills from Chungking, CAT had been airlifting government personnel out of the doomed city since the middle of the month. Conditions became frantic as the end approached. On the afternoon of November 29, operations manager Roger W. Severt loaded company equipment on three remaining CAT transports; as darkness fell, he awaited instructions.

"It was pitch dark," Severt recalled, "and the cold of a Chungking winter was more penetrating than ever. Off over the hills we saw the frequent flash of guns and heard the rattle of fire. Then, at 8:30 P.M., we saw a whole stream of vehicles pouring onto the field from across the runway. It was the final exodus." Severt shut down the radio station, loaded final items of equipment, and made space for several last-minute passengers, including Associated Press correspondent Spencer Moosa. Operating on the theory of "better us than the Communists," enterprising crew members tossed aboard several crates of silver dollars that had been left by the fleeing Nationalists. Company officials did not applaud this act, and two pilots later reluctantly surrendered their treasure. One who failed to do so suddenly found himself unemployed twelve thousand miles from home.[20]

By now, CAT was under intense pressure. "Everything is a mad-house," Cox sighed. The government wanted silver dollars flown to troops in the Southwest; local authorities impounded gasoline and demanded bribes; provincial officials threatened station managers with violence unless granted free air passage. Without regular communications between Hong Kong and outlying stations, the airline's management could do little except worry. "I really was amazed," Willauer reported with pride, "to see our organization stand together under these strains."[21]

No one expected Kunming to last for long, but no one expected the situation to change as quickly as it did. Pressed to make accommodations with the Communists, Governor Lu Han of Yunnan Province told Vice-Consul La Rue R. Lutkins on December 3 that there would be no danger for at least two weeks and promised to give at least three days' notice if it became necessary for Americans to leave. Shortly after midnight on December 10, defecting provincial soldiers occupied Kunming's Chennault Field, trapping four CAT aircraft, crews, and other personnel. Only after Chennault telegraphed a personal plea to Lu Han, reminding the governor of services rendered over the years, did the guards permit the aircraft to leave. Three planes took off shortly after noon. The last C-46, flown by Var M. Green, waited for Vice-Consul Lutkins and his staff, then taxied out for takeoff. The transport used most of the runway before staggering into the air, leaving Captain Green puzzled at the aircraft's sluggish performance. The answer came after arrival at Hainan, when eight stowaway soldiers tumbled out of the C-46's belly cargo compartment.[22]

Stunned by the news that Yunnan had gone over to the Communists and threatened by an attack from the rear, General Pai led his troops toward a last stand on Hainan. It was not to be. Lin Piao attacked before Pai reached his goal and extracted bloody revenge for Tsin-shu-ping. "Right now," Cox wrote to his wife in mid-December, "it looks as tho it's only a matter of days before the Mainland goes. It's awfully discouraging."[23]

CAT had performed spendidly under trying conditions during the last quarter of 1949. Starting with Canton in early October, the airline had evacuated Kweilin, Kweiyang, Liuchow, Nanning, Pakoi, Kunming, Chungking, Chengtu, Hunchung, Amoy, and Swatow. "Each evacuation has cost us heavily," Willauer reported to Corcoran, "but we have never lost enough equipment or personnel to cripple our operations." He took special pride in CAT's safety record, pointing out that only two aircraft had gone down during the frantic three-month period. The first one happened on November 8, when an engine had failed on C-47 XT-805 while en route from Mengtze to Haiphong with a cargo of tin concentrates. Captain Norman R. Jones, who stayed with the aircraft until his crew had bailed out, died in the crash; hostile tribesmen in the isolated border area beheaded radio operator K. V. Chin, leaving copilot M. H. Kung the lone survivor. The other aircraft was lost on December 5, when Captain James B. McGovern in C-46 XT-812 made a forced landing on the Liuchow peninsula. Although no one was injured, Communist soldiers captured the crew.

"It is on account of [McGovern] and boys like him and the type of job that they are willing to do," Willauer concluded to Corcoran, "that the General and I are so proud of our organization and feel that the work we are doing here with this gang is worth-while even though we and our backers have not made a cent out of it and may even have to face bankruptcy one of these days for what some people seem to think as our damn fool stubbornness. Anyhow the General and I were brought up in a school that if you are playing a football game and the score is 51 to 0 against you, it is still your job to try to win the game . . . I hope this does not sound dramatic. It is not meant to be at all. It is just the way he and I and the boys working with us feel about this."[24]

During the waning months of 1949, as the Nationalists faced final defeat on the mainland, CAT officials on both sides of the Pacific fought political and legal battles to keep the bulk of China's air transport fleet out of Communist hands. Their efforts were destined to have far-reaching effects on CAT's future.

Based in Hong Kong since the fall of Shanghai in May 1949, CNAC and CATC had been operating sporadic air service to Nationalist-held areas. Although rumors had been circulating for months about discontent among employees, many of whom feared for the safety of relatives on the mainland should the Nationalist government attempt to relocate the companies on Taiwan, the defection of the general managers of both airlines to Peking with twelve fully manned aircraft on November was a shock. Seventy-one transports, including modern Convairs and DC-4s, remained on the ground in Hong Kong. Communist authorities promptly claimed the aircraft as the "sacred property" of the Chinese People's Republic.[25]

Chennault and Willauer reacted with surprise and dismay to news of the defection. Communist control of the aircraft, they feared, would place the final resistance of Chiang Kai-shek on Taiwan in grave danger. According to their information, the Communists were training paratroopers for an assault on Chiang's last and somewhat shaky redoubt. "We felt," Willauer recalled, "that if [the Communists] got those transport planes and put them together with the Red paratroops, considering the chaos which existed on Formosa [Taiwan] at that time, it would have been a pushover for the Reds to have taken Formosa."[26]

Willauer flew to Taipei on November 10 to consult with Nationalist officials. He found General Chou Chih-jou highly agitated, although the air force commander appeared less concerned over the danger to Taiwan than over the possibility that he might be held personally responsible for the defection of the two general managers, both of whom were former high-ranking air force officers. Conversations with Chou and other senior officials revealed that everyone was "very much distressed" about the situation, but that no one had any idea what to do about it. Willauer realized that it was up to him to formulate a plan of action before a scheduled meeting with Chiang Kai-shek at 8:30 the following morning.[27]

Willauer's last-minute proposal, embodied in a memorandum handed to the generalissimo at their meeting, began by stressing the gravity of the circumstances. Not only did the defection place Taiwan in danger from invasion, but it also represented a severe political defeat that could have fatal effects on Nationalist morale. "Already many people have been constantly worrying about how they can escape if the Communists win," the memorandum warned. "Until the defection of the airlines all these people felt sure they could get out by air. As long as they had this feeling of *ultimate security* they were willing to stay at their jobs and fight to the end. Now this means of escape by air seems cut off. Unless something can be done at once, panic may spread throughout China, Taiwan, and Hainan."[28]

In an effort to prevent the aircraft in Hong Kong from falling under Communist control, Willauer offered the services of CAT. CAT would act as agent for the Nationalist government, with full authority to change title of the aircraft or take any other action necessary to forestall Communist possession of the transports and—it was hoped—to deliver them to Taiwan. Chiang agreed. He made available teletype equipment and codes for speedy communications with Taipei, a high-ranking air force officer for liaison duties, and an official from the Ministry of Finance, who would attempt to freeze the bank accounts of CNAC and CATC.[29]

Returning to Hong Kong, Willauer lost no time in putting his "neutralization program" into effect. On November 13 the Nationalist Civil Aeronautics Administration in Taiwan suspended the registration certificates of the aircraft. Three days later, after "disloyal" employees of the two airlines had been dismissed, a squad of twenty newly hired Sikh guards went on duty to prevent removal of the transports. Willauer personally led a group of CAT pilots and crew chiefs in a midnight foray to the airport, where they immobilized the aircraft, at least temporarily, by letting all the air out of the tires. Willauer also spread rumors that trucks would be driven across the path of any aircraft that attempted to take off. "New things crop up every day," Louise Willauer wrote, "which makes life like an adventure novel."[30]

The aircraft dispute only added to the woes of British authorities in Hong Kong. Nervously eyeing Communist troops massed on the border of the New Territories, fearing invasion or interruption of their vital water supply, and hoping to work out an accommodation with Peking, colonial officials welcomed CAT's intervention in the dispute as they would have an outbreak of the Black Death. But legal formalities, like the ritual of tiffin, had to be observed even under the most trying of circumstances.

On November 17 Sir Alexander Grantham, governor of the colony, announced that no aircraft would be permitted to depart for the mainland until the Sino-British air agreement had been clarified. At the same time, in an effort to avoid trouble with Communist sympathizers, he ordered the removal of CAT's security force. No sooner had the guards left than a number of CNAC and CATC employees, who had declared their allegiance to Peking, took physical possession of the aircraft. The pro-Communist group vowed to stay until the British government recognized the new Chinese regime, which was expected by the end of the year, and the assets of the two airlines passed over to the People's Republic. Although Willauer obtained an injunction from Sir Leslie Gibson, chief justice of Hong Kong, to restrain the defectors from remaining on Kai Tak airport and from removing or tampering with the disputed property, the civil authorities refused to enforce it, fearing a riot that might endanger the security of the colony.[31]

Clearly, the Hong Kong government had no intention of taking action in support of property owned by a discredited Nationalist regime. Colonial officials were prepared to hand over the aircraft to the Communists as soon as London extended formal diplomatic recognition to the People's Republic.

Their plan to act as agents for the Nationalists a failure, Chennault and Willauer realized that the only remaining chance for success lay in transfer of the equipment to American ownership. To do so would require extensive and expensive litigation, as well as support from Washington, and they asked Cox if OPC would be willing to help. Cox favored the idea. Indeed, he was prepared to go further. He recalled:

An urgent recommendation was sent to Washington, strongly recommending that U.S. Govt. assume the initiative in *controlling*, and to the extent necessary underwriting the actions that might have to be taken. It was recognized that this would have to be done covertly, and therefore [I] recommended also that the service of the Willauer-Chennault group be utilized as principal agents, acting ostensibly as private citizens already deeply committed to the ChiNat cause. The reply was simple, direct and firm. Every encouragement should be given to the Corcoran group to continue their efforts as private

citizens, to obtain possession of the CNAC-CATC assets. The U.S. Govt. did
not wish to and did not intend to get involved, not deeming it in the national
interest. This was passed to Willauer and Chennault.[32]

Despite the disappointing news, Chennault and Willauer sought authority
from Corcoran and his associates in the United States to proceed with the
scheme. Corcoran tested the political waters in Washington and came away
impressed. Although the government would not underwrite the project,
considerable sentiment existed for action by CAT. The State Department saw
the issue less as assistance to the Nationalists—which it continued to oppose—than as implementation of overall American civil aviation policy toward the Soviet Union and its satellites as spelled out in NSC 15/1. Applied
to the Far East, this policy opposed establishment of Communist airlines
"which could become instruments of Chinese infiltration into South Asia."
Fearing that such an airline could emerge from the assets of CNAC and
CATC, responsible officials confirmed to Corcoran that it was in the "national
interest" to do everything possible to keep the aircraft from the
Communists.[33]

Because government assistance could be made effective and given openly
only to at least apparent American citizens or corporations, Corcoran put
together a complicated organizational structure for the recovery operation.
At the top of the table of organization stood C.A.T., S.A., incorporated under
liberal Panamanian laws that afforded tax, secrecy, and other desirable benefits. Civil Air Transport, Inc. (CATI), was then incorporated under Delaware
laws to act as C.A.T., S.A.'s nominee in the legal battles to follow. Because
ownership of the disputed aircraft must appear to be American, the relationship between C.A.T., S.A., and CATI was kept secret.[34]

Although the primary purpose of the operation was to deny the aircraft to
the Communists, the corporate documents made provision for the possibility
of recovering all the assets of the two airlines, including their aircraft, frozen
bank balances, and other property. Expenses incurred during the operation
would have first claim on any assets recovered. The remainder, if any, would
be divided equally among the stockholders of C.A.T., S.A.: Chennault,
Willauer, Thomas G. Corcoran, David M. Corcoran, William S. Youngman,
and James J. Brennan.[35]

Armed with the necessary authorization from Corcoran, Chennault and
Willauer began negotiations with the Nationalist government in Taiwan to
purchase CNAC and CATC. Chinese officials, to Willauer's chagrin, insisted
on a purchase price (on paper) equal to the fair market value of the two
companies. The Nationalists obviously would never recoup a penny of their
investment without American assistance, but the negotiators feared that
they would be placed in a bad light should any assets be recovered and the

government not get a fair share. As a result, Willauer signed — on behalf of Chennault and himself — personal promissory notes for $4.75 million. Although the notes were later made the obligation of a corporation, "that was a pretty scary time for me," Willauer recalled, "because I didn't have $4,750,000." The Executive Yuan approved the sale on December 12.[36]

Intense legal and political maneuvering began on two continents. In London former OSS chief William J. Donovan, senior partner in the law firm hired by Corcoran to represent CATI, called at the Foreign Office on December 15 and informed the British that Americans had purchased CNAC and CATC. He spoke about plans to use the aircraft for a "peripheral airline," operating nonscheduled service from Tokyo to Singapore, and he stressed the great strategic value of such airlift capability, especially in case of emergency evacuation. Although obviously not expecting courts to exceed their authority, Donovan said, he did want to urge "all possible speed" in removing legal obstacles to an arrangement that would serve the best interests of Great Britain and the United States.[37]

Chargé Julius Holmes, U.S. State Department representative who accompanied Donovan to Whitehall, expressed the "strong" official interest of the American government in the matter. The United States, he told the British, was concerned "in seeing all precautions taken forestalling transfer [of] equipment and facilities to [the] Communists." He urged "greatest speed possible [in] resolving legal problems." The Foreign Office, cautious as usual, promised to "act immediately" to review the situation in light of recent developments; however, no action could be taken at present.[38]

Activity in Washington centered on securing American registration for the aircraft, an essential step to establish ownership in any legal proceeding and a point the British had raised during the meeting with Donovan. H. F. Amrine of the State Department's Far Eastern division and Civil Aeronautics Administration head Delos W. Rentzel met at the Statler Hotel on December 17 to discuss this problem. Amrine wrote that Rentzel "expressed his desire to cooperate by cutting any corners necessary to expedite placing the aircraft concerned under US registry." In response to Rentzel's query about State's position, Amrine replied "that the Department's chief interest is to see the aircraft moved out of Hong Kong and beyond the reach of Chinese Communist's [sic] legal action through Hong Kong courts or of physical seizure by the Communists." Only one problem stood in the way, Amrine and Rentzel agreed: Pan American Airways still owned 20 percent of CNAC and would no doubt protest transfer of registration. The new American owners had to establish clear title before registration documents could be issued.[39]

William L. Bond, vice-president of Pan American and central figure in CNAC for fifteen years, had little desire to cooperate with Chennault and Willauer. CAT's partners, he believed, operated on the edge of propriety and legality and had deliberately lied to him. But he did not want the aircraft to fall into Communist hands. Above all, the worldwide interests of Pan American dictated cooperation with the American government.[40]

Negotiations between Pan American and the State Department were always delicate. The government did not want to give the appearance of telling a private company how to act or to ask for favors that would have to be repaid. In a meeting with Bond on December 19, Deputy Assistant Secretary Livingston T. Merchant attempted to suggest, with elaborate circumlocution, the department's position.

Bond got the message. The next day, he and T. V. Soong, representing the Nationalist government, negotiated the sale of Pan American's interest in CNAC for $1.25 million. Within hours, the CAA waived airworthiness inspection requirements and granted American registration to the aircraft in Hong Kong.[41]

While lawyers in London and Washington piled up papers and fees, Chennault and Willauer faced a financial crisis. They needed money to pay preliminary legal costs and to bribe Communists with access to the disputed aircraft for information on registration numbers and other data required by the CAA to issue American documentation. "At that time," Cox recalled, "CAT was just about broke. The expense and losses incurred during many successive retreats and eventual withdrawal from the mainland, the termination pays, excessive expenses in HK [Hong Kong], particularly rentals, etc., had just about drained the airline dry." Using authorizations that he held, Cox, wearing his CIA hat, advanced money to Chennault and Willauer. "The amounts involved," he continued, "were in the general range of $10,000 per advance. Advances in higher amounts would have required submission to Washington for prior policy approval, running the risk of everything being brought to a screeching halt. Each advance was fully documented, and had the tacit approval, if not approbation, of my superiors in Washington. As funds became available, these advances were fully repaid by CATI."[42]

Hong Kong authorities, however, remained intransigent. Despite protests by Chennault and Willauer, local courts refused to permit the new owners access to the aircraft. On January 4, 1950, General Donovan and legal associate Richard P. Heppner, wartime head of OSS in China, called on Governor Grantham. Donovan, the governor reported, "insisted that the planes be handed over to him without further ado, for, he said, if it had not been for the United States, Britain would have lost the war. Moreover, he added, if I did not do as he demanded he would make it hot for me with authorities in London." Grantham refused to issue an executive order to deliver the aircraft to their new owners. The following day, at midnight, Great Britain formally recognized the Communist regime.[43]

Officials in Hong Kong came under great pressure from all sides as the courts deliberated on the various claims to the aircraft. The United States, through Consul General Karl L. Rankin, demanded that American property be protected. The Communists threatened to seize a British-owned warehouse in Shanghai for every aircraft denied to them. Under the circumstances, the court's decision never was in doubt. Officials in the colony did not wish to offend the new government in Peking and possibly endanger the safety of Hong Kong. On February 23 a local court dismissed CATI's application for appointment of a receiver, voided all injunctions, and ruled that the aircraft were the rightful property of the People's Republic under the principle of sovereign immunity.[44]

Reaction in Washington was immediate and sharp. Secretary of State Acheson told a press conference on February 24 that the United States had "vigorously protested" to authorities in Hong Kong and London. In a speech to the Senate, influential Republican William F. Knowland termed the release of the aircraft to Peking "one of the greatest blows to the non-Communist world that has been delivered in that part of the world." The United States, Knowland announced, should make it clear to London that "the British can no longer expect assistance from us to help to stop communism in Europe while the British Government, by their recognition of the Communist regime [in China], and by this latest action of turning over 71 planes, actually accelerate the spread of communism in Asia."[45]

Whitehall remained unmoved by Acheson's complaints and Knowland's bombast. The British government, a spokesman for the Foreign Office noted on February 27, could not and would not interfere in the workings of Hong Kong's courts. Two weeks later, the first shipment of one thousand tons of spare parts left Hong Kong by boat for the mainland. At the same time, reports appeared that two thousand residences near Shanghai's Hungjao airport had been commandeered for newly arrived Russian military advisers. The Nationalist government demonstrated its concern by sending agents to Hong Kong to sabotage the aircraft. Time bombs went off at Kai Tak airport on the morning of April 2, damaging seven transports.[46]

American pressure on the British continued unabated. In London, diplomat Arthur R. Ringwalt called almost daily at the Foreign Office to express concern. Senator Knowland led the opposition in Congress and threatened to fight against appropriations for British assistance programs. On March 27 Secretary Acheson asked British Ambassador Sir Oliver Franks to make sure that Governor Grantham was aware "of the importance of the larger issues involved, including US-UK relations." There is even an unconfirmed report that President Truman wrote to Prime Minister Clement Attlee concerning the matter.[47]

Peking was no less active. Foreign Minister Chou En-lai charged on April 4 that the British had been impeding departure of the aircraft and had failed to protect them adequately. The Hong Kong authorities, Chou said, would be held "fully and directly responsible" for any damage to Chinese property. Later Peking indicated that a favorable settlement of this matter was a prerequisite to establishment of full diplomatic relations.[48]

Just as the decision in Hong Kong had been predictable, the response of London authorities to American pressure was a foregone conclusion. On May 10 the government issued an Order-in-Council, instructing Hong Kong officials to retain possession of the disputed aircraft until the question of ownership had been decided "by full processes of the law." The Order ensured a lengthy period of litigation in the Hong Kong courts with final right of appeal to the Privy Council in London, a process that could take years.[49]

Sir Alexander Grantham was not pleased with this turn of events. The Order-in-Council, he later wrote, "overrode the law as it stood and in effect made a new law, which would inevitably pass the planes to the Americans." Nevertheless, the governor had no choice but to comply. Within hours of issuance of the order, police in Hong Kong halted dismantling of the aircraft and seized fifty crates of parts already loaded on board a ship in the harbor, bound for Tsingtao. "Who was I," Sir Alexander asked, "a mere governor of a colonial dependency, to complain, and what good would it have done if I had? Nonetheless I felt unhappy: altogether a sorry business."[50]

Peking protested vehemently. Chang Han-fu, vice-minister for foreign affairs, handed the British chargé a note that expressed the intense displeasure of the Chinese government. Terming the Order-in-Council "a demonstration of a most unfriendly attitude towards the Chinese People's Republic," Chang warned that unless the Order was rescinded, Peking would have cause to doubt the sincerity of London's desire to establish full diplomatic relations.[51]

Chennault, Willauer, and Corcoran celebrated. They had fought a hard battle against great odds. Although a long legal struggle for possession of the aircraft lay ahead, they had achieved their primary objective: the transports had been kept out of Communist hands. After all the defeats on the mainland, victory tasted sweet. It was perhaps just as well that no one could foresee the troubles that lay ahead.

Cox spent a quiet holiday season of 1949 in Hong Kong. On Christmas Eve he shared dinner at a Chinese restaurant with former OSS comrades Richard Heppner and Conrad E. La Gueux. The three men went to midnight mass and listened to the singing, then took a taxi to Brennan's apartment for an early champagne breakfast. Cox paid a few calls on Christmas Day and collected several surprise presents: a cigarette lighter, two ties, a sweater, and a "still unopened" bottle of bourbon. "We have lost all our mainland bases," he wrote to his wife on December 26. He expected to return home after the first of the year.[52]

OPC's project lay in shambles. Although Cox established contact with potential anti-Communist guerrilla forces in border provinces, his attempt to support Nationalist resistance on the mainland had come far too late. Chennault's view notwithstanding, the situation in 1949 was not analogous to World War II. As Governor Lu Han of Yunnan had pointed out in October, the Communists were not the Japanese; they would not be halted by the mountainous terrain of the Southwest because the people did not regard them as invaders.[53]

Willauer also made preparations during the holidays to leave Hong Kong for the United States on a mission that would determine CAT's future. As he packed his bags, he could look back with pride on the airline's remarkable record. Flying through the hazardous skies of civil war, CAT had carried more than three hundred thousand people and piled up nearly 59 million ton-miles during three years on the mainland. Although operational success did not translate into profit because of runaway inflation, CAT always was more than a business venture. "You told me in late September [1949]," he wrote to Corcoran shortly after New Year's Day in 1950, "that you thought my basic function was to use my knowledge of the Far East and the available facilities of CAT to back up the final resistance efforts of the Chinese Government on the mainland; and that if these efforts were not successful to do everything in my power as a private businessman with the facilities of CAT under my control to arrange for resistance by the Chinese on Hainan and Formosa. I have done the best I could under the circumstances and with all due respect I think that the combined efforts of General Chennault and myself have given a breathing spell to the United States in determining their ultimate policy as respects China and the Far East in general."[54]

How the United States used the "breathing spell" so agonizingly earned by CAT would decide if the sustained effort had been worthwhile.

7   The CIA Buys an Airline

CAT faced bankruptcy in January 1950. Ejected from the mainland, with few routes and little business, the airline struggled to survive. Flying hours plummeted from three thousand a month to less than five hundred; employees had to be dismissed or placed on leave without pay in an effort to reduce soaring operating deficits. Unless Willauer could find funds in the United States, CAT would die.[1]

With nowhere else to go, CAT joined Chiang Kai-shek in exile on Taiwan. Taipei, the island's capital and major city, became the center for flight operations, with dispatching, weather, and chief pilot offices at Sungshan airport. By mid-February, thanks to hard work by the airline's staff, Director of Operations Rosbert could report that Taipei "is operating smoothly."[2]

Maintenance was more difficult. CAT'S LST and supply barge, both crammed to the gunnels with a jumble of equipment tossed on board during hasty evacuations, docked at the port city of Kaoshiung, 185 miles south of Taipei. The LST had to be unloaded and parts sorted out before shops could be established. Meanwhile, engineering personnel set up line maintenance at a former Japanese airstrip at Tainan, twenty-six miles away, and began the tedious job of preserving CAT'S numerous unemployed aircraft.[3]

Just before leaving Hong Kong, Willauer had the foresight to hire Hugh L. Grundy, CNAC's chief engineer. Despite the airline's financial woes, he offered the experienced Grundy the job of director of maintenance at a salary of $1,400 a month. Because this was $200 more than the director of operations' salary, Rosbert objected, wanting at least equal pay. He pointed out that Grundy occupied an inferior position on the organization chart. Willauer agreed—and promptly changed the organizational chart. Although displeased with the disparity in salaries, Rosbert had high praise for the taciturn Kentuckian. "The Chief Engineer," he reported to Willauer in February, "is doing an excellent job. This is really the first time that we have had the organization capabilities to set up a genuine, efficient Engineering Department."[4]

CAT desperately needed business. With mainland routes gone, Willauer recalled, "We were like a railroad with no tracks to run on." In January the search for cargo led back to the mainland—with tragic consequences.

Mengtze, tin shipping center in southern Yunnan, had been evacuated by CAT in early December 1949 when Governor Lu Han went over to the Communists. Although the Peking government controlled most of the province, Mengtze remained under tenuous Nationalist authority. Eager to put CAT to work, Chennault decided to take a chance and airlift to Hainan as much as possible of the 472 tons of tin concentrates stockpiled at the airfield.[5]

Operations began on January 13 and continued without incident for two days. For reasons that still remain obscure, Lawrence R. Buol, in charge of the airlift, decided to ignore standing instructions and spend the night at the airfield. He paid a high price for this error in judgment.

Small arms fire broke out near the airfield shortly after midnight and continued for several hours. After the situation quieted down, Captain William J. Welk flew in and attempted to rescue Buol. After landing, Welk turned around and began to taxi toward the end of the runway. A machine gun opened fire. A bullet smashed through the cockpit, hitting copilot Henry Davis in the leg. Welk jammed on full power and roared off. Communist soldiers took Buol into custody later in the day. The former marine flier, who had been one of CAT'S first pilots, received a lengthy prison sentence. Released in September 1955, he died of heart failure the following May.[6]

Termination of the Mengtze-Hainan shuttle left only daily scheduled service between Taipei and Sanya (Hainan), hardly enough to keep the airline in business. Attempting to develop routes on Taiwan, in February CAT began a daily round-the-island service with a "plushed" C-47. The aircraft started at Taipei, crossed rugged mountains to Hwalien on the east coast, then continued south to Taitung before crossing the southern end of the island to Tainan; it returned to the capital via Makung in the nearby Pescadores Islands. Competing with excellent rail and highway service at several points, the route carried only 230 passengers in the first month of operation. Another domestic CAT line opened on March 2 when a five-passenger Cessna 195 inaugurated daily round trips between Taipei and Tainan. "With proper advertising and other business promotion methods," Rosbert predicted, "I am sure that this should show good results."[7]

Efforts to expand beyond the narrow confines of Taiwan bore fruit in February and March, when informal agreement between Chinese authorities in Taipei and British officials in Hong Kong led to daily service between the two points by CAT and Hong Kong Airways. CAT also concluded arrangements with Pacific Overseas Airlines Siam (POAS) for a weekly charter flight between Singapore and Tokyo via Bangkok, Hong Kong, and Taipei.[8]

Nevertheless, money kept pouring out of the company's treasury. Airline executives were forced to take ruthless action to cut expenditures. James Brennan, close associate of Corcoran and collector of Chinese art, led the economy drive and became the target of brickbats from disgruntled employees. Administrative assistant to Representative John J. Dempsey of New Mexico during the 1930s and later congressional liaison for China Defense Supplies, Brennan had played an active role in CAT from the start. Following several lengthy inspection tours for Corcoran, he had moved to Hong Kong in 1949 to assist Chennault and Willauer with financial matters. "He is tremendously helpful as an aide," Willauer had reported in August, "and a very top one at that."[9]

Placed in charge of CAT's budget in January 1950, Brennan realized that personnel costs accounted for nearly one-half of operating expenses. He made few friends when he reduced staff to one hundred foreigners and four hundred Chinese and even fewer when he ordered salaries for foreign personnel cut by 20 percent. The tactless Brennan responded to complaints about the salary reduction by reminding fellow executives that "our personnel are expected to work for CAT because of what CAT is doing and not because of the money they can get from CAT."[10]

Brennan wielded the economic ax with vigor, but deficits continued to climb. The airline reached a low point in February when three hundred revenue hours flown produced a meager income of $20,000. In desperation, Brennan drew on $29,000 of Willauer's personal funds and $25,000 of Chennault's to keep the company going. Loss of his "nest egg" disheartened Willauer; Chennault was furious and even talked for a time about levying charges of embezzlement against Brennan.[11]

"The biggest overall problem is lack of money," Rosbert wrote with depressing accuracy in March. CAT had lost $671,000 during the first three months of 1950. The airline was broke.[12]

Financial succor would have to come from Washington. Indeed, OPC had been CAT's main hope for economic relief ever since Corcoran and General Donovan had developed an imaginative scheme to operate an airline for the CIA on the periphery of Communist China. This plan envisioned the creation of a giant air complex by combining CAT's fleet with the CNAC/CATC aircraft in Hong Kong. Preparing for meetings at OPC, Corcoran explained to Willauer on December 18, 1949: "I think we've got an idea going for our 100 plane line Oregon [CIA] owned but operated by you over the whole peripheral arc from Korea to Japan to Okinawa to Formosa, Manila, Hong Kong, Indo-China, Siam, Malaya, NEI [Indonesia] — and possibly on through Pakistan to Turkey. . . . This is all very hush—but when Donovan comes out [to Hong Kong] he may have this idea developed." In any event, Corcoran continued, it would be best to "get out of ownership and into management of the equipment for Oregon's account—because this is no longer commerce but war."[13]

Awaiting Willauer's arrival in the United States, Corcoran stepped up pressure on OPC. Without immediate financial assistance, he announced at a meeting with OPC officials on January 10, 1950, the airline would have to be liquidated. The government must act immediately if CAT was to be saved for official use.[14]

OPC had $100,000 remaining from its original authorization of $500,000 for CAT's services. Although these funds could be advanced to the airline without going outside the CIA for policy decisions, agency officials were deeply divided on the issue of further assistance to CAT. Individuals concerned primarily with administration had considerable misgivings about the cost of supporting CAT. Their apprehension grew when Robert E. Terhaar, an accountant sent to Hong Kong in December to keep an eye on the agency's financial interests, expressed horror at the condition of CAT's records.

Support for the airline, however, was strong among individuals charged with executing covert projects. Before returning to the United States in January, and no doubt following conversations with General Donovan, Cox had recommended continued association with CAT. The airline, he said, would be of "immeasureable operational value" in providing secure transportation for CIA activities throughout the Far East. In the end, Cox's view prevailed. On February 1 OPC's project subsidy committee approved payment of $100,000 to CAT.[15]

Willauer reached Washington in late January and promptly joined Corcoran in the search for funds. The former government attorney and his well-connected wife moved easily into the capital's social scene, where the line between business and pleasure tends to blur. On January 29 the Willauers attended a buffet party hosted by their old friend the influential columnist Joseph Alsop; the party was also attended by Frank and Polly Wisner. Three days later they had dinner at the Shoreham with Al and Dorothy Cox. Dinner with the Wisners came on February 8. On February 11 the Willauers and Corcorans shared a meal with Admiral and Mrs. Hillenkoetter and others. "Very nice party and good fun," Louise Willauer recorded in her diary, although one guest seemed upset because "the Admiral was drinking and talking too much (to Whitey)." The champagne flowed freely at the Corcorans' tenth wedding anniversary celebration, where the guest list, studded with senators, Supreme Court justices, and all manner of high officials, read like a veritable "Who's Who" of the Washington establishment.[16]

Willauer and Corcoran spent their daylight hours at the State Department, Economic Cooperation Administration, and CIA, arguing the case for CAT. February 20 brought a decisive meeting at OPC. Willauer — according to the CIA's account — dropped a bombshell: CAT's owners would have to act at once on several alternatives. They could sell the company to the Chinese Communists or to a third party who would sell to Peking; they could sell to the United States government, overtly or covertly; or they could liquidate on the open market. Clearly, CAT's owners had no desire to put the airline's assets on the block in a depressed market, and a deal with the Communists seems unlikely, even had such an arrangement been possible. But their threats put Wisner under the gun: OPC would have to make a decision about CAT.[17]

The days following this meeting saw long and heated discussions at the CIA. Unfortunately, available records do not reveal the substance of the decision-making process, but the result is clear. Sometime in early March the CIA concluded that continued support of CAT was in the national interest. On March 13, 1950, the Departments of State and Defense and the Joint Chiefs of Staff (JCS), ratified the decision.[18]

Action on CAT reflected the government's growing concern with Communist advances in Asia and an increasing acceptance of covert operations as one solution. Mao Tse-tung's victory in China increasingly seemed part of a worldwide Communist conspiracy, especially after Peking and Moscow signed a treaty of alliance on February 14. Recognition by both Communist powers of Ho Chi Minh's revolutionaries in Indochina and the movement of arms across the border from China confirmed the worst fears of the growing number of officials in Washington who took the domino theory as gospel. NSC 64, adopted as policy on February 27, embodied these views. Predicting that a Communist triumph in Indochina would place all nearby countries in immediate danger, NSC 64 concluded: "It is important to United States security interests that all practicable measures be taken to prevent further Communist expansion in Southeast Asia."[19]

The State Department responded to NSC 64 by pledging to use all its "political resources" in the battle against Communist aggression. The Joint Chiefs of Staff chimed in with a series of recommendations to counter the spread of revolution. Although the JCS emphasized overt military assistance to friendly governments, their plans included "a program of special covert operations designed to interfere with Communist activities in Southeast Asia."[20]

Taiwan posed special problems for policy makers. "The United States Government," President Truman had announced on January 5, 1950, "will not pursue a course which will lead to involvement in the civil conflict in China." The administration, he continued, would not provide military aid or advice of any kind to Chinese forces on Taiwan. Secretary Acheson, chief architect of the "hands-off" policy, remained adamant in his opposition to Chiang Kai-shek, preferring to allow the historical antagonism between China and Russia to work in America's favor. "We must not undertake to deflect from the Russians to ourselves," he argued, "the righteous anger and the wrath and the hatred of the Chinese people which must develop."[21]

While hoping for the eventual split between the two Communist giants, some officials in the State Department, in the wake of the Sino-Soviet pact, began to register more concern with short-term prospects than with the distant future. The JCS, pointing out that American objectives in Asia could be achieved only by ultimate success in the "vital strategic area" of China, noted evidence of "renewed vitality and apparent increased effectiveness of the Chinese Nationalist forces [on Taiwan]." Intelligence analysts at the CIA also saw glimmers of hope. No doubt Taiwan would fall before the end of 1950, but information received in late February and early March suggested that "the possibility of a somewhat longer survival of the Nationalist regime on that island should not be excluded."[22]

The United States would not reverse its policy toward Taiwan until the Korean War; however, covert activities in support of the Nationalists did not seem to count. Intriguing references to the shadow war can be found in extant documents. On May 25 Assistant Secretary of State Rusk met with Major General Lyman Lemnitzer, director of the Office of Military Assistance, to explore ways of aiding the Nationalists "within existing United States policy." Although the two men agreed that little could be done beyond granting export licenses for military equipment purchased in the United States, a confirming memorandum of the conversation noted: "It was recognized by both sides that covert action in support of resistance on Formosa, while of limited possibilities, is authorized by existing U.S. policies and that augmentation and intensification of the covert effort is desirable." To fund "authorized projects," Rusk agreed to seek presidential release of money available under Section 303 of the Mutual Defense Assistance Act of 1949.[23]

With the air alive with talk of covert action in the Far East, OPC obviously needed a secure, deniable source of transportation to move personnel, airdrop supplies to guerrillas on the mainland, and engage in various clandestine activities. Financial misgivings notwithstanding, CAT seemed ideal for the purpose.

On March 24, 1950, CAT's owners signed an option agreement with Richard P. Dunn, a Washington banker acting as agent for "undisclosed principals." (In intelligence parlance, Dunn was a "cut-out," that is, a friendly outsider used to disguise the CIA's role in the transaction.) The "bankers" advanced $350,000 to clear up arrears in payroll, gasoline bills, outstanding supply accounts, and other debts affecting the owners' equity in the airline. An additional $400,000 would be made available to fund operating deficits until mid-June. The "bankers" then had the option to purchase the business, including physical properties and operating rights, for $1 million.[24]

CAT's value, set after lengthy negotiations, later became a festering source of controversy between the CIA and CAT's owners. Willauer always contended that the CIA had snapped up the airline at a bargain price; he placed the "real" worth of the business at between $4 and $5 million. Critics countered that CAT was a bankrupt company with obsolete equipment and limited prospects that would have folded without agency backing.[25]

During negotiations with the CIA, Corcoran and Willauer implied that other buyers were eager to acquire CAT; however, they probably used this threat as a bargaining ploy. CAT was not a "hot" property in March 1950. Had CAT's owners been forced to liquidate their assets on the open market, they would have been lucky to realize $1 million after payment of debts. The airline owned nineteen C-46s, one C-47, and four Cessna 195s. Seventeen of the C-46s were older "A" and "D" models that would require modification of control surfaces — costing $15,000 each — to bring them up to "F" standards. CAT, in short, would be trying to sell obsolete aircraft on a depressed market. Although the value of other physical assets — spare parts, the LST, shop equipment, real estate, and so forth — is hard to estimate, it could not have amounted to much. CAT no doubt was worth at least $4 million as a going concern on the mainland, and the airline's value increased after the outbreak of the Korean War. But in spring 1950, as Corcoran confirmed, CAT's owners had been forced to make the option commitment "at the bottom." In fact, they had been lucky to find a buyer at any price.[26]

Willauer returned to Hong Kong on April 1, 1950, traveling from Manila with Cox. Chennault met the two men at Kai Tak. "His nose was slightly, but not seriously, out of joint," Willauer reported, "by the fact that he had received NO briefing from me as progress developed." Willauer smoothed over this misunderstanding before giving Chennault the bad news: the agreement with the CIA specifically excluded repayment as prior debt of the general's $25,000 tossed into the breach by Brennan. The craggy-jawed warrior exploded. "I'll fix something," Willauer vowed, "but it's going to be mighty tough."[27]

Chennault had little time for recriminations. He and Willauer had to make good on a commitment to lower the operating budget to $200,000 a month while promoting enough traffic to make CAT self-sufficient by June 15. Brennan already had slashed expenditures to less than $300,000 a month, so there was not much "fat" left.[28]

Chennault promptly reduced CAT's active fleet to six C-46s and one C-47. Each department faced additional cuts that even Chennault termed "hard-boiled and cruel." Flight operations had to make do with Rousselot and twelve American pilots. It would be difficult, Chennault reported to Corcoran, to expand business and remain within budget restrictions. "I do not mean that we have any doubt of our ability to accomplish the objective," he concluded. "We are going to put each department on an overall expenditure limit — and that's that."[29]

Chennault and Willauer looked to the Chinese government for help. Flying to Taipei in early April, they spoke to Madame Chiang Kai-shek, Premier Chen Cheng, Foreign Minister George Yeh (Yeh Kung-chao), and Minister of Communications Ho Chung-han about the need to give CAT enough business to keep going during the crucial days ahead. Later in the month, the two men suggested a plan to cure the airline's financial ills. The Chinese government would engage CAT's entire services for May, June, and July, advancing $250,000 each month. In return, CAT would carry government cargo at "favorable rates." Unused space would be sold to the general public with the revenue going to the government and credited against the monthly advance. A "Chinese lobby group," headed by Wang Wen-san, tried to sell this quixotic scheme to the Nationalists. "Reaction has so far been favorable," the lobby group reported in mid-May; "everyone seems inclined to keep CAT alive and no one has so far opposed." Their optimism proved premature: CAT never received a penny from the Chinese.[30]

Chennault and Willauer divided responsibility for promotional work. Chennault concentrated on territory north of Hong Kong, especially Japan and Korea, while Willauer looked into prospects south of Hong Kong. Loss of Hainan to the Communists in late April, followed by evacuation of the Chusan Islands in mid-May, lent urgency to their task. In addition to increased business, CAT might well require a new home in order to survive.

The fall of Hainan did not come as a surprise. President Li Tsung-jen had visited the island on November 16, 1949, noted that Chiang Kai-shek had ordered the best units transferred to Taiwan, and left depressed. Hoping to establish a major base on the south end of the island, CAT sent the LST to Sanya in November. But Chennault soon came to share Li's pessimism. He ordered the LST to Taiwan in January 1950, reduced staff at Sanya, and prepared to evacuate the station on short notice.[31]

Elements of four Chinese Communist infantry divisions crossed the narrow Chiungchow Straits in 170 motorized junks on the night of April 16/17. Landing on the north coast, General Lin Piao's forces quickly swept aside the dispirited Nationalist defenders. CAT evacuated Sanya on April 24, leaving

CAT's LST at Kaoshiung, Taiwan, 1950

CAT pilots display new uniforms for commercial operations: Douglass H. Smith, Stuart E. Dew, and Chief Pilot Robert E. Rousselot, April 1950

behind valuable radio equipment and provoking angry comments from Chennault. Three days later, the red banner of the People's Republic waved over the island.[32]

The latest Nationalist defeat, Chargé Robert C. Strong reported from Taipei, caused a severe psychological reaction on the beleaguered island. Taiwan's fate appeared sealed. "Gloom and pessimism generally prevailing," he observed, "are matched by weather which for past three weeks could compare on almost even terms with Chungking's lowering winter skies." Willauer shared Strong's sense of foreboding. "Everyone out here, including myself," he wrote, "seems to conclude that we are still rapidly losing the cold/hot war in the Far East." Chennault made arrangements with U.S. Air Force authorities to park up to twenty C-46s at Northwest Air Base on Guam in case Taiwan collapsed.[33]

As the spring days slipped away, Chennault and Willauer scoured East Asia for business. Willauer was constantly on the move, making several trips to Manila to explore a possible domestic cargo service for Philippine Airlines, spending a week in Djakarta to discuss CAT's operation of domestic and international routes for the newly independent Indonesian government, and going to Saigon to draw up plans for air freight service in Indochina in connection with the American military assistance program. Chennault, meanwhile, worked on an arrangement with Korean National Airlines (KNA) for joint operation of domestic and international lines and tried to expand CAT's toehold in Japan. Although intriguing possibilities appeared in all directions, the only solid evidence of progress came on June 6, when Chief Pilot Rousselot inaugurated weekly air freight service between Taipei and Tokyo. Confined to his room by a painful attack of thrombosis in his right leg, Willauer watched in frustation as operating deficits swallowed up the last CIA dollars.[34]

CAT's fate again hung in the balance as Willauer made the wearing trip across the Pacific for discussions with OPC. Arriving in mid-June, he found Washington officials even more concerned with the Communist threat than they had been during his previous visit. Consul General Walter P. McConaughy had returned from Shanghai to tell the State Department that "the top command of the Chinese Communists was thoroughly indoctrinated in Soviet theory and practice and completely loyal to Moscow." The domino theory had been accepted as fact. Military assistance programs were under way for Indochina, Indonesia, Thailand, the Philippines, and Burma, and plans were afoot to send military personnel to these various countries to supervise implementation of the programs. President Truman had approved NSC 68, the major statement of American policy in the Cold War that one historian has termed "a veritable call to arms, both ideological and military, against the further spread of Soviet-directed Communism." Above all, OPC still needed CAT.[35]

Sometime after Willauer's arrival, and probably before the outbreak of the Korean War on June 25, Wisner made his decision. OPC's operations in East Asia, he informed the State and Defense departments and the Joint Chiefs, required continued association with CAT. The CIA intended to acquire the airline in order to implement authorized covert projects and to keep it out of the hands of "uncontrolled purchasers."[36]

Only State raised objections. The diplomats were concerned over the prospect of a government agency competing against Pan American and Northwest Airlines. Wisner and CIA General Counsel Lawrence R. Houston talked to Assistant Secretary Rusk about this problem. Rusk, Houston recalled, "reminded us that it was basic U.S. policy not to get the government in competition with U.S. private industry." They persuaded the assistant secretary that CAT posed no competitive threat to American airlines in the Far East; moreover, a higher national interest was at stake. State insisted, however, that the final purchase agreement contain a provision giving Willauer and Brennan the right to reacquire all stock in CAT between July 1, 1952, and July 1, 1955. "CIA was thus establishing the position," the agency's history observes, "that the purchase was consummated for short-range national policy and operation purposes." It was State's understanding, Houston confirms, "that we would divest ourselves of the private enterprise as soon as such divestment was feasible."[37]

State's reservations overcome, Wisner ordered a new project established to cover the purchase. After CIA Director Hillenkoetter formally approved the project on June 28, General Counsel Houston began to orchestrate the legal and corporate details of the sale. Richard P. Dunn, the Washington banker and agency "cut-out," exercised his option and took title to the airline's assets from Willauer Trading Company, a new company created by CAT's owners to facilitate the transfer. At the same time, Houston formed two companies under liberal Delaware laws, Airdale Corporation and CAT Incorporated. Airdale, the holding company, had three directors, all employees of the CIA's Office of Finance. The same three individuals, together with an agency employee with the airline, formed a majority on CAT Incorporated's seven-man board of directors, thus assuring policy control of the operating company.[38]

Capitalized on August 23, Airdale acquired the airline's assets through Dunn, then transferred them to CAT Incorporated in return for all of the operating company's stock. On August 25 Willauer Trading Company received a check for $750,000, with an additional $100,000 paid on December 14. The remaining $150,000, held until all assets had been transferred, was reduced by negotiation to approximately $100,000 and paid in fall 1951.[39]

Although legal wranglings may have resulted in minor adjustments, division of the $950,000 received by CAT's owners can be detailed with reasonable confidence. First came $44,770 to discharge notes held by former Chinese partners of CAT, concluding arrangements made in October 1949 at the request of Y. L. Wang and K. Y. Chen, two of the airline's original backers, for purchase of their 22 percent interest in the company for $220,000. Chennault received $25,000 and Willauer $29,000 in repayment for personal funds spent without authorization by Brennan earlier in the year. Office expenses for Willauer Trading Company came to $15,000, and the legal firm of Cann and Long (used for the sale) took $35,000. Corcoran and Youngman claimed $100,000 "for the nearly six years past due legal fees" in connection with work for CAT. The balance of $701,230 was divided by the following percentage of ownership:[40]

The American Share	Percentages
Rio Cathay (the Corcoran brothers and Youngman)	28.88
Willauer	17.64
Chennault	14.46
Brennan	8.46
The Chinese Share	
Wang Wen-san	8.315
L. K. Taylor (acquired through Wang Wen-san)	8.315
Yunnan People's Development Corporation	8.11
Shensi Provincial Government	5.86

Several aspects of the purchase led to protracted disputes. The agreement did not include stock held by CAT's owners in the Jardine Aircraft Maintenance Company (later merged with Pacific Air Maintenance to become Hongkong Aircraft Engineering Company Limited); only after a quarter-century of often bitter argument, especially between Corcoran and Willauer interests, was this part of the settlement resolved. Also, the CIA kept its distance from the disputed assets of CNAC and CATC. CATI, the company formed by Corcoran to pursue the case in the courts, would remain separate from CAT Incorporated. Unfortunately, the Chinese government failed to distinguish between the two corporate entities, causing a series of crises in the years ahead. Finally, the repurchase option granted to Willauer and Brennan caused numerous problems for the CIA. Although later changed to a right of first refusal that gave the two men the opportunity to buy the airline at fair market value should the agency decide to sell, the provision — according to Houston — "plagued us for years." Willauer and Brennan, the general counsel complained, made "all sorts of extraordinary claims under

it." Houston noted that these and other problems that later would be criticized as sloppy business procedures were all "a part of the learning curve."
The CIA had never before bought an airline.[41]

The Nationalist defeat on the mainland had doomed CAT as a viable
private economic enterprise. Attempts to find a home and business elsewhere in Asia, even if successful, would have required time and effort to
overcome objections from strongly entrenched local interests. And CAT did
not have time. Driven to the edge of bankruptcy by rapidly mounting operating deficits, the company would have gone under in spring 1950 without
additional financing.

Fortunately, CAT's troubles came at a time of growing concern in the
United States over Communist advances in the Far East. Determined to
counter the possible effects of the domino theory of events, the Truman
administration adopted a wide-ranging course of action that included covert
operations. OPC's projects required secure transportation, and CAT had
performed well in earlier contract work. Initially reluctant to assume ownership of the airline, OPC eventually decided that purchase would be the best
available — or least undesirable — option.

The arrangement pleased CAT's owners — at the time. "I am quite satisfied
with the airline solution arranged by Whitey, you and other associates,"
Chennault wrote to Corcoran. "It is far better than piecemeal liquidation or
pinching down to a size that would satisfy our current operational requirements. We could not operate a competitive airline with our aircraft, and we
didn't have the capital to buy modern transports."[42]

The CIA, as it turned out, had acquired not only a small airline in the Far
East but also the cornerstone for a vast aerial empire that would stretch
around the world. The process of growth began with the Korean War.

The Korean War

The transition from CAT to CAT Incorporated went smoothly. The same initials decorated the fuselages of the airline's C-46s and were used in advertising. (Except where noted, no distinction is made in this volume between CAT and CAT Incorporated.) Chennault remained highly visible in Taipei, moving up to chairman of the board, and Willauer became president. Brennan — rumored to be the source of new money — continued to concentrate on financial matters as executive vice-president. Chief Engineer Grundy, Chief Pilot Rousselot, and other supervisory personnel stayed at their posts. The two CIA employees who took over executive postiions fit in well. Cox, as vice-president, assumed managerial duties with the airline while retaining his reponsibility for OPC's covert activities in East Asia. Terhaar, accountant from the agency's Office of Finance, moved up to treasurer. Both men had been active in the airline's affairs since the end of 1949, so their "promotions" raised few eyebrows. Indeed, no more than a handful of CAT personnel were aware of new owners, much less of their identities.

It soon became clear, however, that significant changes had taken place in the airline's top management. Chennault's position altered dramatically. The general had posed a special dilemma for the CIA, which wanted to capitalize on his friendship with Chiang Kai-shek to assure continued good relations between CAT and the Nationalist government. But Washington distrusted the intimacy between the general and the generalissimo, fearing that certain covert operations involving anti-Communist but not pro-Nationalist groups on the mainland ("third force") might be revealed to Taipei. The CIA attempted to solve this problem by advancing Chennault to chairman of the board — an empty title. Although still able to exert some influence on basic decisions, Chennault had no operational responsibility for the airline and was used, for the most part, only when problems developed with the Chinese government. Whether this arrangement provided the desired security seems problematical.[1]

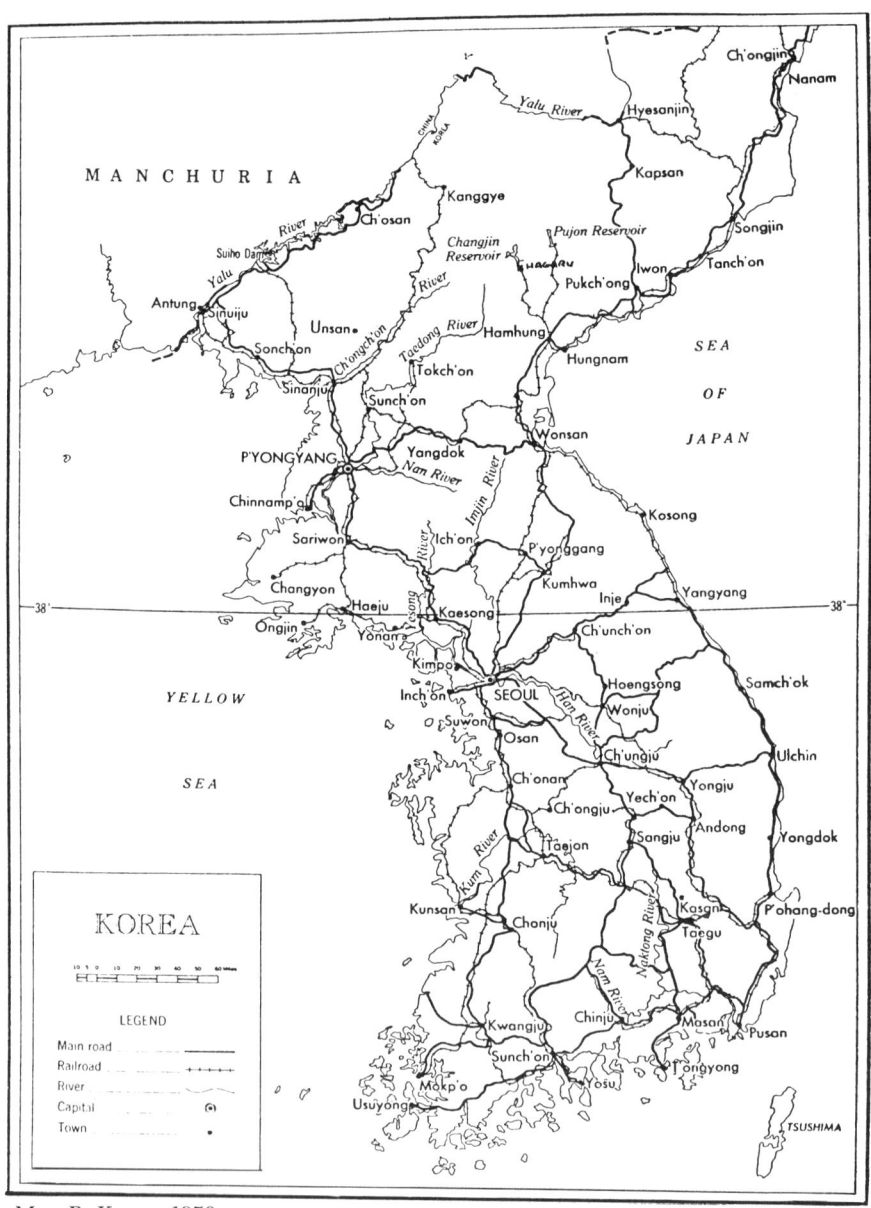

Map B: Korea, 1950

Willauer signed a two-year management contract at $36,000 per year and became CAT's chief operating officer. Based in Hong Kong (which remained the airline's financial and managerial headquarters) and given a fairly free hand in running the company, including authority over personnel and finances, he needed prior approval only for "all major business or operational changes in the nature or locality of the activities of the Company." Willauer of course now reported to the CIA. Corcoran and his Washington associates no longer had any interest in the airline, although they continued active in the affairs of CATI, the company engaged in legal action to recover the disputed aircraft in Hong Kong.[2]

In practice, Willauer delegated responsibility for day-to-day supervision of the airline (except finance) to Director of Operations Rosbert, who was stationed in Taipei. A native of Philadelphia, Rosbert had attended Villanova University on an academic scholarship, graduating cum laude in 1938 with a degree in chemical engineering. He entered the navy's aviation cadet training program in 1939, won his wings, and was assigned to fly PBY patrol bombers on the West Coast. Despite limited experience in fighters, Rosbert joined Chennault's American Volunteer Group in August 1940; he became one of the organization's leading aces, credited with destroying six Japanese aircraft. Hired by the China National Aviation Corporation after the AVG disbanded, Rosbert flew seventy-five round trips over the treacherous "Hump" before his luck ran out. On April 7, 1943, Rosbert crashed into a sixteen-thousand-foot mountain near the Tibetan border. Suffering from a badly broken ankle, the determined young pilot took forty-seven pain-filled days to hobble to safety. After the war, Rosbert became one of the original financial backers of Robert Prescott's Flying Tiger Line. He served as chief pilot and superintendent of operations for the pioneer air freight carrier before joining CAT in 1947. His valuable administrative skills were quickly recognized, and he moved up to director of operations the following year.[3]

Rosbert had little to do at first because business was poor as usual during the early summer of 1950. The war in Korea had little initial impact on the airline. Flying hours remained at the depressed level of five hundred per month, and Willauer once again had to pack his suitcase and set out in search of airlift contracts.

Pakistan, recently split from India, seemed a promising target. Accompanied by Marshall Stayner, Willauer flew to Karachi in late July for a week of talks with high government officials. "I am more favorably impressed with Pakistan than with any other place in the East," he reported. "I'm sure we will have an operation there." But Willauer's optimism proved premature: CAT never operated in Pakistan.[4]

Even more attractive possibilities loomed in Indochina. The transportation-short French needed additional airlift capability to meet combat requirements in their war with the Communist Vietminh. CAT offered a packaged air freight service, including maintenance. Although apprehensive about the Chinese Nationalist registry of the airline's fleet, local French authorities approved the large program. Willauer hastened to Saigon in August and concluded an agreement with the French Air Force. Elated at the prospect of a major operation in Southeast Asia, he continued on to Paris to solicit the required consent of the home government. All came to naught. Despite a strong recommendation from the French air commander in Saigon, Paris vetoed the contract. "I was shocked," Willauer recalled, "when I was turned down on the ground that the French government was afraid that to have CAT in Indochina might make the Commies more irritated and therefore they might fight harder."[5]

The Korean War should have provided full employment for CAT's idle fleet, especially when the Far East Air Force (FEAF) was struggling to meet airlift requirements, but political problems caused initial complications. The airline's equipment continued to bear the flag of Nationalist China despite the change of ownership, and Washington's attitude toward the regime on Taiwan remained ambiguous. Although President Truman extended a measure of protection to the island when the Seventh Fleet moved into the Straits of Formosa in late June, he declined Chiang Kai-shek's offer to send thirty-three thousand troops to Korea, in part, fearing the presence of Nationalist soldiers might provoke a military countermove from Peking. Searching for ways to permit CAT's participation in the war, Burridge suggested to Chennault that Chiang Kai-shek be asked to volunteer transport for the "United Nations" effort in Korea. Taipei then could charter CAT's aircraft for the task. "This will get China's 'foot' officially in," he explained, "and yet would not raise the political complications that other forms of assistance would." The idea never got off the ground.[6]

In July CAT did get a toe if not a foot in the door when Cox made arrangements through intelligence sources for three aircraft to operate between Japan and Korea (Operation AD). Based at Tachikawa, and on twenty-four-hour call, the aircraft transported sensitive personnel and performed other urgent missions. Wider use of CAT in support of covert projects followed.

Fortunately for CAT, urgent military requirements for air transport eventually eroded official concern over registration markings. For nearly two months, the 374th Troop Carrier Wing (two squadrons of four-engine C-54s and one squadron of C-47s), the only transport unit in the Far East, had been making a maximum effort in support of American units in Korea. Relief came in late August with the arrival of the 314th Troop Carrier Group (C-119s) from the United States and formation of the First Provisional Group (C-46s) from aircraft and personnel available in the theater; but the Air Force remained hard-pressed to meet the demands of UN forces. With General Douglas MacArthur planning a bold "end run" offensive for September, and with additional transport squadrons not due in Japan until November, FEAF needed all the help it could find.[7]

On August 25 MacArthur's headquarters approved a major airlift contract for CAT, subject to negotiation of details. This meant, Willauer wrote to Corcoran and Brennan, "that we can look forward to a very busy and I hope profitable fall and winter and even more important that CAT will be used in the anti-Communist drive." As Rosbert arranged to have stored C-46s checked and test flown, Cox and Burridge negotiated with the Air Force's Far East Air Material Command (FEAMCOM). Agreement came on September 8. Under terms of contract AF 92 (504)-5, CAT would fly between points designated by the commanding general of FEAMCOM, carrying cargo and personnel as ordered. Relieved of responsibility for loss of cargo (except in case of gross or willful negligence) and protected against loss of aircraft and/or crew to enemy action, CAT would be paid on a sliding scale, based on monthly use, with a rate of $307 per hour for over five hundred hours a month. The airline was guaranteed four hours daily use for each aircraft called into service. With authority to spend up to $1.5 million, FEAMCOM did not set any time limit for the contract.[8]

In the course of discussions with FEAMCOM, CAT officials led the Air Force to believe that twenty-eight aircraft could be made available on short notice. This error on the far side of optimism would prove troublesome. CAT owned nineteen C-46s and one C-47. Although most of these could quickly be put in flyable condition, the airline needed two C-46s and the C-47 to maintain commercial schedules. CAT also retained custody of eight C-46s that had been leased from the Chinese Civil Aeronautics Administration in May 1948; however, use of these aircraft would require both a new agreement with the CAA and extensive work to remove preservatives ("unpickle"). CAT officials apparently believed they would have ample time for a planned, orderly reconstitution of the airline. They were mistaken. Operation BOOKLIFT began with four aircraft on September 10. Within two weeks, as UN forces in Korea began a rapid buildup following the Inchon landing on September 15, the Air Force ordered full mobilization of the promised twenty-eight aircraft.[9]

The engineering department shouldered the heaviest burden in the struggle to meet FEAMCOM's requirements. Chief Engineer Grundy had to prepare CAT's aircraft for service, install deicing equipment, unpickle the CAA C-46s, set up a line maintenance organization at Tachikawa, and rapidly expand facilities at Tainan. Despite the temptation — and pressure — to cut corners, he maintained rigorous standards of workmanship. In the hectic months ahead, CAT would not suffer a single major accident that could be attributed to mechanical problems.[10]

Recruitment of personnel also took priority in September. Crew strength grew to twenty-five during the month as Rousselot called back pilots from leave without pay and hired locally available airmen. Technical positions on the ground were harder to fill. Because there were few trained mechanics on Taiwan, Grundy and personnel director Reese T. Bradburn went to Hong Kong to look for former CNAC and CATC employees. They had little trouble attracting applicants. Hundreds of qualified people, lured by high wages, sought jobs with CAT, but officials on Taiwan brought recruitment to a virtual standstill by insisting on lengthy political screening to ensure non-Communist backgrounds of prospective employees. Government restrictions, Rosbert complained, "will not allow *sufficient* personnel to come from Hong Kong *quickly* enough." Rumors reaching Hong Kong that Nationalist authorities had seized and executed several new workers did not help recruitment.[11]

Another setback occurred on September 27, when C-46 XT-862 was lost. George V. Calhoun, a newly hired copilot who had flown as a captain with CATC, inadvertently opened the right throttle and left cowl flap, instead of both cowl flaps, after landing at Iwakuni, Japan. The aircraft veered off the runway onto rough ground, the landing gear sheared off, and the left wing crumpled. There were no injuries, but the C-46 would never fly again.[12]

Despite the many problems, flight operations increased dramatically in September. CAT flew 1,665 hours, nearly 300 percent over the number for August and the highest total since fall 1949. "This is a tremendous rate of buildup," Rosbert reported at the end of the month, "but still FEAF is not pleased, because they are demanding *twenty-eight* planes, even though it is impossible to produce this number immediately."[13]

With work on unpickling the CAA C-46s at a standstill because of lack of manpower and with FEAMCOM threatening to cancel its contract, CAT searched the Far East for readily available aircraft. In early October Rosbert worked out an arrangement with Monson W. Shaver, operations manager of Trans-Asiatic Airways, to charter five C-47s, complete with crews. He made a similar agreement with Max A. Springweiler and William A. Dudding, owners and operators of International Air Transport, to lease their single C-47. Painted with CAT insignia, the six aircraft were flying BOOKLIFT missions by October 10.[14]

Unfortunately, charter operations lasted only a week. Following takeoff from Taegu, Korea, in marginal weather, Dudding immediately switched to autopilot, a questionable technique that was observed by a ranking Air Force officer who happened to be on board. When this officer's damning report reached Tokyo, FEAF canceled CAT's authority to carry passengers, charging the airline with violation of several safety regulations. Willauer responded by terminating the C-47 charters on October 17. "This immediately decreased our fleet by six badly needed planes," Rosbert noted, "but it had to be done to save the contract."[15]

For a time, CAT hoped for succor from the Chinese Air Force. Using his influence with Chiang Kai-shek, Chennault obtained permission to charter—for $3,360 a month, each, in advance—twelve flyable C-46s from CAF stocks. The transports arrived in such poor mechanical condition, however, that only three were considered safe enough to be flown to Japan. CAT canceled the lease agreement at the end of the month when the more reliable CAA C-46s came into service.[16]

CAT never managed to station twenty-eight aircraft in Japan during October; nevertheless, flying hours soared to 3,450—double September's total. Demand for air support remained high as UN forces crossed the thirty-eighth parallel and drove toward the Yalu River. Based at FEAMCOM's sprawling complex at Tachikawa, just outside Tokyo, CAT hauled high-priority cargo, mail, and personnel to Korea, bringing back wounded to hospitals in Japan. The airline, writes historian Annis G. Thompson, "carried all types of cargo to practically every airstrip in Korea capable of landing a C-46, including ammunition, gasoline, rations, aircraft parts and engines, medical supplies, tents and cots, machinery, kitchen equipment, weapons, barbed wire and fence pickets. Ammo airlifts included bombs, machine gun and small arms bullets, artillery shells, and napalm tanks and mix."[17]

CAT functioned as a military squadron, performing the same tasks and taking the same risks as Air Force transport units. A typical mission began before dawn at Tachikawa. While Chief Mechanic Ronald E. Lewis supervised predeparture checks of the aircraft, FEAMCOM employees loaded a mixed cargo of mail and aircraft parts. Briefed on weather, loads, and operating conditions by John K. Fogg, a meteorologist who was filling in as operations manager, the sleepy-eyed crew boarded and the C-46 took off into the cool early morning air. Catching a picture postcard glimpse of Mount Fuji, they set a westerly course for Pusan after reaching cruising altitude. Four hours later, the transport touched down on the battered airstrip at K-1 (Pusan). While the crew hunted up sandwiches and coffee, Korean laborers offloaded cargo and prepared the aircraft to carry wounded soldiers. It took less than an hour to cross the Straits of Tsushima and reach Itazuki Air Base on the northern end of Kyushu, where ambulances were waiting to take the wounded to a nearby army hospital at Fukuoka. The C-46 then hopped over to the adjacent airhead at Ashiya and picked up a load of artillery shells for Taegu. Happily, landing at K-2 had become less of an adventure since the 822d Engineering Aviation Battalion had covered the potholed, sod-and-gravel runway with 5,700 feet of pierced steel planking. More wounded came aboard at Taegu. The crew might not return to Tachikawa for several days. Little wonder that, individually, CAT's captains averaged over 150 hours in the air during October.[18]

BOOKLIFT activities increased when CAT received orders to detach six aircraft and ground personnel for service with the Combat Cargo Command at Ashiya. Established on September 10 by Major General William H. Tunner, Combat Cargo imposed order on the chaos of early wartime air transport operations. Tunner, a firm believer in centralized control, relied on techniques perfected during the Berlin Airlift to produce maximum efficient use of aircraft and crews. Gone were the days when pilots would leave Ashiya for Korea at their own discretion, locate a major river near Pusan, then follow the railroad tracks to Taegu. Pilots now adhered to rigorous schedules and flew specific airway channels at set altitiudes. The key to Tunner's system, one historian has emphasized, lay in "a strong headquarters transport movement control center responsible for booking missions for all aircraft, keeping track of movements in flight, and diverting or stopping them from time to time in Korea to fly additional sorties or pick up cargo, personnel or air evacs."[19]

CAT's detachment reached Ashiya on the evening of October 24. James R. Stewart and his staff barely had time to stow their gear in tents and grab a few hours of sleep before operations began at dawn on the twenty-fifth. The first day, CAT flew fifteen round trips from the wind-swept former Japanese fighter strip to Korea, averaging eleven thousand pounds per trip. And this was only a taste of what lay ahead. Caught up in the hectic whirl of Combat Cargo, the six aircraft seemed constantly in the air, shuttling supplies to Kimpo, Pyongyang, and Wonsan as the Eighth Army swept northward. Thanks to the efficiency of Tunner's organization, the Ashiya detachment, with 25 percent of CAT's aircraft in Japan, was doing 75 percent of all BOOK-LIFT flying within three weeks after arrival.[20]

CAT's operations reached a peak in November with twenty-two C-46s and two C-47s assigned to BOOKLIFT. Rousselot had thirty captains and fifty-five copilots on the payroll, enough to handle aircrew requirements for the foreseeable future. Although still short of line maintenance personnel and hard-pressed with engine changes and hundred-hour inspections, engineering now had 464 employees, giving Grundy a small breathing space. "The biggest problem," Rosbert noted, "remains shortage of parts, which becomes more critical every day." CAT had a potential of six thousand hours a month, demonstrated on November 21 when twenty-two aircraft compiled 208 flying hours. But with the lack of critical parts grounding planes for a day or more, the airline accumulated only 3,825 hours during the month.[21]

The war changed dramatically in late November. As early as November 10, intelligence sources had detected large Chinese formations north of

Hamhung, confirming earlier indications that a new enemy had crossed the Yalu and lay concealed in the snowy mountains of north-central Korea. But reports of the Chinese presence between the UN columns advancing up the east and west coasts produced no significant alteration in MacArthur's plans. Like Custer at the Little Bighorn, writes General Matthew B. Ridgway, the supreme commander "had neither eyes nor ears for information that might deter him from the swift attainment of his objective — the destruction of the last remnants of the North Korean Peoples Army and the pacification of the entire peninsula." MacArthur's troops, like Custer's, would pay a high price for the great man's willful blindness.[22]

One new foe was painfully evident. As UN soldiers marched northward, they began to experience the first effects of a North Korean winter. Siberian weather such as most Americans had never known moved into the war zone, blanketing the region with snow and sending blasts of arctic wind to benumb the extremities of the living and freeze the dead where they fell. But the chilled men pressed onward to the Yalu, buoyed by MacArthur's promise to have them home by Christmas.

On November 28 the Chinese struck.

To the blare of bugles and the shrill sound of whistles, masses of Communist troops surged down the icy mountains, overwhelming forward units of the UN advance and throwing MacArthur's campaign into reverse. On the west coast, the Eighth Army fell back, broke contact with the enemy, and hurried southward in relatively good order considering the circumstances. Combat Cargo Command assisted the retreat, first operating from Sinanju, ferrying out Fifth Air Force personnel and equipment along with Eighth Army wounded. The evacuation of Pyongyang soon followed, the last aircraft departing the North Korean capital on December 4. Air Force squadrons throughout Japan, including CAT, mounted an all-out effort in support of the retreating UN forces.[23]

The situation on the east coast was far more perilous. After the initial Chinese onslaught, most units of the battered X Corps retired to safety without serious incident, taking up positions in the Hungham-Hamhung area. Advance elements, however, were not so fortunate. The surging Chinese flowed around and cut off two regiments of the First Marine Division, trapping the Americans in rugged country hard by the icebound Chosin reservoir. Thus was the stage set for the most dramatic episode of the war, with air support playing a crucial role.[24]

The beleaguered marines withstood a series of Chinese frontal assaults. Then, supplied by airdrops, they fought their way in subzero temperatures along a winding mountain road toward divisional headquarters at Hagaru. Exhausted, the two regiments reached the small village, just south of the reservoir, on December 3. Here the trapped men carved a crude airstrip out of the frozen ground that allowed Combat Cargo Command C-47s to establish a twenty-minute air shuttle between Hagaru and Yonpo, the major airfield of the Hungnam-Hamhung perimeter.

General Tunner flew into Hagaru on December 5. "The first sight that met my eyes," he recalled, was "the wounded men, waiting patiently to be loaded on board and flown over the mountains away from this place. Some were on litters, some on crutches. Behind the wounded a tent flap had been erected. Under it were long rows of what appeared to be round mattresses. They were the dead, each corpse placed on a mattress cover, which was then tied around the top. Frozen stiff, the bodies were stacked like logs. They, too, were flown out of Hagaru."[25]

The shuttle airlifted the wounded along with the frozen dead to Yonpo, where C-54s and C-46s waited to fly the casualties to Japan. Altogether Combat Cargo evacuated 4,689 wounded out of Hagaru, losing only two aircraft in the face of treacherous operating conditions. No longer encumbered by their burden of wounded, the marines broke out of Hagaru on December 7, linking up two days later with a task force from the Third Division.[26]

CAT did not take part in the Hagaru-Yonpo shuttle, but the airline's C-46s did assist in evacuation of wounded from Yonpo, losing an aircraft in the process. On December 8 Captain Paul Du Pree in XT-44 crashed at Yonpo in marginal weather. One passenger, a medic from the 801st Medical Air Evacuation Squadron, was killed. The crew suffered minor injuries. With no time to repair the aircraft because of Chinese pressure on the UN perimeter, Rousselot ordered the plane doused with gasoline and burned.[27]

The accident at Yonpo turned out to be only the beginning of CAT's troubles. The following day, a C-46 (XT-852) en route from Tachikawa to Korea plowed into the side of Mount Fuji at the eight-thousand-foot level. Captain Robert Heising, a conscientious pilot who may have been blown into the side of Fuji by high winds, died in the crash, along with copilot Jimmy W. H. Chang and radio operator T. W. Wen. CAT completed the ill-fated cycle of three on December 10, when C-46 XT-846, commanded by Robert L. Brongersma, crashed on takeoff from Taegu after the landing gear had been raised prematurely. Fortunately, there were no injuries, and the aircraft could be repaired.[28]

While CAT labored through this spate of misfortunes, Combat Cargo Command geared up to evacuate from Yonpo X Corps personnel and equipment that would not go by sea. Tunner launched a maximum effort on December 14. In four days of round-the-clock flying, frequently in bad weather, Air Force and CAT aircraft carried to Japan 228 casualties, 3,891 passengers, and 2,088.6 tons of cargo. "The Korean Airlift men," one of their number has written, "were not sorry to leave Yonpo."[29]

The Chinese advance ground to a halt in early January, following the capture of Seoul. The Eighth Army regrouped south of the Han River, then

CAT pilots Paul Holden (left), wounded in the battle of Dien Bien Phu, and Erik Shilling (Courtesy Felix Smith)

Loading supplies at Pusan, Korea, for CIA operations, 1951 (Courtesy H. V. Tofte)

resumed offensive operations in mid-February under the command of General Ridgway. After hard fighting, UN troops entered Seoul on March 15.

CAT's role in direct support of combat units ended as the front stabilized around the thirty-eighth parallel. Always a bit apprehensive about the presence of "civilians" in their bailiwick, Air Force brass — now with sufficient transport to meet any emergency — relegated CAT to the "milk run." For the rest of the war, BOOKLIFT flying consisted primarily of scheduled flights within Japan and to Okinawa, Iwo Jima, Guam, and elsewhere throughout the Far East.[30]

CAT's airlift contribution to FEAF was important but did not compare to its crucial support of OPC operations in Japan and Korea. Hans V. Tofte, head of covert activities, 1950–51, considered the airline "absolutely invaluable" during the early phase of the Korean War.[31]

An OSS veteran with a distinguished wartime record in paramilitary operations, Tofte was recruited by Wisner at the outbreak of the Korean War to take charge of OPC in Japan. He arrived in Tokyo on July 16, 1950, carrying general instructions to establish an escape-and-evasion network to assist fliers brought down behind enemy lines and to begin preparations for guerrilla warfare. Tofte faced a formidable task. OPC's six-man detachment in Japan headed by George E. Aurell, maintained a tenuous liaison with MacArthur's headquarters (SCAP). Only the previous May the CIA had secured permission from a reluctant General MacArthur to enter Japan. The supreme commander had not permitted OSS to operate in his theater during World War II, and he clearly was not happy with the presence of people and activities beyond his control. Major General Charles A. Willoughby, SCAP intelligence chief, barely tolerated Tofte.[32]

Ignoring Willoughby's threats to throw OPC out of the theater, Tofte started work on establishing the infrastructure for future operations. He set up six CIA stations in Japan, the major one at Atsugi Naval Air Station, fifty miles south of Tokyo. Colwell Beers, Tofte's capable deputy, took charge of the Atsugi complex, which included training facilities at Chigasaki, an isolated area on Sagami Bay. OPC activities in Korea centered around a large training base on Yong-do Island in the Bay of Pusan.

Initial operations in fall 1950 emphasized the rescue of American pilots who had been shot down behind enemy lines. Tofte contacted the U.S. Air Force's Office of Special Investigations (OSI), which had responsibility for escape and evasion. Working with Major Julian M. Niemczyk, chief of the OSI's Counter-Intelligence Division, he established a network of agents in North Korea to assist downed American pilots. OPC-trained personnel manned coastal islands on both sides of the Korean peninsula near the thirty-eighth parallel. Pilots in trouble were to head for these sanctuaries. If downed inland, the fliers should try to contact friendly Koreans, who were strung out in a belt across the peninsula. Lookout posts every ten miles along both coasts would radio for assistance when the pilots reached the shore-line.[33]

Tofte used CAT from the beginning. He knew airline personnel and pro-cedures from having worked after World War II as a traffic manager for American Overseas Airlines. Cox had sent three C-46s to Japan in July for "AD" operations. In early September E. V. Wong flew a Cessna 195 from Taipei to Tokyo, adding a light plane to Tofte's growing fleet. The airline performed hundreds of transportation errands, large and small, as OPC quickly became the largest American paramilitary force since OSS.[34]

A classic instance of the freedom of action afforded by the ability to use CAT, Tofte recalled, came during a dispute with MacArthur's headquarters over the use of gold bars for the escape-and-evasion program. Tofte wanted a supply of one-ounce gold bars, bearing the widely recognized chop of the old Bank of China, for pilots to carry and use to pay Koreans for assistance if they were forced down. The bars could be obtained easily on Taiwan, but General Willoughby objected (as he usually did), citing currency regulations that prohibited such imports. Ignoring Willoughby, Tofte took a CAT plane to Taiwan, purchased $700,000 worth of gold bars, and returned to Japan within twenty-four hours. As CAT's chief pilot put it, with evident admiration, Tofte "really got things done."[35]

By the end of 1950 the escape-and-evasion network was in place, the Atsugi-Chigasaki complex had been completed, and OPC had more than a thousand men in Japan. As the battlefield stabilized at the thirty-eighth parallel, emphasis shifted to guerrilla operations in North Korea. Tofte lo-cated thousands of North Korean evacuees in refugee camps around Pusan. After careful screening by South Korean officials, hundreds of these young men were accepted for training on Yong-do Island. CAT flew leaders and skilled personnel to Chigasaki for advanced schooling.

Tofte sent forty-four guerrilla teams and attached intelligence units into North Korea between April and December 1951. Most went by sea; some were parachuted in by CAT. Operating south of the Yalu River from Antung in the west to Rashin and Yuki in the northeast, the guerrillas sabotaged trains and ambushed truck convoys, disrupting the flow of supplies from Manchuria and eastern Siberia. Tofte knew this area well. During the 1930s he had worked in Manchuria for the Danish East Asiatic Company and had taken long big game hunting vacations in the border region. Able to identify vital border crossings along the little-known northern frontier, he could place his units in position to cause maximum damage.

Tofte considered the program "tremendously successful." Although only twelve hundred guerrillas were involved, the CIA intercepted messages from Peking, warning Chinese field commanders in Korea that fifty thousand troops were operating behind their lines.[36]

Within the short space of three months, CAT's flying time increased from five hundred hours a month with three aircraft to nearly four thousand hours with twenty-six aircraft. This explosive growth placed a tremendous strain on the organization. But CAT's staff, from coolies to captains, responded with the "can-do" spirit that had been nurtured on the mainland. In a situation fraught with potential disaster, the untiring efforts of Rosbert, Rousselot, Grundy, and others ensured a relatively smooth transition.

CAT flew more than fifteen thousand BOOKLIFT missions during the Korean War, carrying twenty-seven thousand tons of supplies and mail and thousands of wounded. From September 1950 to January 1951, the airline played an especially important role in direct support of combat operations. "At a time when air transportation was critically short," General Tunner wrote to Willauer, "you made available to us your aircraft and your trained personnel in the quantities required." CAT, he concluded, had done an "outstanding job."[37]

The airline also made a crucial contribution to OPC activities in Japan and Korea. It provided airlift for a variety of covert projects, allowing OPC to ignore SCAP's cumbersome restrictions and shuttle hundreds of guerrillas and agents betweeen CIA training and staging camps throughout the Far East. As Tofte acknowledged, "CIA could never have accumulated an outstanding record in the early stages of the Korean War without CAT."[38]

But CAT's participation in the Korean conflict became even more important following Chinese intervention. When the CIA undertook a secret war against Peking, CAT stood at the center of the action.

 # Covert Operations

OPC mushroomed as the Cold War grew hot. From 302 personnel and a budget of $4.7 million in 1949, the government's covert action arm increased to 2,812 employees and a budget of $82 million in 1952. As former CIA director Colby explained, "Under the impetus of the Korean War, at a time of fierce anti-Communist and anti-Soviet sentiment and rhetoric, covert paramilitary and political action was the name of the intelligence game."[1]

Major organizational changes accompanied this hectic expansion. General Walter Bedell Smith, General Dwight Eisenhower's wartime chief of staff and Truman's postwar ambassador to the Soviet Union, replaced the ineffectual Hillenkoetter as director of the CIA in October 1950. Described as a "tough-minded, hard-driving, often intimidating military careerist," Smith swept through the agency with acerbic vigor. One of his first moves was to end OPC's ambiguous and semiautonomous position in the bureaucracy and place it wholly within the CIA, subject to the director's authority. The general's power and prestige were so great that this action provoked nary a whisper of protest. In August 1952, he overcame strong internal dissent and combined OPC with the Office of Special Operations (OSO), a competing organization that emphasized espionage and counterespionage, to form the Directorate for Plans.[2]

Frank Wisner remained firmly in command of the Clandestine Service under the new regime. Encouraging new projects and driving subordinates with impatient energy, Wisner seemed to flourish in an atmosphere of constant crisis. "He disliked bureaucracy, administration, or planning," one former intelligence officer recalled. "He pondered purpose and then reveled in action." Colonel Richard Giles Stilwell—no relation to General "Vinegar Joe" Stilwell of World War II fame—ran the Far Eastern Division. A career soldier (West Point, 1938) on temporary assignment with the CIA, the future four-star general brought a keen analytical mind to the fastest growing component of OPC. Desmond FitzGerald held down the number two post under

Stilwell. Bright, affluent, cultured, charming, and an avid bird watcher, FitzGerald undertook the deadly business of covert operations with a light-hearted, romantic activism that would become a trademark of OPC/FE during the 1950s.[3]

The chain of command ran from Washington to Hong Kong, where Al Cox had far-reaching responsibilities for developing and implementing OPC projects in East Asia, especially activities that involved CAT. "I think I spend more time sleeping on the floor of an airplane than I do on a bed on the ground," he wrote to his family in September 1950. "As a good infantryman I really don't believe in airplanes, but I sure seem to spend a lot of time in them." Assisting the peripatetic intelligence officer and airline executive were Conrad E. La Gueux, who had served under Cox during the war, and Stuart P. McFadden. La Gueux occupied a variety of head office positions with CAT following his arrival in November 1949; McFadden joined the airline in October 1950 as public relations officer.[4]

An atmosphere of grave apprehension, bordering at times on panic, permeated official Washington during winter 1950–51. Chinese "volunteers" appeared unstoppable as they pushed UN forces out of North Korea and poured across the thirty-eighth parallel. The Joint Chiefs of Staff warned in late December that the enemy was capable of driving the United Nations off the peninsula. General MacArthur agreed. Unless political considerations took precedence, he warned his superiors, UN forces should be withdrawn from Korea "just as rapidly as it is tactically possible to do so." At the State Department, John Paton Davies, Jr., China expert on the Policy Planning Staff, predicted that Peking soon would attack Taiwan, threaten Hong Kong, and extend massive aid to Ho Chi Minh in Indochina. The United States, he concluded, could look forward to seeing its military forces "deeply embroiled from Korea to Cambodia before Spring is over."[5]

W. Stuart Symington, chairman of the National Security Resources Board, struck an especially somber note when he reported to the National Security Council on January 11 that the survival of the United States and the United Nations "is imminently threatened by Communist aggression." The danger was worldwide. Within eighteen months, he predicted, the Soviet Union would have the nuclear capability to "blast the heart out of United States industry." The Communists were winning in Asia because America was attempting to fight a ground war instead of exploiting its air and naval power. Symington recommended that the United States evacuate Korea, blockade Communist China, defend Taiwan, launch air attacks on enemy lines of communication in Korea and China, bomb war industries in Manchuria, promote guerrilla activities in central and southern China, and extend the fullest possible aid to all anti-Communist elements in the Far East. The government at the same time should accelerate mobilization of the nation's military potential to deal with the worldwide Communist menace. "The hour is late," he warned. "The odds may be stacked against the free nations; but it is still possible to take the offensive in this fight for survival."[6]

President Truman stood calm in the midst of storm and ordered General MacArthur to remain in Korea unless forced out by military necessity. He rejected proposals to strike directly at targets in Manchuria and China lest such action lead to a wider war. Aware of Soviet strength and America's limited military resources, Truman agreed with General Bradley that full-scale conflict in Asia would be "the wrong war, at the wrong place, at the wrong time and with the wrong enemy."[7]

While determined to confine the war to Korea, if at all possible, Truman searched for ways to aid hard-pressed UN forces. He therefore proved receptive to an OPC scheme, which may have originated with Cox, to use Nationalist remnants in Burma for an attack on Yunnan. It was hoped the assault would stir up internal resistance to the Communist regime in a border province with a tradition of independence and cause Peking to divert some attention from Korea. CIA Director Smith, according to one undocumented account of the episode, "vigorously opposed the plan, arguing that mainland China had troops aplenty, but Truman overruled him in a White House meeting and insisted that CIA carry out the operation." CAT was about to be put to work.[8]

The origins of what became known as the Li Mi project went back to the last days of the Chinese civil war. In December 1949 scattered remnants of Chiang Kai-shek's defeated army fled across the border from southwestern Yunnan into Burma. General Li Mi led one of the largest contingents, some fifteen hundred men of the Kuomintang (KMT) Ninety-seventh Division. Harassed by the Burmese army, Li Mi eventually settled at Monghsat in the Southern Shan States, about eighty miles from the Thai border. Establishing a base camp and training area in this remote mountainous region, he called on other Nationalist survivors in Burma to join his Yunnan Anti-Communist National Salvation Army. By the end of 1950 Li Mi commanded some four thousand poorly equipped troops.[9]

If OPC hoped to transform Li Mi's ragtag army into a force capable of invading Yunnan with even the slightest chance of success, modern weapons would have to be provided. CAT of course was the perfect — deniable — agent for the covert airlift. Operation PAPER began in early February 1951. Three C-46s and a C-47, flown by Captains Robert L. Brongersma, Charles E. Hayes, Robert C. Snoddy, and Harold W. Wells, picked up arms and ammunition from CIA stocks on Okinawa and carried them to Bangkok on February 7, the first of many such flights. Handling arrangements in Bangkok was Sherman B. Joost, head of Sea Supply Company, the CIA's commercial cover organization in the Thai capital. A Princeton graduate and

CAT pilots in Bangkok during the Li Mi operation: Norman A. Schwartz, unidentified, Robert E. Rousselot, James B. McGovern, and Robert C. Snoddy, February
1951 (Courtesy E. C. Kirkpatrick)

one of the top combat commanders of OSS Detachment 101 in Burma during
World War II, Joost expedited supplies in the Li Mi project, while operational control remained with Cox.[10]

CAT stationed a C-47 at Bangkok's Don Muang airport to transport the
weapons to Chiengmai or Chiangrai in northern Thailand. From there, the
Thai border police arranged delivery to Li Mi. Initially, Chief Pilot Rousselot and Snoddy flew the C-47. After Snoddy accidentally shot himself in
the leg while playing with a pistol, E. C. Kirkpatrick took over as copilot.
Arthur D. Wilson and "Dutch" Brongersma later replaced Rousselot.[11]

Li Mi moved out of Monghsat in April and marched 175 miles north to
Mongmao, CAT airdropping supplies en route. The KMT troops invaded
Yunnan in early May. All went well at first. Li Mi advanced sixty miles into
the border province, joined local guerrillas, and threatened the airfield at
Mengsa. But local Communist units soon reacted sharply and effectively.
The Salvation Army was back in Burma by the end of the month, having
suffered heavy casualties.[12]

A second major incursion into China came two months later. CAT airdrops enabled Li Mi's subordinate, General Liu Kuo-chuan, to set up a staging base at Mongyang, ninety miles north of Monghsat. In July Liu led some two thousand men across the border and headed toward Menglong. Within a week, Communist forces had chased Liu's shattered column out of Yunnan. As discipline and morale collapsed, the dispirited Nationalist troops found it less dangerous and more profitable to plunder peaceful Burmese border villages than to fight Communists.[13]

The Li Mi project had accomplished little. There had been no general uprising in Yunnan, and Peking had not diverted troops from Korea. Support of the Nationalists had only poisoned American-Burmese relations. Ambassador David M. Key, who had not been briefed about the covert operation, cabled a scathing report from Rangoon to Washington on August 15:

> This adventure has cost us heavily in terms of Burmese goodwill and trust. Participation by Americans in these KMT operations well known to GOB [Government of Burma] and constitutes serious impediment to our relations with them, a fact which has become only too apparent to all of us here. Denial of official US connection with these operations meaningless to GOB in face of reports they constantly receiving from their officials in border areas that KMT troops are accompanied by Americans and receiving steady supply American equipment, some of which dropped from American planes, and of reports from their Bangkok Embassy of American support activities going on in Siam, which is an open secret there. Thus American participation in KMT operation, which have brought chaos to eastern Shan States and have been conducted in flagrant disregard Burmese sovereignty, cannot but make a mockery in Burmese eyes of our officially expressed desire to aid in the restoration of internal stability and to strengthen Burmese independence. . . .
>
> Whatever the original justification may have been for these operations . . . it now seems obvious, as far as can be determined here, that they have failed to achieve useful results commensurate with the harm they have done to our interests in Burma. For this reason I feel strongly that the time has come to call a halt to any further American participation in these operations and recommend that the Department endeavor by all means at its disposal to bring this about.[14]

Assistant Secretary Rusk vigorously supported the cover story. After an "exhaustive investigation," he replied to Key on August 22, the State Department was able to authorize the ambassador "categorically to deny to GOB that there is or could be in future any official or unofficial US Govt connection with this force." The department, he promised, would take action to prevent "gunrunning" by private American citizens. CIA Director

Smith took a similar position with the British, stating that the United States government had no association with Li Mi, although he suspected the existence of some American "free lance" support of the Nationalists, possibly connected with General Chennault.[15]

Disguising such a large operation proved impossible. Reporter Seymour Topping had little trouble penetrating the flimsy veil of secrecy. During the summer of 1951 he traced CAT aircraft from their refueling point in Saigon, to Sea Supply in Bangkok, to Li Mi. He went to Rangoon and informed embassy personnel. "They were incensed," he recalled, "considering the whole operation an act of folly from the United States standpoint." Topping filed a dispatch from Singapore that "evoked a chorus of protests around the world," but had little practical effect.[16]

Insistence on the tattered cover story continued to create credibility problems for American diplomats. The most painful episode came in fall 1951 when a group of junior American Foreign Service officers in London, believing the official line on Li Mi, managed to convince their British counterparts that it would be useful if the British ambassador and American chargé in Thailand called on Prime Minister Phibun Songgram and gave joint assurance of noninvolvement.

The British ambassador objected because in an earlier conversation with Phibun, the prime minister volunteered the information that the CIA had asked for facilities to support Li Mi, and Phibun had readily agreed. When the ambassador raised his eyebrows at this disclosure, Phibun said, "Why are you surprised? Aren't you just as interested in killing Communists as I am, or as the Americans are?" When advised of this conversation, the embarrassed American diplomats in London dropped the joint assurance proposal.[17]

The Li Mi project had little to commend it, but the scheme has to be seen as a natural product of the times. It came during the "Hot Button" era at OPC, when the philosophy was "don't just stand there, do something, even if it's wrong." Anxious to confine the war to Korea, Truman had few weapons to use against the Chinese heartland. As one intelligence officer explained, "Li Mi might not have been much, but he was all we had." Perhaps American officials allowed themselves to believe that Li Mi might stir up enough trouble in Yunnan to have an impact on the Chinese effort in Korea. They were wrong, and American-Burmese relations suffered.[18]

The Li Mi scheme formed only part of a larger secret war against Communist China. In February 1951 the Joint Strategic Plans Committee raised with the Joint Chiefs of Staff the possibility of supporting guerrilla forces on the mainland. Although the Nationalists claimed to control and direct 1 million dissidents, a figure used by Chennault in a series of articles for the *New York Herald Tribune*, a study by the Joint Chiefs of Staff's Joint Intelligence

Group (JIG 318) placed total anti-Communist resistance at closer to 600,000. No more than half this number could be counted loyal to Chiang Kai-shek, and control and direction from Taipei were "almost non-existent." Although no significant increase could be expected, assistance to existing groups, Nationalist and non-Nationalist, seemed reasonable. "External logistic support," JIG 318 noted, "would probably accelerate the tempo, increase the combat effectiveness, and widen the area of guerrilla activity." If properly supported, guerrillas could prevent Peking from consolidating its control over southern and central China, tie down many troops, lessen the threat of Chinese action in other parts of Asia, and counter a growing belief in Communist invincibility.[19]

The rosy prospect of achieving significant results at relatively low cost and minimum risk proved as seductive with guerrillas as it had with Li Mi. Although many details of this highly secret program remain obscure, even after three decades, enough fragments exist to piece together the main outlines. The CIA, along with the Air Force, assumed the major responsibilities for implementing the project, and this meant extensive use of CAT. Civilian pilots in unmarked aircraft afforded "official deniability," an important consideration at times in the bizarre rituals of the Cold War.

Support of pro-Nationalist guerrillas transformed Taiwan into a beehive of CIA activities. Joseph Burkholder Smith, who joined OPC's Far Eastern Division in 1951, found the range of activities on the island "rather spectacular." The division, he recalled, "had more than six hundred persons on Taiwan, providing guerrilla training, logistical support, overflight capabilities, facilities for propaganda coverage of the mainland by radio and leaflet balloon, and doing other tasks." Western Enterprises, a fictional company known to intimates as "Western Auto," provided commercial cover for agency personnel. Colonel Raymond W. Peers, OSS Detachment 101 commander in Burma during World War II, directed CIA operations from his headquarters in Wu Chang Villa, a housing complex about ten minutes by car from downtown Taipei that included among its residents Admiral Charles M. Cooke, retired naval officer and military adviser to the Nationalists, and General Chennault. "Having listened to the critics of the Truman administration hammer ceaselessly on the theme that Truman had abandoned Chiang Kai-shek," Smith concluded, "it was a major revelation to me to learn that this was far from the truth. Perhaps, more than anything else, our large-scale efforts with the Chinats [Chinese Nationalists] shaped my appreciation for what I was learning a covert adjunct of foreign policy was evidently meant to be."[20]

Chief Pilot Rousselot was the key link between CAT and the CIA for covert missions. Assigned a task by Cox or La Gueux, Rousselot took charge of operational planning and selection of crew. The chief pilot looked for

Chief Pilot Robert E. Rousselot, 1952 (Courtesy R. E. Rousselot)

capable, responsible individuals, who would complete a mission if at all possible but would abort when necessary. Although the CIA case officer could veto his choice, this rarely if ever happened. The agency might on occasion request particular pilots for a mission, but on the whole they intervened as little as possible in flight operations, content to leave details to the chief pilot's proven judgment. As one former case officer recalled, "Rousselot always delivered."[21]

Born in March 1922, Rousselot grew up on a 120-acre farm in southwestern Missouri, near the small town of Noel. His father was from Kansas City and had worked for the railroad before buying a farm. The oldest of five children, Rousselot helped his parents scratch a living out of the rocky hill country while his character was being shaped by their discipline and determination. The young man attended high school in Noel, where he starred on the baseball team. He entered Joplin Junior College in 1940, enrolling in the premedical program. Rousselot left college in 1942 for the naval aviation cadet program. Choosing the Marine Corps option out of flight school, he became carrier-qualified and saw action in the Pacific as a Corsair pilot with a CVE Air Support Group. At the end of the war he volunteered for a fifteen-month tour in China, hoping to save money for college and medical school or to make a career out of the military. Rousselot enjoyed the life of a marine officer, feeling comfortable with the discipline and sense of order. But the postwar marines, in his view, had become "sloppy." In late 1946 he went to Shanghai and asked Chennault for a job. Although Rousselot had only limited multiengine time, having managed to bootleg a few hours in a C-47, the general liked what he saw. Always more impressed with character than with time in a log book, Chennault hired the determined lieutenant.[22]

Rousselot became chief pilot in 1948. He later recalled those mainland days as the best of times. Unconcerned with politics, life was "easy come, easy go" for the young bachelor. But added responsibilities matured Rousselot. By the early 1950s he ruled the strutting *machismo* world of CAT pilots with an iron hand. The tough former marine belonged to the "follow me" school of leadership; he made it a point to fly the most dangerous missions, at least in the beginning, setting an example for and earning the respect of his fellow airmen. Obligation and personal loyalty were vital in Rousselot's domain. He could be great if he liked a man, one flier observed, and an implacable enemy if he did not. The chief pilot hated sloppiness or lack of discipline, and he was not reticent about expressing his displeasure. Tolerant of misbehavior out of the cockpit, he demanded from his pilots a professional approach to their job when on duty. Gracious, generous, courageous, bull-headed, and petty, Rousselot blended these complex personal qualities to provide dynamic leadership for an extraordinary group of individuals.[23]

Overflights, theoretically at least, were volunteer missions, and not all CAT pilots participated. Rousselot, however, had no trouble finding recruits; perhaps 75 percent of available crew members flew "routine" covert operations at one time or another. Some pilots, Rousselot pointed out, were terrific if used once or twice ("bunters"), others were good for the long haul, and a few were unsuitable. The most hazardous flights were entrusted to a small group of especially responsible pilots, including Norman A. Schwartz, Robert C. Snoddy, Eddie F. Sims, Merrill D. Johnson, William J. Welk, Paul R. Holden, Roy F. Watts, and Cyril M. Pinkava (navigator). Money played little part in attracting men to the dangerous work; extra pay during the early 1950s amounted to $10 an hour — when you could get it. Patriotism and a sense of adventure were more important motivations. As one pilot explained, "I believed in the purpose of the operations."[24]

Many overflights, especially leaflet drops along the Chinese coast or over Hainan, tended to be casual. Briefings were perfunctory, covering little more than location of the drop area. Escape-and-evasion kits consisted of several gold bars to be used for bribes in the event of being forced down. A typical mission, Captain Hugh Hicks recalled, involved heading due west across the Straits of Formosa, then north along the coast of Fukien Province. Over a general drop area, Chinese kickers would toss out bundles of leaflets. Aircraft employed in leaflet drops usually carried Chinese copilots and radio operators. Paid in green dollars by Rousselot, the Chinese crew members were not in the "volunteer" part of the program; they took flights as assigned or looked for other jobs.[25]

Drops involving agents or supplies required more elaborate procedures. Crews assigned to these risky missions operated on precise time schedules and received detailed briefings on Chinese air defenses, coastline penetration points, ground speeds, approach corridors to drop zones, checkpoints for breaking radio silence, and flight paths for return. Because the Communists had no night fighters, evasion procedure usually meant flying in darkness and avoiding large cities. Navigation posed the major problem, and missions were launched on nights with a full moon to facilitate use of ground reference techniques. But accuracy proved difficult. Maps too often were inadequate or unreliable, Captain Watts recalled, and "many of the flights got no closer than twenty miles or so of the assigned DZ [drop zone], especially in the Inner and Outer Mongolia areas."[26]

Long-range penetration missions from Taiwan began in March 1952. Rousselot and Pinkava made two daylight flights, deep into western China, on the fifteenth and seventeenth. On the second mission, they flew in clouds 75 percent of the time and missed their drop zone by sixty-five miles. Although Madame Chiang personally thanked the crew for undertaking the hazardous flight, Nationalist intelligence sources reported that the four parachuted agents had been lost.[27]

Later in the spring Rousselot and Pinkava went to Kadena Air Base, Okinawa, and picked up from the Air Force an unmarked B-17. The World War II bomber, with good altitude and range, was used extensively for long overflights, usually piloted by Rousselot, Welk, or Johnson. In summer 1952 the Air Force covertly turned over to CAT a C-54 (DC-4). The airline promptly announced with appropriate fanfare the "purchase" of its first modern four-engine plane. Bearing the Chinese registration of B-1002, the aircraft began passenger service on routes throughout the Far East. Several times during fall 1952, on nights of the full moon, however, the passenger seats gave way to drop tracks, static line, and signal box. The night flights, Watts remembered, "were hair raisers whose distance and duration were impressive." Watts and Holden claimed the unofficial record for deep penetration missions: fourteen hours and twenty-one minutes.[28]

CAT pilots spent many long and apprehensive hours over mainland China, ears alert for the slightest irregularity in the steady beat of the engines. "There was no real Search & Rescue or Escape & Evasion apparatus that could have in the least have rendered aid or comfort if we went down," Watts pointed out. "The potassium cyanide pills were usually politely turned down when offered in our escape kits." On one flight with Holden, radio operator Charles B. Davenport, and two CIA "cruise directors," Watts lost number three engine on B-1002 about four hours after crossing the coastline. "The engine quit with such a jolt," he noted, "that we thought we had taken a hit." Watts feathered the propeller and completed the mission on three engines.[29]

Thanks to luck, skill, and good maintenance, CAT never lost an aircraft on mainland overflights from Taiwan. Agents sent into China fared less well. Many missions involved "blind" drops of young Chinese agents into unprepared locations where they were expected to establish resistance networks from scratch. Indications are that few survived.[30]

Another part of the guerrilla program involved assistance to non-Nationalist or "third force" elements on the mainland. These operations raised delicate problems between the CIA and CAT, centering on Chennault's relationship with Chiang Kai-shek. The airline owed its existence to the special ties between the general and the generalissimo. Indeed, Chennault *was* CAT in the minds of many high Chinese officials. Operation of an airline that flew the Chinese flag under a Chinese charter depended on the confidence of the Chinese government. Also, as Willauer pointed out, "The extraordinary loyalties of the flight operations personnel of the airline ran to him [Chennault] personally and his presence in Formosa was an indispensable factor in the morale of these men as well as an indispensable factor in the confidence of the Chinese Government in [CAT]."[31]

The CIA recognized from the beginning that some CAT operations would have to be kept secret from the Nationalists, which caused a dilemma because Chennault insisted on a relationship of complete confidence with Chiang Kai-shek. How could Chennault be used to promote the necessary close ties with the Chinese government and at the same time protect the security of certain covert activities? The CIA attempted to solve this problem when it purchased the airline by "promoting" Chenault to chairman of the board and placing Willauer in operational control. From time to time, the agency called the chairman back to Washington for consultations, thus removing him without suspicion from Taiwan "when activities inexplicable to the Chinese were in the planning stage or in actual operation."[32]

The "third force" project was one of those activities unlikely to cause joy in Taipei. As JIG 318 had noted, at least half the guerrillas on the mainland had no connection — and desired none — with the Nationalists. Efforts to support these groups and to introduce new agents with direct ties to American intelligence formed an important part of the secret war against China. The program directed special attention at the two Manchurian provinces adjacent to Korea, Liaoning to the northwest and Kirin to the northeast.[33]

Recruitment of "third force" Chinese began in Hong Kong in 1951. Under the guise of employment with the Far East Development Company for work on Guam, the new agents were flown to the $28 million CIA training complex on Saipan ("Navy Technical Training Unit") or to the more modest facility at Chigasaki, Japan. After instruction in parachuting, small arms, demolition, radio operation, and other basic guerrilla skills, the men were organized into teams and taught how to set up secure bases, prepare drop zones, and establish secret communications networks. Once in Manchuria, they would recruit local dissidents, collect and transmit intelligence and weather information, and rescue any downed American airmen.[34]

CAT involvement in what airline personnel knew as Operation TROPIC began in December 1951 when Captains Snoddy and Schwartz went to Korea and flew indoctrination missions with the Air Force. At the same time, CAT purchased three C-47s from Trans-Asiatic Airways. Given Chinese registration numbers B-813, B-815, and B-817, the aircraft were painted olive drab and equipped with static lines, drop signal systems, and flame suppressors to make them less visible from the ground at night.[35]

In March 1952, shortly after Chennault had been called to Washington for "consultations," Operations Director Rosbert flew to Japan for meetings with Colonel Stilwell and others to make final arrangements for TROPIC. Learning for the first time about the "third force" purpose and goals, Rosbert reacted — privately — with anger. Intensely loyal to Chennault, an admirer of Generalissimo and Madame Chiang, and a close friend of Chiang Ching-kuo, the generalissimo's son, the former AVG ace wrote in his journal: "We'll never learn that you can't win the faith of a people by stupidly dividing the house. Why not get the third force elements into the 1st force? Because we were divided before, the 2nd force (communism) has all the Mainland. I'm really burned on this type of thinking. . . . I'm disgusted with the so-called thinkers in Wash. who work out these utterly stupid plans."[36]

TROPIC got off the ground in spring 1952. Crews assigned to the project lived at the bachelor officers' quarters at Tachikawa or off base if married. Alerted for a mission by telephone, the crew ferried a C-47 from Tachikawa to nearby Atsugi Naval Air Station, headquarters of the Joint Technical Advisory Group. John H. Mason, a highly decorated (Distinguished Service Cross, two Silver Stars, three Bronze Stars, two Purple Hearts) former regimental commander with the Ninetieth Infantry Division in Europe during World War II, had replaced Colwell Beers as chief of JTAG ("Jay Tag"), the CIA cover organization that handled the "third force" and other clandestine programs. The crew usually stayed overnight at Atsugi, where they were briefed by Mason and his air officers, Colonel William Nolan and

Captain Art Dietrich. Flights involved airdrops of supplies or Chinese agents, generally in eastern Manchuria.[37]

The aircraft, identified only by a small tail number that could be read from a distance no greater than about two hundred feet, departed Atsugi for Pusan (K-9) or Seoul (K-16). Cargo door removed to facilitate the drop, the C-47 left Korea at dusk, heading east over the water to avoid detection by U.S. Air Force radar. Beyond radar range, the crew turned north and climbed to ten thousand feet. Near the coastline, the lights of Vladivostok often could be seen off the right wingtip. The crew were careful to avoid large cities because noise was more likely to betray the plan than Chinese radar. Establishing the drop zone by loran, dead reckoning, or a visual signal from the ground, the aircraft came in at low altitude. At a signal from the cockpit, the two or three CIA agents who were on board as PDO's (parachute dispatch officers) pushed the cargo or people out the side. The crew then retraced the route back to home base and debriefing.[38]

Captains Snoddy and Schwartz, primary crew for TROPIC, did most of the covert work during spring and summer 1952. In addition to the C-47, they often flew solo over the mainland in a sanitized B-17 that was assigned to the project. Schwartz, a native of Louisville, had a happy-go-lucky personality. Single, excellent golfer, and star pitcher on Chennault's Shanghai softball team, the former marine had flown only fighters before joining CAT in 1948. Snoddy, in contrast, brought extensive multiengine experience to China. A wartime B-24 pilot in the navy, he had been with Hawaiian Airlines and Trans-Pacific Airlines before signing on with CAT in 1948. Although a bit wild on the ground, Snoddy was strictly business in the air and made frequent suggestions for improving techniques. His wife Charlotte became pregnant with their first child during his assignment to TROPIC.[39]

John T. Downey often shared with Snoddy and Schwartz the perils of night flights over Manchuria. The son of a Connecticut probate judge, Downey was in many ways typical of the young intelligence officers with the "third force" project. He was in his senior year at Yale, planning a legal career, when a CIA recruiter visited the campus and spun tales of parachuting behind enemy lines, setting up resistance networks, and all manner of derring-do. "Hey," Downey recalled, "that was as glamorous as anything we could hope for. A large number of the outstanding people in my class applied." Downey joined the CIA in June 1951. Following three months of training at Fort Benning, Georgia, he was sent by the agency to Atsugi for the "third force" program.[40]

One of Downey's first assignments was to set up a resistance network in Kirin Province. He visited the CIA training complex on Saipan in spring 1952 and selected Chinese agents for the task. Working with the group at Chigasaki, he put together a four-man team (Team Wen), led by Chang Tsaiwen, a twenty-eight-year-old native of Kirin. CAT delivered Team Wen to Manchuria in July.[41]

Delivering people to Manchuria, though always hazardous, was not overly difficult; bringing them out was the real problem. OPC, however, had high hopes for a novel in-flight pickup system. Two poles were set in the ground and a wire strung between them. Attached to the wire was a line leading to a harness in which the person to be picked up was strapped. Approaching slightly above stall speed (at about sixty miles per hour), the aircraft hooked onto the wire and jerked the man up to flying speed, then reeled him into the aircraft. One can only marvel at the courage of those intrepid individuals who agreed to sit impassively in harnesses, awaiting possible decapitation, whiplash, or other serious injury. Snoddy and Schwartz practiced with this system in fall 1952, and it seemed to work.[42]

OPC attempted the first operational pickup on November 29, 1952. It resulted in a disaster that would reverberate for two decades.

Li Chun-ying, who had been dropped into Kirin in October to observe Team Wen in action, radioed that he was ready to come out. Snoddy and Schwartz, together with Downey and Richard G. Fecteau (an inexperienced intelligence officer who had been with the CIA only five months), boarded C-47 B-813 on the evening of November 29 to make the pickup. Three hours after takeoff from Seoul, the olive drab transport approached the rendezvous. Everything appeared normal as the aircraft neared the pickup wire. A minute later Snoddy and Schwartz were dead, shot down by Communist gunfire. Downey and Fecteau survived the crash and were captured. Team Wen had been penetrated.[43]

When Snoddy and Schwartz failed to return, CAT put out a cover story that B-813 had disappeared over the Sea of Japan while on a routine flight from Korea to Japan. Authorities ordered an air-sea rescue search. The Communists kept silent for two years. Finally, on November 23, 1954, Radio Peking announced that thirteen Americans had been sentenced to prison for espionage. Eleven of the thirteen were B-29 crew members who had been shot down on January 12, 1953, while on a covert mission (not involving CAT) over Liaoning Province; the other two were Downey (sentenced to life) and Fecteau (twenty years). The Chinese identified Downey and Fecteau as CIA agents and released extensive details about their background and mission.[44]

Washington promptly and vigorously denied the charges. Downey and Fecteau, the State Department insisted, were civilian employees of the Department of the Army who had disappeared on a "routine" flight between Korea and Japan. Unable to explain how the men had fallen into Communist hands, department spokesman Lincoln White dismissed the spy story as "old hat from radio Peiping." The United States demanded release of all Americans "forthwith."[45]

United Nations chief delegate Henry Cabot Lodge cited the incident as another reason why the "unspeakable gang from Peiping" should not be given a seat in the international body. The British government termed the sentencing "outrageous." "It is perfectly clear," a *New York Times* editorial declared, "that the Americans have been imprisoned as a deliberate means of making the United States 'lose face' . . . in the eyes of Asia and thus enhance Peiping's prestige." Senator Knowland wanted to blockade the mainland.[46]

Stung by the criticism, Peking released additional information. The Chinese claimed that their security forces had seized from enemy agents six mortars, 998 rifles, 179,000 rounds of ammunition, ninety-six radio sets, secret codes, invisible ink, fake passes, and gold bars. Of the 212 Chinese agents who parachuted into the mainland between 1951 and 1953, 101 had been killed and 111 captured. Most had surrendered on arrival, and some had been killed by "outraged peasants." Five Americans had died (three B-29 crew members and Snoddy and Schwartz, whose names never appeared, perhaps because their bodies bore no identification) and thirteen had been captured (the men sentenced on November 23).[47]

The overwhelming majority of Americans rejected the Chinese version of events. Americans knew about "brainwashing" that produced confessions under pressure and radically altered behavior. The hated Chinese, skilled at such devious manipulation, could not be trusted. The CIA North Asia Command of course knew better; it assumed that Downey and Fecteau had told their captors everything. "When they were released many years later," writes E. Howard Hunt of Watergate fame, who served with the North Asia Command in 1955, "the assumption proved to have been correct."[48]

Faced with rising public anger, Secretary of State John Foster Dulles attempted to calm the situation. In a nationwide radio broadcast on November 29, Dulles ruled out any warlike retaliation such as a naval or air blockade. The first duty of the United States, he emphasized, "is to exhaust peaceful means" to secure release of the imprisoned Americans.[49]

In summer 1955, at the start of the Geneva Conference on Indochina, Peking freed the eleven B-29 crew members and several other Americans, including CAT's Lawrence R. Buol, who had been captured at Mengtze in January 1950. But Downey and Fecteau remained in jail. The two men were seen on occasion through the years. Visited by a touring group of American youths in September 1957, Fecteau readily admitted that he had worked for the CIA. Washington did not respond. The mothers of the two agents visited China by special permission in January 1958, but Chou En-lai rejected a tearful plea for release of their sons. The United States, Dulles announced, would never yield to emotional blackmail. On December 12, 1971, two months before President Richard M. Nixon's scheduled trip to Peking, the

Chinese quietly released Fecteau. He had served nineteen years of his twenty-year sentence.[50]

When President Nixon reached Peking early in 1972, he took the opportunity to discuss Downey's case with Chinese leaders. At the dawn of what was hoped to be a new era of friendly Sino-American relations, a compromise was struck. At a press conference in February 1973 Nixon acknowledged that Downey was a CIA agent who became a prisoner after his *military* aircraft had been *forced down* in Chinese territory. Satisfied, Peking set Downey free on March 12, 1973.[51]

The U.S. government never acknowledged the death or role of Snoddy and Schwartz. They lie buried, probably in unmarked graves, somewhere in Manchuria. Any CAT pilot who flew the deniable overflights could have met the same fate.[52]

The project to support guerrilla activity on the mainland during the Korean War apparently caused few problems for Peking. As noted by the intelligence component of the CIA in Special Estimate 20, issued on December 15, 1951, "The Chinese Communists have succeeded in greatly reducing the strength of guerrilla forces throughout China and these forces do not now have a significant operational capability. Even if guerrilla capabilities were developed, the guerrillas could be employed effectively only in conjunction with other course of action directed against Communist China." Informed commentators have agreed: American-trained Chinese agents sent into the mainland, writes retired CIA operative Harry Rositzke, found no signs of the "extensive resistance" claimed by the Nationalists. One well-informed intelligence officer has termed the "third force" project a complete failure. If a dropped team managed to establish radio communications with JTAG, one could be sure that a double agent was at work. There may have been infiltration successes during the Korean War, but they surely were few and far between—and kept *very* secret.[53]

The Korean War, Karalekas emphasizes, "established OPC's and CIA's jurisdiction in the Far East and created the basic paramilitary capability that the Agency employed for twenty years. By 1953, the elements of that capability were 'in place'—aircraft, amphibious craft, and an experienced group of personnel. For the next quarter-century paramilitary activities remained the major CIA covert activity in the Far East."[54]

CAT was an essential component of this paramilitary capability. As the air arm of the CIA in East Asia during the 1950s, the airline provided safe, secure, deniable transportation for a variety of covert projects. Whether involved in such large operations as the abortive Li Mi affair or conducting "black" flights in Indonesian waters with a PBY, CAT performed with professional excellence. The airline's civilian pilots made more than one hundred perilous overflights of mainland China without the protection and benefits of a uniform, risking capture, long imprisonment, and death. Rewards were few for these secret soldiers of the Cold War, but they got the job done. As one former CIA case officer remarked, with feeling, "CAT never let us down."[55]

 # Managerial Turmoil

CAT's operational efficiency during the Korean War occurred despite managerial turmoil. Although often complicated and clouded by personality clashes, at the heart of the controversy lay fundamental questions of control and direction. The CIA had purchased CAT because OPC wanted secure transportation for covert activities in East Asia, but the business side of the airline demanded attention lest costs become excessive. Application of sound business principles to such a unique enterprise posed difficult challenges for an organization geared to the collection of intelligence. As the agency quickly and painfully discovered, buying an airline was far easier than running one.

At first the CIA hoped to avoid managerial burdens by giving Willauer executive responsibility for the company's affairs, subject to overall direction from headquarters. Washington expected to use the airline for operational purposes without worrying about mundane business details. Although initially pleased with Willauer, the agency soon grew restless over lack of information from the field. With subsidies increasing at an alarming rate, and CAT's president failing to submit timely financial reports, OPC sent a strong memorandum of complaint to Hong Kong on November 8, 1950. Willauer, at least in OPC's view, replied in curt, almost insulting terms, causing Washington to wonder who was in charge.[1]

Two months later, a more significant incident took place. CATI, the Corcoran-Chennault-Willauer group involved in the legal dispute over CNAC and CATC aircraft in Hong Kong, recovered $1.8 million from CNAC dollar holdings in American banks. CATI wanted to use the money to pay outstanding legal fees and finance the continuing lawsuits, but powerful Chinese creditors promptly laid claim to the funds. The Central Bank of China pressed for immediate repayment of $1.25 million that had been advanced in 1949 to purchase Pan American's share in CNAC, the Bank of Taiwan sought $500,000 loaned to CNAC and CATC, and the Central Bank of Communications wanted $140,000 that CATI had borrowed to finance legal action. Willauer and Brennan, under intense Chinese pressure, agreed in January 1951 to "loan" the Bank of Taiwan $500,000. A disconcerted CIA learned about the transaction only three weeks after the event. Willauer had neither given Washington notice nor sought approval. "Instead of improving," the agency's history notes, "CIA's control over the proprietary seemed to be slipping."[2]

Willauer and the CIA obviously held different views about CAT. Because of his rights to reacquire the airline between July 1, 1952, and July 1, 1955, Willauer considered agency ownership temporary. In the meantime, he intended to manage the company as he had in the past, that is, with minimum interference from people in Washington who could not possibly understand the manifold and complex problems of operating an airline in the Far East. Willauer believed the agency had little cause to complain about his arrangements regarding CATI. "This whole baby of CNAC/CATC," he stated, "has been offered to and refused by the Bankers [CIA] on several occasions." If they did not want financial responsibility, they could not call the shots.[3]

The CIA did not agree with Willauer's interpretation. CAT was their airline, bought and paid for, and Willauer was their employee. They expected the airline's president to follow Washington's direction without question. Although Willauer had been given a good deal of independence in running the company, there should have been no questions in his mind about who was in command. Furthermore, CAT had intimate ties with CATI, certainly in the minds of Chinese officials. Because actions involving CATI had a direct effect on CAT, the agency expected Willauer to keep his superiors closely informed about such developments.[4]

The situation came to a head in spring 1951. The shift to covert action following Chinese intervention in Korea increased the CIA's interest in CAT's day-to-day affairs. Before long the agency concluded that operational considerations demanded less independent management. The airline's ability to absorb money also encouraged a change. As Treasurer Terhaar reported in April, "Our financial situation is progressively getting worse and worse." With the CIA well on the way to providing a subsidy of $2 million during the first fiscal year of ownership, Willauer committed a major error in timing, if not judgment, when he spent $18,800 on a converted PT boat, plus $10,308 for radio equipment. Willauer easily justified acquisition of the lovely *Narcissus*: with Hong Kong threatened by imminent Communist attack, the PT boat afforded an avenue of escape for top personnel. In addition, it could be used for recreation and business entertainment. Perhaps Willauer was right, but many at CIA headquarters saw the *Narcissus* as a glaring example of extravagant mismanagement.[5]

In mid-May the CIA decided to limit Willauer's authority and sent someone more directly responsible to headquarters to take control of CAT. A carefully orchestrated transfer of power began on June 4 with a prearranged top secret memorandum from Willauer to the CIA. CAT's president pointed to the airline's transformation from a commercial venture to "almost purely a government operation," and he acknowledged that "long-range plans were being formulated for continued use of CAT as the government's operational instrumentality." In light of the new circumstances, the CIA replied, Willauer's management contract would have to be amended. The agency would assume direct control over the company's financial affairs and provide a new assistant manager who would gradually relieve Willauer of day-to-day operational burdens. A right of first refusal replaced the option agreement held by Willauer and Brennan. Should the CIA decide to sell CAT, the two men would be given first opportunity to purchase the airline at a "fair and reasonable" price.[6]

CIA consultants, after an extensive search, selected Clarence H. ("Dutch") Schildhauer for the difficult and demanding job of managing CAT. The retired navy captain brought distinguished qualifications to the task. After graduation from Annapolis in 1918, Schildhauer had become expert in the operation of large flying boats and set world's records in a Dornier DO-X, a huge twelve-engine machine. His exploits caught the attention of Juan T. Trippe of Pan American Airways. Hired by Trippe to pioneer transoceanic air routes, Schildhauer served as operations manager of the Pacific (1934–37) and Atlantic (1937–39) divisions. In May 1951, following discussions with agency officials, Schildhauer accepted the position of vice-president and assistant general manager of CAT at a salary of $25,000 a year.[7]

CIA headquarters set out specific guidelines for Schildhauer to follow once he reached the Far East. CAT's fleet would be limited to twenty-six aircraft with a maximum potential of three thousand hours a month. Development of air cargo would be emphasized, keeping only enough passenger business to maintain operating franchises and existing routes. CAT was not to make any long-term commitments that would remove equipment and personnel from the Japan-Thailand area. Charters beyond this region could be accepted only if they were short term and small scale. Above all, the CIA stressed, strict economy must be practiced.[8]

Schildhauer stopped in Hawaii on his way across the Pacific for a series of meetings with Chennault, Willauer, and Cox. Honolulu provided a relaxed setting for what could have been an awkward gathering. Willauer seemed to enjoy the surroundings. "I have discovered a new sport — expensive of course!" he wrote to his wife. "I really love surfboarding." The business conferences, he continued, had gone well and had resulted "in much 'meeting of the minds.'" Schildhauer, however, "made only a mediocre first impression on Al [Cox]. . . . Personally I like him, but his caliber and ability to take over remain to be seen."[9]

CAT's new vice-president reached Taiwan on July 24. Accompanied by Willauer, he met the airline's staff, toured the LST and maintenance complex at Tainan, and took a round-the-island flight. Two weeks later, Schildhauer assumed command of the operations and supply divisions. Willauer, in Hong Kong, remained responsible for supervision and promotion of new activities. Schildhauer, based in Taipei, would consult with Willauer on all important policy matters.[10]

Suffering from a recurrence of a painful thrombosis in the foot, Willauer at first relinquished operational control of CAT with relief. "I personally am taking things so easy that I am positively bored half the time," he wrote to his wife. "While I realize that is what I am supposed to do, for my own good — and to give Dutch something to do — I do miss the extrovert aspect of the day to day banging out of decisions and handling of problems. Actually, for the moment it seems the struggle we have been fighting for the last year and a half to put CAT on an organized basis has finally paid off. So long as we don't have real emergencies, CAT pretty nearly can run itself — except for the large promotions and the big political questions." Willauer began to give serious thought to retiring from CAT in July 1952 and embarking on new ventures, perhaps in Central America.[11]

The era of good feelings proved brief. Within weeks of Schildhauer's arrival, Willauer developed reservations about his ability to do the job. "I am giving him every possible support, and so is Jim [Brennan] — but I fear the stuff just isn't there; and I know the experience in our type of problems and politics is not only lacking but will probably never be effectively acquired." Moreover, Willauer objected strongly to the restrictive guidelines that Schildhauer had brought from Washington. Harmony soon gave way to hostility as the two men tried to move CAT in different directions.[12]

Willauer had an opportunity to air his grievances at a series of meetings in Hong Kong from September 8 to 14, 1951. Participants in the conferences, held at Willauer's apartment on the Peak, included Schildhauer, Cox, Brennan, Terhaar, and agency consultants Roger C. Hyatt and Thomas Jones. Issues discussed ranged from personnel problems to financial reorganization, with major attention paid to plans for developing new business, Schildhauer's economy program, concentration of top executives on Taiwan, and the degree of autonomy to be granted field management.

Restricting CAT to Japan-Thailand, Willauer complained, would not promote the airline's economic health. Schildhauer, acting on instructions from Washington, was trying to increase revenue by emphasizing the development of commercial business within this area. Willauer pointed out that scheduled operations and charters in the Japan-Thailand region amounted only to 6.5 percent of CAT's flying. Even if the airline acquired long-sought landing rights at Naha (Okinawa) and Bangkok, increased load factors (already running at 85 percent), and placed more emphasis on regional charters, maximum additional monthly revenue would amount to only $40,000. Deducting the $14,000 spent on salaries to man the new Traffic and Sales Division, the total was not impressive.[13]

Willauer proposed a variety of alternatives. CAT, he argued, should join with other regional air carriers in plans to develop a domestic Japanese airline. CAT's share in the program would be $50,000 and three aircraft. He recommended purchase, for $250,000, of Trans-Asiatic Airlines, through which CAT would acquire an airline flying the Philippine flag, four C-47s currently under lease, and a 70 percent interest in TAA's subsidiary in Thailand, Trans-Asiatic Airlines (Siam), a company with two C-47s. Possibilities for operating an air cargo service in Pakistan should be explored; an excellent opportunity existed to obtain a contract from the Indonesian government for air-sea rescue and smuggling prevention work; and New Zealand wanted CAT to operate a charter service. The best course, he concluded, would be "an overall policy that we should promote in any place where there is an economically sound vacuum for using our services."[14]

Willauer predicted that Schildhauer's emphasis on retrenchment through personnel reduction and salary cuts would not work. Operating efficiency and morale could not be maintained if more than 5 percent of these "bits and pieces" fell to the budgetary ax. Much greater savings could be made in parts procurement and gasoline purchases. The 40 percent markup from list price on parts bought from the Air Force for BOOKLIFT flying had cost CAT an average of $10,000 a month for the past year. Surely the CIA should be able to negotiate more favorable arrangements with its government colleagues. Willauer also noted that the agency had been alerted some nine months previously to the possibility of negotiating a gasoline contract with Standard Oil, which could result in a substantial savings in CAT's $120,000 monthly fuel bill, the single largest operational expense.[15]

Schildhauer's desire to concentrate the airline's top management on Taiwan led to another dispute. Although the argument for concentration looked good at first glance, Willauer acknowledged, the idea was in fact "highly dangerous." Problems would arise about security of records and taxation. CAT's operations were far-flung, and experience had shown that regional autonomy produced results. "Effective and real delegation of authority to local area managers with a minimum of top level interference in the day to day handling of their jobs," he argued, "has created a spirit and an intense interest in the affairs of CAT which is probably CAT's greatest single asset. If the feeling of independent initiative and the right of operational decisions on the spot is removed by cumbersome head office controls, the Bankers [CIA] will find very shortly that their investment is reduced to the liquidating value of the tangible assets and that they have lost the major asset for which they contracted — i.e. *the ability to get things done in seemingly impossible situations which can only arise from high morale and spirit of teamwork.*"[16]

Willauer firmly believed in the virtues of autonomy, not only within CAT but also in the relationship between Washington and the field. "It can hardly be expected," he said, "that the present management of the Bankers' affairs can devote enough time or can remain sufficiently familiar with the operations to give the quick and businesslike action required to control the fast moving affairs of an airline 10,000 miles away." Willauer supported a scheme under which CIA headquarters would formulate major policies, then lay down quarterly or semiannual budget limitations. Field management would be given a free hand to implement the policies within the budgetary restrictions. Board-of-directors-level supervision would be vested in "an established commercial house," which would keep track of operations through "continuous correspondence and inspection."[17]

Consultants Hyatt and Jones returned to Washington in mid-September with tales of CAT's continuing managerial woes. At the same time, CIA headquarters received a gloomy report on the airline's finances from a team of auditors connected with Lybrand Ross Brothers & Montgomery, one of the country's leading audit firms. Sent to the Far East in July to survey CAT, the team had been unable to make a physical inventory of assets and certify an audit. Its report criticized the airline's accounting procedures, called for expansion and reorganization of the fiscal division, and raised questions that led to the dismissal of one accountant for misuse of company funds.[18]

Kilbourne Johnston, retired army colonel and deputy director of plans, decided that the time had come to take a hard and close look at the agency's proprietary. He called all parties concerned, together with CAT's management, for a week-long conference beginning on October 22 at CIA headquarters. All agreed that inadequate communications between Washington and the field had led to numerous misunderstandings and must be improved. In addition, the discussions emphasized that a divided CIA lacked a consistent policy toward the airline. CAT's dual roles as an instrument for covert action and a business enterprise were not always compatible. OPC, designed to conduct covert operations, had neither the time nor the staff to provide CAT with the required business direction.[19]

Hoping to promote managerial efficiency, Johnston sought assistance from the agency's administrative section. OPC, especially the Far Eastern Division, would remain in charge of the airline's operational use and requirements. Walter R. Wolfe, deputy director for administration, was given responsibility for business management. In practice, Ernest W. Pittman, Wolfe's assistant, took on the task of overseeing the airline.[20]

CAT executives: Whiting Willauer, Louise Willauer, Mr. and Mrs. Samuel S. Walker, C. Joseph Rosbert, A. Lewis Burridge, Alfred T. Cox

Recruited by Wolfe, a friend and former business associate, to look after the agency's growing list of commercial proprietaries, Pittman had extensive experience in industry and government. President of Interchemical Corporation before retirement, the sixty-one-year-old executive and chemical engineer had been wartime chief of the United States Strategic Bombing Survey's rubber and chemical section and had led the American Rubber Mission to the Soviet Union in 1942. According to one well-informed source, Pittman was responsible for the idea of increasing headquarters' control over CAT through a strengthened board of directors. The new board consisted of eleven members, three of whom (Chennault, Willauer, and Schildhauer) would reside abroad and rarely attend meetings. An executive committee of six members held real power. Two of these men, Samuel S. Walker and William Read, were "business-friends" of the agency and would act primarily as advisers; the other four formed a management group that supervised the airline on a day-to-day basis. Initially, the management group consisted of Ward M. French, prominent Washington attorney Brackley Shaw, and businessmen-consultants Hyatt and Jones.[21]

French, the only CIA employee on the board, held the important secretarial post. A graduate of the University of Pennsylvania's prestigious Wharton School of Finance and Commerce, French had taken a law degree at Temple University. He specialized in corporate law and was employed at one time as house counsel by the Scott Paper Company. He served during the war with the Air Transport Command, rising to the rank of lieutenant colonel. A slender six feet four inches tall, with bow tie, glasses, short haircut, and well-tailored suit, he appeared to many as the archetypal lawyer. Skilled at administration and apparently content with legal work, he never tried to use his key position (astride communications between the agency and the board and between the board and the field) as a stepping stone for advancement into a policy-making role. Perhaps, as an intelligence officer once remarked, French lacked the combination of nastiness and drive that seemed to be among the necessary qualities to rise to power in the agency's bureaucracy.[22]

Colonel Johnston approved Pittman's plan to gain a tighter grip on CAT and confirmed Schildhauer's authority. The airline's vice-president promptly renewed his efforts to implement the agency's guidelines, leaving a restless and angry Willauer to simmer in Hong Kong. Calling on employees to reduce operating costs and overhead, Schildhauer announced: "With an aggressive sales organization, geared to intensive effort, together with efficient Operations, Maintenance, and Supply Divisions, that goal of efficiency and economy will be reached."[23]

Schildhauer and Treasurer Terhaar developed budgetary controls for the airline's various divisions and required detailed and frequent reports. A reorganized fiscal department took shape, based on the auditors' recommendations, that included a controller's office, cost accounting section, and internal auditor's office. The airline adopted a regional accounting system, with branch offices maintaining records based on the Uniform System of Accounts as prescribed by the U.S. Civil Aeronautics Board. The branches reported monthly to the central office in Hong Kong on schedules of incomes and expenses and trial balances of assets and liabilities. The controller's office consolidated the reports and issued a monthly balance sheet and profit-and-loss statement.[24]

CAT's main economic problem, Schildhauer realized, arose from the peculiar nature of the enterprise. Most flying was done on a demand basis, and the demand could not be predicted. CAT had to maintain excess capacity in order to meet anticipated requirements, which meant heavy overhead expenses. "To conduct our operations at minimum cost," Schildhauer argued, "a network of commercial air transport operations must be developed together with a maintenance operation that will assist in reducing the overall operating costs."[25]

Schildhauer took advantage of new bilateral air agreements, long in the works, to expand CAT's scheduled international service. Following conclusion in November 1951 of a Sino-Thai accord and designation of CAT as the Republic of China's flag carrier, the airline began twice-weekly flights between Taipei and Bangkok. A similar agreement with Korea in March 1952 added Pusan to CAT's route structure. The airline also obtained commercial landing rights at Naha, Okinawa. Flying hours for scheduled international operations increased from 262 in July 1951 to 550 in July 1952, while revenue went from $43,514 to $172,349, far in excess of Willauer's earlier prediction. Schildhauer recommended that CAT acquire two DC-4s with high-density seating capacity. Four-engine equipment would enable the airline to compete more effectively against other regional air carriers that were operating modern aircraft and to take greater advantage of the lucrative Hong Kong market, where the airline landed under a special exchange agreement with Hong Kong Airways but was restricted to four scheduled arrivals and departures a week.[26]

Contract maintenance work promised even better results. CAT's Tainan facility had come a long way since crew chief George C. Stubbs had led the first arrivals to the sleepy southern city in November 1949. Newcomers had not been impressed with the former Japanese Air Force experimental base. Heavy bombing during the war had left little but the runways. Isolated, damp in spring, hot in summer, and dusty-cold in winter, Tainan offered only limited housing and entertainment for foreigners. "We've got maintenance here," one supervisor allowed, "but brother, maintenance is all we do have here."[27]

By mid-1951 expansion induced by the Korean War had caused many changes, at least in facilities. Chief Engineer Grundy had set up a maintenance area in the shape of a horseshoe around the inside of a bombed-out hangar. Quonset huts that housed shops, supply, mess hall, and operations faced a cement ramp where as many as a dozen aircraft could be parked and worked on at one time. Instrument and other specialized shops remained on the LST at Kaoshiung, necessitating constant traffic between the two points. Grundy's twenty foreign supervisors and 380 Chinese, Taiwanese, and Filipino workers could maintain five thousand flying hours a month at a time when CAT was averaging half that total. "The entire aircraft maintenance program," Schildhauer observed, "can be based on our present physical plant with perhaps a small additional outlay for equipment to make use of our overall potential."[28]

Aware that Air Force maintenance requirements in the Far East amounted to eight million man-hours a year, Schildhauer tried to tap the military market. In December 1951 CAT signed a contract with FEAMCOM to overhaul eight Air Force C-46s (CAT project MS-1). Carried on by Schildhauer's successors, the maintenance program grew to substantial and lucrative proportions. By the end of 1954 CAT had overhauled seventy-three C-46s and had secured contracts to work on C-119s and C-54s. Man-hours on the C-46 project increased from 16,000 a month in early 1952, to 54,300 in summer 1954. The maintenance division expanded from four hundred out of the airline's sixteen hundred employees in 1951 to a thousand out of two thousand in 1954. A milestone was reached on August 10, 1954, when Harold J. Carrick of the U.S. Civil Aeronautics Administration presented Grundy with a certificate that made CAT the only CAA-approved air frame, propeller, radio, instrument, and accessory repair station in the Far East. Grundy, thanking his workers and supervisors for making the award possible, had reason to be proud: a CAA certificate meant that CAT had met the highest possible standards of maintenance excellence.[29]

Although Schildhauer had worked hard to set CAT on the road to economic progress, his tenure as operational head of the airline ended on a sour note. From the beginning, his cautious, methodical style of management, coupled with a constant demand for reports, had irked airline personnel who were accustomed more to action than administration. The situation worsened as time passed. Schildhauer had not gone through the mainland bonding experience and was resented as an outsider. Moreover, he came from Pan American, known throughout the industry for its arrogant and intolerant attitude toward lesser airlines. Middle-level management complained of the vice-president's dictatorial behavior, cooperated with reluctance, and schemed to replace him. After discussing the situation with Burridge on March 7, 1952, Rosbert noted in his journal: "Lou and I [are] in agreement on CHS's [Schildhauer] ultimate disposition — out."[30]

Concerned about the pervasive discontent within CAT, CIA headquarters began to doubt Schildhauer's managerial ability. They faulted him for breaches of security, which were at least in part the agency's fault for not briefing him fully on the details of CAT's covert activities. No wonder that he stepped on Cox's toes! "Our present relationships in Bangkok," Cox warned Schildhauer at one point, "are of such nature that it would be ill advised to have any persons outside of CAT become aware of either our activities or of our intimate relationships with various officials in Bangkok." Therefore, the CIA was receptive when Willauer recommended Schildhauer's dismissal in spring 1952.[31]

Unaware that his fate had been decided, Schildhauer returned to the United States for a board meeting in New York City on May 23. "Just previous to this meeting," he recalled, "I was advised by Mr. E. P. [Pittman] that Mr. Willauer had made certain recommendations to the Board and that they would be accepted and which would require me to sever my connections with CAT, Incorporated."[32]

Schildhauer's dismissal was viewed from the field as a triumph for Willauer and produced a sense of relief throughout the airline. "This is the first real opportunity I've had to write since your victory in Washington," Rosbert enthused on July 18. "Needless to say, we who know the situation are completely overjoyed, without exception." But congratulations were premature. Even if Willauer had wished to resume operational control of CAT, and there is considerable doubt that he did, CIA headquarters had no intention of returning to the situation that had existed before Schildhauer had taken over. To make this point clear, Washington in July "promoted" Willauer out of the presidency to vice-chairman of the board. Wisner then asked Cox to manage CAT. Assured that he could concentrate on airline duties, Cox accepted.[33]

CIA General Counsel Houston, testifying before a congressional committee in 1976, recalled that the agency had to learn "the hard way" about managing proprietaries. CAT raised difficult problems for the intelligence organization: Who should control the airline? What policies should be applied to its operation? How should headquarters and the field divide responsibilities? "The struggle within the Agency," Houston noted, "ranged all the way from sort of quiet management discussions as to what was good management, to sometimes rather vociferous arguments of who's in charge here. And the operators always said, 'Well, we need to call the shots because it's our operation.'"[34]

The first two years of ownership saw the CIA making slow and painful progress toward the goal of managerial efficiency. At first, control of CAT was lodged in a desk at OPC's Far Eastern Division and tended to be casual. By mid-1952, largely because of a worsening economic situation, the clandestine services and administration had agreed to share responsibility for the proprietary, using a strengthened board of directors to exercise supervision. Yet despite the organizational changes, the agency continued to have trouble with the airline.

Headquarters never doubted that Washington should "call the shots," but the CIA's indecisiveness contributed to confused relations with the field. It had been a mistake to give Willauer broad executive powers, then expect him meekly to administer policy handed down from above. With strong ideas about how to run the airline that he and Chennault had created, Willauer found it impossible to defer to "inexperienced bureaucrats." Once Washington decided that Willauer was concerned more with autonomy than economy, it brought in Schildhauer to replace him. Resented from the start as an outsider, the former naval officer never stood a chance. However well his managerial style might have worked at Pan American, it did not suit the peculiar conditions at CAT. Schildhauer was a good "number two" man, more skilled at administration than decision making, trying to function without a "number one" man. The result was unfortunate—and predictable.

Important questions of management and control remained unanswered as Cox assumed the acting presidency of CAT. Washington wanted an economic operation responsive to directions from headquarters, but considerable ambiguity existed about the best way to achieve it. Although Cox would soon be caught up in the managerial maelstrom, he did have time to catch his breath before being swept away.

11 French Indochina

CAT's new acting president brought an élan to the job that contrasted sharply with Schildhauer's ponderous managerial style. A dynamic leader, widely admired and respected, Cox inspired loyalty and devotion among subordinates. Agreeing with Willauer that autonomy produced results, he remained in Hong Kong and let Rosbert, promoted to vice-president and assistant general manager, once again handle day-to-day operations.

Despite the change in personnel, policy remained constant. CIA headquarters continued to insist on the basic guidelines that had been laid down the previous year. Like Schildhauer, Cox fostered the growth of contract maintenance at Tainan and built up international schedules. Acquisition of a DC-4 (B-1002), placed into service in September 1952, enabled CAT to increase seating capacity on its four trips a week to Hong Kong and offer weekly nonstop seven-hour flights between Taipei and Tokyo. CAT's acting president negotiated a new BOOKLIFT contract, calling for two round trips a week from Japan to the Philippines via Taiwan and Okinawa, one round trip a week between Tachikawa and Chitose (on Hokkaido), once weekly service from Japan to Guam via Iwo Jima, plus special missions as requested. The Air Force budgeted $4,415,600 for BOOKLIFT in 1953; CAT would be paid $294 per flying hour.[1]

On January 19, 1953, the board elected Cox president, general manager, and a director of CAT Incorporated. "Mr. Walker, the other vice chairman of the Board [with Willauer], who was just here on an inspection trip," Dorothy Cox wrote to her parents early in the year, "told us he was very pleased and impressed with the job Al is doing." The situation was too good to last.[2]

Two coincident events dominated Cox's presidency. The first, to be surveyed in subsequent chapters, involved problems with the Chinese government over franchise renewal and settlement of CATI and the continuing attempts by CIA headquarters to define managerial functions. The second concerned the operational deployment of CAT to meet a series of crises in French Indochina.

CAT's interest in the French colony began with the tin lift from Mengtze to Haiphong in 1949. Willauer saw attractive economic prospects in the region and hoped to involve CAT in the French war effort. Interviewed in Saigon in October 1950, he spoke about plans to operate a freight service with seven C-47s. "Mr. Willauer," the press report noted, "emphasized that the Americans [pilots], though willing to carry war materials and drop them to French garrisons, would take no part in actual fighting. He told newsmen arrangements would be purely a matter of business." As noted earlier, Paris rejected the scheme. Although disappointed, Willauer never lost sight of opportunities in Indochina, and CAT kept a full-time representative in Saigon to promote business.[3]

Frank L. Guberlet, CAT's man in Saigon, had been in Indochina since February 1949. A wartime naval carrier pilot with a degree in biology, Guberlet had been working with the United Nations in Tsingtao as a fisheries expert when approached by CAT. Hired as a pilot, he started out in operations but never flew for the airline. When the tin lift started, Chennault sent Guberlet, one of CAT's two French-speaking employees, to open a station at Haiphong. In June 1950 he moved to Saigon, making contacts in an attempt to drum up business. For a time, he had high hopes for CAT's participation in a local airline, but the scheme fell through. Guberlet explained to Rosbert, "Air France and pro-French members of the Vietnamese government have created a new company, Air Vietnam, which has been given a complete monopoly on all profitable routes in Indochina." A proposal to perform maintenance work for the French Air Force also failed to materialize.[4]

Guberlet's first breakthrough came in December 1950, when he contracted with the United States Special Technical and Economic Mission (STEM) to airlift several tons of urgently needed medical supplies from Tokyo to Hanoi. The airlift went smoothly, but the problem of internal distribution remained. Robert Blum, chief of the CIA-connected STEM and member of a wartime OSS team that had worked with the counterintelligence section of Britain's MI-6, wanted to use CAT so that American aid would go directly to the people rather than through the French. Colonial authorities, however, opposed both direct distribution of American aid and use of the Nationalist-tainted airline. Blum managed to overcome these objections, and Felix T. Smith and Max Springweiler arrived in Hanoi on Christmas morning to begin the operation. Having opened the door a crack, CAT quietly slipped through and established a small but lasting presence in

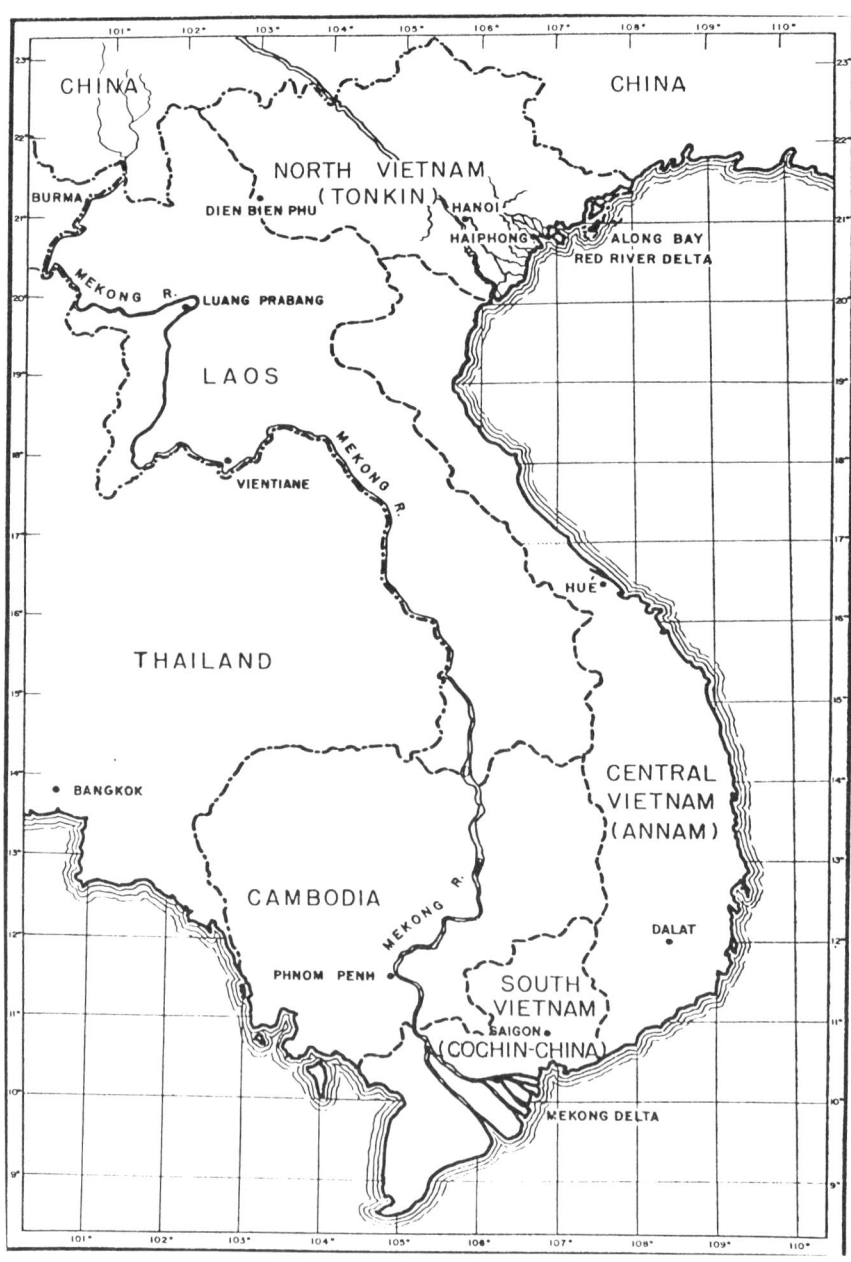

Map C: French Indochina, 1953

Indochina. Early in the new year, Blum contracted with Guberlet for a C-47 to be permanently assigned to Saigon for STEM.[5]

James B. McGovern, Jr., took over CAT's C-47 in September 1951 and remained in Indochina until spring 1953. Best remembered of all the airline's pilots, McGovern stood out in a crowd. He was five feet ten inches tall, and his weight varied from 225 to 300 pounds. Tales of McGovern's strength abounded, and he became known as "Earthquake McGoon," the embodiment of Al Capp's cartoon character. He loved buttered lima beans, peanuts, chili, Chinese food, and good times. A two-fisted drinker, forbidding when challenged by outsiders, McGovern laughed easily with friends. With a heart to match his girth, "McGoon" seemed most at ease with children. "You knew he was real," Felix Smith recalled, "but you almost couldn't believe it." Al Kindt, CAT's Manila station manager, once celebrated the legendary figure in verse:

> The rumor is growing apace
> Of a behemoth creature who flies in the skies
> With a lecherous smile on his face.
> His three hundred pounds shake the earth when he walks,
> Yet he soars with the grace of a loon.
> Through all the Far East this fabulous beast
> Is known as Earthquake McGoon.[6]

Separating the man from the myth grew more difficult as time passed. Writers depicted him as a wartime ace with the Fourteenth Air Force, a *bon vivant* who once won a troupe of Russian dancing girls in a poker game, a pilot who always landed tail high because he could not pull the yoke of a C-46 past his protruding stomach, and such an irascible individual that he was able to talk his way out of a Communist prison. The real McGovern, revealed in his personnel file, was at least as interesting as the legendary "Earthquake McGoon" and much more believable.

Born on February 4, 1922, in Elizabeth, New Jersey, McGovern graduated from Thomas Jefferson High School, then trained as an aircraft mechanic at the Casey Jones School of Aeronautics. He worked for two years at the Wright Aircraft Engineering Company in Paterson, operating an engine test stand. Enlisting in the aviation cadet program at the beginning of World War II, he arrived in China in November 1944 and saw action as a P-51 pilot with the Twenty-Third Fighter Group. Official records credit him with the destruction of two Japanese planes on January 20, 1945. McGovern remained in China after the war, transferred from fighters to the 332d Troop Carrier Squadron in Peking, and accumulated 475 hours of multiengine time.[7]

McGovern took his discharge in China and joined CAT on April 12, 1947, at a base salary of $560 a month. On promotion to captain in April 1948, his salary went up to $850 for sixty hours of flying and $10 an hour for overtime. McGovern usually logged more than one hundred hours a month, so he often made over $1,200, a substantial sum for a young bachelor in postwar China.[8]

McGovern's great failing was indolence. An excellent airman when he put his mind to the task, he had sloppy habits guaranteed to drive check pilots to distraction. "Pilot very lazy and has to be told to do all of his duties," Captain Bigony complained. Captain Buol reported after a route check with McGovern on June 23, 1948: "This pilot went on this check ride without so much as carrying a map or let down procedure. By a quirk of luck he flew close enough to TYN [Taiyuan] to locate the town. I would not call this confidence but stupidity. I assume he flies all the time without standard equipment. He is a very lazy pilot and takes much for granted. He definitely isn't responsible enough to be a good captain and unless he overcomes this attitude [I] recommend he be given more co-pilot time."[9]

Although less than the ideal professional pilot, McGovern had redeeming features that overshadowed his faults. Willauer, writing to Corcoran about CAT's last days on the mainland, singled out McGovern for special praise. The former fighter pilot, who "now tips the scale at an even 270 and is ugly to boot," had been a leader at Weihsien, Taiyuan, Mukden, and "in all the other tough flying jobs" that CAT had done. "He has won the respect of his fellow pilots and the management," Willauer concluded, "from his willingness to do anything reasonable even though dangerous if it is in line of duty."[10]

McGovern came through the most hazardous flying of the civil war without so much as a scratched wingtip, but his luck ran out on December 4, 1949. He left Hong Kong for Kunming at sunset on this bleak winter day, carrying a load of mixed cargo and two passengers, Mrs. James Liu and her six-month-old daughter. Russian-born wife of a Chinese citizen, Mrs. Liu had been ordered deported by British authorities because she did not have proper entry documents. The Hong Kong–Kunming trip, a seven-hundred-mile flight over enemy territory without en route radio aids to navigation, was typical of CAT's operations at a time when Communist forces had captured most of the mainland. Approaching Kunming, McGovern picked up the station's radio beacon on his automatic directional finder (ADF), but he could not obtain accurate heading information because of the distortion caused by "night effect" on low-frequency radio waves. Unable to locate Kunming, he altered course to the southeast and flew toward Hainan. At 1:40 A.M., after more than eight hours in the air and with less than forty gallons of fuel remaining, McGovern belly-landed his C-46 on a sandbar in a river in Kwangsi Province, about one hundred miles short of Hainan.[11]

Taken prisoner by the Communists, McGovern and his two Chinese crew members were interned at the Great Asia Hotel in Nanning. Mrs. Liu and her daughter, both uninjured, were not seen again after capture. M. L. Lay, the copilot, escaped in January and brought word that McGovern was in good health. "He has lost considerable weight," Chief Pilot Robert E. Rousselot wrote to McGovern's mother, "but knowing Mac as we do, this loss of weight is quite understandable and, I am sure, permissible." Chennault appealed through the American consulate in Hong Kong for McGovern's release; CAT pilots raised money for a possible bribe attempt. Nothing was heard for several months. Then, without warning, the Communists set him free.

A somewhat gaunt, bearded McGovern reached Hong Kong on May 31. Despite bad food and attempts at indoctrination, he had not been badly treated. Like some big men, however, he was cursed with tiny feet. The pain of walking when first captured, he later recalled, had been the worst part of the ordeal.[12]

Stories soon began to circulate that the Communists had released McGovern because they had found the irrepressible pilot too difficult to handle. Although this seems unlikely, there is no adequate explanation why McGovern and two military fliers should have been freed while Captain Buol, captured in January 1950, and other Americans remained in custody. Consul General McConaughy, back from Shanghai, saw the incident as part of the conflicting signals being sent out by Peking. Although Communist behavior on the whole had been antagonistic toward the United States, some moves, such as the release of McGovern, "could even be considered semi-conciliatory." The Communists, he concluded, "present many baffling contradictions."[13]

McGovern took a lengthy home leave before returning to duty in October 1950. He had regained the lost seventy-five pounds and more. Although outwardly unchanged, the young airman had been shaken by his experience. Close friends noticed a new and militant anticommunism. When McGovern spoke about communism, Felix Smith recalled, he "became serious. He hated their regime because it subdued and sometimes crushed people's spirits. He vowed never to be recaptured."[14]

Whether a result of the trauma of imprisonment or of a natural maturation, McGovern's flight checks improved considerably. Chief Pilot Rousselot, who had spent many long and wearing hours trying to "shape up" an anarchistic McGovern in the Marine Corps image, reported on May 6, 1951: "McGovern gave me a nice flight. However, at times he has to be 'jacked-up' about both his flying and conduct—has shown much improvement in *both* during past 3 yrs., however *only* after constant attention—has been called to these things by Chief Pilot—he has flown many hazardous flights in good order."[15]

In fall 1951 McGovern volunteered to fly CAT's C-47 in Indochina. He was one of several CAT pilots who enjoyed detached service in Southeast Asia. Mostly bachelors and nonconformists, they adapted well to local conditions, accepting a measure of hardship in return for freedom from authority. Indochina did not have the advantages of Japan, where CAT crews lived in American style, complete with PX privileges and additional amenities, but adventurous spirits found other compensations. Despite occasional terrorist attacks, Saigon retained a certain charm. An American newspaperman based there during the early 1950s recalled "a pleasant, vividly colored city of treelined streets and boulevards, with sidewalk cafes and restaurants serving superb food and wine. . . . French Union soldiers in a melange of uniforms, many of them Foreign Legionnaires, African Senegalese, Moroccan Goumiers or French paratroopers, crowded the streets looking for women, bars, gambling, and they were rarely disappointed."[16]

McGovern shared an apartment with Frank Guberlet in the Eden Cinema Building in downtown Saigon, across from the old opera house. Air conditioning was virtually unknown, the city's electrical system was erratic, and the phones were worse; but girls and cognac were inexpensive, excellent, and readily available—and McGovern enjoyed both in full measure. He strolled the Rue Catinat, where the café terraces were crammed as many of the city's thirty thousand French residents observed the ritual of apéritif. He avoided the new Majestic Hotel, built on the banks of the Saigon River in 1950; hulking and expensive, its only good feature was the superb view from the windows of the enormous barnlike bar on the seventh floor. He often took a pedal rickshaw to Cholon, two miles from the center of town at the end of Boulevard Gallieni, for "Chinese chow," and he spent a lot of time in "Jean's" bar, which he and Guberlet had helped to finance. Reminders of the war were everywhere: barbed wire surrounded the golf course, iron bars in front of restaurants protected against grenades, and barricades, searchlights, and machine guns guarded Tan Son Nhut airport. About once a month, he flew to Hong Kong, had the aircraft serviced, and loaded up with glass containers of chili from Gingle's restaurant. All in all, it was a good life.[17]

McGovern flew throughout Indochina in connection with the American economic aid program, administered after October 1951 by the Mutual Security Agency. He carried technicians and material to support projects in disease control, agriculture, forestry, fisheries, transportation, power, and public works. Sometimes Ambassador Donald R. Heath or visiting officials from Washington used the aircraft. Averaging eighty hours of flying a month,

McGovern grew familiar with airports at Dalat, Donghoi, Tourane (Danang), Hue, Hanoi, Haiphong, Nhatrang, Vientiane, and Phnon Penh.[18]

In addition to overt flying, there was a small covert side to operations in Indochina. Issued motion picture cameras, McGovern and other CAT pilots were expected to photograph all areas of possible interest, including new landing sites. From time to time, Guberlet replaced McGovern's Chinese copilot for special photographic assignments, which had to be done with great care because the French did not welcome CIA activities in their bailiwick.[19]

American military and economic assistance to Indochina increased during the early 1950s. Intended to strenghten Bao Dai's native government, promote a spirit of nationalism, and turn the tide of battle in favor of French Union forces, it failed miserably on all counts. "The situation in Indochina," Blum reported with depressing candor in 1952, "is not satisfactory and shows no substantial prospect of improving, that no decisive military victory can be achieved, that the Bao Dai government gives little promise of developing competence and winning the loyalty of the population . . . and that the attainment of American objectives is remote." In October three Vietminh divisions struck French positions in the Black River valley of northwestern Tonkin and threatened Laos. The French, under intense pressure, evacuated smaller outposts west of the Red River, reinforced garrisons at Na San and Son La, and launched a counteroffensive. In mid-November, when logistical problems brought the French drive to a halt, the Communists renewed their attack, focusing on Na San. Thanks to a massive aerial supply operation, the garrison held out, inflicting heavy casualties on General Vo Nguyen Giap's forces. The Vietminh broke off the battle and spent the winter reorganizing their supply service for a spring offensive.[20]

French colonial rule in Indochina moved swiftly toward its inevitable end during 1953. General Giap, learning from past mistakes, assigned one regiment to contain the garrison at Na San and ordered his remaining troops to advance into Laos on April 9. Within weeks, the Vietminh had invested the royal capital of Luang Prabang and turned southward toward the administrative center of Vientiane. Two Communist divisions surrounded a French blocking force in the Plaine des Jarres, leaving the trapped soldiers dependent for supplies upon an airlift from Hanoi, 250 miles away. A beleaguered French Air Force, hard-pressed to maintain the increasing number of isolated posts in northwestern Tonkin and Laos, cried out for assistance. The French in Indochina had only forty-nine C-47s and fifteen JU-52s (German prewar three-motored transports), not enough to meet the new airlift demands.[21]

Secretary of State John Foster Dulles called at the White House on the afternoon of April 23 to discuss developments in Asia with President Dwight D. Eisenhower. Just returned from a NATO meeting in Paris, Dulles reported that the French were gravely concerned about the situation in Laos. They wanted to borrow U.S. Air Force C-119s and crews to fly tanks and heavy equipment into Laos. "Having such equipment," the French had emphasized, "might mean the difference between holding and losing Laos." The secretary noted that sending American military personnel on combat missions into Indochina "was a decision which would have repercussions and would raise many problems." But there was an alternative: perhaps civilian pilots could fly the C-119s. Dulles had made inquiries earlier in the day and determined that pilots were available on Taiwan who might undertake the missions. "This possibility," he told Eisenhower, "was being explored on an urgent basis."[22]

Dulles of course had checked with his brother, Allen, new head of the CIA. The Director of Central Intelligence (DCI), in turn, contacted Cox in Hong Kong. Cox answered the query from Washington about the use of CAT pilots in Indochina with a prompt "can do." In light of the reduced risk of untoward domestic and international reactions, Eisenhower approved the project. Although at first the French objected, fearing that Peking might consider CAT's ties with Nationalist China more provocative than direct American assistance, they reluctantly agreed to the arrangement after being assured that only American pilots would fly the aircraft.[23]

CAT pilots Felix T. Smith, Eugene P. Babel, Harold W. Wells, Steve A. Kusak, E. G. Kane, and N. N. Forte received word in Tokyo early Friday morning, May 1, to leave on the 9:30 A.M. flight for Taipei. Accustomed to abrupt departures, the men tossed a few extra clothes and shaving tackle into suitcases, then headed out to Haneda. Paul R. Holden, Eddie F. Sims, George Kelly, Cyril M. Pinkava, William J. Welk, and Monson W. Shaver joined the group in Taipei. The tired but excited airmen, alive to the sense of urgency, received a short briefing on their mission before continuing on to Clark Air Force Base in the Philippines. With hardly a pause for breath, the pilots were swept up in a whirlwind seventy-two hours of concentrated ground school and flight training on the unfamiliar C-119s. Meanwhile, personnel of the 483d Troop Carrier Wing prepared six of the twin-tailed "Flying Boxcars" for service in Indochina by carefully removing all traces of American markings, then painting on the tricolored roundels of the French Air Force. Together with eighteen U.S. Air Force mechanics in civilian clothes, the CAT group left Clark for Indochina at dawn on May 5. Operation SQUAW—the airline's name for the project—got under way the next day.[24]

Bernard B. Fall, legendary journalist-scholar who wrote about the war with unmatched skill and understanding, recorded one SQUAW mission in his classic study, *Street Without Joy*. Fall was in Hanoi on Sunday, May 31, when asked if he would like to go along on a flight. He eagerly accepted. Picked up by a French Air Force jeep at dawn, he drove through the quiet streets of the sleeping city, crossed the Doumer Bridge, and continued to Gia-Lam air base, just outside Hanoi. The C-119s were parked on the ramp, tail gates removed, taking on cargo for an airdrop at Ban-Ban in Laos. It was already hot, even before the sun had fully risen, and everyone was dressed casually. Fall met the pilot, Steve Kusak, then boarded the aircraft for takeoff.[25]

Kusak headed due west, toward the mountains of Laos. Fall squeezed into the cockpit with the pilots and French navigator and watched the countryside unfold beneath him. The symmetrical beauty of rice paddies quickly gave way to dense jungle. "Viet territory," the navigator said. An hour later, as the aircraft approached Ban-Ban, Fall went back into the cargo hold and watched two French riggers unchain six tons of artillery ammunition. A loud buzzer sounded: five minutes to target. The riggers grew apprehensive, glancing at the ground four thousand feet below, alert for last-minute turbulence or ground fire.

"Here we go," Fall writes. "The plane goes into a shallow dive and, as we hit the Drop Zone, sharply noses upward. The two riggers, warned by buzzer, jump up on the sides of the plane as the whole load in a roar of clanking metal and whooshing static lines leaves the plane in a few seconds. All of a sudden, the picture of the sky through the tail gate is replaced by that of lush vegetation, by what seems to be a small city and a few huge white and yellow flowers which seem to blossom out under us: the cargo chutes are opening."

Kusak put the aircraft into a sharp turn and climbed steeply away from the drop zone. Fall returned to the cockpit in time to see the parachutes land close to a large white "T" on the ground. Kusak had placed the load within French lines. Fall continues:

Then it happens: A slight tremor on our left wing and some holes appear in it, seemingly out of nowhere. Communist flak. It's an odd feeling for I'd never been in an airplane in a combat zone and feel so damn' naked. The Boxcar, lightened of all its load, again turns on its wing and again climbs steeply. Kusak reaches back, taps my shoulder and points his thumb downward. I look out the window but see nothing. He yells: "Fighters." Sure enough there were two French fighters, way below us, looking tiny like toys against the backdrop of the jungle. They had been on a covering mission, and our navigator had informed them of the ack-ack. Their conversations came through clearly on the intercom, since our navigator had switched to the fighter channel.

"Now, how do you like that? Get that ass of yours out of the way. I want to make a pass at the village."

"Can't see a darn' thing. Do you see anything?"

"Can't see anything either, but let's give it to them for good measure."

Another swoop by the two little birds and all of a sudden a big black billow behind them. It was napalm—jellied gasoline, one of the nicer horrors developed in World War II. It beats the conventional incendiaries by the fact that it sticks so much better to everything it touches.

"Ah, see the bastards run now?"

Now the village was burning furiously. The two fighters swooped down in turn and raked the area with machine guns. As we veered off, the black cloud just reached our height. Scratch one Lao village—and we don't even know whether the village was pro-Communist or not.

The way back is uneventful. Jokes are passed around, Kusak is congratulated for the perfect drop—some of the stuff actually hit the "T"—and then the navigator switched to the Voice of America in Manila for its Sunday jam session. Back in Hanoi just in time for a late lunch at the Air Force Officers Mess: red wine at will, cold cuts, sirloin steak with French-fried potatoes, green salad, cake and coffee; thirty-five cents. Oh, yes, debriefing. A French Air Intelligence Officer with an American "civilian" from "CAT." "How was it, Al?"

"Oh, just the routine crap, some pretty accurate machinegun fire. They're getting better, you know?"

"Got to make one more trip today, Al."

"Geez, man, let me at least have my lunch. I'm pooped." So we did, and later Al went back with a new crew of French paratroop riggers for one more round of the "routine stuff."[26]

The Vietminh returned to their bases in Tonkin during May and June, leaving guerrilla units in Laos to harass the French. General Giap had achieved his main objective. As the Intelligence Advisory Comittee noted, Giap had forced the French "to withdraw the bulk of their offensive striking power from the Tonkin delta and disperse it in isolated strong points, dependent upon air transport for logistic support." The Communists, confident of ultimate victory, retained the strategic initiative.[27]

Major General Chester E. McCarty, commander of the 315th Air Division and member of the Joint Military Mission to Indochina, led a survey party to Southeast Asia in late June and early July. He came away appalled by the profligate use of SQUAW aircraft. The French concept of air transport, McCarty reported, was "extravagant in the extreme, measured by USAF standards," with C-119s being employed to carry such nonessential items as champagne, ice, and furniture. He concluded that it would be a mistake to provide transports to the French on a long-term basis because they "probably would join the 'barnstorming' fleet in Indochina unless they are strictly controlled and removed immediately following the combat operation for which they are loaned." Instead, McCarty supported the temporary loan of C-119s for specific projects that would last no more than five days. Ferried to Indochina and maintained by U.S. Air Force personnel, the aircraft would be flown by French crews. Washington accepted these recommendations and authorized a training program for French pilots.[28]

SQUAW continued until July 16. As the Vietminh offensive waned and the pace of operations slackened with the onset of the monsoon season in late spring, landed loads become more common than the airdrops described by Fall. CAT pilots, no strangers to battle, were not impressed with the French military effort. The dispirited colonial army fought a casual war, complete with midday siestas, and without any sense of purpose. As one French fighter pilot commented to Felix Smith, "This country is not worth dying for." The high command appeared disorganized and indifferent. During evacuations, the pilots watched with disgust as the French brought out their household effects and concubines but left behind valuable equipment. An incident in early July raised disturbing questions about the promiscuous violence that characterized this baffling conflict. A U.S. Air Force liaison officer arranged to borrow a C-119 (with a French crew) for a napalm demonstration. A village outside Haiphong was designated Vietminh — arbitrarily it seemed — and destroyed. Appalled and alienated, most CAT pilots left Indochina with relief, unaware that they were fated to return for the last act of the French war.[29]

DCI Dulles sent Cox a special commendation for SQUAW. Although he appreciated the award, all was not well with CAT's president. Worn down by his many responsibilities, Cox was exhausted. Despite Wisner's assurances, the CIA had not allowed him to concentrate on running the airline. Furthermore, after La Gueux's return to headquarters in spring 1952, Washington had failed to send competent assistants for the covert side of his work. "Poor Al is sunk & so overworked and spreading himself so thin," Dorothy Cox informed her parents on May 10, "that I'm quite concerned for him. If you will recall, when we came out here the understanding was that Al was completely through with his old job and his sole job was the airline. As I might have suspected, due to the fact that they've never bothered to send a replacement for his old job, Al still does the *two* jobs — and if something isn't done soon the poor fellow is going to collapse."[30]

Dorothy Cox's apprehension proved justified. Cox, drinking heavily, returned from Indochina the following week and collapsed from overwork and exhaustion. He spent a week in the hospital, then returned to the office on a restricted schedule. The Coxes flew to Japan in July for a much-needed three-week vacation. "Al's beginning to relax I think," Dorothy wrote to her parents from the Kawana Hotel in Izu, "still not sleeping well, but I do hope another 10 days of this will be sufficient for him — seems to be enjoying himself and he's certainly taking it easy — also off liquor except for one drink before dinner, which is a good thing."[31]

Cox needed his strength. The Republican victory in 1952 had brought a new regime to power at the CIA, and change was in the wind. Challenging problems lay ahead for CAT's tired president.

12   A New Regime

Allen W. Dulles took over the CIA in February 1953 with a sense of destiny fulfilled. A wartime OSS operative who had fallen in love with the intelligence game, the pipe-smoking minister's son had joined the agency in fall 1950, just in time to assist General Smith with reorganization. Extroverted, gregarious, and destined to leave an indelible stamp on the CIA, the new DCI savored the operational details of covert schemes but neglected administration. As a result, internal management of the agency gradually fell into the willing and capable hands of his deputy director, General Charles P. Cabell.[1]

Member of a prominent Dallas family, Cabell had graduated from West Point in 1925, then undergone Air Corps primary and advanced flying training. When his father, owner and operator of a large dairy business, fell on hard times during the Great Depression, Cabell took a leave of absence and tried to keep the company afloat. The young Air Corps officer did everything from scooping ice cream to keeping books. The company survived. Later, Southland — the Seven-Eleven chain — absorbed the prosperous concern.[2]

Having learned a valuable lesson in business management, Cabell returned to military duties. He commanded a combat wing of the Eighth Air Force in Europe and later served as director of operations and intelligence of the Mediterranean Allied Air Forces. Following the war, Cabell held a variety of staff positions in Washington, rising to director of Air Force intelligence in 1948. He was serving with the Joint Chiefs of Staff when offered the CIA post.

According to one report, Cabell found the agency in appalling administrative condition when he came aboard in April 1953. With Dulles's warm approval, the precise, hard-driving, taciturn West Pointer set out to impose order. On the basis of his Air Force background, Cabell soon assumed special responsibility for the CIA's air operations. These dual interests soon brought CAT to the general's attention. In May he sent Ernest W. Pittman, the agency's expert on proprietary organizations, on an inspection trip to the Far East with instructions to review all aspects of the airline's affairs, especially the vexing franchise problem.[3]

The franchise issue had been a source of concern to the agency since 1950. CAT's right to operate rested on a personal arrangement, first concluded in 1947 and subject to yearly renewal, between the Chennault-Willauer partnership and the Nationalist Chinese Ministry of Communications. Although the CIA had sought a more secure franchise after purchasing the company, the Chinese steadfastly refused to accept any departure from the status quo. As far as Taipei was concerned, a change in CAT's ownership did not affect the agreement directly with Chennault and Willauer as individuals.[4]

Trouble first appeared in July 1952 when the Executive Yuan passed the draft of a new civil aviation law. Patterned on similar legislation in other countries, including the United States, it required majority Chinese ownership for airlines operating under the code. Henry Yuan, who handled government relations for CAT, saw no immediate problem. Although the Ministry of Communications, charged with administering the new regulations, remained a hotbed of narrow, nationalistic sentiment and could be counted on to oppose an American-owned airline, responsible officials in Taipei had assured him that CAT's services were needed. Nevertheless, the law boded ill for the future. "No one is seriously interested in CAT's well-being beyond its minimum needs to stay in business," Yuan advised, "and as new rules are made or new contracts are signed, CAT gradually becomes more and more dependent upon the Chinese Government's patronage rather than upon any kind of legitimate footing."[5]

Brackley Shaw, prominent Washington attorney and influential member of the airline's board of directors, proposed a legalistic solution to the problem. He wanted to form a company under Chinese law that would hold as assets the name Civil Air Transport, a franchise from the government to operate international air routes, and a long-term management contract with CAT Incorporated. The Chinese promptly rejected this scheme on the understandable grounds that the majority-owned Chinese company, which held no real assets, was a façade for American ownership.[6]

In March 1953 the board placed Willauer in charge of franchise negotiations. Working with Saul G. Marius, CAT's legal counsel, he devised a plan for a single company, limited by shares, to take over the airline's business and equipment. Chinese nationals would hold 55 percent of the stock in the new company, obtaining loans in the United States to purchase this interest by pledging their shares as security. The majority Chinese-owned company would then be in a position to obtain from the government the right — valid for five years and renewable — to operate international air routes. Eventually, the Chinese might obtain full ownership of the airline under some mutually satisfactory arrangement.[7]

Although this scheme no doubt would have complied with Chinese law, the CIA rejected it on the grounds that it did not adequately protect the airline's assets. "The bankers seem to have changed their minds again about the Chinese company," Willauer informed his wife, "and now they think they don't want one. I feel they are wrong, but it's up to them."[8]

With matters at an impasse, Cabell ordered Pittman to look into the problem. Willauer met the former chemical executive in Tokyo on May 30, shortly after the new civil aviation code had been promulgated. The two men spent the afternoon in Pittman's room at the Imperial Hotel, reviewing the franchise situation. Progress in resolving the issue, Willauer said, had come to a standstill because a controversy over CATI had angered officials in Taipei. As Pittman knew, the Corcoran-Chennault-Willauer group in 1952 had been awarded possession of the seventy disputed CNAC/CATC aircraft in Hong Kong, following a lengthy legal battle that ultimately had reached the Privy Council in London. The Nationalist government immediately had pressed CATI for payment of the $4.75 million in promissory notes that had been signed at the time of original purchase in December 1949. CATI in turn had advanced over $10 million in counterclaims against the government, including $3 million for foreign exchange that had been promised but not provided on the mainland and $2.5 million for legal and other expenses connected with recovery of the CNAC/CATC assets.[9]

Two weeks earlier, Willauer explained to Pittman, CATI had offered to compromise. Presenting a proposal that had been formulated mainly by Corcoran, Willauer had pointed out to the Chinese that CATI had sold only fifteen of the seventy aircraft. The cash proceeds from the sale had been spent to finance lawsuits, remove the aircraft from Hong Kong, and recondition them for sale. Current expenses already had cost CATI's partners $500,000 out of their own pockets, and at least an additional $2.9 million was needed to put the remaining aircraft in salable condition. Under the circumstances, Willauer observed, the Chinese had two choices. They could wait until all the aircraft had been sold and take their chances on sharing in the profits, if any, or they could accept $1.25 million in cash "in full and complete settlement."[10]

CATI, Willauer continued, expected that its offer would be viewed as the beginning of a negotiation process; he had expected the Chinese to counter with a proposal to take half the remaining aircraft plus real estate holdings on Taiwan. But the government had been insulted by the initial offer and flatly refused to bargain. Because Taipei insisted on linking CATI and CAT, the franchise question had become a political football.[11]

Pittman decided to seek State Department support on the franchise issue. Following discussions between Pittman and diplomatic officials in Taipei on June 17, the American Embassy sent a note of "deep concern" to the Ministry of Foreign Affairs about the possible adverse impact on CAT of provisions in the new aviation law that prohibited foreign ownership of airlines. Not only did CAT perform vital services for American military forces in the Far East, but it also represented "the largest single private investment in Free China." It would set a "most unfortunate precedent" if the company "were to receive unfavorable treatment as a result of Chinese legislative action." The continued operation of CAT "without substantial change in its present status" would serve the best interests of both Free China and the United States.[12]

Willauer was not optimistic about the CIA's approach to the problem. "Right now," he wrote to his wife on June 19, "I am in the middle of a multitude of problems which stem from the attempt of the Chinese to play off the CATI situation against the desire of CAT to have a more stable basis than the C-W [Chennault-Willauer] franchise; whereas at the same time the bankers are now unwilling to transfer the assets to a Chinese company." Pittman had mobilized the State Department on CAT's behalf, and official communications were flying back and forth between the two governments. "All of this is probably a mistake in the long run," Willauer concluded, "but in my junior equity position I am accepting the bankers' policy and actively assisting, up to the point where I am brain trusting the activities."[13]

Pittman and Willauer went to the Ministry of Foreign Affairs on June 24 for an embassy-arranged meeting with Chinese diplomatic officials. Minister George K. C. Yeh, Pittman reported to Washington, "was most affable, cordial, and reassuring in his manner." The Amherst and Cambridge (England) educated former professor of English told Pittman that CAT remained vitally important to China. The government at present did not have the money to establish its own airline and did not expect to have such funds for many years to come. CAT's franchise, he promised, would be extended without any difficulty and for a longer term. In fact, Yeh confided, the Ministry of Economic Affairs was considering a statute to facilitate foreign investment that would provide amply legal security for CAT and other foreign enterprises. Pittman was delighted. "It seems to me," he concluded, "that these events have greatly improved our political position in Formosa."[14]

While working with Pittman, Willauer's thoughts had often turned to the future. "Ernie [Pittman] seems to think the bankers ought to have their heads examined if they don't keep using my twelve years of experience in these parts," he wrote to his wife. "I have told him that I could possibly be interested in staying on in an active post only if they had plans for further investments and promotional effort in this field." Willauer also thought about a diplomatic post in Central America. In any event, he agreed with

Pittman "that I must come home very soon to explore the possibilities and come to a final decision."[15]

On June 30 Cox came to see Willauer. With tear-filled eyes he relayed the sad news that Willauer's youngest son had been killed. Tommy, the precocious youngster who had braved the cold Shanghai winds in January 1947 to greet the aircraft from Manila and become CAT's first passenger, had been digging a cave in a sand dune near the Willauers' summer home on Nantucket. The cave had collapsed, and he was buried in the sand. Willauer hurried home, where emotional shock caused a severe embolism. Following a lengthy recovery, he was persuaded to accept an ambassadorship to Honduras and did not return to the Far East. He formally severed all ties with CAT in February 1954, after his appointment had been approved by the U.S. Senate.[16]

During the course of his inspection tour, Pittman had led Willauer and Cox to expect he would make a glowing report on CAT's field management. "It really is gratifying to see the enthusiasm of Ernie [Pittman] after he has seen our setup and has gotten to know our people," Willauer had told his wife. "You know all the problems of the bankers and their worries that we have a crazy bunch. He now feels that they have invested in a fine set of people from top to bottom, and is apologetic about previous misinformation from some prejudiced sources."[17]

Dorothy Cox also had been delighted. Pittman, she had told her parents, was a "great guy," who had been "completely sympathetic" to Cox's problems. "Thanks to him," she had written, "I believe some really constructive steps will be taken now and Al can finally be sure of real backing and cooperation at home. He seems greatly impressed with the job Al is doing and says he cannot stress strongly enough how valuable Al is to them and what a great job he's done."[18]

Pittman's recommendations to Cabell are not known, but the deputy director obviously did not share the optimism of Willauer and Cox. In mid-July Cabell persuaded George A. Doole, Jr., experienced airline executive and longtime friend, to become a permanent CIA employee and take charge of looking after CAT.

Few people recall Doole with dispassion. Ambitious, arrogant, irascible, thin-skinned, vengeful, and flawed in many ways, he was a superbly talented airline executive and skilled bureaucratic infighter who merits a place in aeronautical history alongside Eddie Rickenbacker of Eastern, Juan Trippe of Pan American, William Patterson of United, C. R. Smith of American, and other giant figures of the industry. As head of Air America during the 1960s, Doole faced monumental and unique challenges. His management of the CIA's giant proprietary will be long remembered by friends and foes alike.[19]

Doole was born on August 12, 1909, in Quincy, Illinois, where his father ran a bank and owned real estate. He received a bachelor of science degree in business administration from the University of Illinois in 1931. A member of the school's elite ROTC cavalry unit, he was an accomplished rider. Graduating in the midst of the Great Depression, Doole found job offers few and far between. In fact, he recalled, there were only two options: his father's bank or the military. Doole chose the latter. Accepted into the highly competitive aviation cadet program, he spent a year at training fields in Texas, earning his wings and a second lieutenant's commission. He was assigned to Luke Field, Honolulu, then to a bombardment squadron at France Field on the Atlantic side of the Panama Canal Zone. In addition to regular squadron duties at France Field, he often flew a Douglas Dolphin seaplane for Colonel Lewis H. Brereton. Doole made many lasting friendships with junior officers destined for high command, including Lieutenants Jacob E. Smart and Charles P. Cabell. Later, he introduced Cabell to Jacklyn De Hymel, whom Cabell married in 1934.[20]

With assistance from Brereton, Doole joined Pan American Airways when his active duty ended in 1934. He went first to the Western Division at Brownsville, Texas, and flew DC-2s to Mexico City as a flight mechanic/apprentice pilot. He underwent an intensive training program, learned all phases of aircraft maintenance, worked for a second-class radio telegraph license, and took comprehensive courses leading to a rating of master pilot. He also volunteered for administrative chores. "We were getting the pilots from the Air Force," Chief Pilot George Kraigher recalled. "They were of superior qualifications and one of them was George Doole. Further, he was one of the few pilots interested in ground work and I had him as an assistant between the flights." Sent to Central America in 1936, Doole operated a Ford trimotor from Guatemala to Panama. For a time, he managed Panama Airways and flew the shuttle across the Canal Zone.[21]

Doole returned to Brownsville in 1937 and participated in the inauguration of DC-3 service to South America. In fall 1939 he took a leave of absence and enrolled in Harvard's noted graduate business administration program, where he completed one year of the two-year course before Pan American recalled him to duty. Juan Trippe, at the request of the State Department, had taken over SCADTA, a German-owned airline in Colombia. Doole went with the company, renamed Avianca, as chief pilot. He remained in Colombia until September 1942, then joined the Atlantic Division as assistant chief pilot, an important promotion. In 1946, with some thirteen thousand hours of command time in his log book, Doole gave up flying and became Pan American's regional director for the Middle East and Asia. A colonel in the Air Force Reserve, Doole was called to active duty in 1951 and served under

Cabell as chief of estimates for the Middle East, working closely with the CIA.[22]

No sooner had Doole accepted Cabell's offer to join the CIA when CAT once again became a contentious issue at headquarters. With the end of the Korean War, General Counsel Houston raised the question of whether the agency's mission in the Far East required continued ownership of the airline. Houston's query led to a full-scale debate on CAT's future.[23]

On September 15, 1953, Cabell convened a high-level meeting at CIA headquarters to consider the issue. Some twenty people attended, including Doole, Houston, Deputy Director of Plans Wisner, Richard Helms (Wisner's chief of operations), Lyle T. Shannon (Wisner's chief administrative officer), Director of Administration Lawrence K. White, Assistant General Counsel John Warner, George E. Aurell (chief of the Far Eastern Division in the Directorate of Plans), and Desmond FitzGerald (Aurell's assistant). Doole recalls "a monstrous fight" on the question of retaining CAT, with strong opinions expressed on both sides. One faction had opposed acquisition of the airline from the beginning, contending that a small, inexperienced group of aviation enthusiasts in the agency had been taken advantage of by Corcoran, Willauer, and other sharp entrepreneurs. Now was the time, they argued, to wind up the money-draining mess. Another group, led by FitzGerald, emphasized the proprietary's operational advantages to the agency. CAT's usefulness had been demonstrated during the recent crisis in Indochina, and DCI Dulles had been impressed.[24]

Cabell finally sided with FitzGerald and recommended retention of CAT. DCI Dulles concurred. CAT would be maintained, the CIA's "History of Air America" records, "as an Agency instrumentality to be continually available for utilization in the national interest."[25]

Cabell might have been persuaded that CAT should continue, but he was determined to end the constant administrative and economic problems created by the proprietary. He clarified lines of authority and responsibility within headquarters by creating a CAT management committee — not to be confused with the board's management group — that included Wisner, Chief Administrative Officer Shannon, General Counsel Houston, and Secretary of CAT Incorporated French. At the same time, he ordered Doole to "clean up the mess." The airline would be run efficiently and placed on a cash break-even basis or it would be liquidated.[26]

Doole agreed that CAT was in appalling financial condition. The airline, he later recalled, had lost $6 million since 1950, outside accountants were unwilling to certify an audit, and rumors abounded about fraud and deception at the highest managerial levels. The Chinese, moreover, were unhappy, and CATI was a scandal. Doole felt that his work was cut out.[27]

Accompanied by Brackley Shaw, in October 1953 Doole set out to take a firsthand look at his new challenge. The inspection tour confirmed everything he had heard. CAT's executives did not seem to understand that the commercial side of the airline existed only for cover; they talked about "nothing but expansion." Doole had to halt plans for a project in the Middle East and discourage other ambitious ventures. CAT's relationship with Korean National Airlines must be straightened out. CAT had helped KNA get started in spring 1951, providing aircraft, crews, maintenance, and credit for the purchase of gasoline and other supplies. Over the years, however, CAT's influence over KNA's operations had declined almost in direct proportion to the Korean carrier's mounting indebtedness, which now was approaching $450,000. Doole blamed Burridge for allowing the situation to get out of hand, seeing it as yet another instance of gross mismanagement.[28]

Doole returned to Washington and began to tighten the screws on field management. At his request, the board ordered Cox to obtain prior approval for all capital improvements costing more than $1,000. Doole further recommended that the airline's personnel and supplies be tailored to a monthly capacity of twenty-three hundred hours instead of the then current three thousand hours. The CIA, he observed, indicated a need for five to seven hundred hours, BOOKLIFT amounted to six hundred hours, and commercial flying averaged a thousand hours. Although field management would be responsible for initiating the necessary adjustments to conform with the 23 percent reduction in operational capacity, he expected to be kept fully informed.[29]

While in the Far East, Doole and Shaw discussed with Cox the problem of franchise renewal. In July CAT had obtained from the Ministry of Economic Affairs a draft of the proposed law to encourage foreign investment. Marius forwarded the draft to Washington along with comments on how the airline might comply with the statute. Shaw took the material and drew up a plan for corporate reorganization. The Washington attorney noted that the draft law permitted CAT to establish a wholly American-owned Chinese corporation to operate air services under the Nationalist flag. He pointed out that such an arrangement would not conform with the standard provisions in most bilateral air transport agreements "that either party has the right to refuse to accept or to withdraw its acceptance of the airline designated by the other party if it is not satisfied that substantial ownership and effective control of the designated airline are in the hands of Nationals of the designating nation."[30]

To deal with this problem, Shaw proposed a two-company arrangement. CAT of China, wholly American-owned, would be incorporated under Chinese law. It would acquire CAT's personnel, equipment, and other assets, exclusive of nonflying equipment used in Japan for BOOKLIFT. Civil Air

Transport, also incorporated under Chinese law, would issue a majority of its stock to "friendly" Chinese nationals in return for a nominal capital contribution. The stock would be pledged back to ensure de facto American control. A dry company without real assets, Civil Air Transport would obtain an air route franchise from the Chinese government, then contract with CAT of China to operate the services. "Under such an arrangement," Shaw concluded, "there would be at least colorable authority for the position that the airline was substantially owned and effectively controlled by Nationals of China since its name, good-will, and franchise, without which it could not operate, would be so owned and controlled." Taipei thus would be in position to nominate Civil Air Transport as its national flag carrier in bilateral discussions.[31]

Doole, who had had extensive experience in negotiating international air agreements, liked the plan. Securing board approval, he delivered it to Cox in October. Although CAT's franchise had to be renewed by the end of the year, there was no sense of urgency. The draft law on foreign investment, upon which the Shaw plan depended, was winding its way through legislative channels, Minister Yeh had given his assurances that franchise renewal was only a technicality, and Colonel H. Y. Lai in the CAA indicated that the current agreement would be extended if the new investment law had not been approved by the end of the year. "Al is working here on an important settlement with the Nationalist government, greatly affecting the airline," Dorothy Cox wrote home on October 12. "He feels it is moving along smoothly but may take two or three months."[32]

In mid-November a cabinet crisis shattered the calm. Chiang Kai-shek, after a flurry of resignations, ordered the dismissal of Dr. Wang Shih-chieh, secretary-general of the president's office. According to a Reuters dispatch, Wang had lost his post because he had failed to inform the generalissimo about the results of CATI litigation. "President Chiang," the report continued, "was enraged when he learned that several million US dollars were turned over to CATI after the General's [Chennault] firm won the lawsuit."[33]

Two weeks later, the CAA notified CAT that the Chennault-Willauer franchise agreement would not be renewed. The airline's present organization, an accompanying memorandum pointed out, was illegal under Chinese law; a new, majority Chinese-owned company would have to be formed if CAT's principals wished to continue doing business on Taiwan. Twisting the knife even deeper, the government alluded to the availability of $4.75 million in Chinese capital—that is, the CATI promissory notes—to finance such a Sino-American enterprise. Should this solution be unacceptable, other methods would be adopted to ensure continued operation of China's air routes without CAT's participation.[34]

Colonel Lai, in a private conversation a few days later, said that the memorandum had been drawn up in the Ministry of Communications and hinted that it had been personally approved by the "Supreme Authority." The MOC, center of nationalistic opposition to CAT, was discussing problems connected with CAT's demise. Lai then offered some friendly advice. There were rumors that CAT planned to form a Chinese company, without assets, in order to comply with the civil aviation law. The MOC, he warned, would oppose such a move. Any Chinese company would have to own a minimum of five aircraft in order to operate routes authorized by the CAA.[35]

Obviously, CATI's problems had enabled the MOC to secure Chiang Kai-shek's support of a scheme to abolish the hated CAT. "Nationalism is a MOC complex," Henry Yuan earlier had explained, "and, like all complexes, it prevails over realism at unpredictable times." Foshing Airlines, a small Chinese-owned company and favorite of Minister of Communications Ho Chung-han, waited in the wings, eager to take over from CAT.[36]

Word that CAT's franchise would not be renewed, the official "History of Air America" emphasizes, "threw CIA Headquarters into a panic." Cox, who was in Washington for a board meeting, met with DCI Dulles, Cabell, and other senior officials, then hurried across the Pacific to deal with the crisis. Working with Rosbert, he drew up contingency plans, to be placed in effect should the airline be forced to leave Taiwan. BOOKLIFT would continue, with excess aircraft flown to Okinawa for storage, surplus personnel placed on leave without pay, and efforts made to obtain New Zealand registry for the airline's C-46s.[37]

Meanwhile, Cox tried to persuade the Chinese to permit CAT to continue. He spoke to Pai Ch'ung-hsi, while Rosbert and Burridge went to see Yen Hsi-shan. Cox enlisted the support of American diplomatic and foreign aid officials, and pressure was brought to bear on the ministries of Foreign Affairs and Economic Affairs. The situation was saved, however, through Chennault's relationship with Chiang Kai-shek. Only after Chennault had convinced the generalissimo that he had been misinformed about CATI's affairs were forces in the Chinese government opposed to the MOC able to operate effectively. On December 28, as instructed, Chennault wrote to Colonel Lai and requested a continuation of the present franchise while a permanent solution was being worked out. Three days later, the CAA extended CAT's operating rights until April 1, 1954; a reorganization proposal would have to be submitted by February 15.[38]

"Poor Al has had a grueling past six weeks," Dorothy Cox wrote from Hong Kong to her parents on January 3. "It's all very involved and CAT is the goat although CATI (Corcoran) is responsible for all the mess. Anyway, I've seen Al only 4 days out of the past six weeks while he's been turning himself inside out to keep the airline alive and get some sort of settlement. He arrived back [from Taipei] yesterday . . . with the welcome news that he'd got a three month extension out of the Nationalists and is now quite optimistic about a favorable eventual settlement. But it took a lot of starch out of Al. . . . I'm hoping he can stay put here for a few days now—but with fresh troubles in Indo China I suppose he'll be heading there too before long."[39]

13   Dienbienphu

When North Korean and American negotiators met at Panmunjon in July 1953 and brought an end to thirty-seven months of bitter warfare, President Eisenhower announced: "We have won an armistice on a single battlefield, not peace in the world." He was right. The ink scarcely had dried on the armistice agreement before supplies began pouring across the border from China to General Vo Nguyen Giap's six infantry and one support divisions in French Indochina. As Chinese assistance increased from four hundred to three thousand tons a month, including trucks, heavy artillery, and anti-aircraft guns, the United States stepped up its support for French Union forces. Impressed with the Navarre Plan—intended to enlarge Franco-Vietnamese forces and wrest the strategic initiative from the Communists—Washington programmed $785 million in aid for fiscal 1954, amounting to 78 percent of total war costs.[1]

Général de corps d'armée Henri Navarre, concerned about growing enemy strength and the threat to Laos, wanted to lure the Vietminh into a setpiece battle in which superior French firepower could be used to good effect. On November 20, 1953, French paratroopers occupied Dienbienphu, 220 miles behind enemy lines and 10 miles from the Laos border, then enlarged a small airstrip. Confident that the isolated position could be supplied by air, as had Na San earlier in the year, Navarre decided to accept battle if the Communists would cooperate. "It was an incredible gamble," Bernard Fall has pointed out, "for upon its success hinged not only the fate of French forces in Indochina and France's political role in Southeast Asia, but the survival of Viet-Nam as a non-Communist state and, to a certain extent, that of Laos and Cambodia as well."[2]

From the beginning, Navarre counted on American help to keep Dienbienphu supplied. The U.S. Air Force responded to initial French requests for air transport by launching Project IRONAGE on December 5. In accordance with General McCarty's previous recommendation, twelve C-119s, to be flown by French crews, were made available for short-term use. Between December 7 and 21, as the paratroopers and Legionnaires dug in at Dienbienphu, the aircraft delivered 1,070 tons of equipment to the garrison, including barbed wire, tent stakes, and 105mm howitzer ammunition. Although McCarty had planned to withdraw the C-119s by Christmas, reports that four Vietminh divisions were moving into the area caused a change of mind. The aircraft remained in Indochina and delivered another 2,500 tons of priority cargo to Dienbienphu by the end of January.[3]

The air transport situation worsened early in the new year as Vietminh attacks throughout Indochina produced additional calls for aerial support. Colonel Jean-Louis Nicot, head of the French Air Transport Command in Indochina, was unable to handle the increased demands. French airlift capabilities already were strained to the limit. Aircrew shortages caused the main problem: Nicot could put his hands on seventy C-47s for a maximum effort, but he had only fifty-two military crews for the aircraft. The C-119 situation was no better. Although the U.S. Air Force had trained twenty-two French crews during the second half of 1953, Nicot could count on only ten at any one time. With mounting complaints of pilot fatigue and no prospect of direct American participation in the war, the French once again looked to CAT for assistance.[4]

Washington alerted CAT for SQUAW II in early January. Cox immediately sent twenty-one pilots to check out in C-119s at Ashiya Air Base, Japan. Meanwhile, the Eisenhower administration kept the worsening situation in Southeast Asia under constant review. On January 29, 1954, the President's Special Committee on Indochina met at the Pentagon to discuss urgent French requests for aircraft and personnel. The committee approved prompt shipment of twenty-two B-26 attack-bombers, together with two hundred uniformed Air Force mechanics needed to maintain B-26s and C-47s. DCI Dulles then asked about the CAT pilots. "It was agreed," a record of the meeting states, "that the French apparently wanted them now, that they should be sent, and CIA should arrange the necessary negotiations with the French in Indochina to take care of it."[5]

Desite increasing Vietminh pressure on Dienbienphu, French negotiations with CAT moved at a leisurely pace. The contract, signed by James R. Kelly in Saigon on March 3, called for twenty-four pilots to operate twelve C-119s. The aircraft, loaned and maintained by the U.S. Air Force, were to be flown "under the colors and insignia of France, and to be used exclusively for the benefit of the Expeditionary Corps." CAT personnel would serve under the direction of military authorities and be expected to fly "all missions of a logistical nature which might be required, exclusive of any combat missions. Bombardment and dropping napalm will never be required." The

C-119 taxiing out for airdrop at Dienbienphu from Cat Bi airfield, Haiphong, March 20, 1954 (Courtesy E. C. Kirkpatrick)

Flight line, Cat Bi airfield, Haiphong, March 23, 1954 (Courtesy E. C. Kirkpatrick)

French agreed to pay CAT $70 per flying hour with a minimum monthly guarantee of sixty hours.[6]

A C-46 brought the first CAT contingent from Taipei to Haiphong on March 9. In addition to pilots Forte, Shaver, and Pinkava, who had flown C-119s in SQUAW I, newcomers included Hugh H. Hicks, Neese D. Hicks, Roy F. Watts, A. L. Judkins, Hugh L. Marsh, Eric F. Shilling, Thomas C. Sailer, M. K. Clough, and mechanic George C. Stubbs. Unlike the previous year, when pilots had carried little more than a small suitcase apiece, this group came well prepared. A truck was needed to haul their trunks, suitcases, bags of every size and description, cases of food, and one large white electric refrigerator to the Majestic Hotel in Haiphong. "Within thirty minutes after moving into the CAT hotel," one account notes, "there was music coming from several tape recorders, the refrigerator was humming, and a snack and refreshment bar had been set up in Eric Shilling's room."[7]

Briefings got under way the next day. Operations, the pilots learned, would be conducted from Cat Bi airport, located four miles southeast of Haiphong, where the main runway was an ample 8,000 by 170 feet of asphalt and concrete with steel matting in the center. A shorter secondary runway, 3,875 by 160 feet, was constantly under repair and would not be of much use. The men studied maps, especially the ones that detailed the terrain between Haiphong and Dienbienphu. Communications procedures, complicated by the language barrier, seemed potentially troublesome. CAT shared an operations building with a French squadron that flew C-119s, while a smaller adjoining structure served as a crew lounge. A jeep and three new weapon carriers provided ample ground transportation, although the vehicles lacked canvas tops, a necessity in the persistent showers of the *crachin* (spitting) season of Tonkin.[8]

Flying was scheduled to begin on March 11 but was canceled because of rain and haze. The weather cleared the next day, and several pilots went on familiarization missions. An hour and thirty minutes after takeoff from Cat Bi, they arrived over the isolated French outpost, located in a north-south valley close to the Laos border. The main position, centered around the airstrip, consisted of interconnected strong points, surrounded by barbed wire. Colonel Christian Marie Ferdinand de la Croix de Castries, pilot, champion horseman, noted gambler and womanizer, and commander of the Legion of Honor, had his headquarters on the west side of the Nam Yum River, just south of the approach end of runway 33.[9]

Dienbienphu, at first glance, appeared to sleep in the sun. On closer inspection, however, ample evidence of accurate enemy artillery fire could be seen. Beginning with a single 75mm howitzer on February 1, the Vietminh now had a dozen 105mm guns registered on the airfield. The smouldering wreckage of a C-119, destroyed when its French crew was forced to

Loading baggage on Taiwan during the early 1950s (Courtesy A. L. Burridge)

Control tower, Cat Bi airfield, Haiphong, April 1954 (Courtesy E. C. Kirkpatrick)

remain overnight on March 11 for engine repairs, attested to their accuracy, as did the remains of a C-46, crippled by enemy gunfire earlier in the morning. Still, no antiaircraft capability could be detected. Unless conditions changed, airdrops should be "a piece of cake" for the experienced CAT pilots.[10]

The situation changed dramatically twenty-four hours later. On the afternoon of March 13, 1954, the earth shook as hundreds of Vietminh heavy guns poured fire into the French positions. The battle of Dienbienphu had begun in earnest.

General Giap, assisted by Chinese advisers, had surrounded the French garrison of ten thousand with forty thousand battle-tested troops. After months of backbreaking labor, the Vietminh had in place more than two hundred guns over 57mm caliber, including more than one hundred 105mm artillery pieces; the French had only sixty. A Chinese antiaircraft regiment moved into place in early March, adding sixty-four 37mm guns to the sixteen that Giap had concealed in caves east and north of the French outpost. Chinese soldiers brought supplies into the battle area from Yunnan and Kwangsi provinces, driving Russian-made Molotova trucks and captured American 6 x 6's over existing and newly constructed roads to base camps near Dienbienphu, where tens of thousands of coolies waited to carry the shells to advanced positions. From the beginning, French Union forces were outnumbered, outgunned, and outsmarted.[11]

CAT pilots joined French military and civilian crews in airlifting personnel, food, medical supplies, ammunition, dismantled artillery pieces, tons of barbed wire, and other supplies. The C-119s, which could drop seven tons in a single pass, usually made two three-hour round trips a day, arriving over Dienbienphu at about 10:00 A.M. and 3:00 P.M. Initially, CAT airdropped pallet loads of one ton or more from less than five thousand feet. Within a short time, however, the garrison asked for smaller packages because it was too difficult to move the large ones under heavy shellfire.

Weather posed greater problems than antiaircraft fire for the first few days. But this changed on March 24. Caught by Communist flak over Dienbienphu, a French C-47 crashed in a nearby rice field and the crew was killed. Enemy gunners brought down another C-47 on March 26 and two more the next day. Reporting the losses to General Henri Lauzin, commander of the French Far Eastern Air Force, Colonel Nicot concluded: "It is hardly necessary to insist on the necessity of stopping that carnage. But the air crews, in addition to an obvious physical fatigue, have suffered a psychological shock. . . . It is necessary to immediately stop low-level parachute drops and I have given the order to do so as of tonight."[12]

When drop altitudes rose to 6,500 feet, the French tried to maintain accuracy by means of a powder train delay fuse—a small explosive charge

James B. McGovern, Cat Bi airfield, Haiphong, March 25, 1954 (Courtesy E. C. Kirkpatrick)

that would open a parachute at a preset altitude. The first attempt to use this device, on March 31, ended in failure. Captain Jean Pouget (former aide-de-camp to General Navarre, who would jump into Dienbienphu at the end to share the fate of his First Colonial Parachute Battalion) noted that 50 percent of the cargo fell outside French lines, augmenting the enemy's supply of ammunition. "Catastrophic," Pouget commented.[13]

CAT crews made some eighty-seven airdrops over Dienbienphu during the second half of March, contributing significantly to the daily average of 126 tons received by the garrison. Although the pilots suffered no casualties in trying to meet the defenders' daily need for 170 tons of ammunition and thirty tons of food, their battle-damaged C-119s attested to the intensity and accuracy of Vietminh antiaircraft fire. Nearly every aircraft bore the scars of .50 caliber bullets. Hugh H. Hicks commanded one of the first C-119s hit by 37mm fire. Flak shredded the fuselage and punctured both engine nacelles. Despite extreme vibration and loss of aileron tab control, Hicks completed his drop and returned safely to Cat Bi. A short time later, 37mm fire pierced the tail boom and rudders of a C-119 flown by Thomas C. Sailer. He also finished his mission before heading for home base.[14]

Franco-American cooperation broke down in early April. CAT crews, Colonel de Castries complained from his headquarters at Dienbienphu, did not follow instructions from ground controllers when over the drop zone; they released their cargo prematurely, and it ended up in Vietminh hands. As Bernard Fall explained, "Since the crews spoke no French and most of the French air control personnel spoke no English, communications were often difficult." Saigon cabled Paris in frustration that all C-119s should be commanded by French personnel.[15]

CAT pilots were equally displeased. They had been led to expect air cover, but except for an occasional F6F off the carrier *Arromanches*, French fighters rarely were seen below ten thousand feet. French Air Force officials refused to modify the 10:00 A.M. and 3:00 P.M. drop schedule. Reports reached U.S. Air Force intelligence sources that the pilots were "unhappy and want to quit." Lest the grumbling flare into rebellion, Cox and Rousselot flew to Indochina on April 6 and attempted to calm the situation. "The pitch that Al Cox gave at the briefing," one pilot recalled, "consisted of a heavy dose of flag waving and admonition that we were doing a great service to the United States and the French Government." Cox also promised better fighter support and detailed, daily briefings.[16]

To cope with linguistic problems, Cox ordered Frank Guberlet, CAT's French-speaking operations manager who was in northern Thailand in connection with the evacuation of Li Mi's forces (see chapter 14), to return to Haiphong. Guberlet immediately began attending the French Air Force's twice-daily intelligence briefings, which he interpreted to CAT crews before

C-119 showing 37 mm battle damage, Cat Bi airfield, Haiphong, April 1954 (Courtesy E. C. Kirkpatrick)

The CIA's George A. Doole (Courtesy David A. Hickler)

they departed on missions. He also compiled a map, showing the coordinates of known enemy antiaircraft positions. Flak suppression improved after Guberlet met with French pilots off the *Arromanches* and recommended closer cooperation with airdrops. For a time, Rousselot toyed with the idea of having Guberlet accompany the drop missions to interpret French ground controllers' instructions, but this became unnecessary when English-speaking Legionnaires took over as controllers during CAT airdrops. "It was because of those British Legionnaires," Guberlet recalled, "that the percentages of accurate drops continued and kept improving until the end of the operation when visibility became so bad it was impossible for our crews and the controllers to see each other."[17]

Airdrop efficiency reached a peak in mid-April. Supplies dropped into Dienbienphu between April 1 and 15 had averaged 137 tons a day. On the fourteenth however, with increased fighter protection, 220 tons fell into the valley. Thanks to better delayed-action fuses and improved communications, most of the cargo landed within French lines. April 15 saw 250 tons dropped and only 15 percent lost—the largest single-day total during the siege and close to the daily maximum reached by the German air force at Stalingrad. Another 215 tons tumbled out of transport aircraft on the sixteenth, adding to the three-day record. Hanoi could now report to Paris that CAT crews were participating in the airlift with great spirit (*avec beaucoup de cran*), setting an example being followed by French civilian crews flying C-47s.[18]

CAT suffered its first casualty on April 24. Paul R. Holden, one of the airline's original pilots, who had been promoted to chief pilot in March when Rousselot became director of operations, elected to occupy the right—or copilot's—seat on departure from Cat Bi. On his left sat a new copilot, Wallace A. Buford. As the C-119 approached the drop zone at Dienbienphu, Vietminh antiaircraft fire filled the air. Enemy gunners quickly bracketed the twin-tailed aircraft. One 37mm shell went through the tail boom without exploding. Another blew up inside the cockpit, destroying the top part of the compartment near the escape hatch and severely wounding Holden in the right arm. Buford, a twenty-eight-year-old veteran of the Korean War, completed the drop and returned to Cat Bi. French surgeons wanted to amputate Holden's arm, but he insisted on evacuation to an American military hospital at Clark Air Force Base. U.S. Air Force surgeons saved his arm, and Holden returned to duty several months later.[19]

Vietminh antiaircraft fire grew intense the last week of April. On the twenty-sixth the French lost two B-26s, brought down from ten thousand feet by radar-controlled weapons, and a C-47. In all, enemy guns destroyed eight aircraft in April and inflicted major damage on forty-seven others. As French positions shrank, creating a smaller drop zone, the situation could only worsen.

CAT pilots completed 428 missions in April, flying through flak concentrations that one observer considered "as dense as anything Allied planes encountered over the German Ruhr toward the end of World War II." The three minutes over Dienbienphu could seem like three hours as machine gun slugs and flak peppered tail booms, rudders, wings, and fuselages. Although their C-119s took sixty direct hits, CAT pilots continued to lead the way. "It had become common knowledge among the troops at Dien Bien Phu," Fall reported, "that the American civilian pilots were in many cases taking greater chances than the transport pilots of the French Air Force."[20]

All prospect of American intervention faded by the end of April. Admiral Arthur W. Radford, chairman of the Joint Chiefs of Staff, for a time had encouraged the French to believe that a massive B-29 strike on Vietminh artillery positions might be possible, but domestic and international political considerations, as well as military realities, prevented the Eisenhower administration from taking such a step. General Navarre, who earlier had ruled out the possibility of a rescue attempt, could only hope that the impending Geneva Conference on Indochina might produce a cease-fire and save the garrison. Navarre of course had misjudged the enemy from the beginning.[21]

Vietminh artillery pounded the doomed outpost unmercifully on May 1 as General Giap prepared for the final assault. The main French redoubt, just south of the airstrip, had been reduced to the size of a baseball field. Daytime airdrops, now conducted from ten thousand feet because of the intense antiaircraft barrage, more often than not missed the tiny target. Nightime low-level drops by French C-47s, Colonel Nicot reported, "are subjected to automatic weapons fire coming from all directions, and bursts of tracer bullets converge on the pilots who are also blinded by Viet-Minh illuminating shells, searchlights, and Bangalore torpedoes." Captain Pouget noted that the enemy claimed 50 percent of the 128 tons dropped on May 2. "Level of supplies," he recorded in his journal: "Food 5 days; 5 105 fire units; 3 155 fire units; 3 120 fire units; in the trenches, 60 centimeters of mud."[22]

Bad weather associated with the beginning of the monsoon season and a stand-down by French civilian pilots reduced airdrops to fifty-seven tons on May 4 and forty tons on May 5. Skies cleared on the sixth and French civilian crews returned to their aircraft, permitting the largest effort in nearly three weeks. Despite heavy antiaircraft fire, the transports managed to drop 196 tons of food and ammunition to the desperate defenders.[23]

Several CAT pilots volunteered to fly low-level daytime drops of badly needed artillery pieces to Legionnaires who were holding out in strongpoint Isabelle, seven thousand yards south of the main French position. During one mission, Arthur D. Wilson took a 37mm hit in the aft section of the left tail boom and lost elevator control. He completed his drop before limping back to Cat Bi. James B. McGovern was not as lucky.[24]

After a year's absence, "Earthquake McGoon" had returned to Indochina to participate in SQUAW II. Heavier than ever, with a severe crew cut and wearing a multicolored "Aloha" shirt over nondescript shorts, McGovern was hard to miss, even in the middle of an unusual cast of characters. Flying with Wallace Buford on May 6, he reached the valley without incident, then began to spiral down over Isabelle in the face of mounting antiaircraft fire. The artillery piece, fastened to three parachutes, would have to be dropped close to the ground if it were to fall within the minuscule French perimeter, and McGovern was determined to get the job done. The C-119 penetrated a curtain of flak. A metal shard hit the left engine, and the aircraft shuddered. Just as McGovern feathered the propeller, enemy fire ripped large pieces out of the tail section. Unable to hold the aircraft level, McGovern restarted the damaged engine, grateful even for its limited power. The C-119 yawed badly and lost altitude. Steve Kusak, who watching McGovern's struggle from a nearby aircraft, suggested over the radio that he parachute out of the damaged aircraft and take a chance on being picked up by a rescue helicopter. No, McGovern replied, he did not want to risk capture and "do all that walking again." He would stick with the airplane.[25]

McGovern put up a good fight, but the C-119 kept losing altitude. Kusak directed him to a narrow, winding river where a belly landing might be attempted. The aircraft staggered over a series of ridges, edging closer to the ground. Approaching the river and out of altitude, McGovern radioed to Kusak: "Looks like this is it, son." His left wing dug into the steep slope of the riverbank, the C-119 flipped over twice, and exploded. Miraculously, two French kickers survived the crash, but McGovern and Buford perished.

McGovern's death shook the CAT pilots as nothing else had done. There was talk of a stand-down. Fortunately, rain on the morning of May 7 cancelled operations and prevented a confrontation between management and the pilots. Dienbienphu surrendered later in the day.[26]

Estimates of supplies dropped to the besieged garrison between March 13 and May 7 vary from 6,410 to 6,900 tons. Vietminh and Chinese gunners shot down 48 aircraft and severely damaged 167. "Considering that these losses were inflicted in five months upon an air force which never had more than 100 supply and reconnaissance aircraft and 75 combat aircraft available for Dien Bien Phu," Bernard Fall has pointed out, "they were extremely heavy."[27]

CAT pilots flew some 682 airdrop missions (see Appendix C for a complete listing). Day after day, they had risked their lives on combat operations. "Every C-119 Flying Boxcar that we have in Indo-China," Fairchild Aircraft's technical representative reported, "is marked with battle damage, some not as bad as others, but they show that they have gone through hell." Rewards were few. Despite rumors to the contrary, the pilots were not well paid for the hazardous work; basic pay ranged from $800 to $1,000 for sixty flying hours a month with a combat bonus of $10 an hour. The CIA might have owned the airline, but the pilots were not considered government employees and therefore were not eligible for the benefits that went with federal service. They flew through the flak-filled skies over Dienbienphu out of patrioism, personal pride, and because the *esprit de corps* that Chennault earlier had nurtured in the American Volunteer Group (Flying Tigers) had passed over to CAT. At times strained, the "CAT spirit" never broke.[28]

CAT operations in Indochina continued after the fall of Dienbienphu. Between mid-May and mid-August, C-119s dropped supplies to isolated French outposts and delivered landed loads throughout the country. At one point, CAT responded to an emergency call and airlifted tear gas from Okinawa to Saigon for riot control.[29]

The Geneva Agreement, signed on July 21, 1954, divided Vietnam roughly along the seventeenth parallel. As the French left, the Vietminh would assume control of the northern half, leaving Ngo Dinh Diem to establish a non-Communist government in the south. The agreement permitted free movement of civilians from one zone to the other for a specified period of time. Chinese officials on Taiwan immediately chartered two CAT C-46s to evacuate Nationalist supporters who wanted to leave North Vietnam before the Communists took over. During a month-long airlift, pilots Harry B. Cockrell and John R. Plank carried 1,526 refugees from Hanoi to Saigon.[30]

With CIA help, CAT also contracted with French authorities to assist in the massive exodus of people from the north. Signed by E. C. Kirkpatrick on August 18, the agreement called for twelve C-46s to be available for two months. The French would pay $262 per flying hour for the aircraft and crew, plus other allowances, with a monthly guarantee of a thousand hours.

Project COGNAC began on August 22 under the direction of Robert L. Brongersma and A. V. Ozorio. From the beginning, Brongersma had trouble with local French officials. By September 5, Regional Director Var M. Green reported, CAT was receiving "little or no cooperation at all." With the number of evacuees dwindling and commercial air carriers from France competing for business, "the confusion at both Haiphong and Hanoi is extremely critical." It was hoped that Colonel Nicot might be able to resolve the difficulties. The French Air Transport commander, Green pointed out, "is more than pleased with the results of our activity and in fact was amazed at our ability to make as many flights as we have completed with the number of aircraft assigned." But as the French began to load bar stools and refrigerators to make up full loads, the need to reduce the number of aircraft became obvious. Kirkpatrick and Colonel Bardou agreed on September 18 that seven

C-46s would be adequate to complete COGNAC. Between August 22 and the end of operations on October 4, CAT flew 19,808 men, women, and children out of North Vietnam.[31]

Besides transportation of refugees, COGNAC also involved close cooperation between CAT and the CIA's Saigon Military Mission (SMM). Headed by Edward G. Lansdale, the SMM had entered Indochina after Dienbienphu to organize resistance to the Vietminh. While one team established bases in the south, another set up stay-behind paramilitary networks in the north, intended to harass the new Communist regime after the French departed. "CAT," Lansdale explained, "asked SMM for help in obtaining a French contract for the refugee airlift, and got it. In return, CAT provided SMM with the means for secret air travel between the North and Saigon."[32]

The northern team, led by Lucien Conein, a former OSS officer who had fought against the Japanese with *maquis* groups in Tonkin in 1945, entered Hanoi as part of the U.S. Military Assistance and Advisory Group charged with supervising the flow of refugees. Conein's men worked closely with the CAT airlift, performing their cover duties with great enthusiasm if not skill. "One day," Lansdale recalled, "as a CAT C-46 finished loading, they saw a small child standing on the ground below the loading door. They shouted for the pilot to wait, picked the child up and shoved him into the aircraft, which then promptly taxied out for its takeoff in the constant air shuttle. A Vietnamese man and woman ran up to the team, asking what they had done with their small boy, whom they'd brought out to say goodbye to relatives. The chagrined team explained, finally talked the parents into going south to Free Vietnam, put them on the next aircraft to catch up with their son in Saigon."[33]

On occasion, CAT carried more lethal cargo from Saigon to Hanoi. SMM smuggled into the north fourteen agent radios, three hundred carbines, ninety thousand rounds of carbine ammunition, fifty pistols, ten thousand rounds of pistol ammunition, and three hundred pounds of explosives, Lansdale reported, "mostly with the help of CAT." Because the Vietminh likely had agents among the refugees, CAT no doubt brought Communist paramilitary specialists to Saigon on the return flights.[34]

Conein's team sabotaged buses and rail lines, identified targets for future operations, and organized several local guerrilla groups. But prospects were not encouraging. "The northern SMM left with the last French troops," Lansdale observed, "disturbed by what they had seen of the grim efficiency of the Vietminh in their takeover."[35]

Dienbienphu had been CAT's finest hour, but sustained combat operations had placed the organization under enormous strain. Fortunately, the situation in Asia grew quiet after the Communist victory in Indochina, and the airline had time to lick its wounds. As Rousselot wrote to Willauer in November, the hiatus "has given us an opportunity to regain our balance and smooth out the rough edges."[36]

CAT was not finished with Indochina. Although reduced to a single air-craft, attached to the U.S. Operations Mission in Saigon, CAT would remain in that troubled land. Later, as Air America, the airline would join an ex-panding war—and pay a price in blood that would make Dienbienphu pale in comparison.[37]

 # End of an Era

Operation REPAT—the evacuation of Nationalist troops from Burma—could not match the drama of Dienbienphu. Nevertheless, the airlift ranks as one of the major achievements of Cox's presidency. Despite the fiasco of 1951 (see chapter 9), the CIA had continued to support Li Mi, although Taipei assumed primary responsibility for the Yunnan Anti-Communist National Salvation Army. Reinforcements from Taiwan, flown in by CAT, increased Li Mi's force from six thousand to eight thousand men by summer 1952. In August two thousand troops made a foray from Mongyang into Yunnan. They were beaten back into Burma within a week. Li Mi returned permanently to Taiwan in October 1952, turning over command to General Liu Kuo-chuan. It was clear by early 1953 that the KMT irregulars were more interested in carving out a permanent sphere in Burma and controlling the drug trade in the Golden Triangle than in fighting Communists.[1]

The Burmese government, impatient with Washington's feeble efforts to pressure Taipei into resolving the festering problem, terminated the American aid program in March 1953 and appealed to the United Nations for help. Nationalist China's delegation denied any association with the troops despite overwhelming evidence to the contrary. "Do carbines and anti-aircraft guns grow on trees?" asked the exasperated Burmese ambassador, U Myint Thein. "My country is a fertile country but even in the productive region of Monghsat only rice and opium grow." After passing a watered-down resolution condemning the presence of "foreign troops" in Burma, the UN approved an American proposal and created a Four Nation Military Committee (United States, Burma, Thailand, and Nationalist China) to investigate. Ambassador to Thailand William J. Donovan, former OSS chief, conducted negotiations in Bangkok that led to an evacuation agreement. CAT, in its overt role of commercial air carrier, received the airlift contract.[2]

The evacuation posed major operational difficulties for CAT. Because political problems prevented refueling stops in French Indochina or Hong Kong, auxiliary fuel tanks had to be placed in the bellies of eight C-46s to make possible the 1,678-mile trip. Even with the added fuel, a Thailand-Taiwan nonstop flight would place the aircraft at the limit of their range.

An advance guard of fifty KMT soldiers reached the Thai-Burma border at Tachilek on November 8, 1953. Thin and hungry, the troops carried a large portrait of Chiang Kai-shek but no weapons. Ambassador Donovan welcomed the group, saw them boarded on trucks for the ninety-mile ride to Lampang, then fired off a testy cable to Taiwan, demanding that the troops be instructed to bring out their arms.[3]

CAT began Operation REPAT from a short, grass airstrip at Lampang in northern Thailand as soon as the morning ground fog cleared on November 9. Appropriately, Chief Pilot Rousselot, who had delivered the initial load of arms and ammunition to Li Mi in February 1951, was at the controls of the first evacuation flight. After nearly nine hours in the air, Rousselot landed at Taipei's Sungshan airport, where his tired passengers received a gala welcome.[4]

The airlift continued until December 8. CAT carried to Taiwan 1,925 troops and 335 dependents. Despite pressure by Donovan, UN observers reported only an "insignificant amount of small arms and crew-served weapons . . . turned in." The rifles that were brought out, Burmese officials complained, were model 1907 antique pieces; also, some of the evacuees were Shan and Lahu tribesmen, not Chinese. Urged by the Burmese government, the UN passed a resolution on November 28, calling upon the United States to work for removal of the remaining KMT troops.[5]

Further negotiations brought about a second evacuation. Using the airfield at Chiangrai, CAT carried out 2,962 troops, many of them armed, and 513 dependents between February 14 and March 20, 1954. Smaller groups crossed into Thailand over the following months and were flown to Taiwan on special CAT charters. In all, CAT airlifted to Taiwan 5,583 soldiers, 1,040 dependents, 1,000 rifles, 69 machine guns, and 22 mortars. Most flights made the lengthy nonstop trip without incident, although several were forced to land at Hong Kong. The British imposed tight security, ringing the aircraft with troops during refueling; officially, they averted their eyes to the incidents.[6]

Operation REPAT meant profits for CAT: the airline collected $128 for every evacuee. The money was welcome because Cox faced continuing financial woes. For a time, the airline's economic outlook had appeared promising. CAT lost only $107,476 during the five-month period from July to November 1953. But December brought a loss of $191,004. January was even worse: nonscheduled flying was down by 30 percent and CAT suffered a deficit of $243,317. "Operations during the past month," Controller Harold B. Newell reported to Cox, "emphasize particularly the volatile and hazardous character of nonscheduled operations — the maintenance of a fleet and organization in waiting for much higher utilization." Later in the year, CIA headquarters tried to solve this problem by establishing a standby fleet of twelve C-46s, segregated from the airline's normal requirements and funded — up to $600,000 a month when in use — out of CIA reserves. Unfortunately, this adjustment came too late to help Cox's bookkeeping.[7]

Although unable to prevent losses when CAT's full capacity was not in use, the airline's president had a better grasp of the financial picture than had his predecessors. Fiscal reorganization, begun under Captain Schildhauer during winter 1951–52, continued under Cox. CIA headquarters finally responded to repeated requests from the field and sent out a number of talented accountants. Lindsey B. Herd, John Weigers, and James T. McElroy arrived in the Far East between June and September 1952 and joined local employee Edgar L. Mitchell, Jr., to form the nucleus of a first-rate staff.[8]

Cox's main concern in 1953 was a lack of leadership at the top of CAT's fiscal structure. Harold R. Colvin had replaced Terhaar, who had a severe drinking problem, in summer 1952, but the new treasurer did not last many months into the new year. CAT's president thus had to rely on financial adviser George K. Hyslop, whose ability left much to be desired. Aware of growing problems, in mid-1953 the agency hired Harold B. Newell on a three-year contract to take over as controller.[9]

Newell proved a happy choice for the job. A tart-tongued six-footer who listed his chief hobby as work, the new controller had an extensive background in accounting. Educated in his profession at the Elmira (New York) Business Institute and Chicago's Walton School of Commerce, Newell had held responsible fiscal positions with several private companies, gaining public accounting experience with the noted New York firm of Ernst & Ernst. He had been working as a consultant to the Air Force at Wright-Patterson Air Force Base, wrestling with problems of true depreciation, when approached by Ward French about the job with CAT.[10]

Before leaving for the Far East, Newell spoke with officials at CIA headquarters and with Lybrand accountants in New York. "My instructions," he recalled, "were to straighten out the accounting mess and devise a proper system of control for the head office and branches. Throughout all interviews emphasis seemed to be directed to immediacy and getting the job done."[11]

Cox met Newell at Kai Tak when he reached Hong Kong in early August 1953. They went at once to the airline's offices on Hysan Avenue, where Cox introduced Newell to Hyslop. The new controller spent several hours with Hyslop, trying to find out why financial statements were four months in arrears. Finally, he reported to Cox that the situation was hopelessly muddled. "As a result," Newell has written, "he dismissed Hyslop late on the first day of my being on the job."[12]

Newell decided that it would be a waste of time to work up statements for the delinquent months; instead, he pressed for a current statement. He called branch accountants to a meeting in Hong Kong, where he set forth reporting procedures. Head office staff then compiled a consolidated report. "During this early period twelve hour days were common, including Sundays," Newell remembers. "The organization had an objective; it became an integrated group, frustration seemed to have disappeared and directed toward a common purpose." Within a short period, monthly financial statements appeared regularly.[13]

Newell joined CAT just in time to get caught up in Lybrand's yearly attempt to certify an audit. In 1951 the accounting firm, noting the absence of any semblance of inventory, had refused to issue a certified statement, settling instead for a tentative balance sheet. The following year, the auditors insisted on a complete, verifiable count of all property. Subsequently, CAT accountant Lindsey Herd went to Tainan with the audit team to inspect aircraft parts that had been valued in the 1950 sale. He saw one pile of parts, about ten feet high, twenty to thirty feet in circumference, covered by a tarpaulin. "When the corner was lifted," Herd recollects, "it was so greasy and damp that the cover was put back." He asked maintenance personnel if the nomenclature, condition, and possible worth of the parts ever had been determined. No, they replied, no one was qualified to make such an inventory. He found other parts in large wooden crates, obviously thrown together during hasty evacuations from the mainland. Again, no one was able to verify their current condition or potential reparation. The auditors sighed. Only after placing on the books a $1 million valuation reserve against recorded inventory did they agree to issue a qualified certification.[14]

By the time of Newell's arrival, accounting procedures had improved tremendously, and Grundy had brought enough order to the spare parts situation for him to meet with Newell and determine possible usage. After writing off $600,000 in unverifiable assets, the auditors supplied CAT with its first certified statement. The airline had come of fiscal age.[15]

Newell found little corruption in CAT. A Chinese cashier who had had his hand in the till was identified, prosecuted, and jailed; an American employee left the company to avoid questioning about financial irregularites. But these were the only instances. CAT was losing money unnecessarily because of lax procedures in loading practices and reporting, but only small sums were involved, and the leaks were quickly plugged. Newell did locate and solve a more serious problem. Working with Richard M. Barmon, who joined CAT in 1953 with extensive airline accounting experience, he corrected a lack of control on payment of aviation gasoline and oil bills. The U.S.

Air Force, unintentionally, had occasionally double-billed CAT for gasoline purchases. Barmon not only developed procedures to verify future billings but also organized a staff to examine all payments for gasoline since 1950. As a result, CAT recovered from the government $250,000 in overpayments.[16]

By June 1954, when the board elected Newell treasurer-controller, CAT's fiscal organization had made substantial progress toward becoming one of the strongest areas of the CIA's proprietary. "It was my privilege under Al Cox to work at this situation," Newell recalls. "The beginnings were not easy and only by the loyalty and drudgery of long hours by an inspired staff, did we finally turn the corner. Al Cox supported my initiatives and to my knowledge he never let me down, nor I him."[17]

If accounting was one bright spot during Cox's presidency, accident prevention was another. Although faced at times with unusual and hazardous conditions, CAT maintained an excellent safety record during 1953 and 1954. Recognizing that CAT had suffered no passenger fatalities since establishing scheduled commercial service in 1950, in mid-1954 the Chinese CAA awarded the airline China's first Air Safety Citation. In addition to losing McGovern and Buford in combat at Dienbienphu, the airline recorded only one major accident in charter operations. This involved a C-47 (B-811) that CAT kept in Bangkok under charter to Sea Supply, the CIA's commercial cover organization in Thailand. Sea Supply, among other activities, supported a special police unit that conducted clandestine missions in border areas. While returning from a night parachute training exercise on October 20, 1954, pilot Harry Kaffenberger dipped a wingtip into the water during a low-level turn over the Gulf of Siam. Kaffenberger survived, but copilot Y. C. Kan (Kan Yao-chung), radio operator Y. Z. Chen (Chen Yao-Ziang), CIA agent James McCarthy, Jr., and three Thai policemen died in the crash.[18]

Dienbienphu, REPAT, and the many details connected with running an airline occupied most of Cox's time and energy during the early months of 1954, but franchise renewal remained a festering problem that demanded constant attention. Under terms of the three-month extension, Cox had to submit a reorganization proposal by February 15. In accordance with the board's wishes, he offered the two-company plan that had been drafted by Brackley Shaw in August 1953. The scheme did not fare well. Shaw's plan had been premised on passage of the proposed foreign investment law, but objections from the Ministry of Communications had delayed legislative action. The MOC now rejected CAT's proposal, terming it "inconsistent with the principles of foreign investment as desired by our Government." Furthermore, the ministry pointed out, because the majority Chinese-owned half of the two-company plan would own neither aircraft nor equipment, "it is impossible for our Government to permit it to be formed."[19]

CAT officials returned with another proposal. Put together mainly by Saul Marius, the new scheme was designed to protect American assets, while conforming to the civil aviation code. Two companies would be formed under Chinese law: Company "A," wholly American-owned, would hold the airline's engineering assets and conduct the maintenance side of its business. Company "B," owned 51 percent by Company "A" as a Chinese juristic person and 49 percent by Americans, would take over and operate CAT's flight equipment and air routes. The two companies would be interrelated by long-term contracts, interlocking directors, and other devices. In late March Cox submitted the Marius plan as a preliminary proposal and asked the ministry for a further six-month extension while a definitive scheme was being formulated.[20]

The MOC, not overly sympathetic with CAT's problems, registered its displeasure by terminating the Chennault-Willauer franchise as of March 31. The airline would be permitted to continue operations for three months under the name of Promotion Office of Civil Air Transport; a final reorganization plan must be ready by May 15.[21]

Although the MOC declined comment on the Marius plan, preferring to wait for a final proposal, Joseph C. Twanmoh, an influential Chinese attorney retained by CAT to handle sensitive matters with the government, found fault with it. Although technically complying with the civil aviation code through the use of Company "A" as a Chinese juristic person, the Marius plan failed to meet the "substantial ownership and effective control" requirements of international air agreements. Wang Wen-san, original CAT financial backer and important advisor on government relations, supported Twanmoh. "To operate CAT without even a semblance of *Chinese nationals'* participation and control," he warned, "is raw material for international disputes, if not conflicts."[22]

Cox acknowledged that Twanmoh and Wang had raised an important point, but he was not overly concerned. The problem, he believed, could be raised with appropriate Chinese officials well in advance of final reorganization. Meanwhile, the best course would be to play for time.[23]

As the May 15 deadline approached, Cox informed the board that he planned to seek another extension. A new cabinet was due to take office at the end of the month, he explained, and it would be far better to deal with the new minister of communications than with Ho Chung-han, "who can not be classified as a friend of CAT." Moreover, Cox argued, a delay would allow additional time for the legislature to pass the long-awaited foreign investment law. He had been assured by high Chinese officials, including Foreign Minister Yeh, that this approach was sound. "The Foreign Minister," he continued, "has advised me that he personally would like to see a single 100% American owned company as provided by the proposed new [foreign investment] law, and agrees with me that the separation into two companies [under the Marius plan] is wasteful and bulky."[24]

On May 7 Shaw telephoned Hong Kong and conveyed to French, who had replaced Marius as field counsel in March, the board's mounting anger with events on Taiwan. The Chinese knew, Shaw said, that CAT's owners could not comply with the civil aviation code and still adequately protect their assets. Indeed, high officials in the government, acknowledging the problem, had led the board to believe that the new foreign investment law would afford the necessary security. But the Chinese were continuing to press for a definitive reorganization proposal before passage of the investment statute. Although earlier in favor of delay, Shaw now believed that the time had come to take a stronger position. The CIA's management committee and the board of directors, he warned, "are in full agreement that the Company would cease operations before submitting to any 'give away.' In other words, it was their desire to make it plain that the Company would do nothing in the absence of an acceptable foreign Investment Law." This policy, Shaw continued, "has been confirmed on the topmost echelon of Management."[25]

In retrospect, Shaw's trans-Pacific telephone call marked a crucial turning point in Washington's attitude toward franchise negotiations. Doole and Cabell obviously had agreed to adopt a tougher stance with the Chinese, even at the risk of folding up CAT. But Cox did not appear to understand the change of direction. Caught in the emotional trauma of Dienbienphu, he was unable to focus on lesser issues. Shaw's call came the day after McGovern's death. "I was in the office when word was received that 'Earthquake' McGoon [McGovern] was killed," secretary Lillian Chu later wrote to Louise Willauer, "and Al just went to pieces, I mean literally to pieces." Drinking heavily, a distracted Cox came to rely increasingly on the advice of subordinates.[26]

As French puzzled over ways to comply with the civil aviation code while protecting American assets, Henry Yuan, now vice-president for general affairs, offered soothing advice. The problem, Yuan assured French on May 19, was academic. Responsible officials in the government recognized CAT's situation; the forthcoming foreign investment law would cure all difficulties. On his recommendation, Cox sought and obtained a delay until June 15.[27]

Three weeks later, Yuan called on Colonel Lai. The CAA director was on his way to brief Yuan Chou-chien, new minister of communications, and wanted to know what plans CAT was making to meet the June 15 deadline. The airline, Henry Yuan said, had a concrete proposal ready to submit, but it was contingent upon passage of the foreign investment law. Because it now appeared that the legislature would not begin debate on the statute until after June 15, he would welcome Colonel Lai's advice on how best to handle the matter. The colonel suggested that CAT ask for another delay.[28]

Cox accepted Lai's advice, as relayed by Yuan. On June 14 he informed the CAA that CAT's work on a concrete reorganization plan had been hampered by the absence of a foreign investment law; he asked for a further delay while the legislature considered the new statute. CAT, the CAA responded, would have until August 15 to submit a definitive proposal; however, this would be the final extension.[29]

As if Cox did not have enough to worry about, CATI once again raised its ugly head to complicate matters. The Chinese government had written to CATI early in 1954 and demanded immediate settlement of note indebtedness, based on an assessment of $5.2 million in assets. CATI replied with a suggestion of dividing equally the remaining CNAC/CATC aircraft, real estate, and current bank balance of $215,000. When this offer was rejected, CATI offered $1.25 million in cash, plus real estate on Taiwan. Chennault called on Chiang Kai-shek to explain the situation. "He was not happy about the [proposed] CATI settlement," the general wrote to Willauer, "but I am sure that I convinced him that the net worth of CATI is far below his reports."[30]

The Chinese, however, continued to hold out for a better deal, enlisting the support of Ambassador Karl L. Rankin in an effort to bring pressure on CATI. Corcoran decided that the time had come to play political hardball. In early June, in a vituperative telegram to Foreign Minister Yeh, he expressed great dissatisfaction with the government's unreasonable attitude, threatened to withdraw from the entire business, and implied disastrous political repercussions for Taiwan.[31]

The new minister of communications, Cox informed Willauer in the wake of Corcoran's missive, "once again is confusing CATI with the CAT franchise." The Chinese, in fact, were not at all happy about "the rather harshly worded cables" that had been received. "Tom [Corcoran]," Cox explained, "is apparently making no bones about waiting for the November Elections and is confident that with a Democratic victory he can deal with the Chinese with a very high hand. All of this, of course, does not make life every easy for us."[32]

Cox could only smile his crooked, sad smile and add CATI to a growing list of woes. Among other irritations, Doole's efforts to place tighter controls on field management remained a source of constant distress for CAT's president. The latest blow had come in May, when the CIA's management committee, acting under direct orders from General Cabell, approved a set of ten "ground rules" which placed severe limits on Cox's authority. Henceforth, Cox needed prior board approval for long-range charter operations outside the Far East, contractual arrangements with foreign or American government agencies, purchase of new capital items costing more than $5,000, or improvements to existing items costing more than $1,000; for initiation of lawsuits; changes in depreciation or other balance sheet adjustments; setting up of bank accounts; employment of senior personnel; promotion and longevity pay; and "other activities impinging on policy or creating obligations." When Cox complained about "excessive controls which bind our hands on almost everything," the board not only reaffirmed the "ground rules" but elected Doole vice-president, vice-chairman of the board, and chief executive officer in the United States, effective July 1, 1954.[33]

The new chief executive made his presence felt at once. Cox, following Minister Yeh's earlier suggestion, had drawn up a simplified version of the Marius plan that called for a single company, organized under Chinese law and 100 percent American owned, to succeed CAT. On July 10 he forwarded the plan to Washington for approval. "We would like to know how," Doole replied, "under such a scheme, you plan to meet the requirements that substantial ownership and effective control of the airline concerned must be in Nationals of the country whose flag the airline bears. . . . If you have developed a method whereby the requirements of the bilateral agreements can be met within a single 100% American owned company, we would of course be delighted to hear about it." Because it seemed unlikely that the single-company plan would work, Doole continued, the management committee was inclined to revert to the Shaw two-company plan. The chief executive enclosed a copy of the Shaw plan "just so that there may be no misunderstanding as to what we are talking about."[34]

Cox asked Yuan to sound out Chinese officials on the two-company proposal. "The general reaction," Yuan reported, "was unfavorable." The CAA and MOC continued to insist that the majority Chinese-owned company possess aircraft in order to operate franchised routes. Also, Foreign Minister Yeh, "who as you know has remained CAT's friend throughout these troublesome 8 months, and on whom we have depended a good deal for advice and guidance during this crucial period," did not like the plan. Yeh promised to do everything he could to support it, but he warned CAT to expect strong opposition. Yuan concluded:

> My own evaluation of the situation is this: because the Government has already rejected the plan in question . . . it would seem almost an effrontery to send in practically a carbon copy of the same paper after 5 months of protestations about protection of assets, etc., while waiting for the all-cure Foreign Investment Law. If it is the Board's idea merely to satisfy itself of its unacceptablility before trying something else, the situation seems too delicate for such frivolous tactics, considering all that has taken place and considering the personal reactions we have already ascertained. On the other hand if the Board is absolutely bent on the set-up and will have nothing else, then some timely diplomacy is obviously necessary to make it more palatable.[35]

Pressure on Cox became intense as August 15 drew near. The CIA's management committee, Doole cabled on August 5, had "fully approved" the two-company plan. Six days later, Colonel Lai, noting that the foreign investment law had at last been promulgated, reminded CAT that August 15 was the last date to submit a reorganization proposal. Cox seemed damned if he did and damned if he didn't. He had a copy of the Shaw plan translated into Chinese, but at the last minute he held it back and asked the CAA for another delay. He then wrote a lengthy explanation to Doole, detailing Yuan's discussions with Chinese officials. "From the foregoing," Cox concluded, "you can see that we are faced with a delicate problem of negotiations and that it is desirable for future company purposes, for us to present our plan in the most palatable fashion possible. Quite obviously we should do nothing to adulterate the favourable political position occupied by the company." Cox went on to request discretionary authority to present the details of the board's plan at a time and in a way best calculated to achieve the board's overall objectives. He also asked for permission to vest title to no more than five aircraft in the majority Chinese-owned company in order to satisfy the CAA and Ministry of Communications.[36]

Doole exploded. Up to this point, communications with Cox had been polite and formal, filled with suggestions and requests. On August 26, however, Doole adopted a new tone of command. The two-company plan, he cabled Cox, would protect American assets and meet bilateral treaty requirements. Prior objections to the scheme had been removed by passage of the foreign investment law. He ordered: "UNLESS YOU CAN CABLE US COMPELLING REASON FOR FAILURE TO COMPLY YOU DIRECTED IMMEDIATELY SUBMIT APPROVED PLAN AS RESPONSE TO CAA LETTER STOP COMMITTEE REQUIRES COMPLIANCE WITH REQUIREMENTS ESTABLISHED BY CHINESE GOVERNMENT AND DOES NOT WANT TO BE IN POSITION OF ASKING FOR ANY DELAYS OR EXTENSIONS ON DEADLINE STOP."[37]

Despite Rosbert's earlier warning that Yuan was "not very effective in those major cases where he is most needed." Cox continued to listen to his dubious advice. CAT's president held his ground and refused to submit the two-company plan. Doole, in turn, brought the issue to a special meeting of the board. Results were predictable. The board took the matter out of Cox's hands and ordered Doole to assume direct control of negotiations.[38]

Doole arrived in Taipei on September 7, 1954, four days after the Communists had begun a massive artillery bombardment of Nationalist positions on the offshore island of Quemoy. On the thirteenth, now qualified as a foreign investor under the new law, CAT Incorporated applied to the Ministry of Economic Affairs to establish two companies. Asiatic Aeronautical Company Limited (CAT of China in the original Shaw plan), wholly American-owned, would hold all the airline's assets except BOOKLIFT ground equipment in

Japan. Civil Air Transport Company Limited, owned 60 percent by private Chinese investors (who would deposit deeds of trust with the CIA in return for their shares), would operate air routes authorized by the Chinese government, contracting with Asiatic Aeronautical for assistance. Both companies would be capitalized at a nominal NT$400,000 (US$25,000).[39]

The following day, September 14, a letter of agreement from James Brennan to Minister Yeh settled CATI. According to one report, the State Department had become involved in the matter following Corcoran's threatening June telegram to Yeh. Howard P. Jones, counselor of the Embassy in Taipei, and Walter McConaughy, director of the Office of Chinese Affairs in Washington, apparently put together a lengthy report that reflected ill on CATI's partners. Assistant Secretary of State Walter S. Robertson called Corcoran and Chennault to the State Department, and in a blunt, table-thumping session demanded an immediate, equitable settlement with the Chinese.[40]

The final agreement was more favorable than previous CATI offers, but it fell far short of Taipei's expectations. To liquidate obligations arising out of the $4.75 million in promissory notes, CATI agreed to pay $1,296,928.32 in cash. CATI received credit for $1,913,373.43 in claims against the government. Other rights and assets accruing to the Chinese were given a paper value of $1,539,698.25. This last category included real estate on Taiwan and a promissory note for $500,000, payable out of funds to be realized from the sale of stock in a new company having as assets Bailey's Shipyard and other property in Hong Kong formerly owned by CNAC and CATC. In short, the Chinese had settled for approximately $2 million in real value.[41]

Chennault was not happy with the final arrangement, but he felt that nothing else could have been done. "I hope this will be a lesson to both you and me," he wrote to Willauer, "never to interfere in the future when we learn that an airline is defecting to the Communists." Although relieved that CATI finally had been resolved, Willauer shared Chennault's sentiments. He replied:

I only hope the boys will be able to sell enough airplanes so that we can keep up with our commitments to the Chinese Government and perhaps have a dollar or two left over for all the sweat and tears we had put into this quixotic gesture. Despite the Hell we went through I know you agree with me that we did very probably save Formosa, if not from a takeover by parachuters, from a very nasty situation which would have prevailed in 1950 had the Communists been in possession of the CATI assets. I don't suppose you feel any better than I do that we never have been given full public credit by the Chinese Government on this score but rather have been maligned because of the troublesome financial aspects which the Chinese choose to misunderstand in their own favor. I am not bitter about it but sure am disillusioned.[42]

Available records do not reveal the final amount realized by CATI's partners following sale of all aircraft and payment of expenses, but it could not have been great. Duncan C. Lee, a lawyer close to the case, pointed out that legal expenses were enormous. CATI had hired the best lawyers in Hong Kong, London, and San Francisco. "This was going first class," he noted, "but that was the only way to go." In addition, removing the aircraft from Hong Kong and preparing them for sale had cost a large sum. Having sat in the salty air for nearly three years without protection or preservatives, the planes were in poor condition. "I am convinced," Lee concluded, "that the shareholders netted very little from the operation in terms of money, certainly nothing commensurate with the talent and time they put into it."[43]

Settlement of CATI at least removed a sizable obstacle in resolving the franchise problem, and international events were creating a more congenial climate for negotiations. Escalation of fighting around the offshore islands drew the Nationalist government close to the United States. Talks were under way in October that would lead to the signing of a mutual defense treaty by the end of the year. On October 30 Doole learned that the government had approved the two-company plan, with the understanding that Civil Air Transport Company Limited would own at least three aircraft.[44]

A jubilant Doole left for Washington on November 2, convinced that his negotiating skill had brought about a happy solution to the vexing problem. Chennault thought differently. "Mr. Doole," the general informed Corcoran, "is completely confident that he obtained government approval practically as a result of his own efforts. As a matter of fact, he would still be sitting here for a much longer time had it not been for calls made by Al Cox and me on Madame Chiang and my calls alone on the Generalissimo, Premier and the Governor."[45]

No matter where credit should be assigned, Cox clearly was odd man out. "The Pineapple King [Doole] paid us a 6-week visit," CAT's president wrote to Willauer in mid-November, "and I can't say that it was a very enjoyable one, and I am afraid that he will be extremely critical of many things before the Board." In fact, Cox's demise had been long coming. He had made no secret of his discontent with the growing restrictions on field management. His complaints to agency personnel passing through Hong Kong, asking them to raise questions in Washington, angered the officials at headquarters who were responsible for the proprietary. Cox fell behind on required reports; he resisted orders to move the airline's executive offices from Hong Kong to Taipei. Rumors of his heavy drinking reached Cabell's ears. Headquarters sent General Counsel Houston to the Far East to investigate. His report added another nail to Cox's coffin. After detailing Cox's strengths and weaknesses, Houston concluded that it would be prudent to begin thinking of a successor.[46]

Hugh L. Grundy, Alfred T. Cox, and Claire L. Chennault

The CIA's management committee called Cox to the United States to attend a board meeting scheduled for December 17. When he arrived, Lyle T. Shannon, chief administrative officer in the Directorate of Plans, informed him that he was being removed as president of CAT, effective December 31. Cox registered shock and dismay. Even Doole was surprised at the timing and method of dismissing Cox, but he concurred with the move.[47]

Corcoran smelled a rat. "Tom reacted violently to [your dismissal]," Willauer informed Cox. "As you know, he has made no secret of his own personal suspicion that at some time somebody will try to sell the outfit to one of the bigger companies such as Pan American." Chennault shared Corcoran's view. "In my opinion," he wrote to Willauer, "the whole thing was managed by George Doole and approved by Cabell. . . . I am confident that George's objective is to eventually make CAT an affiliate of Pan American, and undoubtedly he hopes to become Vice President of Pan Am thereby."[48]

Corcoran and Chennault were wrong on all counts. Doole did not have to engineer Cox's dismissal—the former OSS officer had cut his own throat. The connection with Pan American existed only in Corcoran's mind, conditioned by long years in Washington to suspect plots everywhere. Cox was unable to live with the revised corporate structure that headquarters was intent upon imposing. Accustomed to autonomy, Cox fought against Washington's detailed control over field management, making his removal inevitable. Besides, Cox's drinking was out of hand despite the best efforts of fiercely loyal subordinates to protect him.[49]

Doole returned to the Far East on December 22, followed the next day by Cox. The chief executive announced on December 27 that Cox would depart in January on an "extended leave" and that Hugh Grundy, head of technical services, would take over as acting president. In January the Chinese government granted charters to Civil Air Transport Company Limited and Asiatic Aeronautical Company Limited. On March 1, 1955, after Asiatic Aeronautical sold three C-46s to Civil Air Transport Company Limited and the Ministry of Communications issued all necessary permits and air route licenses, the new companies commenced operations.[50]

"Morale is at bottom low," secretary Lillian Chu wrote to the Willauers in summer 1955, "and as far as I am concerned they might as well not use the name of CAT, as it now is not the organization that 'CAT' stood for and has certainly no spirit de corps [sic] as in the past. . . . I wish they would just have another name instead of CAT, so that people won't think it is the same as the old CAT."[51]

Lillian Chu was right. Although a change of name did not take place until 1959, when CAT Incorporated became Air America, the old CAT had ended with Cox's dismisssal.

Chennault, Willauer, and Cox were cut from the same cloth. Sharing an activist temperament, their style of management emphasized personal leadership and personal loyalty. They flourished in an atmosphere of independence, where the challenges were operational in nature. Such an approach, however, did not satisfy the CIA. General Cabell wanted administrative efficiency. The proprietary had to set its financial house in order, and field managers had to follow directions set by Washington. Given this view of the enterprise, Doole's rise was inevitable. Employees who could conform to the changed style of management — Grundy is the best example — prospered under the new conditions, whereas such individualists as Burridge, Rosbert, and Rousselot were soon gone.

The new regime could not erase the past, although efforts were made to do so. Some of the people, a bit of the style, and many of the memories of the old CAT did pass over to the organizations that formed the CIA's aerial empire in East Asia during the 1960s. The "CAT spirit" survived.

Conclusion

Civil Air Transport occupies a unique and intriguing place in the history of aerial enterprises. It began as an anachronism, founded in China by two adventurer-entrepreneurs at a time when Western domination of the storied Middle Kingdom was drawing to a close. Chennault and Willauer came last in a long line of foreigners who traveled to China in search of fame, profit, and excitement. In common with many of their predecessors, the two Americans developed a deep affection for the ancient land and its people. Functioning in what Jonathan Spence has aptly described as "that indefinable realm where altruism and exploitation meet,"[1] they wanted to help the Chinese government bring peace and stability to the war-ravaged country and at the same time build their own fortunes.

CAT quickly became caught up in China's civil war. While maintaining the trappings of a commercial airline, it more often than not served as a paramilitary adjunct of the Chinese Air Force. The company's pilots fought long and hard on the Nationalist side. They flew troops and supplies into battle, carried out the wounded, evacuated valuable technicians from besieged cities, airdropped supplies to isolated garrisons, and performed numerous other vital tasks. Although their efforts may have delayed a Communist victory, the Red tide proved unstoppable. The Nationalist government had lost the mandate of heaven; a cycle of Chinese history had come to an end.

Fighting in a losing cause, CAT shared the fate — and exile — of Chiang Kai-shek's defeated regime. No longer economically viable, the airline teetered on the verge of collapse when the CIA came to its rescue. As the United States moved toward a policy of containment in the Far East during the early months of 1950, resulting in an expanded role for the CIA's paramilitary forces, officials in Washington purchased CAT with the idea of employing it in the growing secret struggle against Asian communism.

CIA covert operations grew rapidly in size and scope during the Korean War, and CAT time and again proved a valuable acquisition. The airline provided cover for CIA personnel, enhanced the secrecy of clandestine projects, and afforded a freedom and flexibility that would have been impossible if the CIA had had to rely on other government agencies for air transport. CAT delivered guns to Li Mi in Burma, made numerous overflights of China in support of guerrillas, carried hundreds of sensitive personnel between CIA bases in Saipan, Okinawa, Japan, and Korea, and provided secure airlift for a bevy of secret operations throughout East Asia.

Although it is difficult to judge the efficacy of the CIA's clandestine operations on the basis of available documentation, large paramilitary projects apparently accomplished few worthwhile results. The Li Mi affair was a fiasco; support of guerrillas on the Chinese mainland did not deter Peking from prosecuting the war in Korea or consolidating its power at home. One suspects — but cannot prove — that smaller covert projects fared better. Intelligence officers who worked in the field are positive about CAT's usefulness.

If an operational boon to field personnel, the agency's first air proprietary seemed at times an administrative headache to harried officials in Washington. "There are built-in difficulties in running what appears to be normal business for operational purposes," CIA General Counsel Lawrence Houston recalled.[2] Cover had to be maintained; CAT had to give the impression of being a viable business. Also, CIA headquarters developed a distinct aversion to huge subsidies. Above all, administrators sought to exert tighter fiscal and operational control over the company. Although by 1955 Washington had won this struggle for power over field managers, a host of other problems continued to plague CAT, including the often complicated and always difficult relationship with the Chinese Nationalist government.

The CIA never fully resolved what Houston termed a proprietary's "built-in dichotomy," but the airline's operational advantages continued to outweigh its administrative complications. "Of course, there were individual problems from time to time with certain aspects of the operation," CIA Director William Colby has written, "but I think these should never be exaggerated into a question as to the overall contribution these assets made."[3] Indeed, CAT was only the beginning. The small airline that first flew in postwar China for "relief and rehabilitation" purposes turned out to be the flagship company in a long line of CIA air proprietaries that would flourish in East Asia — and elsewhere — during the 1960s.

Epilogue

Chennault remained chairman of CAT Incorporated's board of directors under the Doole-Grundy regime, but the old warrior's advice was rarely sought. His complaints to DCI Dulles about restrictive controls on field management were ignored. As the CIA's "History of Air America" states, Chennault "was speaking of a former age. Headquarters preferred to listen to the reports of Grundy and Doole on how well the organization had worked and how the management had been tightened."[1]

A heavy smoker, Chennault suffered from chronic bronchial problems that worsened through the years. A physical examination in August 1956 detected a tumor on his left lung; it proved cancerous. The general fought the malignancy for nearly two years, becoming progressively weaker. On July 25, 1958, as he struggled for breath at the Ochsner Foundation Hospital in New Orleans, the White House announced that Chennault had been awarded the third star of a lieutenant general. He told his wife that it had come ten years too late. He died two days later.[2]

Willauer became ambassador to Honduras in 1954 and took part in CIA activities that led to the overthrow of Guatemala's leftist government. Among other duties, he made arrangements for "borrowed" CAT pilots to fly for the "rebel" air force. After four years in Tegucigalpa, he moved south and served as ambassador to Costa Rica for two years. Willauer's final assignment came in winter 1960–61, when he returned to Washington as special assistant to the secretary of state and reviewed plans for the Bay of Pigs adventure. His concern about lack of air cover over the invasion beaches was ignored by the incoming Kennedy administration. He died of an embolism at his summer home on Nantucket on August 6, 1962. His wife buried him on the island, next to Tommy.[3]

Cox stayed with the CIA, which, he found, tended to accept alcoholism as an occupational disease. Although he never returned to field work, Cox became an expert in counterinsurgency doctrine and later worked as a contract historian. Too proud to seek help, Cox never solved his drinking problem. Alcohol ruined his marriage and eventually killed him in July 1973. General Stilwell composed a moving eulogy to his old friend, which was delivered at the Fort Myer Post Chapel by Corcoran, but Dorothy Cox deserves the last word on her husband:

> Al Cox was one of the most complex human beings many of us have ever known and one of the most valuable and promising. Whatever the personal demons were that began to gnaw at him as early as his Fort Benning days, and eventually caused his tragic destruction, he was never able to express or talk about them and was a deeply reticent and inhibited man emotionally. He seemed always driven by two powerful inner forces, one inexplicable — toward serving his country and toward his own self destruction. His gentle, genial manner covered a fervent patriotism along with the instincts of a true adventurer and soldier of fortune — he was a man of *action*, perhaps unusual in one who also had such a strong intellectual bent. He worked best under pressure, craved it seemingly, and drove himself relentlessly, yet under too much pressure he eventually broke. I really do not understand him now and certainly was not mature enough or wise enough to in those days, and was unable to reach his demons (could anyone really? — many tried), but I loved him for his unfailing kindness and generosity of spirit, his courage and personal integrity, his wit and fine mind. He was a truly lovable man and a human being of great worth even in the later terrible years when our own personal life could no longer be held together. . . . I think of him with gratitude for all the good and memorable things — and with deep pain for his inner torment, loneliness and too early disintegration of a bright star.[4]

CAT continued to operate its unique combination of normal commercial business and clandestine missions under the new managerial team. Major covert projects during the late 1950s involved aerial assistance to dissident forces in Indonesia and Tibet. With increasing American involvement in Southeast Asia during the 1960s, the CIA rapidly expanded its air proprietaries to cope with a variety of new tasks. Operating under the name of Air America, the agency's air force dropped rice and guns and transported supplies and troops to a thirty-six-thousand-man army of Hmong tribesmen and their three hundred American case officers in the not-so-secret war in Laos. Air America also flew rescue missions for downed American military pilots, contracted with U.S. government agencies for overt commercial work in support of the war effort, and undertook numerous deeply secret ("black") flights throughout Southeast Asia and into China.[5]

The CIA relegated CAT to a "cover" role during the 1960s. Serving as international flag carrier for the Republic of China, the airline used a single Convair 880 jet transport (later replaced by a Boeing 727) to operate commercial passenger service along routes extending from Tokyo to Bangkok. CAT also maintained several DC-4s and C-46s for domestic service on Taiwan and for charter flights. An accident involving the airline's jet transport, and the subsequent controversy over responsibility, finally put CAT out of business in 1968.[6]

Appendix A

Operating Statistics
January 1947 to November 1949

Month	Hours Flown	Passengers	Revenue Ton-miles (Cargo and Passengers)
1947			
January	50	*	18,700
February	167	*	40,117
March	310	*	91,343
April	506	*	109,517
May	776	*	286,343
June	833	125	322,820
July	1,386	497	617,963
August	1,880	3,830	762,251
September	1,629	4,692	690,948
October	2,179	*	1,149,115
November	1,727	*	1,176,053
December	2,151	*	1,722,224
	13,594	27,644 (est.)	6,987,394
1948			
January	2,902	5,958	1,806,457
February	2,127	6,984	1,289,455
March	2,665	10,563	1,969,653
April	3,127	14,277	3,161,624
May	3,308	17,959	2,919,293
June	3,612	15,428	3,289,616
July	3,303	17,885	2,953,446
August	3,404	31,520	2,392,191
September	3,849	34,726	2,796,368
October	3,462	24,057	2,560,126
November	3,370	16,020	3,104,850
December	2,441	8,097	2,409,163
	37,570	203,474	30,652,242

Month	Hours Flown	Passengers	Revenue Ton-miles (Cargo and Passengers)
1949			
January	3,460	6,207	4,257,608
February	2,828	4,940	3,167,207
March	4,508	8,404	5,194,825
April	3,485	9,456	3,198,745
May	1,706	2,136	249,906
June	1,721	6,216	800,373
July	2,321	11,283	1,114,629
August	2,869	13,174	1,422,982
September	1,967	5,614	883,988
October	1,747	5,816	929,581
November	1,482	8,165	744,721
	28,094	81,411	21,964,565

*No figures available.

Sources: Certified Statement of C. L. Chennault, April 26, 1950, Willauer Papers; *China Handbook, 1950* (New York, 1950), p. 631; United Nations Relief and Rehabilitation Administration, *Operational Analysis Papers, No. 51,* "Industrial Rehabilitation in China" (Washington, D.C., 1948), p. 19; *CAT Bulletin* 1 (February 15, 1948):9; "Operational Statistics for the Year 1947," Rosbert Papers.

Appendix B

The Panzer Notes

During the course of my research, I learned about the existence of an "official" history of the CIA's air complex in the Far East. Several individuals with agency connections who had read the document assured me that it was the definitive treatment of the topic. I attempted to obtain a copy of the history—or at least an expurgated version—through the Freedom of Information Act. George W. Owens, information and privacy coordinator at the CIA, replied "that the history to which you refer was never completed. I regret that we will therefore be unable to assist you in this matter."

Fortunately, at least for my purposes, the CIA decided to use the "History of Air America, 1946–1971" to defend the government in legal proceedings before the Civil Service Commission. At issue was the claim for civil service credit that had been made by several former employees of the agency's proprietary. Irving R. M. Panzer, attorney for David H. Hickler and other former airline employees, sought and obtained access to the "History" in 1980.

Granted the necessary security clearances, Panzer went to CIA headquarters to review the document. It was brought to the general counsel's office, and he was allowed to take notes. The "History," divided into four chapters, consisted of more than one thousand pages of unbound typescript, replete with numerous strikeovers, and obviously intended for "in-house" purposes. Panzer went through it carefully and took forty-seven pages of detailed notes on legal size paper, including lengthy quotations. The notes were submitted for security review, at which time about 10 percent were excised. Panzer then used the notes to prepare a lengthy memorandum, "Summary of the History of Air America, from the Official 'Secret' History Prepared by the C.I.A."

Through the courtesy of Mr. Panzer, and with the kind permission of Mr. Hickler, I obtained copies of the memorandum and original notes. Needless to say, I am most grateful to both gentlemen.

The "History of Air America," as the Panzer notes make clear, is a scholarly work, obviously compiled by agency historians. Based to a large extent on documents generated in Washington, the "History" reflects a view of the air complex as seen from CIA headquarters, especially the Directorate of Administration. Although an essential source of information for understanding the nature of the proprietary, it is by no means a definitive treatment of the topic.

Appendix C

Airdrops at Dienbienphu
March 13 to May 7, 1954

Pilot	Missions	Pilot	Missions
A. L. Judkins	64	D. R. Price	39
S. A. Kusak	59	A. D. Wilson	36
H. L. Marsh	58	E. F. Shilling	34
E. W. Cedergren	57	R. F. Watts	33
A. L. Pope	57	C. E. Hayes	32
N. D. Hicks	56	W. D. Gaddie	29
J. M. Verdi	56	F. F. Walker	21
C. M. Pinkava	54	W. C. Buttons	14
D. D. Carden	52	S. E. Dew	13
K. L. Milan	49	D. A. Lampard	13
M. K. Clough	48	J. R. Dexheimer	12
N. N. Forte	48	R. N. Duke	12
F. L. Hughes	48	R. S. Richardson	11
M. W. Shaver	48	H. J. Hudson	16
J. B. McGovern	46	E. L. Porter	9
M. McCallum	41	W. P. Hobbs	6
T. C. Sailer	41	P. R. Holden	5
R. L. Brongersma	39	J. G. Anastasakes	4
H. H. Hicks	39	S. McDonnel	2
J. R. Plank	39		

Source: Holden to Newell, "Squaw Flight Time—March 1954," "Squaw Flight Time—April 1954," and "Squaw Flight Time—May 1954," all dated June 21, 1954, copies in McGovern's personnel file.

Appendix D

Equipment List
February 1954

Aircraft type (CAT or Leased)	Chinese Registration	Manufacturer's Serial Number	Army Air Force Serial Number	Empty Weight	Operational Limitations	Special Modifications
C-47B CAT	B-801	20681	43-16215	18,873	Plushed; ordinarily used as passenger plane	1. Static line installed.
C-47A (L)	B-809	15437	43-15466	18,909	Plushed; ordinarily used as passenger plane	2. Light and bell signal system.
C-47A (L)	B-811			17,475	Wings and fuselage registration symbols for Indo-China and visible in flight. Deicer boots will not be installed.	3. Radio installation includes Dual ADF but no APH-2.
						4. Unmarked.

Type	Designation	No.	Serial	Weight	Notes	Equipment
C-47A (L)	B-815	19258	42-100795		Now undergoing #3 service and conversion of seating configuration and exterior markings as a replacement of B-811.	1. Light and bell signal system. 2. Removable aircraft registration plate on fin. 3. Unmarked.
C-47A (L)	B-817	19256	42-100793	17,414		1. Static line installed. 2. Removable aircraft registration plate on fin. 3. Removable navigator's table installed. 4. Unmarked.
PBY-5A CAT	B-819	55		21,216	Not winterized.	1. Modified bow. 2. Blisters removed; large cargo door portside. 3. 8 JATO units. 4. Fuel dump system. 5. Navigator's station. 6. 18 canvas seats. 7. Cargo flooring. 8. Aux. power plant (long-running). 9. Spare parts carried for sustained operations. 10. Unmarked (silver).
C-47A (L)	B-823			17,377	Deicer boots will not be installed.	1. 202-gallon cabin tank. 2. Static line.

Aircraft type (CAT or Leased)	Chinese Registration	Manufacturer's Serial Number	Army Air Force Serial Number	Empty Weight	Operational Limitations	Special Modifications
PBY-5A CAT	B-825	48441		22,436		1. Fully winterized. 2. Two jettisonable external aux. fuel tanks available. 3. 8 JATO units. 4. Fuel dump system. 5. Navigator's station. 6. Compressed air supply with pressure regulator (for rubber boat inflation). 7. Port blister padded. 8. Aux. power plant. 9. Spare parts carried for sustained operations. 10. Unmarked (navy blue).
C-46D CAT	B-840	22359	44-78536	30,959	Standard markings.	
C-46D CAT	B-842	22363	44-78540	31,329	Standard markings. Used as standby for passenger service.	
C-46D CAT	B-844	22353	44-78530	30,939	Standard markings.	

Type	Reg.	No.	Serial	Weight	Remarks
C-46D CAT	B-846	22215	44-78392	30,758	1. Unmarked
C-46A CAT	B-848	347356	43-47356	32,752	Plushed; ordinarily used as passenger plane (and for light cargo) only. Standard markings; now undergoing #40 service.
C-46F CAT	B-850	22451	44-78628	31,253	Standard markings.
C-46D CAT	B-854	33372	44-77976	32,867	Plushed; ordinarily used as passenger plane (and for light cargo) only. Standard markings.
C-46D CAT	B-856	32950	44-77554	31,256	
C-46D CAT	B-858	22228	44-78405	32,679	Plushed; ordinarily used as passenger plane (and for light cargo) only. Now undergoing #40 service. Standard markings.
C-46D CAT	B-860	22236	44-78413	30,989	Standard markings.
C-46D CAT	B-864	22362	44-78539	30,792	Standard markings.
C-46D CAT	B-866	22366	44-78543	31,008	1. 202-gallon aux. fuel tank installed in aft belly compartment.
C-46D CAT	B-870	22232	44-78409		Standard markings.
C-46D CAT	B-872	32878	44-77756		1. Unmarked. 2. 202-gallon aux. fuel tank installed in aft belly compartment.

Aircraft type (CAT or Leased)	Chinese Registration	Manufacturer's Serial Number	Army Air Force Serial Number	Empty Weight	Operational Limitations	Special Modifications
C-46D CAT	B-874	33132	44-77736	30,551		1. Unmarked. 2. 202-gallon aux. fuel tank installed in aft belly compartment. 3. Static lines. 4. Light and bell signal system.
C-46D CAT	B-876	33153	44-77757	31,362		1. Unmarked. 2. 202-gallon aux. fuel tank installed in aft belly compartment. 3. Static lines. 4. Light and bell signal system.
C-46F (L)*	B-130	22379	44-78556	30,758	Standard markings.	
C-46F (L)	B-136	22465	44-78642	31,213		1. Unmarked. 2. 202-gallon aux. fuel tank installed in aft belly compartment. 3. Static lines. 4. Light and bell signal system.

Type	No.	Number	Serial	Weight	Markings	Remarks
C-46F (L)*	B-138	22500	44-78677			1. Unmarked. 2. Static lines. 3. Light and bell signal system.
C-46F (L)*	B-146	22461	44-78638	30,968	Standard markings.	1. 202-gallon aux. fuel tank installed in aft belly compartment.
C-46F (L)*	B-148	22510	44-78687	30,927	Standard markings.	1. 202-gallon aux. fuel tank installed in aft belly compartment.
C-46F (L)*	B-150	22526	44-78703	31,063	Standard markings.	1. Static lines. 2. Light and bell signal system. 3. Dump chute 11″ x 11½″ installed.
C-46F (L)*	B-154		44-78547	30,713	Standard markings.	
C-54A CAT	B-1002	3078	41-37387	42,788	Special plush markings.	1. Quick removable seats, flight rug, draft partition, etc., for cargo use. (Cargo doors retained.) 2. Modified for easy installation of jump door. 3. Dump chute, 10″ x 12″ permanently installed. 4. Brackets for static line installed (line available). 5. Light and bell signal system. 6. Floor suitable for cargo conveyor (roller-type) usage.

Aircraft type (CAT or Leased)	Chinese Registration	Manufacturer's Serial Number	Army Air Force Serial Number	Empty Weight	Operational Limitations	Special Modifications
C-54G CAT	B-1004	36072			Special plush markings. Now undergoing #4A service and plushing.	7. Blackout curtains available. 8. Carries spare parts for sustained operations. 9. Removable flag.

*Leased from Chinese Civil Aeronautics Administration.

Sources: "Aircraft Data Report for February 1954," Nantucket Papers, and memorandum, Rousselot to French, "Registration of Fleet Aircraft," February 17, 1955, Air America legal files 1.3.5.

Notes

Prologue

1. The details for this mission were taken from an operational memorandum, "Eagle Flight," October 1951, in the Papers of C. Joseph Rosbert, in his possession, Franklin, N.C.

Chapter 1

1. Arnold to Chief of Staff General George C. Marshall, February 5, 1943, reprinted in Riley Sunderland and Charles F. Romanus, eds., *Stilwell's Personal File: China-Burma-India, 1942–1944*, 5 vols. (Wilmington, Del., 1976), 1:360.

2. The Chennault Papers, located at the Hoover Institution, Stanford University, contain only limited biographical information. Boyd H. Bauer, "General Claire Lee Chennault and China, 1937–1958" (Ph.D. dissertation, American University, 1973), surveys existing literature on the controversial airman. In the absence of detailed, reliable studies, Chennault's memoirs, *Way of a Fighter* (New York, 1949), remain the best source of background information on his early life and career, but see also Wanda Cornelius and Thayne Short, *Ding Hao: America's Air War in China, 1937–1945* (Gretna, La., 1980), pp. 27–91.

3. Chennault, *Way of a Fighter*, pp. 4–8. Information on Chennault's background—even the year of his birth—is contradictory. The problems will not be resolved until a scholarly biography appears.

4. Ibid., pp. 9–11.

5. Ibid., pp. 11–13.

6. Ibid., pp. 18–31.

7. Ibid., pp. 32–86. See also Gordon K. Pickler's excellent study, "United States Aid to the Chinese Nationalist Air Force, 1931–1949" (Ph.D. dissertation, Florida State University, 1971).

8. Chennault, *Way of a Fighter*, pp. 32–86.

9. The Chennault Papers contain a wealth of information on the operational aspects of the AVG. See also Charles F. Romanus and Riley Sunderland, *Stilwell's Mission to China* (Washington, D.C., 1953), and Arthur N. Young, *China and the Helping Hand, 1937–1945* (Cambridge, Mass., 1967). A reliable, scholarly account of the organization remains to be written.

10. For some contemporary views of Chennault and the AVG, see *Time*, June 8, 1942, p. 30; *Collier's*, July 4, 1942, pp. 16ff; and *Life*, August 10, 1942, pp. 70–77.

11. Theodore H. White, *In Search of History* (New York, 1978), pp. 132–44; Stilwell to Marshall, October 18, 1942, in Sunderland and Romanus, eds., *Stilwell's Personal File*, 1:360.

12. Books on the Chennault-Stilwell controversy, generally hostile to Chennault's position, abound. Barbara Tuchman, *Stilwell and the American Experience in China, 1911–45* (New York, 1972), is the most popular; Michael Schaller, *The U.S. Crusade in China, 1938–1945* (New York, 1979), is the most recent. Indispensable are the volumes of Romanus and Sunderland: *Stilwell's Mission to China*, *Stilwell's Command Problems* (Washington, D.C., 1956), and *Time Runs Out on CBI* (Washington, D.C., 1959). See also Jonathan Spence's perceptive essay in *To Change China: Western Advisers in China, 1620–1960* (Boston, 1969), pp. 228–78.

13. Wedemeyer to Robert C. Taylor, December 15, 1964, Chennault Collection, Albert F. Simpson Historical Research Center, Air University, Maxwell Air Force Base, Alabama. On Chennault's relationship with Chiang Kai-shek, see Brian Crozier, *The Man Who Lost China* (New York, 1976), p. 233.

14. Willauer to Norman D. Cann, December 2, 1950, the Papers of Whiting and Louise Willauer, in the possession of Louise Willauer Jackson at Nantucket, Mass. Hereinafter, this collection will be referred to as Nantucket Papers to distinguish it from the Papers of Whiting Willauer at Princeton University, referred to as Willauer Papers.

15. Interview with Louise Willauer Jackson, June 27–28, 1981.

16. There is abundant biographical material on Willauer in both the Willauer Papers and the Nantucket Papers.

17. Interview with Louise Willauer Jackson, June 27–28, 1981. The report card, dated December 22, 1916, is in the Willauer Papers.

18. Interview with Louise Willauer Jackson, June 27–28, 1981; clipping from the *Nantucket Inquirer and Mirror*, October 24, 1953, Nantucket Papers.

19. Interview with Louise Willauer Jackson, June 27–28, 1981; George Van-Deurs, *Wings for the Fleet* (Annapolis, 1966), pp. 118–20, 157–58.

20. The biographical material is from the Willauer Papers. A copy of Willauer's senior thesis is in the library at Princeton University.

21. Interview with Louise Willauer Jackson, June 27–28, 1981; Louise Willauer to the author, March 25, 1971. Sally Jackson Willauer was born on April 28, 1934, and Thomas Jackson Willauer on March 19, 1940.

22. Interview with Louise Willauer Jackson, June 27–28, 1981; biographical information in Willauer Papers. The quotation is from Willauer memorandum, February 1962, Willauer Papers.

23. Interview with Louise Willauer Jackson, June 27–28, 1981; Willauer, taped memoir, December 1, 1960, Willauer Papers.

24. Interview with Thomas G. Corcoran, April 21, 1967.

25. Willauer to Louise R. Willauer, September 23, 1943, March 18, 1946, Willauer Papers.

26. Willauer, "Biographical Data," n.d. [ca. 1960]; Willauer to Louise R. Willauer, March 18, 1946; both in Willauer Papers.

27. Willauer to Corcoran, April 5, 1947, and Willauer to Norman D. Cann, November 10, 1950, Nantucket Papers; C. Bedell Monro, president, Pennsylvania Central Airlines, to Willauer, December 10, 1945, Willauer Papers.

28. Willauer to Norman D. Cann, December 2, 1950, Nantucket Papers.

29. For postwar Shanghai, see John Hersey, "Letter from Shanghai," *The New Yorker*, February 9, 1946, pp. 82–90, and "A Reporter in China," ibid., March 23, 1946, pp. 32–36.

30. Willauer to Louise R. Willauer, January 4, 9, 15, 1946, Willauer Papers.

31. Willauer to Louise R. Willauer, January 15, 1946, Willauer Papers.

32. Ibid.; Willauer to Henry R. Luce, March 16, 1946, Willauer Papers.

33. See my study of civil aviation in China, *The Dragon's Wings: The China National Aviation Corporation and the Development of Commercial Aviation in China* (Athens, Ga., 1976), especially pp. 193–96.

34. Great China Aviation Corporation, sponsored by the San Min Chu I Youth Corps, included on its board of directors the personal secretary to Chiang Kai-shek, an adviser to the Ministry of Communications, the head of the Farmers Bank, and the director of the Central Trust. See Walter S. Robertson, minister-counselor for economic affairs, Chungking, to the secretary of state, October 2, 12, 1945, State Department File 893.796, United States Department of State Archives, National Archives, Washington, D.C. (hereinafter cited simply by SD File number).

35. Willauer to Louise R. Willauer, April 11, 1946, Willauer Papers; Norman D. Cann to commissioner of internal revenue, July 3, 1950, Nantucket Papers.

36. Arthur N. Young, memoranda, May 14, August 3, 1946, Papers of Arthur N. Young, Hoover Institution, Stanford University, Stanford, Calif.

37. Willauer to Louise R. Willauer, March 4, 1946, Willauer Papers. Olmstead wrote to me May 17, 1967, about the distribution problems and the origins of the airline: "I went to China on a survey trip in October 1945 and spent about six weeks touring China. We visited Kweilin, Chungking, Canton, Hengyang, Changshaw, Tientsin, Peking, Hankow and Shanghai. At that time a severe famine was in progress in the central valley, i.e. Hengyang and Changshaw areas. In these communities the people had eaten all the grass and foilage and were eating clay to fill their stomachs. Of course, hundreds were found dead of starvation each morning. At the same time there was a substantial surplus of rice in Szechwan Province and hundreds of thousands of tons of UNRRA supplies were arriving in Shanghai and being stored in godowns (warehouses) because of inadequate distribution facilities.

I came back to the United States about mid December 1945 and, after reviewing the situation, returned to Shanghai in February 1946 as Director of Operations of UNRRA to endeavor to solve this part of the problem. . . . Shortly after my arrival I recommended that top priority be given to a transportation system consisting of CNRRA Air Transport, CNRRA Water Transport and CNRRA Highway Transport. . . . General Chennault and Whiting Willauer were in Shanghai at the time and I called upon them to provide the know-how for establishing and operating CNRRA Air Transport."

38. Willauer to Louise R. Willauer, March 15, 18, April 11, 15, 25, 1946, Willauer Papers; Willauer to Corcoran, April 5, 1947, Nantucket Papers. Contrary to rumor, Soong at no time had a financial interest in CAT. For Soong's background and insight into the workings of the Nationalist government, see Parks M. Coble, Jr., *The Shanghai Capitalists and the Nationalist Government, 1927–1937* (Cambridge, Mass., 1980).

39. Willauer to Louise R. Willauer, May 13, 1946, Willauer Papers.

40. Ibid.

41. Olmstead to the author, May 17, 1967; Willauer to Louise R. Willauer, May 13, 1946, and Willauer, taped memoir, December 1, 1960, Willauer Papers.

42. Willauer to Henry R. Luce, March 16, 1946, Willauer Papers.

43. Corcoran to Chennault, October 2, 1946, Nantucket Papers. In his famous attack on the China lobby, Charles Wertenbaker discusses the origins of Cat: "Arguing the prospect of a serious airline in the interior in 1946, Chennault and Willauer . . . enlisted the support of T. V. Soong and Mme. Chiang for a proposal that UNRRA provide the equipment for an airline to fly relief supplies to remote provinces. Chennault was to run the airline. Since China already had tow airlines, the proposition was opposed as wasteful by all responsible UNRRA officials, and was turned down by LaGuardia. Chennault and his old friend., Tommy Corcoran, however, continued to high-pressure LaGuardia, and shortly before he resigned as director [of UNRRA] he was called in for consultation by the State Department and told that both Soong and Madame Chiang had insisted on the need for the airline. LaGuardia reversed himself" (The China Lobby," *The Reporter*, April 15, 1952, p. 9).

44. The figure was later reduced to $1.17 million for aircraft and $505,000 for foreign exchange (*China Press*, April 29, 1947).

45. *Shanghai Evening Post and Mercury* (American edition), November 8, 1946; United Nations Relief and Rehabilitation Administration, *Operational Analysis Papers, No. 51*, "Industrial Rehabilitation in China" (Washington, D.C., 1948), pp. 18–26.

46. *New York Times*, October 26, 1946; *China Press*, October 17, 1946. For later critical accounts of CAT's origin, see William Paget, "C.A.T. —Chennault's Airline," *China Weekly Review*, February 25, 1950, pp. 182–84, and Graham Peck, *Two Kinds of Time* (Boston, 1950), p. 720.

47. *China Press*, October 18, 1946.

48. Willauer, "How CAT Really Got Going," *CAT Bulletin* 5 (February 1952):1.

49. Willauer to Louise R. Willauer, April 15, 1946, and Louise R. Willauer to her family, September 9, 1946, Willauer Papers; Willauer to Corcoran, April 5, 1947, and Corcoran to Willauer, January 10, 1947, Nantucket Papers.

50. *New York Times*, October 6, 1946; John R. Rossi (a close associate of Prescott) to the author, March 26, 1981; interview with C. Joseph Rosbert, April 26, 1979.

51. Corcoran to Willauer, October 3, 1946, Nantucket Papers.

52. Willauer, taped memoir, December 1, 1960, and Willauer, annotation to letter of July 4, 1946, Willauer notes, 1962, Willauer Papers; Willauer to Norman D. Cann, November 10, 1950, Nantucket Papers.

53. Corcoran to Willauer, January 10, 1947, Nantucket Papers.

54. Willauer to Corcoran, April 5, 1947, Nantucket Papers. Corcoran eventually settled for 27.9 percent (Willauer to Corcoran, June 5, 1948, Nantucket Papers).

55. Louise R. Willauer to A. Osborn Willauer, November 9, 1946, Nantucket Papers.

56. Willauer to Daisy Day Whiting, February 2, 1946, Willauer Papers.

57. For a fascinating glimpse of Corcoran at work as a lobbyist for United Fruit, see Thomas P. McCann, *An American Company: The Tragedy of United Fruit* (New York, 1976), pp. 50–55. See also Joseph C. Goulden, *The Superlawyers* (New York, 1972).

58. Louise R. Willauer to A. Osborn Willauer, November 9, 1946, Nantucket Papers.

Chapter 2

1. Lincoln C. Reynolds, a Pan American Airways official, to his wife, January 2, 1947, copy supplied by Reynolds; Hugh L. Woods, CNAC's operations manager at the time, to the author, April 27, 1979; Quentin Roosevelt to Harold M. Bixby, April 7, 1947, Quentin Roosevelt Papers, in the possession of Mrs. Quentin Roosevelt, Oyster Bay, N.Y. See also Leary, *Dragon's Wings*, pp. 200–204.

2. Woods to the author, April 27, 1979; *North China Daily News*, January 9, 1947; Y. F. Soo, "Improvements Urged for China's Civil Aviation Operations," *China Weekly Review*, January 25, 1947.

3. *New York Times*, January 7, 14, 27, 30, 1947.

4. McConnell, memorandum, "Civil Aviation in China," for Ambassador J. Leighton Stuart, January 15, 1947, SD File 893.796.

5. Memorandum for the secretary of state, "Re: Chennault Airlines," May 23, 1947, SD File 893.796; *CAT Bulletin*, "Anniversary Supplement," October 1947, pp. 12–15; taped reminiscences of Rossi, Burridge, and Bigony, October 20, 1978, *CAT Association Bulletin* 4 (November/December 1978–January/February 1979):4–6; Norman D. Cann to the commissioner of internal revenue, July 3, 1950, Nantucket Papers.

6. By mutual consent, designated flight equipment later became three C-47s and fifteen C-46s (*CAT Bulletin* 9 [October 1956]:4–5).

7. John Denson and Charlotte Knight, "The World's Most Shot-at Air Line," *Collier's*, August 11, 1951, pp. 35, 65–69; Var M. Green, "The 'Impossible,'" *CAT*

Bulletin 9 (October 1956):11; Burridge, taped reminiscence, October 20, 1978, *CAT Association Bulletin* 4:4.

8. Phyllis Altamire, "Reminiscences of CAT's Beginning," *CAT Bulletin* 1 (February 1, 1948):3; Thomas E. Freeman, "CAT's First Airfield," *CAT Bulletin* 4 (December 1951):5.

9. Louise R. Willauer to her family, January 30, 1947, Willauer Papers; *North China Daily News*, January 26, 28, 1947; Louise R. Willauer's movies of the arrival, Nantucket Papers. The company insignia, designed by Bruno Braga, included the side view of a "tiger-cat," a stylized Chinese sun, and an American star, all on a blue background.

10. *CAT Bulletin* 10 (February 1957):4–5; Louise R. Willauer to her family, January 30, 1947; *North China Daily News*, January 31, 1947.

11. *CAT Bulletin* 10:4–5; UNRRA, *Operational Analysis Papers, No. 51*, p. 19.

12. Louise R. Willauer to her children, February 2, 1947, Willauer Papers; Ed Souder, Jr., "Highlights in the History of Civil Air Transport," typescript, 1950, copy in Rosbert Papers.

13. Taped reminiscences of Robert Lee and Ronald E. Lewis, October 20, 1978, *CAT Association Bulletin* 4:4–5.

14. Sue Buol, "How It Feels to Work Five Years with an Outfit Called CAT," *CAT Bulletin* 5 (December 1951):8–11; taped reminiscences of Sue Buol Hacker and C. J. Rosbert, October 20, 1978, *CAT Association Bulletin* 4:7–8.

15. Rossi to the author, March 26, 1981; *China Press*, March 3, 1947. After arriving in China, the C-46s were stripped of 3,700 pounds of wartime equipment, and 300 pounds of deicing and other gear were added. The aircraft operated with a maximum takeoff weight of 48,000 pounds for cargo and 46,000 pounds for passengers, giving a payload of 12,000 and 10,000 pounds (*Aviation Week*, July 19, 1948, p. 51).

16. Francis G. Jarvis, American consulate general, Shanghai, to the secretary of state, April 12, 1947, SD File 893.796. See Appendix A for operating statistics, 1947–49.

17. Louise R. Willauer to her children, March 15, 1947, Willauer Papers.

18. *North China Daily News*, March 23, May 28, June 15, 1947.

19. Willauer to Corcoran, April 5, 1947, Nantucket Papers; *CAT Bulletin*, "Anniversary Supplement," p. 9.

20. *CAT Bulletin*, "Anniversary Supplement," pp. 9–10.

21. Willauer to Corcoran, April 5, 1947.

22. Ibid.

23. Jarvis to the secretary of state, April 12, 1947; Willauer to Louise R. Willauer, March 9, June 29, 1947, Willauer Papers.

24. Lincoln Au, "'Problem Base' Gets Going," *CAT Bulletin* 1 (November 15, 1947):12; Willauer to Corcoran, April 5, 1947; Willauer to Louise R. Willauer, May 28, 1947, Willauer Papers.

25. Youngman to Willauer, October 3, 1946, Nantucket Papers.

26. Willauer to Corcoran, April 5, 1947; Willauer to Louise R. Willauer, May 28, June 22, 29, August 18, 1947, Willauer Papers.

27. Willauer to Louise R. Willauer, July 13, 1947, Willauer Papers.

28. *CAT Bulletin* 1 (February 1, 1948):3, (August 1947):2, 3; Willauer to Louise R. Willauer, June 29, August 14, 1947, Willauer Papers.

29. *CAT Bulletin* 1 (February 15, 1948):2; interview with Rousselot, November 11–12, 1981; Willauer to Louise R. Willauer, September 7, 1947, Willauer Papers.

30. Willauer to Louise R. Willauer, September 14, 1947, and Willauer's annotation on the letter, 1962, Willauer Papers.

31. *China Handbook, 1950* (New York, 1950), pp. 439–74; Willauer to Louise R. Willauer, August 18, September 1, 14, 1947, Willauer Papers.

32. Willauer to Louise R. Willauer, July 13, September 1, 28, 1947, Willauer Papers; Willauer to Corcoran, June 5, 1948, Nantucket Papers.

33. Willauer to Louise R. Willauer, September 28, 1947, Willauer Papers.

34. *CAT Bulletin* 1 (January 1, 1948):2, (January 15, 1948):2, (November 15, 1947):2–3, (December 15, 1947):4.

35. Memorandum by Clarence J. Spiker, consul general, Tsingtao, to General A. C. Wedemeyer, n.d. [ca. August 1947], U.S. Department of State, *Foreign Relations of the United States, 1947*, vol. 7 (Washington, D. C., 1972), pp. 710–11 (hereafter cited as *FRUS*); *CAT Bulletin* 1 (November 1, 1947):2; *China Handbook, 1950*, p. 618.

36. *CAT Bulletin*, "Anniversary Supplement," pp. 10–11; Souder, "Highlights."

37. *CAT Bulletin* 1 (December 1, 1947):5, (December 15, 1947):9, (November 15, 1947):6.

38. Ibid. (November 1, 1947):3, (December 15, 1947):9.

39. Ibid. (December 15, 1947):9.

40. Ibid. (January 15, 1948):7; Strong to the author, July 21, 1981; Felix T. Smith to the author, February 3, 1979.

41. *CAT Bulletin* 1 (January 15, 1948):3.

42. CAT learned in April 1947 that CNRRA would terminate all activities at the end of the year (*China Press*, April 29, 1947; *Shanghai Evening Post and Mercury*, January 2, 1948; Willauer to Louise R. Willauer, July 4, 10, 1947, Willauer Papers).

43. A copy of the "Anniversary Supplement" is in my collection.

44. Willauer to Corcoran, June 5, 1948.

45. *Shanghai Evening Post and Mercury*, January 2, 1948; James Pilcher, consul, Shanghai, to the secretary of state, December 2, 1947, SD File 893.796.

46. Saul G. Marius to Brackley Shaw, quoting the Ministry of Communications, January 1, 1953, Air America legal files, temporarily in my possession; Willauer to Corcoran, June 5, 1948.

47. Corcoran to Willauer, February 4, 1948, Nantucket Papers.

48. *CAT Bulletin* 1 (February 15, 1948):2; certified statement of Chennault, April 26, 1950, Willauer Papers; *China Economist* 1 (May 31, 1948):267–68; interview with Corcoran, April 21, 1967.

Chapter 3

1. U.S. Department of State, *United States Relations with China, with Special Reference to the Period 1944–1949* (Washington, D.C., 1949), pp. 311–59; F. F.

Liu, *A Military History of Modern China, 1924–1949* (Princeton, 1956), pp. 255–60; Lionel Max Chassin, *The Communist Conquest of China: A History of the Civil War, 1945–1949*, trans. Timothy Osato and Louis Gelas (Cambridge, Mass., 1965), pp. 165–82; Angus I. Ward, consul-general, Mukden, to the secretary of state, December 23, 1947, *FRUS, 1947*, 7:413–14.

2. James Pilcher, consul, Shanghai, to the secretary of state, January 12, 1948, U.S. Department of State, *Foreign Relations of the United States, 1948*, vol. 7 (Washington, D.C., 1973), p. 25; Pilcher to the secretary of state, January 14, 1948, SD File 893.796; *CAT Bulletin* 1 (January 15, 1948):1.

3. *Shanghai Evening Post and Mercury*, February 28, 1948; *CAT Bulletin* 1 (February 1, 1948):2; *New York Times*, January 21, 1948.

4. *CAT Bulletin* 9 (October 1956):15.

5. *U.S. Relations with China*, p. 267; Souder, "Highlights."

6. John F. Melby, *The Mandate of Heaven: Record of a Civil War, China, 1945–1949* (Toronto, 1968), pp. 213–14.

7. *Shanghai Evening Post and Mercury*, March 19, 1948; *North China Daily News*, March 20, 1948; Louise R. Willauer Diary, March 13, 14, 19, 1948, Nantucket Papers; Louise R. Willauer to her family, April 25, November 7, 1948, Willauer Papers.

8. *CAT Bulletin* 1 (November 1, 1947):2, (November 15, 1947):6, (December 15, 1947):9, (February 1, 1948):4–5, "Anniversary Supplement," pp. 18–19.

9. My account of CAT at Weihsien is drawn from the following sources, not all of which agree on details: Louise R. Willauer to her family, April 20, 1948, Willauer Papers; Louise R. Willauer Diary, April 12, 13, 14, 15, 1948, Nantucket Papers; Robert C. Strong's untitled memoirs, excerpts supplied by Ambassador Strong; *China Press*, April 22, 1948; William P. Gray, "Chennault Flies Again," *Life*, June 7, 1948, pp. 13–14, 16, 19; interview with Rousselot, November 11–12, 1981. The incident was featured in a novel by a former CAT pilot: Bruno Skoggard, *China Hand* (New York, 1979). See also the testimony of General Barr in U.S. Senate, Committee on Armed Services and Committee on Foreign Relations, *Military Situation in the Far East*, 82d Cong., 1st sess., 1951, pp. 2967–68.

10. Strong, consul, Tsingtao, to the secretary of state, April 12, 1948, *FRUS, 1948*, 7:189.

11. Willauer, taped memoir, December 1, 1960, Willauer Papers.

12. Louise R. Willauer to her family, April 25, 1948, Willauer Papers.

13. Ibid.; Strong, untitled memoirs.

14. McAfee's draft of a memorandum, Butterworth to the secretary of state, and draft of a telegram, secretary of state to the embassy in Nanking, no dates, SD File 893.796.

15. Memorandum, Butterworth to the secretary of state, May 4, 1948, SD File 893.769. For American policy toward the Chinese civil war, see Tang Tsou, *America's Failure in China, 1941–50* (Chicago, 1963); William Whitney Stueck, Jr., *The Road to Confrontation: American Policy toward China and Korea, 1947–1950* (Chapel Hill, 1981), an excellent recent study; and Thomas G. Paterson, "If Europe, Why Not China? The Containment Doctrine, 1947–49," *Prologue* 13 (1981):19–38.

16. Cabot to Butterworth, February 6, 1948, U.S. Department of State, *Foreign Relations of the United States, 1948*, vol. 8 (Washington, D.C., 1973), pp. 467–71. See Cabot's obituary in the *Washington Post*, February 25, 1981.

17. Memorandum, Butterworth to the secretary of state, June 19, 1948, *FRUS, 1948*, 8:66–67; *U.S. Relations with China*, pp. 945–46; *China Press*, May 18, 1948.

18. Willauer commented, "We have concluded an operating contract for these with fairly favorable provisions." CAT leased the aircraft for $6.25 an hour and 12 percent of gross revenue (Willauer to Corcoran, June 5, 1948, Nantucket Papers).

19. Ibid.; *CAT Bulletin* 2 (October 1, 1948):2; "Air Transport Booms in China," *Aviation Week*, July 19, 1948, pp. 51–52. The two airlines ahead of CAT were Slick and American.

20. Willauer to Corcoran, June 5, 1948.

21. Willauer to Louise R. Willauer, June 28, 1948, Willauer Papers.

22. Willauer to Corcoran, June 5, 1948; Willauer, "CAT and ISC," *CAT Bulletin* 2 (October 1, 1949):6.

23. Badger, commander of United States Naval Forces in the Western Pacific, to the chief of naval operations, May 3, 1948, *FRUS, 1948*, 8:310–11; Strong to the secretary of state, April 12, 1948, *FRUS, 1948*, 7:189; *U.S. Relations with China*, p. 331.

24. *CAT Bulletin* 1 (August 1, 1948):2.

25. Chennault to General Douglas A. MacArthur, April 26, 1950, Willauer Papers.

26. Burridge, "Evacuation of Tsinan," *CAT Bulletin* 2 (October 1, 1948):2, 8.

27. William T. Turner, consul-general, Tsingtao, to the secretary of state, September 23, 1948, *FRUS, 1948*, 7:470–71; Turner to the secretary of state, October 1, 1948, ibid., p. 480; Strong, untitled memoirs.

28. *CAT Bulletin* 2 (March 1, 1949):2, (October 1, 1948):2; Souder, "Highlights"; *U.S. Relations with China*, pp. 331–35.

29. *U.S. Relations with China*, p. 335; Mao Tse-tung, *Selected Works, 5 vols.* (Peking, 1961–71), 4:287; Stuart to the secretary of state, November 6, 1948, *U.S. Relations with China*, p. 894.

30. *China Handbook, 1950*, pp. 471–72; Souder, "Highlights"; Stuart to the secretary of state, August 23, 1948, *U.S. Relations with China*, pp. 877–78.

31. *U.S. Relations with China*, pp. 333–36; Chassin, *Communist Conquest*, pp. 192–99; Liu, *Military History*, pp. 260–64.

32. Chassin, *Communist Conquest*, p. 194.

33. *U.S. Relations with China*, p. 334.

34. *Shanghai Evening Post and Mercury*, November 29, 1948; *China Press*, November 27, 30, 1948; Willauer, taped memoir, December 1, 1960, Willauer Papers.

35. Dew, XT 832, en route Hsuchow-Shanghai, to Rousselot, November 30, 1948, Rosbert Papers.

36. Melby, *Mandate*, p. 292; *CAT Bulletin* 2 (December 15, 1948):2–3. Mrs. Willauer commented on the move: "This is quite annoying as the overhaul was previously done down there [Canton], but everything was moved up here [Shang-

hai] while Whitey was away this summer although he had strongly advised against it" (Louise R. Willauer to her family, November 7, 1948).

37. Willauer to Louise R. Willauer, December 2, 1948, Willauer Papers.

38. *China Press*, December 2, 1948; Willauer to Louise R. Willauer, December 11, 1948, Willauer Papers. A copy of Tu's message is in the Rosbert Papers.

39. Seymour Topping, *Journey between Two Chinas* (New York, 1972), p. 43.

40. Radiogram, Tseng to CAT Operations, Shanghai, January 11, 1949, Rosbert Papers.

41. *CAT Bulletin* 2 (March 1, 1949):11; Willauer, taped memoir, December 1, 1960.

42. Souder, "Highlights."

Chapter 4

1. Donald G. Gillin, *Warlord: Yen Hsi-shan in Shansi Province, 1911–1949* (Princeton, 1967), is excellent.

2. A. Doak Barnett, *China on the Eve of Communist Takeover* (New York, 1963), pp. 157–80.

3. *New York Times*, July 19, 20, 28, 1948.

4. *Time*, November 15, 1948, pp. 33–34. A photo spread appeared in *Life*, November 22, 1948, pp. 38–41, that included a picture of Yen displaying the vials of potassium cyanide. The photograph of Chennault is clearly visible on Yen's desk.

5. Chennault, testimony before the House Committee on Foreign Affairs, March 10, 1948, in U.S. Congress, House, Committee on International Relations, *United States Policy in the Far East: Selected Executive Session Hearings of the Committee, 1943–50*, vol. 7 (Washington, D.C., 1976), pp. 241–68.

6. Cabot to the secretary of state, December 8, 1948, *FRUS, 1948*, 8:296.

7. Stuart to the secretary of state, November 18, 1948, ibid., p. 292; Walter Millis, ed., *The Forrestal Diaries* (New York, 1951), pp. 533–34.

8. Butterworth, memorandum, November 29, 1948, *FRUS, 1948*, 8:294–95.

9. Butterworth to Carter, December 4, 1948, ibid., pp. 295–96.

10. Cabot to the secretary of state, December 8, 1948, ibid., p. 296; Strong to Stuart, December 10, 1948, SD File 893.796.

11. Rosbert notes, November 1, 2, 3, 4, 5, 1948, Rosbert Papers.

12. *China Daily Tribune*, November 23, 1948; Combined Military Service Command to CAT, December 31, 1948, quoting telegram from Yen, December 29, 1948, Rosbert Papers; John Denson and Charlotte Knight, "The World's Most Shot-at Air Line," *Collier's*, August 11, 1951, pp. 35, 65–69.

13. Willauer pocket diary, December 28, 29, 1948, January 6, 7, 8, 1949, Nantucket Papers.

14. Ibid., January 9, 11, 1949; operational plan for Project Demonstration, n.d. [ca. January 1949], Rosbert Papers.

15. Interview with Rousselot, November 11–12, 1981; Cabot to the secretary of state, January 13, 1949, Declassified Document Reference Service Catalog, 1975, 90C; Willauer pocket diary, January 12, 13, 1949, Nantucket Papers.

16. Willauer notebook, January 6, 1949, Nantucket Papers; Willauer to Louise R. Willauer, January 14, 21, 1949, Willauer Papers.

17. CAT's contract required 6,930 pounds on each flight, 6,030 for rice and 900 for soldiers to push the rice sacks out the door. CAT, however, usually carried 8,400 pounds of rice per trip without extra charge (*CAT Bulletin* 2 [March 1, 1949]:1). The letter from Burridge to his family was placed in the Appendix of the *Congressional Record* by Representative Albert J. Engel of Michigan, 81st Cong., 1st sess., pp. A1687–89.

18. Roy F. Watts to the author, May 24, 1980.

19. Yen to CAT, January 8, 1949, and Burridge to Rosbert, January 13, 1949, both in Rosbert Papers. Burridge is quoted in Denson and Knight, "World's Most Shot-at Air Line."

20. Watts to the author, May 24, 1980; radiogram, Loane to all planes, January 16, 1949, Rosbert Papers.

21. Willauer to Louise R. Willauer, January 21, 1949, Willauer Papers.

22. Louise R. Willauer to Willauer, January 23, 1949, Willauer Papers.

23. Willauer, taped memoir, December 1, 1960, Willauer Papers. Rousselot paid Randall S. Richardson a bonus of $100 to accompany the flight into Taiyuan with another planeload of "black powder." He recalls Richardson huddling in a cave as Communist mortar shells fell around the entrance. "No money is worth this," Richardson muttered as a dead guard was dragged into the cave (interview with Rousselot, November 11–12, 1981).

24. Willauer, "Notes for Conference with Marshal Yen," n.d. [January 1949], Willauer pocket diary, Nantucket Papers.

25. Radiogram, Rousselot to Operations, January 26, 1949, Rosbert Papers; interview with Rousselot, November 11–12, 1981.

26. Souder, "Highlights," p. 33; radiogram, David Tseng to Sue Pollock, January 15, 1949, Rosbert Papers; Cabot to the secretary of state, January 28, 1949, SD File 893.7965; Quentin Roosevelt to Harold M. Bixby, November 23, 1948, Roosevelt Papers.

27. Willauer to Chennault, February 20, 1949, Willauer Papers; Denson and Knight, "World's Most Shot-at Air Line."

28. Denson and Knight, "World's Most Shot-at Air Line"; Burridge to Willauer, n.d. [February 1949], Willauer Papers.

29. Burridge to Willauer, n.d. [February 1949].

30. Stuart to the secretary of state, February 19, 1949, U.S. Department of State, *Foreign Relations of the United States, 1949*, vol. 8 (Washington, D.C., 1978), p. 136.

31. Yen to Willauer, February 28, 1949, Rosbert Papers.

32. Willauer to Louise R. Willauer, February 20, 1949, Willauer Papers.

33. Souder, "Highlights," p. 37; *CAT Bulletin* 2 (May 1, 1949):4.

34. *CAT Bulletin* 2 (April 1, 1949):8.

35. Denson and Knight, "World's Most Shot-at Air Line." Gillin, *Warlord*, p. 288, suggests that Yen had no plans to return to Taiyuan.

36. The radiograms are from the Rosbert Papers.

37. Gillin, *Warlord*, pp. 288–92; *New York Times*, April 23, 1949.

38. Gillin, *Warlord*, pp. 288–92; biographical material on Yen in the Rosbert Papers. Yen died in 1960.

39. Tong Te-kong and Li Tsung-jen, *The Memoirs of Li Tsung-jen* (Boulder, Colo., 1979), p. 514.

40. Chennault to Willauer, April 23, 1949, Willauer Papers.

Chapter 5

1. Chennault, *Way of a Fighter*, pp. vii–viii.

2. There is abundant material in the Chennault Papers on the general's lobbying activities. For a sample of his articles, see "Last Call for China," *Life*, July 11, 1949, pp. 25–28. See also Stueck, *Road to Confrontation*, pp. 127–31.

3. For Chennault's statement, see *Congressional Record*, 81st Cong., 1st sess., May 3, 1949, pp. 5480–84.

4. See Chennault's testimony before the House Committee on Foreign Affairs, June 30, 1949, published in U.S. Congress, House, Committee on International Relations, *United States Policy in the Far East*, vol. 8, pt. 2, pp. 285–326.

5. Dean G. Acheson, *Present at the Creation: My Years in the State Department* (New York, 1969); Warren I. Cohen, "Acheson, His Advisers, and China, 1949–50," in Dorothy Borg and Waldo Heinrichs, eds., *Uncertain Years: Chinese-American Relations, 1947–1950* (New York, 1980), pp. 13–52. See also Paterson, "If Europe, Why Not China?"

6. Cohen, "Acheson, His Advisers, and China."

7. Ibid.; interview with Dean Rusk, February 11, 1981. For rumors of Chennault's dishonesty, see Tyler Abell, ed., *Drew Pearson: Diaries, 1949–1959* (New York, 1974), pp. 59–60.

8. Webb to Butterworth, May 10, 1949; Butterworth to Webb, May 10, 1949; memorandum of conversation, May 11, 1949; all in U.S. Department of State, *Foreign Relations of the United States, 1949*, vol. 9 (Washington, D.C., 1974), pp. 517–23. Chennault earlier had testified: "I believe that the present [1948] Chinese Government is honest. I know many of the Cabinet members well. I have known them for many years. I have confidence in their honesty. . . . The generalissimo is a simple, trustful man. He believes in friends" (U.S. Congress, House, Committee on Foreign Affairs, *United States Policy for a Post-War Recovery Program*, 80th Cong., 2d sess., 1948, pp. 2209–38.

9. Webb to Stuart, May 25, 1949, and Stuart to Webb, May 30, 1949, *FRUS, 1949*, 9:524–25.

10. Clark to the secretary of state, June 6, 1949, ibid., pp. 526–27.

11. See Acheson's testimony before the House Committee on Foreign Affairs, June 23, 1949, in U.S. Congress, House, Committee on International Relations, *United States Policy in the Far East*, vol. 8, pt. 2, p. 260.

12. For Helliwell's wartime career, see Archimedes L. A. Patti, *Why Vietnam?* (Berkeley, 1980). For the CIA's initial contact with CAT, see notes by Irving R. M.

Panzer on the Central Intelligence Agency's "History of Air America, 1946–1971." This document is discussed in Appendix B.

13. My account of the OPC is drawn primarily from Anne Karalekas, "History of the Central Intelligence Agency," which is part of U.S. Congress, Senate, Select Committee to Study Governmental Operations with Respect to Intelligence Activities, *Supplementary Detailed Staff Reports on Foreign and Military Intelligence*, Senate Report 94–755, 94th Cong., 2d sess., 1976. See also Lyman B. Kirkpatrick, Jr., *The Real CIA* (New York, 1968); Ray S. Cline, *Secrets, Spies, and Scholars* (Washington, D.C., 1976); and Thomas Powers, *The Man Who Kept the Secrets: Richard Helms and the CIA* (New York, 1979).

14. William Colby, *Honorable Men: My Life in the CIA* (New York, 1978), p. 73. See also E. Howard Hunt, *Undercover: Memoirs of an American Secret Agent* (New York, 1974), p. 63.

15. Karalekas, "History of the CIA," pp. 11, 35.

16. Panzer notes, "History of Air America."

17. Ibid.

18. A copy of the memorandum, unsigned, on plain white paper, and without date or identification, is in SD File 893.796. There is no doubt about the document's author or origins; it obviously "fell through the cracks."

19 O. Edmund Clubb, consul general, Peking, to the secretary of state, December 20, 1948, enclosing a report on CAT's activities in the Northwest by Vice-Consul Philip W. Manhard, November 28, 1948, SD File 893.796; *CAT Bulletin* 2 (May 1, 1949):3; Amos Landman, "Feeder Routes for Remote China," *Aviation Week*, May 9, 1949, pp. 35–36.

20. Willauer pocket diary, January 6, 1949, Nantucket Papers; Willauer to Louise R. Willauer, January 14, February 15, 1949, Willauer Papers.

21. Souder, "Highlights"; *CAT Bulletin* 2 (May 1, 1949):3; "Briefcase Memorandum," n.d. [April 1949], Willauer Papers. For CAT's public (and differing) view of events in the Northwest, see Chennault's statement before the Senate's Committee on Armed Services, May 3, 1949, *Congressional Record*, 81st Cong., 1st sess., pp. 5483–84.

22. "Briefcase memorandum." See also Howard L. Boorman and Richard C. Howard, eds., *Biographical Dictionary of Republican China*, 4 vols. (New York, 1967–71), 2:747–75.

23. "Briefcase memorandum"; see also Boorman and Howard, eds., *Biographical Dictionary*, 2:468–69.

24. "Briefcase memorandum."

25. Ibid.

26. Anna Chennault, "Journey to the Northwest," *CAT Bulletin* 2 (April 15, 1949):5–6.

27. Ibid.; *Congressional Record*, 81st Cong., 1st sess., May 3, 1949, pp. 5483–84.

28. See Appendix A for operating statistics, 1947–49.

29. Souder, "Highlights"; *CAT Bulletin* 2 (May 15, 1949):6, (September 1, 1949):4; Willauer to Chennault, June 17, 1949, Nantucket Papers.

30. Willauer to Chennault, June 30, 1949, Willauer Papers.

31. Ibid.

32. *CAT Bulletin* 2 (July 15, 1949):7. Norwich, a serious New Englander with limited piloting experience, had been working hard to develop his skills when caught in weather he could not handle (interview with Rousselot, November 11–12, 1981).

33. C.Y.W. Meng, "Tin Industry in Yunnan," *China Monthly* 8 (1947):314–17.

34. Souder, "Highlights."

35. American consulate, Hanoi, to the secretary of state, March 31, 1949, SD File 893.796; interview with Frank L. Guberlet, October 1, 1981.

36. *CAT Bulletin* 2 (July 15, 1949):2; "A Chinese Tin-Lift," unidentified clipping in Willauer Papers; Willauer to Louise R. Willauer, July 11, 1949, Willauer Papers.

37. Willauer to Louise R. Willauer, July 11, 1949.

38. Chassin, *Communist Conquest*, p. 230; Clark to the secretary of state, July 27, 1949, *FRUS, 1949*, 8:461.

39. Souder, "Highlights"; *CAT Bulletin* 2 (July 15, 1949);5, (August 15, 1949):2–3.

40. Stayner to Rosbert, May 24, 1949, Rosbert Papers; *Time*, June 27, 1949, pp. 25–26; Chassin, *Communist Conquest*, pp. 225–26.

41. Clark to the secretary of state, August 15, 1949, *FRUS, 1949*, 8:489–90. Theodore A. Wahl, vice-consul at Chungking, visited Lanchow in late July. He returned pessimistic about prospects to defend the area against the Communists. The efforts of the defending armies were uncoordinated, the province was bitterly divided along historic Han-Moslem lines, and Ma Hung-k'uei was unpopular. Despite the best efforts of Ma Pu-fang to bridge the difficulties with the Han majority (80 percent), most agreed that "Han Chinese still hate and fear Moslems." Some people, Wahl reported, recalling past cruelties by Moslems, would prefer Communist to Moslem rule. Wahl's report can be found in Stanley A. McGeary, vice-consul, Chungking, to the secretary of state, August 3, 1949, ibid., pp. 468–69.

42. Clark to the secretary of state, August 17, 1949, ibid., pp. 493–94. The words are Clark's.

43. Willauer to Louise R. Willauer, August 14, 1949, Willauer Papers.

44. Tong Te-kong and Li Tsung-jen, *Memoirs of Li Tsung-jen*, pp. 546–48; McGeary to the secretary of state, August 30, 1949, *FRUS, 1949*, 8:511, and September 3, 1949, ibid., pp. 518–19; Strong to the secretary of state, August 9, 1949, ibid., pp. 523–24; Willauer to Louise R. Willauer, August 29, September 18, 1949, Willauer Papers.

45. Willauer to Louise R. Willauer, September 18, 1949; Tong Te-kong and Li Tsung-jen, *Memoirs of Li Tsung-jen*, pp. 547–48.

46. Clark to the secretary of state, August 16, 1949, *FRUS, 1949*, 8:493; Willauer to Louise R. Willauer, September 18, 1949; La Rue R. Lutkins, vice-consul, Kunming, to the secretary of state, September 3, 1949, *FRUS, 1949*, 8:519.

47. For NSC 48/1, see *The Pentagon Papers* (Gravel edition), 4 vols. (Boston, 1971), 1:82.

48. Cohen, "Acheson, His Advisers, and China," pp. 37–38; Waldo Heinrichs, "Roosevelt and Truman: The Presidential Perspective," in Borg and Heinrichs,

eds., *Uncertain Years*, pp. 11–12; memorandum by Davies, August 24, 1949, *FRUS, 1949*, 9:536–40.

49. Panzer notes, "History of Air America"; Willauer to Louise R. Willauer, August 29, 1949.

50. Dorothy Borg, "Summary of Discussion," in Borg and Heinrichs, eds., *Uncertain Years*, pp. 174–75; testimony by Gross, August 30, 1949, in U.S. Congress, Senate, Committee on Foreign Relations and Committee on Armed Services, *Military Assistance Program, 1949, Joint Hearings Held in Executive Session*, 81st Cong., 1st sess., Historical Series (Washington D.C., 1974), pp. 475–76: Tsou, *America's Failure in China*, pp. 511–13; "Mutual Defense Assistance Act of 1949," *United States Code: Congressional Service*, 81st Cong., 1st sess., 1949, Chapter 626 — Public Law 329. See also Butterworth to the secretary of state, October 21, 1949, and Butterworth to Webb, October 24, 1949, *FRUS, 1949*, 9:568–76.

51. Panzer notes, "History of Air America."

52. Ibid. George Kennan wrote to me, November 6, 1980: "My recollection is that the Policy Planning Staff, of which I was then Director, had no authority to authorize or order action by the Office of Policy Coordination, but that we merely supplied, from among our officers, the State Department's representation on an inter-departmental committee set up to advise the Office of Policy Coordination on its work." Former CIA official Lyman B. Kirkpatrick, however, wrote, October 21, 1980: "Using Kennan's memo as authority was indeed common practice at the time. This was long before a formalized procedure for approving covert operations had been established."

53. Panzer notes, "History of Air America."

Chapter 6

1. Cox to Dorothy Cox, October 4, 1949, Letters of Alfred T. and Dorothy B. Cox, in the possession of Dorothy Cox Ingram, High Point, N. C.

2. Cox to Dorothy Cox, October 14, 1949, ibid.

3. Interview with Dorothy Cox Ingram, May 18, 1980; interview with Francis A. Cox, April 2, 1979.

4. Richard G. Stilwell, "Eulogy for Alfred T. Cox," October 26, 1973 (delivered by Thomas G. Corcoran), copy in Cox Letters; Lehigh University, *Epitome* (1940).

5. Cox to the author, December 7, 1971; Cox, "Resumé," n.d. [ca. 1970], copy supplied by Francis T. Cox. For information on Operational Groups, see *War Report of the OSS* [1947], 2 vols. (New York, 1976), 1:223–25; and R. Harris Smith, *OSS* (Berkeley, 1972), pp. 28–29.

6. Cox. *Operational Report, Company "B," 2671st Special Reconnaissance Battalion, Separate (Prov.)* (Grenoble, France, 1944). I am indebted to Francis A. Cox for a copy of this document.

7. Dorothy Cox Ingram to the author, November 6, 1979; interview with Dorothy Cox Ingram, May 18, 1980.

8. Elizabeth P. MacDonald, *Undercover Girl* (New York, 1947); Cox to Dorothy Branson, May 21, 1945, Cox Letters.

9. *War Report of the OSS*, 2:454–57; "Citation for Oak Leaf Cluster to the Legion of Merit," n.d. [1945], copy supplied by Francis A. Cox.

10. Dorothy Cox Ingram to the author, May 30, 1980; interview with Dorothy Cox Ingram, May 18, 1980.

11. Elizabeth MacDonald McIntosh to the author, July 19, 1981; interview with Dorothy Cox Ingram, May 18, 1980; Colby, *Honorable Men*, pp. 74–77. Cox became an appointed employee of the Central Intelligence Agency on April 13, 1949. See James M. Harris, assistant general counsel, CIA, to Thomas A. Tinsley, Civil Service Commission, enclosing "Annex A," December 5, 1978. I am indebted to David H. Hickler for a copy of this letter.

12. Willauer to Corcoran, January 6, 1950, and Willauer, taped memoir, December 1, 1960, Willauer Papers; *CAT Bulletin* 3 (November 15, 1949):2–3. Without Chennault's knowledge, Dr. Thomas Gentry persuaded Rousselot to go back to Canton on October 12 to pick up the general's gun collection. Rousselot landed without incident, then waited at the airport while Gentry took a cab into town. He returned with the guns, and they left Canton without any problem (interview with Rousselot, November 11–12, 1981; see also Louise R. Willauer Diary, November 2, 1949, Nantucket Papers).

13. *CAT Bulletin* 3 (November 15, 1949):8; Willauer, taped memoir, December 1, 1960.

14. Willauer to Corcoran, January 6, 1950.

15. Boorman and Howard, eds., *Biographical Dictionary*, 3:51–56; Liu, *Military History*, pp. 129, 261.

16. Chassin, *Communist Conquest*, p. 229; Liu, *Military History*, p. 268; Tong Te-kong and Li Tsung-jen, *Memoirs of Li Tsung-jen*, p. 527.

17. Robert Strong to the secretary of state, November 5, 1949, *FRUS, 1949*, 9:578–79; Karl L. Rankin, consul-general, Hong Kong, to the secretary of state, ibid., p. 555; Cox to Dorothy Cox, October 19, 1949, Cox Letters; Pai Ch'ung-hsi to Chennault, October 15, November 13, 15, 1949, Chennault Papers.

18. Pai to Chennault, November 15, 1949; Cox to Dorothy Cox, October 19, 1949.

19. King C. Chen, *Vietnam and China, 1938–1954* (Princeton, 1969), pp. 201–11; Tong Te-kong and Li Tsung-jen, *Memoirs of Li Tsung-jen*, p. 544; Souder, "Highlights"; Willauer to Corcoran, January 6, 1950.

20. Souder, "Highlights"; Willauer to Corcoran, January 6, 1950; interview with Merrill D. Johnson, April 4, 1981. Severt is quoted in Victor Black, "Chennault's CAT," *Flying* 55 (February 1954):15, 45.

21. Cox to Dorothy Cox, n.d. [ca. late November 1949], Cox Letters; Willauer to Corcoran, January 6, 1950.

22. La Rue Lutkins to the secretary of state, December 4, 1949, *FRUS, 1949*, 8:620; *CAT Bulletin* 9 (October 1956):16–17; Souder, "Highlights."

23. Liu, *Military History*, pp. 269–70; Tong Te-kong and Li Tsung-jen, *Memoirs of Li Tsung-jen*, p. 546; Cox to Dorothy Cox, n.d. [ca. mid-December 1949], Cox Letters.

24. Willauer to Corcoran, January 6, 1950.

25. For an earlier account of this episode, see William M. Leary, Jr., "Aircraft and Anti-Communists: CAT in Action, 1949–52," *China Quarterly* 52 (1972):654–69, and *Dragon's Wings*, pp. 220–22.

26. John Gittings, *The Role of the Chinese Army* (London, 1967), pp. 40–44; Willauer, taped memoir, December 1, 1960.

27. Willauer to Corcoran, December 27, 1949, Willauer Papers.

28. Willauer, memorandum, "Informal Notes for Talk with H.E. The Generalissimo," November 11, 1949, Willauer Papers.

29. Ibid.; Willauer to Corcoran, December 27, 1949.

30. Willauer, taped memoir, December 1, 1960; Louise R. Willauer to Sally Willauer, November 16, 1949, and Louise R. Willauer Diary, November 12, 13, 14, 1949, Nantucket Papers.

31. *The Times* (London), November 18, 25, 1949; Willauer notes, n.d. [ca. 1961], Willauer Papers.

32. Cox to the author, December 7, 1971.

33. Memorandum, Donald D. Kennedy, deputy director, Office of South Asian Affairs, to Philip D. Sprouse, chief, Division of Chinese Affairs, "Current Status of Chinese National Aviation Corporation as it may bear upon efforts to Implement NSC 15/1 in South Asia," November 16, 1949, and Sprouse to Kennedy, December 6, 1949, SD File 893.796; unsigned memorandum [probably written by Willauer], "Background Statement to Rio Cathay, S.A., C.A.T., S.A. and Civil Air Transport, Inc. (Del.) Corporate Papers," July 15, 1953, Willauer Papers.

34. "Background Statement."

35. Ibid.

36. Willauer, taped memoir, December 1, 1960.

37. Julius Holmes, chargé in the United Kingdom, to the secretary of state, December 16, 1949, SD File 893.796.

38. Ibid.

39. Amrine, "Memorandum of Conversation," December 17, 1949, SD File 893.796.

40. Interview with William L. Bond, August 24, 1967.

41. Merchant, "Memorandum of Conversation with W. L. Bond," December 19, 1949; Merchant to Butterworth, December 21, 1949; Merchant, "Memorandum of Conversation with W. L. Bond," December 22, 1949; Acheson to Rankin, December 20, 1949; all in SD File 893.796.

42. Cox to the author, December 7, 1971.

43. Rankin to Merchant, December 10, 1949, and Rankin to the secretary of state, December 30, 1949, SD File 893.796; Alexander Grantham, *Via Ports* (Hong Kong, 1965), p. 162.

44. *Washington Daily News*, February 24, 1950; *The Times* (London), February 25, 1950; "In the Privy Council," n.d. [ca. 1952], Willauer Papers. For an American view of the diplomatic atmosphere in Hong Kong during the winter of 1949–50, see Karl Lott Rankin, *China Assignment* (Seattle, 1964).

45. *New York Times*, February 28, 1950; *Congressional Record*, 81st Cong., 2d sess., February 24, 1950, p. 233.

46. *New York Times*, February 28, March 15, April 2, 1950. Taipei's responsibility for the sabotage, officially denied, is detailed in Willauer, memorandum, "CAT Equitable Claims Against the Chinese Government," January 31, 1953, Willauer Papers.

47. Oral History Interview with Arthur R. Ringwalt, June 5, 1974, and memorandum of conversation between Acheson and Franks, March 27, 1950, in the Harry S. Truman Library, Independence, Missouri; *Congressional Record*, 81st Cong., 2d sess., March 28, 1950, pp. 223–24; Willauer, taped memoir, December 1, 1960. I am indebted to Professor William W. Stueck, Jr., for supplying the material from the Truman Library.

48. *New York Times*, April 4, May 11, 1950.

49. Ibid., May 11, 1950; "In the Privy Council," Willauer Papers.

50. *New York Times*, May 13, 1950; Grantham, *Via Ports*, p. 163.

51. *New York Times*, May 20, 1950; *The Times* (London), May 22, 1950.

52. Cox to Dorothy Cox, December 26, 1949, Cox Letters.

53. Lutkins to the secretary of state, October 28, 1949, *FRUS, 1949*, 8:569.

54. Willauer to Corcoran, January 6, 1950, Willauer Papers.

Chapter 7

1. Willauer, taped memoir, December 1, 1960, Willauer Papers.

2. Rosbert to Chennault, February 10, 17, 1950, Rosbert Papers; *CAT Bulletin* 3 (November 1, 1950):2.

3. Rosbert to Chennault, February 10, 17, March 23, 1950, Rosbert Papers; *CAT Bulletin* 3 (May 15, 1950):5.

4. Rosbert to Willauer, February 14, 1950, Rosbert Papers; interview with Rosbert, April 20, 1980; *CAT Bulletin* 3 (March 15, 1950):7.

5. Willauer, taped memoir, December 1, 1960.

6. Louise R. Willauer to her family, November 16, 1950, enclosing a report by Lincoln Sun, station manager at Mengtze who had been captured with Buol but escaped in October, Willauer Papers; *CAT Bulletin* 3 (February 15, 1950):16, 8 (October 1955):1, 15.

7. Rosbert to Chennault, March 2, 1950, Rosbert Papers; *CAT Bulletin* 3 (May 15, 1950):8.

8. Rosbert to Chennault, March 2, 1950; *CAT Bulletin* 3 (November 1, 1950):7–8.

9. Chennault to Corcoran, April 12, 1950, and Willauer to Louise R. Willauer, August 14, 1949, Willauer Papers; interview with Corcoran, April 21, 1967.

10. *CAT Bulletin* 3 (May 15, 1950):1; Rosbert to Chennault, February 10, 1950; Reese T. Bradburn, director of personnel, to McGovern, June 5, 1950, personnel file of James B. McGovern, Jr., temporarily in my possession. Brennan is quoted in Rosbert to Willauer, February 14, 1950.

11. Chennault and Willauer, "Petition to the Government of the Republic of China," April 23, 1950, and Rosbert to Chennault, March 23, 1950; Louise R. Willauer Diary, March 6, 1950, Nantucket Papers; Willauer to Louise R. Willauer, April 3, 1950, Willauer Papers.

12. Rosbert to Chennault, March 23, 1950, and Chennault and Willauer, "Petition."

13. Julius Holmes, chargé in the United Kingdom, to the secretary of state, December 16, 1949, SD File 893.796; Corcoran to Willauer, December 18, 1949, Willauer Papers.

14. Panzer notes, "History of Air America."

15. Ibid.

16. Louise R. Willauer Diary, January 29, February 1, 8, 11, March 4, 1950, Nantucket Papers.

17. Panzer notes, "History of Air America."

18. Ibid.

19. "Report by the National Security Council on the Position of the United States with Respect to Indochina" [NSC 64], February 27, 1950, *Pentagon Papers* (Gravel edition), 1:361–62. See ibid., pp. 82–83, for discussion of the document.

20. Rusk to Major General James H. Burns, March 7, 1950, and General Omar N. Bradley to Secretary of Defense Louis Johnson, April 10, 1950, ibid., 1:363–66.

21. *New York Times*, January 6, 1950; Acheson's speech to the National Press Club, January 12, 1950, reprinted in *Congressional Record*, 81st Cong., 2d sess., January 20, 1950, pp. 672–76.

22. Stueck, *Road to Confrontation*, pp. 146–51; Rusk memorandum, "CIA Reappraisal of Formosa," April 17, 1950, U.S. Department of State, *Foreign Relations of the United States, 1950*, vol. 6 (Washington D.C., 1976), p. 330; Bradley to Johnson, April 10, 1950.

23. Burns to Rusk, May 29, 1950, *FRUS, 1950*, 6:346–47. Rusk and Lemnitzer testified in an executive session of the House Committee on Foreign Affairs on June 20, 1950. Rusk stated that $50 million of Section 303 funds had been expended and proceeded to give a breakdown. He referred to $6.5 million "which General Lemnitzer can explain." Lemnitzer did so, but off the record. Presumably, these funds were used for covert projects (U.S. House of Representatives, Committee on International Relations, *United States Policy in the Far East*, vol. 8, pt. 2, pp. 492–93).

24. Panzer notes, "History of Air America"; "Statement of Account with CATI," June 28, 1954, Air America legal files 1.3.2 (these files are temporarily in my possession); Willauer, "Working Paper — CAT — 15 March to 15 June 1950," April 9, 1950, Willauer Papers.

25. Panzer notes, "History of Air America"; Willauer to Corcoran, July 1, 1962, Nantucket Papers; interview with George A. Doole, Jr., April 21, 1980.

26. "Fleet Registration and Serial Numbers," May 18, 1950, and Corcoran to Chennault, July 10, 1950, Willauer Papers; Rosbert to Chennault, February 17, 1950, and Grundy to Rosbert, February 27, 1950, Rosbert Papers.

27. Willauer to Louise R. Willauer, April 1, 3, 1950, Willauer Papers.

28. Willauer, "Working Paper," and Chennault to Corcoran, April 12, 1950, Willauer Papers.

29. Ibid.

30. Ibid.; Chennault and Willauer, "Petition," and "Summary of a Report on the Progress Made in CAT's Appeal to the Chinese Government for Financial Aid," May 14, 1950, Rosbert Papers.

31. Tong Te-kong and Li Tsung-jen, *Memoirs of Li Tsung-jen*, pp. 544–45; John J. Macdonald, consul general at Taipei, to the secretary of state, November 23, 1949, *FRUS, 1949*, 8:605–6; Chennault to Rosbert, April 28, 1950, Rosbert Papers.

32. Chassin, *Communist Conquest*, p. 237; Chennault to Rosbert, April 28, 1950, and Rosbert to Chennault, May 1, 1950, Rosbert Papers.

33. Strong to the secretary of state, April 27, 1950, *FRUS, 1950*, 6:335–39; Willauer to Louise R. Willauer, May 1, 1950, Willauer Papers; Major General John M. Weilert, vice-commander, Far East Air Forces, to CAT, May 16, 1950, Rosbert Papers.

34. Willauer to L. K. Taylor, April 25, 1950, and Willauer to Louise R. Willauer, May 1, 1950, Willauer Papers; *CAT Bulletin* 3 (July 1, 1950):5, 13–14; Burridge to Chennault, June 20, 1950, Rosbert Papers; Louise R. Willauer Diary, June 6, 7, 8, 1950, Nantucket Papers.

35. "Record of an Interdepartmental Meeting on the Far East at the Department of State," May 11, 1950, *FRUS, 1950*, 6:87–91; John H. Ohly, deputy director of the Mutual Defense Assistance Program, to Lemnitzer, June 1, 1950, ibid., pp. 98–100; Stueck, *Road to Confrontation*, p. 148.

36. Panzer notes, "History of Air America."

37. Ibid.; Houston, testimony, Select Committee to Study Governmental Operations with Respect to Intelligence Activities, *Foreign and Military Intelligence*, Final Report of the Committee, 94th Cong., 2d sess., 1976, pp. 221–22.

38. Panzer notes, "History of Air America."

39. Ibid.; CAT Incorporated, "Statement of Account with CATI," June 28, 1954, Air America legal files 1.3.2; Willauer to the board of directors, CAT Incorporated, September 13, 1951, copy in the Papers of Clarence H. Schildhauer, in possession of the Schildhauer family, Owings Mills, Md.

40. Purchase agreement of October 26, 1949, and Youngman to Willauer, enclosing memorandum of settlement with L. K. Taylor, November 20, 1951, Nantucket Papers. Available records do not explain why the figures total 100.04 percent.

41. Samuel Becker, attorney for Corcoran, to Robert M. Beckman, attorney for Louise Willauer Jackson, October 27, 1965, and Wang Wen-san to Louise Willauer Jackson, December 28, 1968, Nantucket Papers; interview with Louise Willauer Jackson, June 21, 1981; Houston, testimony, *Foreign and Military Intelligence*, pp. 221–22.

42. Chennault to Corcoran, July 18, 1950, Willauer Papers.

Chapter 8

1. "Affidavit of Whiting Willauer" (drawn up by Corcoran and Willauer), July 13, 1959, and Corcoran to Willauer, July 18, 1959, Nantucket Papers.

2. CAT Incorporated to Willauer, July 10, 1950, Willauer Papers.

3. Rosbert to Willauer, January 23, 1951, Rosbert Papers; interview with Rosbert, April 26, 1979. For Rosbert's epic tale of survival after the crash in the Himalayas, see his "Only God Knew the Way," *Saturday Evening Post*, February 12, 1944, pp. 11ff.

4. Willauer to Louise R. Willauer, July 20, 28, 1950, Willauer Papers.

5. Willauer to Chennault, August 25, 1950, Rosbert Papers; Willauer, taped memoir, December 1, 1960, Willauer Papers.

6. Stueck, *Road to Confrontation*, pp. 183–84; Truman Diary, June 30, 1950, in Robert H. Ferrell, ed., *Off the Record: The Private Papers of Harry S. Truman* (New York, 1980), p. 185; Burridge to Chennault, July 27, 1950, Rosbert Papers; Willauer to Louise R. Willauer, August 6, 1950, Nantucket Papers.

7. Annis G. Thompson, *The Greatest Airlift* (Tokyo, 1954), pp. 1–11.

8. Willauer to Corcoran and Brennan, August 25, 1950, Nantucket Papers; Joseph E. Weiss, "History of the 374th Troop Carrier Wing (Heavy)," Albert F. Simpson Historical Research Center, Air University, Maxwell Air Force Base, Ala.

9. Lt. Gen. George E. Stratemeyer, commanding general, FEAF, to Chennault, October 8, 1950, Chennault Papers; Rosbert to executive management committee, September 20, 1950, and Rosbert to Willauer, October 7, 1950, Rosbert Papers.

10. Rosbert to executive management committee, September 20, 1950.

11. Rosbert to executive management committee, October 3, 1950, Rosbert Papers; *Hong Kong Standard*, October 9, November 7, 1950.

12. Rosbert to executive management committee, October 3, 1950.

13. Ibid.

14. Rosbert to Willauer, October 7, 1950, Rosbert Papers; interviews with Rosbert, April 26, 1979 and April 20, 1980; *Hong Kong Standard*, October 9, 1950.

15. Rosbert to executive management committee, October 31, 1950, Rosbert Papers; interview with Eddie F. Sims, April 12, 1981.

16. Rosbert to executive management committee, October 16, 1950, and Rosbert to Willauer, October 7, 1950, Rosbert Papers.

17. Rosbert to executive management committee, October 31, 1950; Thompson, *Greatest Airlift*, p. 449.

18. Rosbert to executive management committee, October 31, 1950. The description of operations is taken from Thompson, *Greatest Airlift*, and Robert F. Futrell, *The United States Air Force in Korea, 1950–1953* (New York, 1961).

19. Thompson, *Greatest Airlift*, pp. 11–12, 400; William H. Tunner, *Over the Hump* (New York, 1964).

20. James Holt, "Sojourn at Ashiya," *CAT Bulletin* 4 (June 1951):3; Rosbert to executive management committee, November 20, 1950, Rosbert Papers.

21. Rosbert to executive management committee, November 20, December 2, 1950, Rosbert Papers. FEAF also had a spare parts problem. See Tunner, *Over the Hump*, pp. 250–51.

22. Matthew B. Ridgway, *The Korean War* (New York, 1967), p. 73.

23. Thompson, *Greatest Airlift*, pp. 57–58.

24. The story of the marines is best told by Lynn Montross and Nicholas A. Canzona, *The Chosin Reservoir Campaign*, vol. 3 of *U.S. Marine Operations in Korea, 1950–1953* (Washington, D.C., 1957).

25. Tunner, *Over the Hump*, p. 256.

26. Thompson, *Greatest Airlift*, pp. 58–63; Futrell, *USAF in Korea*, pp. 238–42.

27. Rosbert to executive management committee, December 18, 1950, Rosbert Papers. The accident was blamed on pilot error, and DuPree was fired (interview with Rousselot, November 11–12, 1981).

28. Rosbert to executive management committee, December 18, 1950; *Hong Kong Standard*, December 10, 1950; interview with Sims, April 12, 1981. On Heising's background, see Gregory Boyington, *Baa Baa Black Sheep* (New York, 1958), pp. 23–27.

29. The statistics are from Futrell, *USAF in Korea*, p. 241. Thompson, *Greatest Airlift*, pp. 58–63, gives slightly different figures.

30. Thompson, *Greatest Airlift*, p. 450; Weiss, "History of the 374th Troop Carrier Wing."

31. Interview with Hans V. Tofte, March 28, 1982.

32. Ibid. A more complete account of Tofte's activities in Japan and Korea can be found in Joseph C. Goulden, *Korea: The Untold Story of the War* (New York, 1982), pp. 464–75.

33. Interview with Tofte, March 28, 1982; Niemcyzk to the author, August 4, 1982.

34. Interview with Tofte, March 28, 1982; Rosbert to executive management committee, September 20, 1950.

35. Interview with Tofte, March 28, 1982; interview with Rousselot, April 1, 1982.

36. Interview with Tofte, March 28, 1982; Tofte to the author, May 2, 1982.

37. Thompson, *Greatest Airlift*, p. 454; Tunner to Willauer, January 19, 1951, published in *CAT Bulletin* 4 (February 1951):cover.

38. Tofte to the author, March 8, 1982.

Chapter 9

1. Karalekas, "History of the CIA," pp. 31–32; Colby, *Honorable Men*, p. 104.

2. Karalekas, "History of the CIA," pp. 11–12, 36–38; Kirkpatrick, *Real CIA*, p. 90.

3. David Atlee Phillips, *The Night Watch* (New York, 1977), pp. 96–97, 123–24; Joseph B. Smith, *Portrait of a Cold Warrior* (New York, 1976), pp. 76–77 and passim; Colby, *Honorable Men*, p. 147; *New York Times*, July 24, 1967; interview with a retired intelligence officer. For a glimpse of Stilwell, see his testimony in U.S. Congress, Senate, Select Committee on Intelligence, *National Intelligence and Reform Act of 1978*, 95th Cong. 2d sess., 1978, pp. 308–21.

4. Cox to his family, September 25, 1950, copy supplied by Francis A. Cox; interview with a retired intelligence officer.

5. Ridgway, *Korean War*, p. 99; Davies, memorandum, January 23, 1951, U.S. Department of State, *Foreign Relations of the United States, 1951*, vol. 1 (Washington, D.C., 1979), pp. 7–20.

6. W. Stuart Symington, "Report to the National Security Council: Recommended Policies and Actions in Light of the Grave World Situation," January 11, 1951, *FRUS, 1951*, 1:7–20.

7. Ridgway, *Korean War*, p. 100; U.S. Congress, Senate, Committee on Armed Services and Committee on Foreign Relations, *Military Situation in the Far East*, 82d Cong., 1st sess., 1951, p. 732.

8. Interview with a retired intelligence officer; Powers, *Man Who Kept the Secrets*, p. 81.

9. For the background of this episode, see John F. Cady, *A History of Modern Burma* (Ithaca, N.Y., 1958); Robert H. Taylor, "Foreign and Domestic Consequences of the KMT Intervention in Burma," *Data Paper Number 93* (Southeast Asia Program, Department of Asian Studies, Cornell University, 1973), an excellent study; Kenneth Ray Young, "Nationalist Chinese Troops in Burma — Obstacle in Burma's Foreign Relations: 1949– 1961" (Ph.D. dissertation, New York University, 1970); Oliver E. Clubb, Jr., "The Effects of Chinese Nationalist Military Activities in Burma on Burmese Foreign Policy" (Rand Corporation Study P-1595-RC, January 20, 1959); and David Wise and Thomas B. Ross, *The Invisible Government* (New York, 1964), pp. 129– 35. There is extensive documentation on the incident in Government of the Union of Burma, Ministry of Information, *Kuomintang Aggression against Burma* (Rangoon, 1953), copy available in the library of the Department of State, Washington, D.C.

10. CAT's early role can be seen in a series of radiograms, February 1951, in the Rosbert Papers; see also Cox to Joseph Brent, an American aid official in Bangkok, May 5, 1951, Rosbert Papers. The information on Joost is from Richard Dunlop, *Behind Japanese Lines: With the OSS in Burma* (Chicago, 1974), p. 315; Daniel Mudrinich to the author, January 25, 1981; and Joseph E. Lazarsky to the author, March 17, 1981. An interesting glimpse of Sea Supply can be caught in an article headlined "IRS vs. CIA," *Wall Street Journal*, April 18, 1980.

11. Interview with E. C. Kirkpatrick, August 24, 1980.

12. Burma, *Kuomintang Aggression*, pp. 13– 14.

13. Ibid.

14. Key to the secretary of state, August 15, 1951, *Foreign Relations of the United States, 1951*, vol. 6 (Washington, D.C., 1977), pp. 288– 89.

15. Rusk to Key, August 22, 1951, ibid., pp. 289– 90; memorandum of conversation by Deputy Assistant Secretary of State for Far Eastern Affairs Merchant, August 10, 1951, ibid., pp. 287– 88. Ambassador Key wrote to me, May 20, 1980: "Subsequently, I was informed that the reason that I was misled was that this would make it easier for me to hide the truth!"

16. Topping, *Journey between Two Chinas*, pp. 129– 30.

17. Memorandum by Merchant, November 28, 1951, *FRUS, 1951*, 6:316– 17.

18. William R. Corson, *The Armies of Ignorance* (New York, 1977), p. 313; interview with a retired intelligence officer.

19. Joint Strategic Plans Committee to the Joint Chiefs of Staff, "Courses of Action Relative to Communist China and Korea," February 16, 1951, and Joint Intelligence Group, "Estimate of the Effectiveness of Anti-Communist Guerrilla Operations in China," February 19, 1951; both in U.S. Joint Chiefs of Staff, *Records of the Joint Chiefs of Staff*, pt. 2, 1946– 53, "The Far East," microfilm edition

(Washington, D.C., 1979). The Chennault articles appeared in *New York Herald Tribune*, March 26, 27, 28, 29, 30, April 1, 1951.

20. Smith, *Portrait of a Cold Warrior*, p. 77; Smith, *OSS*, p. 265; interview with Rosbert, April 13, 1980.

21. Interview with Rousselot, November 11–12, 1981; interviews with several retired intelligence officers.

22. Interview with Rousselot, November 11–12, 1981.

23. Ibid.

24. Ibid., and interviews with Kirkpatrick, April 26, 1980, Sims, April 12, 1981, and Rosbert, April 26, 1979. The quote is from Sims.

25. Interviews with Hugh H. Hicks, August 24, 1980, and H. Y. King (in Taipei), March 1, 1980.

26. Interview with a retired intelligence officer; Roy F. Watts to the author, May 24, 1980; "First Amended Complaint," May 10, 1977, *Roy F. Watts* v. *United States of America, et al.*, civil action 76-0385, United States District Court for the District of Columbia.

27. Rosbert journal, March 22, 1952, and Chennault to Rosbert, April 1952, in Rosbert Papers; interview with Rousselot, November 11–12, 1981.

28. Interview with Rousselot, November 11–12, 1981; interview with a retired intelligence officer; interview with Watts, August 25, 1980; and Watts to the author, May 24, 1980.

29. Watts to the author, May 24, 1980.

30. Interview with a retired intelligence officer.

31. "Affidavit of Whiting Willauer" (drawn up by Corcoran and Willauer), July 13, 1959, and Corcoran to Willauer, July 18, 1959, Nantucket Papers.

32. Ibid.

33. Interview with a retired intelligence officer.

34. Ibid.; Edward G. Lansdale to Maxwell D. Taylor, n.d. [ca. July 1961], in *Pentagon Papers* (Gravel edition), 2:643–49; E. J. Kahn, Jr., *A Reporter in Micronesia* (New York, 1966), pp. 39–40; U.S. Consulate General, Hong Kong, "Survey of the China Mainland Press," November 24, 1954 (microfilm).

35. Rousselot to Rosbert, November 27, 1951; Rosbert, "Report on Tropic Operation," December 26, 1951; Grundy to Rosbert, May 26, 1952; all in Rosbert Papers.

36. Rosbert journal, March 22, April 2, 1952, Rosbert Papers.

37. Interview with Kirkpatrick, April 26, 1980. For a sketch of Mason's military career, see *CAT Bulletin* 7 (December 1954):9. Chatham Clark was chief of JTAG between Beers and Mason (interview with Hans V. Tofte, March 28, 1982).

38. Interview with Kirkpatrick, April 26, 1980.

39. Kirkpatrick to the author, June 3, 1981; interview with Rosbert, April 26, 1979; interview with Sims, April 12, 1981; *CAT Bulletin* 5 (April 1952):14.

40. An interview with Downey appeared in *People* December 18, 1978, pp. 45–46, 49–50.

41. U.S. Consulate General, Hong Kong, "Survey of the China Mainland Press," November 24, 1954 (microfilm), reporting the trial of Downey and Fecteau. The trial judgment is conveniently reprinted in Jerome Alan Cohen and Hungdah Chiu,

eds., *People's China and International Law: A Documentary Study*, 2 vols. (Princeton, 1974), 1:625–28.

42. Interview with a retired intelligence officer.

43. Ibid.; Downey interview in *People*.

44. Ibid.; interview with Rosbert, April 26, 1979; *New York Times*, November 24, 1954; *Washington Post & Times Herald*, November 24, 1954.

45. *New York Times*, November 24, 1954; *Washington Post & Times Herald*, November 25, 26, 1954.

46. *Washington Post & Times Herald*, November 26, 1954; *New York Times*, November 25, 1954.

47. *Washington Post & Times Herald*, November 25, 1954.

48. Hunt, *Undercover*, pp. 102–4.

49. *Washington Post & Times Herald*, November 20, 1954.

50. *New York Times*, August 2, 1955, September 8, 9, 10, 1957, January 10, 25, July 2, 1958, December 13, 1971.

51. *New York Times*, March 1, 1972, February 1, 1973, March 12, 1973.

52. There are rumors that Roberta Snoddy, born after the death of her father, received money toward her college education following Downey's release, perhaps through the efforts of an Oregon congressman. I have been unable to confirm these rumors.

53. CIA Special Estimate 20, "The Probable Consequences of Certain Possible US Courses of Action with Respect to Communist China and Korea," December 15, 1951, in Declassified Document Reference Service, Catalog, 1980, 16A; Harry Rositzke, *The CIA's Secret Operations* (New York, 1977), p. 173; interview with a retired intelligence officer.

54. Karalekas, "History of the CIA," p. 36.

55. Interview with Rosbert, April 20, 1980; interview with Rousselot, November 11–12, 1981; interview with Kirkpatrick, April 26, 1980; Lansdale to Taylor, n.d. [ca. July 1961]; interview with a retired intelligence officer. The PBY (B-819), flown mainly by Donald E. Teeters and Connie W. Seigrist, was based in the Philippines and undertook numerous covert missions to Indonesia and adjacent areas.

Chapter 10

1. CAT Incorporated to Willauer, July 10, 1950, Willauer Papers; Panzer notes, "History of Air America."

2. J. K. Twanmoh, memorandum, "CATI Problems," September 8, 1951, and Willauer to Louise R. Willauer, August 29, 1951, Willauer Papers; Louise R. Willauer to Robert M. Beckman, discussing the circumstances of the "loan," October 23, 1965, Nantucket Papers; Panzer notes, "History of Air America."

3. Willauer to the board of directors, September 13, 1951, Schildhauer Papers.

4. Panzer notes, "History of Air America."

5. Ibid.; Terhaar to Rosbert, April 9, 1951, Rosbert Papers; unsigned memorandum, "Narcissus," n.d. [ca. May 1951], and "Stenographic Record of Meeting Held

September 13, 1951 at 10:00 A.M. at the Willauer Apartment," Schildhauer Papers; Willauer's 1962 annotation of a letter to his wife, July 28, 1951, Willauer Papers.

6. Panzer notes, "History of Air America"; "Memorandum of Agreement between Whiting Willauer and Airdale Corporation," n.d. [ca. June 1951], Nantucket Papers.

7. Chicago Aero Commission, *Who's Who in Aviation, 1943 – 43* (Chicago, 1942), p. 376; Schildhauer, memorandum, "C. H. Schildhauer vs. CAT Incorporated," October 1952, Schildhauer Papers.

8. Willauer to board of directors, September 11, 1951, Schildhauer Papers; Thomas E. Freeman to all CAT executives and department heads, July 5, 1951, Rosbert Papers.

9. Willauer to Louise R. Willauer, July 17, 1951, Willauer Papers.

10. Willauer to Louise R. Willauer, July 28, 1951, Willauer Papers; Willauer to all concerned, August 11, 1951, Schildhauer Papers.

11. Willauer to Louise R. Willauer, August 15, 29, 1951, Willauer Papers.

12. Willauer to Louise R. Willauer, August 29, 1951.

13. Willauer to board of directors, September 10, 1951, Schildhauer Papers.

14. Ibid.; "Stenographic Record of Meeting held September 11 [1951] at 10:00 A.M. at Mr. Willauer's Apartment," Schildhauer Papers. For the Japanese domestic airline, see *CAT Bulletin* 4 (October 1951):8 – 11, and Burridge to Schildhauer, September 7, 1951, Schildhauer Papers.

15. "Stenographic Record of Meeting held September 13, 1951 at 10:00 A.M. at the Willauer Apartment," and "Record of Meeting in Hong Kong, September 14, 1951, at the Willauer Apartment," Schildhauer Papers.

16. Willauer to board of directors, September 9, 1951, Schildhauer Papers; Willauer's emphasis.

17. Willauer to board of directors, September 10, 1951.

18. CAT Incorporated, Balance Sheet, June 30, 1951, and "Stenographic Record of Meeting held at 10:00 A.M. September 12, 1951, at the Willauer Apartment," Schildhauer Papers; Lindsey Herd to the author, December 1980; Panzer notes, "History of Air America."

19. Panzer notes, "History of Air America." Colonel Johnston was the son of General Hugh Johnson, head of the National Recovery Administration during the 1930s; he adopted a different spelling of the family name.

20. Panzer notes, "History of Air America."

21. Ibid.; Pittman's obituary in the *New York Times*, April 18, 1970; Steuart L. Pittman to the author, September 8, 1980; interview with a retired intelligence officer.

22. French was profiled in *CAT Bulletin* 7 (August 1954):5; interview with a retired intelligence officer.

23. Schildhauer, "As the VP-AGM Sees It," *CAT Bulletin* 5 (February 1952):14.

24. "Record of Meeting in Hong Kong, September 14, 1951, at the Willauer Apartment," and Schildhauer, memorandum to divisional and regional directors, "Efficiency Program," February 19, 1952, Schildhauer Papers; M. D. Malloy, "Accounting for CAT," *CAT Bulletin* 6 (March 1953):9.

25. Schildhauer, memorandum, May 23, 1952, Schildhauer Papers.

26. Ibid.; statistics on revenue and flying hours in the Schildhauer Papers; *CAT Bulletin* 4 (December 1951):15, 5 (January 1952):8–9, (April 1952):1, (May 1952):8–19, (June 1952):1.

27. *CAT Bulletin* 4 (May 1951):7.

28. Ibid.; Schildhauer, memorandum, May 23, 1952.

29. Schildhauer, memorandum, May 23, 1952; *CAT Bulletin* 7 (October 1954):5, 8 (April 1955):10–11, 16.

30. Interview with Rosbert, April 26, 1979; Rosbert journal, March 7, 1952, Rosbert Papers. The CIA's "History of Air America" states incorrectly that Schildhauer and Willauer were not on speaking terms. See Schildhauer's diary, Schildhauer Papers.

31. Panzer notes, "History of Air America"; Cox to Schildhauer, August 10, 1951, Rosbert Papers.

32. Schildhauer, memorandum, "C. H. Schildhauer vs. CAT Incorporated," October 1952. Schildhauer, whose resignation became effective on January 1, 1953, returned to the Far East and spent several months as a consultant to CAT. See Cox to Burridge, June 13, 1952, Rosbert Papers.

33. Rosbert to Willauer, July 18, 1952, Rosbert Papers; Willauer to board of directors, June 30, 1952, Nantucket Papers; Panzer notes, "History of Air America."

34. Houston, testimony, *Foreign and Military Intelligence*, p. 221.

Chapter 11

1. *CAT Bulletin* 5 (October 1952):7; Weiss, "History of the 374th Troop Carrier Wing (Heavy)."

2. Dorothy Cox to her parents, February 15, 1953, Cox Letters.

3. *Hong Kong Standard*, October 29, 1950.

4. Interview with Guberlet, October 1, 1981; Guberlet to Rosbert, November 28, 1950, Rosbert Papers.

5. Richard M. Bissell, acting administrator, Economic Cooperation Administration, to the ECA Mission in France, May 6, 1950, *FRUS, 1950*, 6:809–12; Topping, *Journey between Two Chinas*, p. 138; interview with Guberlet, October 1, 1981. Smith, *OSS*, p. 165, gives Blum's background and identifies STEM as "CIA-connected."

6. Felix Smith, "CAT Captain Earthquake Magoon and Friends," *CAT Association Bulletin* 3 (August 1977):1, 3–6. Kindt's poem is quoted in Corey Ford, "The Flying Tigers Carry On," *Saturday Evening Post* February 5, 1955, pp. 24–25, 57–58, 60, and February 12, 1955, pp. 30, 99–102. Ford's article passes along many of the myths that surrounded McGovern, together with other tall tales. Rousselot wrote to Willauer on April 20, 1955: "I certainly concur with your conclusions inasmuch as that there were some tales *I* had not heard prior to the publication of the article — and as you said, 'I don't believe them now that I have read them'" (Willauer Papers).

7. The background information is from employment applications in McGovern's personnel file, temporarily in my possession.

8. Pay records in McGovern personnel file.

9. McGovern personnel file.

10. Willauer to Corcoran, January 6, 1950, Willauer Papers.

11. Ibid.; *CAT Bulletin* 3 (July 1950):2–3.

12. Rousselot to Mrs. James B. McGovern, Sr., February 10, 1950, McGovern personnel file; *CAT Bulletin* 3 (February 1950):2, (July 1950):2–3; interview with Guberlet, October 1, 1981.

13. Christopher Robbins, *Air America* (New York, 1979), p. 53; "Remarks on the Situation in China by Consul General McConaughy at the Inter-departmental Meeting on the Far East," June 1, 1950, *FRUS, 1950*, 6:352–56.

14. Smith, "CAT Captain Earthquake Magoon."

15. McGovern personnel file.

16. Topping, *Journey between Two Chinas*, p. 110.

17. Lucien Bodard, *The Quicksand War: Prelude to Vietnam*, trans. Patrick O'Brien (Boston, 1967), pp. 71–85; interview with Guberlet, October 1, 1981.

18. Interview with Guberlet, October 1, 1981; U.S. Mutual Security Agency, *Dateline Saigon* (Washington, D.C., 1952); "Flight Time Record," McGovern personnel file.

19. Interview with Guberlet, October 1, 1981.

20. Blum is quoted in *Pentagon Papers* (Gravel edition), 1:73. See also Robert Shaplen, *The Lost Revolution* (New York, 1965), pp. 86–91. Events in Indochina are covered well by Joseph Buttinger, *Vietnam: A Dragon Embattled*, 2 vols. (New York, 1967); for developments in 1952–53, see 2:787–92.

21. Buttinger, *Vietnam*, 2:791–92. French Air Force strength is detailed in Annex "C" to National Intelligence Estimate 91, June 4, 1953, in *Pentagon Papers* (Gravel edition), 1:402–3.

22. Department of Defense, *United States–Vietnam Relations, 1945–1967*, 12 books (Washington D.C., 1971, book 9, p. 38.

23. Panzer notes, "History of Air America."

24. *CAT Bulletin* 6 (May 1953):20; *New York Times*, May 11, 1953, Robert L. Lovelace and Evelyn B. Simonson, "Narrative Report of 315th Air Division (Combat Cargo) Participation in French Indo-China," September 1, 1954, Albert F. Simpson Historical Research Center, Air University, Maxwell Air Force Base, Ala.

25. Bernard B. Fall, *Street without Joy* (Harrisburg, Pa., 1961), p. 107.

26. Ibid., pp. 109–11.

27. National Intelligence Estimate 91, "Probable Developments in Indochina through Mid-1954," June 4, 1953, *Pentagon Papers* (Gravel edition), 1:391–404; Buttinger, *Vietnam*, 2:792–93.

28. Lovelace and Simonson, "315th Air Division."

29. Felix T. Smith to the author, May 13, 1979; interview with Eddie F. Sims, April 12, 1981; interview with Guberlet, October 1, 1981. Guberlet reported the napalm incident to Chennault. Later he was told that the U.S. Air Force officer had been court-martialed.

30. Panzer notes, "History of Air America"; Dorothy Cox to her parents, May 10, 1953, Cox Letters.

31. Dorothy Cox to her parents, May 17, 23, July 14, 1953, Cox Letters.

Chapter 12

1. Karalekas, "History of the CIA," pp. 43–45; Leonard Mosley, *Dulles* (New York, 1978).

2. Cabell's career is outlined in *Who Was Who in America*, vol. 5: 1969–1973 (Chicago, 1973), p. 107. My account of Cabell during the Great Depression comes from an interview with George A. Doole, Jr., April 27, 1980. Peter Wyden, *Bay of Pigs* (New York, 1979), and Phillips, *Night Watch*, contain unflattering accounts of Cabell's career. A retired intelligence officer, who agreed to provide background information, was more complimentary.

3. Interview with Doole, April 27, 1980; interview with a retired intelligence officer.

4. The background of the problem is detailed in Saul G. Marius to Brackley Shaw, January 19, 1953, Air America legal files 1.3.1.

5. Henry Yuan, "Memorandum," July 6, 1952, ibid.

6. Shaw, memorandum, "Suggested Organization of Chinese Company," August 8, 1952, ibid.

7. Ward French to Willauer, May 7, 1953, ibid.; Willauer's draft of a proposal for Chen Cheng, president of the Executive Yuan, n.d. [ca. April 1953], Willauer Papers.

8. Willauer to Louise R. Willauer, June 2, 1953, Willauer Papers.

9. Pittman, "Report to Board of Directors on Results of Field Trip, May 27–July 15, 1953," n.d. [ca. July 1953], Willauer Papers; Leary, "Aircraft and Anti-Communists."

10. Pittman, "Report," and Willauer to P. Y. Hsu and R. C. Chen, May 16, 1953, Willauer Papers.

11. Pittman, "Report"; Twanmoh to Premier Chen Cheng and Wang Shih-chieh, secretary-general, Office of the President, May 27, 1953, Willauer Papers.

12. A copy of the note is in Pittman, "Report." See also Karl L. Rankin to the secretary of state, "Negotiations with Foreign Ministry on Status of Civil Air Transport (CAT) Airline," June 29, 1953, copy in Nantucket Papers.

13. Willauer to Louise R. Willauer, June 19, 1953, Willauer Papers.

14. Pittman, "Report."

15. Willauer to Louise R. Willauer, June 9, 1953, Willauer Papers.

16. Dorothy Cox to her parents, July 1, 1953, Cox Letters; Willauer, taped memoir, December 1, 1960, Willauer Papers; "Minutes of Meeting of Board of Directors of CAT Incorporated," February 15, 1954, Nantucket Papers; interview with Louise Willauer Jackson, June 28, 1982. The CIA's "History of Air America," according to the Panzer notes, incorrectly states that Willauer was fired in June 1952 by CAT Incorporated's board of directors.

17. Willauer to Louise R. Willauer, June 19, 1953.

18. Dorothy Cox to her parents, July 1, 1953.

19. Doole's background is sketched in *CAT Bulletin* 7 (September 1954):4. See also Victor Marchetti and John D. Marks, *The CIA and the Cult of Intelligence* (New York, 1974), pp. 150–53.

20. Interview with Doole, April 27, 1980; General Jacob E. Smart to the author, January 14, 1981.

21. Interview with Doole, April 27, 1980; George Kraigher to the author, June 13, 1980. For an excellent picture of Pan American's Western Division during the early 1930s, see Francis Jacobs, "Brownsville, Texas, 1933," in Horace Brock, ed., *More About Pan Am* (Lunenburg, Vt., 1980), pp. 21–31.

22. Interview with Doole, April 27, 1980; John C. Leslie to the author, April 13, 1979; Panzer notes, "History of Air America."

23. Panzer notes, "History of Air America."

24. Ibid.; interview with Doole, April 27, 1980; Doole to the author, August 14, 1980.

25. Panzer notes, "History of Air America."

26. Ibid.; interview with Doole, January 26, 1979.

27. Interviews with Doole, January 26, 1979, April 21, 27, 1980.

28. Ibid.; Pittman, "Report"; Lindsey B. Herd to the author, December 1980; R. L. Orlowski to Rosbert, n.d. [ca. October 1953], Rosbert Papers.

29. Panzer notes, "History of Air America"; memorandum from the management committee to the board of directors, December 21, 1953, Willauer Papers.

30. Marius, "Comments on Draft Regulations Governing Foreign Investments," July 29, 1953, and Shaw, "Proposed CAT Corporate Reorganization," August 27, 1953, Air America legal files 1.3.2.

31. Ibid.

32. Dorothy Cox to her parents, October 12, 1953, Cox Letters.

33. A copy of the Reuters dispatch is in the Rosbert Papers. See also *New York Times*, November 19, 1953.

34. Lai to Chennault and Willauer, November 30, 1953, and Rosbert notes, Rosbert Papers.

35. R. T. Kiang to Chennault, December 2, 1953, Rosbert Papers.

36. Yuan, "Memorandum," July 6, 1952, Air America legal files 1.3.1; Rosbert notes, Rosbert Papers.

37. Panzer notes, "History of Air America"; Rosbert notes, Rosbert Papers. The New Zealand government expressed interest in using CAT to operate an international air freight service. See Rosbert to Cox, March 17, 1954, Rosbert Papers.

38. Chennault to Lai, December 28, 1953, and Rosbert notes, Rosbert Papers; Chennault to Willauer, April 16, 1954, Willauer Papers.

39. Dorothy Cox to her parents, January 3, 1954, Cox Letters.

Chapter 13

1. David Rees, *Korea: The Limited War* (New York, 1964), pp. 432–33; George C. Herring, *America's Longest War: The United States and Vietnam, 1950–1975* (New York, 1979), pp. 22–23; Buttinger, *Vietnam*, 2:795–96.

2. Bernard B. Fall, *Hell in a Very Small Place* (New York, 1966), p. ix.

3. Lovelace and Simonson, "315th Air Division."

4. Ibid.; Fall, *Hell in a Very Small Place*, pp. 2–3, 303–4; information provided by Service Historique de l'Armée de l'Air.

5. Memorandum for the record, "Meeting of the President's Special Committee on Indochina," January 29, 1954, *Pentagon Papers* (Gravel edition), 1:443–47; Harry B. Cockrell, acting director of operations, "Monthly Report of the Operations Division for January 1954," Nantucket Papers.

6. I am indebted to Général de Brigade Aérienne Christienne, chef du Service Historique de l'Armée de l'Air, for a copy of the contract. Jean Pouget, *Nous étions à Dien-Bien-Phu* (Paris, 1964), p. 363, states incorrectly that CAT pilots made napalm drops on March 24. After March 22, when Admiral Arthur W. Radford, chairman of the Joint Chiefs of Staff, lifted a ban on the use of C-119s for such missions, French crews flew numerous napalm drops, pouring 770 tons on Vietminh artillery positions around Dienbienphu by mid-April. But CAT personnel did not take part in these operations. One C-119, carrying four thousand gallons of napalm, crashed on takeoff from Cat Bi when the copilot retracted the gear prematurely. Although there was no explosion, the C-119 suffered such extensive airframe damage that it could not be repaired. See Lovelace and Simonson, "315th Air Division"; Robert F. Futrell and Martin Blumenson, *The United States Air Force in Southeast Asia: The Advisory Years to 1965* (Washington, D.C., 1981), p. 19; Jules Roy, *The Battle of Dienbienphu* (New York, 1965), pp. 194–95; interview with E. C. Kirkpatrick, April 26, 1980.

7. *CAT Bulletin* 7 (April 1954):1, 4–5.

8. Ibid.; Lovelace and Simonson, "315th Air Division."

9. Fall, *Hell in a Very Small Place*, pp. 54–56.

10. Ibid., pp. 134–35.

11. Ibid., pp. 127, 133–34; Chen, *Vietnam and China*, pp. 296–97.

12. Interview with E. C. Kirkpatrick, April 26, 1980; interview with Hugh H. Hicks, August 24, 1980; Fall, *Hell in a Very Small Place*, pp. 169, 183–85.

13. Lovelace and Simonson, "315th Air Division"; Pouget, *Dien-Bien-Phu*, pp. 265, 374.

14. Information provided by Service Historique; Holden to Newell, "Squaw Flight Times — March 1954," June 21, 1954, McGovern personnel file; Lovelace and Simonson, "315th Air Division"; Stubbs, "Battle Damage — Operation Squaw," n.d. [1954], copy provided by Kirkpatrick; CAT, "C-119 Battle Damage — Indo-China Theatre," n.d. [1954], copy provided by Theron Rinehart, historian and archivist, Fairchild Republic Company, to whom I am indebted.

15. Fall, *Hell in a Very Small Place*, pp. 241–42; information provided by Service Historique.

16. E. C. Kirkpatrick to the author, April 15, 1981; interview with Hicks, August 24, 1980; Air Defense Command, U.S. Air Force, *Weekly Intelligence Review*, no. 16 (April 28, 1954), Simpson Center; Rosbert schedule for 1954, Rosbert Papers; Watts to the author, May 24, 1980; Frank L. Hughes to the author, June 7, 1981.

17. Guberlet to the author, August 30, 1982.

18. Information provided by Service Historique; Fall, _Hell in a Very Small Place_, pp. 247, 253–54, 256.

19. Stubbs, "Battle Damage—Operation Squaw"; CAT, "C-119 Battle Damage"; _South China Morning Post_, April 28, 1954; Edie Holden to the author, April 10, 1979; _CAT Bulletin_ 7 (May 1954):8. Fall, _Hell in a Very Small Place_, pp. 332–33, 346–47, and Lucien-Max Chassin, _Aviation Indochine_ (Paris, 1954), p. 213, state that CAT pilots refused to fly after Holden was wounded and did not return to duty until April 30. Futrell and Blumenson, _USAF in Southeast Asia_, p. 26, repeats the story, citing Fall's book. Kirkpatrick and Guberlet, both of whom served in operations at Cat Bi in late April, deny the story. Rousselot, in a recent interview, termed the report of a pilot stand-down "a goddamned lie."

20. Fall, _Hell in a Very Small Place_, pp. 327–28; Holden to Newell, "Squaw Flight Time—April 1954," June 21, 1954, McGovern personnel file; G. T. Ewart, Fairchild's technical representative with CAT, as quoted in "C-119 Battle Damage."

21. Dwight D. Eisenhower, _Mandate for Change, 1953–1956_ (New York, 1963), pp. 348–51; Stephen Jurika, ed., _From Pearl Harbor to Vietnam: The Memoirs of Admiral Arthur W. Radford_ (Stanford, 1980), pp. 390–416; Fall, _Hell in a Very Small Place_, p. 339.

22. Fall, _Hell in a Very Small Place_, pp. 349, 359; Pouget, _Dien-Bien-Phu_, p. 419.

23. Fall, _Hell in a Very Small Place_, pp. 361, 367, 371.

24. Stubbs, "Battle Damage."

25. My account of McGovern's last flight, which varies in some details from the one that appeared in Fall, _Hell in a Very Small Place_, pp. 373–74, is based on interviews with Rosbert, April 26, 1979, E.C. Kirkpatrick, April 26, 1980, _CAT Bulletin_ 7 (June 1954):2, and information provided by Service Historique.

26. Interview with Rosbert, April 26, 1979; interview with E. C. Kirkpatrick, April 26, 1980.

27. Fall, _Hell in a Very Small Place_, pp. 452–53, 455.

28. Holden's reports to Newell on "Squaw Flight Time," McGovern personnel file; CAT, "C-119 Battle Damage."

29. Lovelace and Simonson, "315th Air Division"; Watts to the author, February 13, 1981; Ernest W. Cedergren, "I Flew at Dien Bien Phu," _Flying_ 56 (February 1955):26–27, 66–67.

30. _CAT Bulletin_ 7 (August 1954):4, (October 1954):23.

31. Green to Rosbert, September 11, 1954, Rosbert Papers; _CAT Bulletin_ 7 (October 1954):28, (November 1954):4; contract between CAT and the French government, August 18, 1954, and "Official Statement of a Meeting Held at the French Air Force Headquarters between Colonel Bardou . . . and Mr. Kirkpatrick," September 18, 1954, both documents courtesy of Kirkpatrick.

32. Lansdale's report on the Saigon Military Mission, n.d. [1955], is in _Pentagon Papers_ (Gravel edition), 1:573–83.

33. Ibid.

34. Ibid.

35. Ibid.

36. Rousselot to Willauer, November 24, 1954, Nantucket Papers.

37. Air America lost at least eighty-four crew members in Southeast Asia between 1960 and 1975. These casualty figures were compiled from a variety of sources and reflect only the deaths of American citizens. Information on crew members who were not U.S. citizens is not available.

Chapter 14

1. *Burma, Kuomintang Aggression*, pp. 10–11, 15; Taylor, "Foreign and Domestic Consequences of KMT Intervention," pp. 39–40; Young, "Nationalist Chinese Troops in Burma," pp. 56–57, 102.

2. *Burma, Kuomintang Aggression*, p. 41; Taylor, "Foreign and Domestic Consequences of KMT Intervention," pp. 45–49.

3. "Out of Burma to Join Chiang," *Life*, December 7, 1953, pp. 60–62, 65–66; *New York Times*, November 9, 1953; Alfred W. McCoy, *The Politics of Heroin in Southeast Asia* (New York, 1972), p. 133.

4. *CAT Bulletin* 6 (December 1953):4–5, 7 (January 1954):18–19.

5. McCoy, *Politics of Heroin*, p. 133; *New York Times*, November 28, 1953; "Final Report of the Joint Military Committee for the Evacuation of Foreign Forces from Burma," September 28, 1954, United Nations Publications, General Assembly, General Series, Document A2740.

6. The totals are from "Final Report of the Joint Military Committee." Cox gives the slightly higher figure of 6,908 in *CAT Bulletin* 7 (November 1954):4. For later problems with the KMT remnants in Burma, see McCoy, *Politics of Heroin*, pp. 134–35.

7. "Minutes of Meeting of Board of Directors of CAT Incorporated," February 15, 1954, and Newell to Cox, March 25, April 2, 1954, Nantucket Papers; Panzer notes, "History of Air America."

8. McElroy to the author, September 20, 1980; Herd to the author, December 1980.

9. Schildhauer diary, March 29, 1952, Schildhauer Papers; Panzer notes, "History of Air America."

10. *CAT Bulletin* 7 (August 1954):5.

11. Newell to the author, June 8, August 1, 1980.

12. Ibid.

13. Ibid.

14. "CAT Incorporated Balance Sheet, June 30, 1951," and accompanying report, Schildhauer Papers; Herd to the author, December 1980, January 27, 1980.

15. Newell to the author, June 8, 1980; interview with Doole, April 27, 1980.

16. Newell to the author, June 8, August 1, 1980; Barmon to the author, July 13, 1980.

17. *CAT Bulletin* 7 (August 1954):5; Newell to the author, June 8, 1980.

18. *CAT Bulletin* 7 (September 1954):1, (October 1954):11; *Bangkok Post*, October 21, 22, 23, 1954; *New York Times*, October 24, 1954; interview with a retired intelligence officer.

19. Cox to Lai, February 13, 1954, and Lai to Chennault, March 1, 1954, Air America legal file 1.3.2.

20. Cox and Chennault to Lai, March 27, 1954, ibid.

21. Lai to Chennault and Cox, March 29, 1954, ibid.

22. Twanmoh to French, April 15, 1954, ibid; Wang to Willauer, April 17, 1954, Nantucket Papers.

23. French to Shaw, April 22, 1954, Air America legal file 1.3.2.

24. Cox to Shaw, May 1, 1954, ibid.

25. Memorandum, French to Cox, "Conversation with Brackley Shaw on the Evening of May 7, 1954," May 8, 1954, ibid. Shaw earlier had expressed support for the tactic of delay in a memorandum to the board of directors, CAT Incorporated, March 15, 1954, Nantucket Papers.

26. Lillian Chu (Mrs. Robert P. Finnerty), to Louise Willauer, September 1966, Nantucket Papers.

27. French to Cox, May 21, 1954, and Cox to Lai, May 21, 1954, Air America legal file 1.3.2.

28. Yuan to Cox, June 9, 1954, ibid.

29. Cox to Lai, June 14, 1954, and Lai to Cox, July 1, 1954, ibid.

30. "Minutes of Meeting of Board of Directors of CAT Incorporated," February 15, 1954; Chennault to Willauer, April 16, 1954, Willauer Papers.

31. Memorandum, Yuan to Cox, "C.A.T.I.," June 10, 1954, Air America legal file 1.3.2; Brennan to Willauer, June 25, 1954, and attached memorandum, June 5, 1954, Nantucket Papers.

32. Cox to Willauer, June 26, 1954, Nantucket Papers.

33. Ibid.; Panzer notes, "History of Air America"; Shaw to Cox, July 2, 1954, Air America legal file 1.1.3.

34. Doole to Cox, July 19, 1954, Air America legal file 1.3.2.

35. Yuan to Cox, August 16, 18, 1954, ibid.

36. Doole to Cox, August 5, 1954; Lai to Promotion Office of Civil Air Transport, August 11, 1954; Cox to Doole, August 21, 1954; all in ibid.

37. Doole to Cox, August 26, 1954, ibid. 1.3.1.

38. Rosbert to Cox, March 14, 1954, Rosbert Papers; Panzer notes, "History of Air America"; interview with Doole, April 27, 1980.

39. Panzer notes, "History of Air America"; *CAT Bulletin* 8 (April 1955):8.

40. Brennan to Yeh, September 14, 1954, Air America legal file 1.3.1; interview with Doole, April 27, 1980. When I contacted Ambassador McConaughy, he declined to comment on the episode.

41. Brennan to Yeh, September 14, 1954.

42. Chennault to Willauer, October 18, 1954, and Willauer to Chennault, December 15, 1954, Willauer Papers.

43. Duncan C. Lee to the author, November 8, 1980. Cox also stressed heavy legal expenses in a letter to the author, December 13–14, 1971.

44. Doole to Shaw, October 30, 1954, Air America legal file 1.3.2.

45. Chennault to Corcoran, November 2, 1954, Nantucket Papers.

46. Cox to Willauer, November 16, 1954, Nantucket Papers; interview with Doole, April 27, 1980; Panzer notes, "History of Air America."

47. Interview with Doole, April 27, 1980; Panzer notes, "History of Air America"; Chennault to Willauer, February 4, 1955, Cox Letters.

48. Willauer to Cox, January 24, 1955, Nantucket Papers; Chennault to Willauer, February 4, 1955.

49. Interview with Dorothy Cox Ingram, May 18, 1980; Dorothy Cox Ingram to the author, May 30, 1980.

50. *CAT Bulletin* 8 (April 1955):8; bills of sale for B-874, B-876, and B-872, March 1, 1955, Air America legal file 1.3.2.

51. Lillian Chu to the Willauers, August 12, 1955, Nantucket Papers.

Conclusion

1. Spence, *To Change China*, introduction.

2. *Foreign and Military Intelligence*, p. 255.

3. Colby to the author, June 12, 1980.

Epilogue

1. Panzer notes, "History of Air America."

2. Interview with Anna C. Chennault, April 14, 1982. The story of Chennault's final days is told movingly by his wife: Anna Chennault, *A Thousand Springs* (New York, 1962).

3. Interview with Louise R. Willauer Jackson, June 28, 1981. For Willauer's role in the Bay of Pigs episode, see his testimony in U.S. Congress, Senate, Committee on the Judiciary, *Communist Threat to the United States through the Caribbean*, 87th Cong., 1st sess., 1962, pt. 13, pp. 861–88, and *Operation Zapata: The 'Ultra-sensitive' Report and Testimony of the Board of Inquiry on the Bay of Pigs* (Frederick, Md., 1981). The CAT pilots who flew in Guatemala in 1954 were D. Bussard, M. D. Johnson, E. F. Sims, H. Wells, and W. Welk.

4. Dorothy Cox Ingram to the author, November 6, 1979. A copy of Stilwell's eulogy is in my collection.

5. For a glimpse of the air proprietary's later operations, see *Foreign and Military Intelligence*, an article by Richard Halloran in the *New York Times*, April 5, 1970; Marchetti and Marks, *The CIA and the Cult of Intelligence;* and Robbins, *Air America*, an interesting if erratic study. A professionally produced, ninety-one-minute color film entitled *Flying men, Flying Machines* details aspects of Air America's operations in Southeast Asia. The reasons why the air complex's normally secretive management commissioned this fascinating documentary remain obsure.

6. Arnold Dibble, "The Nine Lives of CAT," *Saturday Review*, May 11, 1968, pp. 44, 49–50, and May 18, 1968, pp. 50, 55–56, outlines CAT's final demise.

Glossary

AD: CAT's designation for CIA-related flying in Japan and Korea during the early phases of the Korean War.

Airdale Corporation: a Delaware corporation, formed by the CIA in 1950 to act as the holding company for the assets of its newly acquired airline.

AVG: American Volunteer Group, popularly known as the Flying Tigers, a semi-official American aviation mission in China headed by Claire L. Chennault that flew against the Japanese in 1941–42.

BOOKLIFT: CAT's designation for its contract with the U.S. Air Force to airlift men and supplies between designated points throughout the Far East.

CAA: Civil Aeronautics Administration (Chinese or American, as identified in the text).

CAF: Chinese Air Force.

CAT: Civil Air Transport (CNRRA Air Transport, 1946–47), the airline operated by Claire L. Chennault and Whiting Willauer on the mainland of China that was purchased by the CIA in 1950.

CATC: Central Air Transport Corporation, an airline owned by the Chinese government that flew commercial routes throughout China during the postwar period.

CATI: Civil Air Transport, Inc., a company incorporated under the laws of Delaware in 1949 to act as C.A.T., S.A.'s nominee in the legal battles to acquire the aircraft in Hong Kong and other assets of CNAC and CATC.

CAT Incorporated: a Delaware corporation formed by the CIA in 1950 to act as the operating company for its newly acquired airline. "CAT Incorporated" was the designation used when doing business with other U.S. government agencies; otherwise, "CAT" continued as the airline's primary business identification. (Except where noted, no distinction is made in this volume between CAT and CAT Incorporated.)

C.A.T., S. A.: a Panamanian corporation formed in 1949 by Thomas Corcoran and associates to control any assets that might be recovered during efforts to acquire the aircraft in Hong Kong and other holdings of CNAC and CATC.

CDS: China Defense Supplies, a wartime agency of the Chinese government that coordinated lend-lease activities.

CIA: Central Intelligence Agency.

CNAC: China National Aviation Corporation, a Sino-American airline that dominated commercial aviation in China.

CNRRA: Chinese National Relief and Rehabilitation Administration, an agency of the Chinese government that was formed to work with the UNRRA in the distribution of relief supplies

CNRRA Air Transport: the airline formed by Claire Chennault and Whiting Willauer in 1946 to operate in China; succeeded in 1947 by Civil Air Transport.

COGNAC: CAT's designation for the airlift of refugees from North to South Vietnam following the Geneva agreement in 1954.

DCI: Director of Central Intelligence, chief officer of the CIA.

DDP: Directorate of Plans, the covert operations section of the CIA. 1952–73.

ECA: U.S. Economic Cooperation Administration.

FEAF: U.S. Far East Air Force.

FEAMCOM: U.S. Air Force's Far East Air Material Command.

ISC: International Suppliers' Corporation, a company, partially owned by CAT, that was used to stimulate export cargo from interior areas of the Chinese mainland.

JAMCO: Jardine Aircraft Maintenance Company of Hong Kong, in which CAT held a 20 percent interest.

JCS: U.S. Joint Chiefs of Staff.

JTAG: Joint Technical Advisory Group, the CIA "cover" for its paramilitary forces in Japan, with headquarters at Atsugi Naval Air Station.

KMT: Kuomintang, the political party of the Chinese Nationalists; commonly used to designate Chinese Nationalist elements such as Li Mi's forces in Burma.

KNA: Korean National Airlines.

MOC: Ministry of Communications of the Chinese government.

NSC: U.S. National Security Council.

OPC: Office of Policy Coordination, the U.S. government's covert action arm, 1949–52. Initially attached to the CIA but reporting to the departments of State and Defense, OPC came under CIA control in 1950. In 1952 it was absorbed into the newly created Directorate of Plans.

OSS: Office of Strategic Services, U.S. intelligence agency from 1942 to 1945.

PAPER: CAT's designation for operations in support of Li Mi's forces in Burma.

REPAT: CAT's designation for the airlift of Nationalist troops from Burma/Thailand to Taiwan in 1953–54.

Rio Cathay-S.A.: a Panamanian corporation, owned by Thomas and David Corcoran and William S. Youngman, that was formed for the purpose of pursuing postwar business ventures in China and South America.

Sea Supply: the CIA's commercial "cover" organization in Bangkok, Thailand.

SMM: Saigon Military Mission, the CIA's forces in Indochina in 1954, led by Edward G. Lansdale.

SQUAW: CAT's designation for operations in support of French forces in Indochina in 1953.

SQUAW II: CAT's designation for operations in support of French forces in Indo-china in 1954, especially during the siege of Dienbienphu.

STEM: U.S. Special Technical and Economic Mission in French Indochina.

TROPIC: CAT's designation for operations in support of guerrillas in Manchuria during the Korean War.

UNRRA: United Nations Relief and Rehabilitation Administration, an international agency designed to aid war-ravaged countries.

Bibliography

Manuscripts

Air America. Legal files. In the temporary possession of the author, Athens, Georgia.

Chennault, Claire L. Collection. Albert F. Simpson Historical Research Center, Air University, Maxwell Air Force Base, Alabama.

Chennault, Claire L. Papers. Hoover Institution, Stanford University, Stanford, California. Microfilm edition available at the Library of Congress.

Civil Air Transport and Air America. Documents. In the possession of the author, Athens, Georgia.

Cooke, Charles M. Papers. Hoover Institution, Stanford University, Stanford, California.

Cox, Alfred T. and Dorothy B. Letters. In the possession of Dorothy B. Cox Ingram, High Point, North Carolina.

McGovern, James B., Jr. Personnel file. In the temporary possession of the author, Athens, Georgia.

Roosevelt, Quentin. Papers. In the possession of Mrs. Quentin Roosevelt, Oyster Bay, New York.

Rosbert, C. Joseph. Papers. In the possession of Mr. Rosbert, Franklin, North Carolina.

Schildhauer, Clarence H. Papers. In the possession of the Schildhauer family, Owings Mills, Maryland.

United States Department of State. Archives. National Archives, Washington, D.C.

Willauer, Whiting. Papers. Firestone Library, Princeton University, Princeton, New Jersey.

Willauer, Whiting and Louise R. Papers. In the possession of Louise R. Willauer Jackson, Nantucket, Massachusetts.

Young, Arthur N. Papers. Hoover Institution, Stanford University, Stanford, California.

Unpublished Works

Bauer, Boyd H. "General Claire Lee Chennault and China, 1937–1958." Ph.D. dissertation, American University, 1973.

Clubb, Oliver E., Jr. "The Effects of Chinese Nationalist Military Activities in Burma on Burmese Foreign Policy." Rand Corporation Study P-1595-RC, January 20, 1959.

Lovelace, Robert L., and Evelyn B. Simonson. "Narrative Report of 315th Air Division (Combat Cargo) Participation in French Indo-China," September 1, 1954. Albert F. Simpson Historical Research Center, Air University, Maxwell Air Force Base, Alabama.

Panzer, Irving R. M. Notes on Central Intelligence Agency, "History of Air America, 1946–1971." [See Appendix B.]

Pickler, Gordon K. "United States Aid to the Chinese Nationalist Air Force, 1931–1949." Ph.D. dissertation, Florida State University, 1971.

Weiss, Joseph E. "History of the 374th Troop Carrier Wing (Heavy)." Albert F. Simpson Historical Research Center, Air University, Maxwell Air Force Base, Alabama.

Young, Kenneth Ray. "Nationalist Chinese Troops in Burma—Obstacle in Burma's Foreign Relations. 1949–1961." Ph.D. dissertation, New York University, 1970.

Published Documents

Government of the Union of Burma. Ministry of Information. *Kuomintang Aggression against Burma*. Rangoon, 1953. Available in the library of the Department of State, Washington, D.C.

China Handbook, 1950. New York, 1950.

Operation Zapata: The "Ultrasensitive" Report and Testimony of the Board of Inquiry on the Bay of Pigs. Frederick, Md., 1981.

The Pentagon Papers (Gravel edition). 4 vols. Boston, 1971.

Sunderland, Riley, and Charles F. Romanus, eds. *Stilwell's Personal File: China-Burma-India, 1942–1944*. 5 vols. Wilmington, Del., 1976.

U.N. Relief and Rehabilitation Administration. *Operational Analysis Papers, No. 51*. "Industrial Rehabilitation in China." Washington, D.C., 1948.

U.S. Commission on CIA Activities within the United States. *Report to the President, June 6, 1975*. Washington, D.C., 1975.

U.S. Congress. House. Committee on Foreign Affairs. *United States Policy for a Post-War Recovery Program*. 80th Cong., 2d sess., 1948.

———. Committee on International Relations. *United States Policy in the Far East: Selected Executive Session Hearings of the Committee, 1943–50*. Vols. 7 and 8. Washington, D.C., 1976.

U.S. Congress. Senate. Committee on Armed Services and Committee on Foreign Relations. *Military Situation in the Far East*. 82d Cong., 1st sess., 1951.

————. Committee on Foreign Relations. *Economic Assistance to China and Korea; 1949–50*. Hearings Held in Executive Session. 81st Cong., 1st and 2d sess. Historical Series, Washington, D.C., 1974.

————. Committee on Foreign Relations. *United States Security Agreements and Commitments Abroad: Republic of China*. *Hearings before the Subcommittee on United States Agreements and Commitments Abroad*. 91st Cong., 2d sess., 1970.

————. Committee on Foreign Relations and Committee on Armed Services. *Military Assistance Program, 1949: Joint Hearings Held in Executive Session*. 81st Cong., 1st sess. Historical Series, Washington, D.C., 1974.

————. Select Committee on Intelligence. *National Intelligence and Reform Act of 1978*. 95th Cong., 2d sess., 1978.

————. Select Committee to Study Governmental Operations with Respect to Intelligence Activities. *Foreign and Military Intelligence*. Final Report of the Select Committee. 94th Cong., 2d sess., 1976.

————. Select Committee to Study Governmental Operations with Respect to Intelligence Activities. *Supplementary Detailed Staff Reports on Foreign and Military Intelligence*. Senate Report 94-755, 94th Cong., 2d sess., 1976. [Contains Anne Karalekas, "History of the Central Intelligence Agency."]

U.S. Department of of Defense. *United States–Vietnam Relations, 1945–1967*. 12 books. Washington, D.C., 1971.

U.S. Department of State. *Foreign Relations of the United States, 1947*. Vol. 7: *China*. Washington, D.C., 1972.

————. *Foreign Relations of the United States, 1948*. Vol. 7: *China*. Washington, D.C., 1973.

————. *Foreign Relations of the United States, 1948*. Vol. 8: *China*. Washington, D.C., 1973.

————. *Foreign Relations of the United States, 1949*. Vol. 8: *China*. Washington, D.C., 1978.

————. *Foreign Relations of the United States, 1949*. Vol. 9: *China*. Washington, D.C., 1974.

————. *Foreign Relations of the United States, 1950*. Vol. 6: *East Asia and the Pacific*. Washington, D.C., 1976.

————. *Foreign Relations of the United States, 1951*. Vol. 1: *National Security Affairs*. Washington, D.C., 1979.

————. *Foreign Relations of the United States, 1951*. Vol. 6 (2 pts.): *Asia and the Pacific*. Washington, D.C., 1977.

————. *United States Relations with China, with Special Reference to the Period 1944–1949*. Washington, D.C., 1949.

U.S. Joint Chiefs of Staff. *Records of the Joint Chiefs of Staff*. Part 2: 1946–53. "The Far East." Microfilm edition. Washington, D.C., 1979.

U.S. Mutual Security Agency. *Dateline Saigon*. Washington, D.C., 1952.

War Report of the OSS. [1947] 2 Vols. New York, 1976.

Correspondence and Interviews

Ames, James B., correspondence, August 24, 1980.

Baca, Olga, correspondence, April 29, 1981.

Barmon, Richard M., correspondence, July 13, 1980.

Bisson, Gary B., correspondence, February 24, 1982.

Bond, William L., correspondence, December 19, 1979; interview, August 24, 1967.

Burridge, A. Lewis, correspondence, January 8, 1979, June 15, 1982; interview, July 15, 1979.

Chennault, Anna C., correspondence, March 15, April 22, 1982; interview, April 14, 1982.

Colby, William E., correspondence, June 12, 1980.

Corcoran, Thomas G., interview, April 21, 1967.

Cox, Alfred T., correspondence, September 14, December 7, 13/14, 1971; interview, April 21, 1967.

Cox, Francis A., interview, April 2, 1979.

Doole, George A., Jr., correspondence, August 14, 1980, interviews, January 26, 1979, April 21, 27, 1980.

Fink, Jerry, interview, August 24, 1980.

Finnerty, Lillian Chu, correspondence, July 10, 1981.

Fowler, David F., correspondence, September 7, 1980.

Guberlet, Frank L., correspondence, July 2, 1980, August 30, 1982; interview, October 1, 1981.

Herd, Lindsey B., correspondence, January 27, December 1980, March 23, 1982.

Hickler, David H., correspondence, September 14, 1980.

Hicks, Hugh H., interview, August 24, 1980.

Holden, Edie, correspondence, April 10, 1979, January 29, 1981.

Hughes, Frank L., correspondence, June 7, 1981.

Ingram, Dorothy B. Cox, correspondence, November 6, 1979, May 30, 1980; interview, May 18, 1980.

Jackson, Louise R. Willauer, correspondence, 1967–82; interview, June 27–28, 1981.

Johnson, Merrill D., interview, April 4, 1981.

Kennan, George, correspondence, November 6, 1980.

Key, David M., correspondence, May 20, 1980.

King, H.Y., interview, March 1, 1980.

Kirkpatrick, E. C., correspondence, April 15, 26, 1981; interviews, April 26, August 24, 1980.

Kirkpatrick, Lyman B., correspondence, October 21, 1980.

Kraiger, George, correspondence, June 13, 1980.

Lazarsky, Joseph E., correspondence, March 17, 1981.

Lee, Duncan C., correspondence, November 8, 1980.

Leslie, John C., correspondence, April 13, 1979.

Marius, Saul G., correspondence, September 23, 1980.

McCarthy, Walter B., correspondence, February 25, 1982.

McElroy, James T., correspondence, September 20, October 3, November 3, 1980.

McIntosh, Elizabeth MacDonald, correspondence, July 19, 1981.

Mudrinich, Daniel, correspondence, January 25, 1981.

Newell, Harold B., correspondence, June 8, August 1, 1980.

Niemczyk, Julian M., correspondence, August 4, 1982.

Olmstead, Ralph W., correspondence, May 17, 1967.

Pittman, Steuart L., correspondence, September 8, 1980.

Reimer, Ward, correspondence, August 23, 1979.

Reynolds, Lincoln C., correspondence, June 3, 1968.

Rosbert, C. Joseph, interviews, April 26, 1979, April 13, 20, 1980, April 22, 1981.

Rossi, John R., correspondence, March 26, 1981, May 5, 1982.

Rousselot, Robert E., interviews, November 11–12, 1981, April 1, 1982 (telephone).

Rusk, Dean, interview, February 11, 1981.

Schildhauer, Clarence H., correspondence, February 24, April 7, 1979.

Sims, Eddie F., interview, April 12, 1981.

Smart, Jacob E., correspondence, January 14, 1981.

Smith, Felix T., correspondence, February 3, May 13, 1979.

Springweiler, Max, correspondence, May 1, 1981.

Strong, Robert C., correspondence, July 21, 1981, April 9, 1982.

Tofte, Hans V., correspondence, March 8, May 2, 1982; interview, March 28, 1982.

Watts, Roy F., correspondence, May 24, 1980, February 13, 1981; interview, August 25, 1980.

Woods, Hugh L., correspondence, April 27, 1979.

In addition, I interviewed several retired intelligence officers directly concerned with the operational use of CAT who provided background information.

Newspapers and Periodicals

Aviation Week, 1947–55

CAT Association Bulletin, 1977–81

CAT Bulletin, 1947–59

China Economist, 1948

China Press (Shanghai), 1946–49

Hong Kong Standard, 1949–54

New York Times, 1945–59

North China Daily News, 1947–49

Shanghai Evening Post and Mercury, 1946–49

The Times (London), 1949–52

Books

Abell, Tyler, ed. *Drew Pearson: Diaries, 1949–1959.* New York, 1974.

Ambrose, Stephen E. (with Richard H. Immerman). *Ike's Spies: Eisenhower and the Espionage Establishment.* Garden City, N.Y., 1981.

Barnett, A. Doak. *China on the Eve of Communist Takeover.* New York, 1963.

Bodard, Lucien. *The Quicksand War: Prelude to Vietnam.* Translated by Patrick O'Brien. Boston, 1967.

Boorman, Howard L., and Richard C. Howard, eds. *Biographical Dictionary of Republican China.* 4 vols. New York, 1967–71.

Borg, Dorothy, and Waldo Heinrichs, eds. *Uncertain Years: Chinese-American Relations, 1947–1950.* New York, 1980.

Brock, Horace, ed. *More About Pan Am.* Lunenburg, Vt., 1980.

Buttinger, Joseph. *Vietnam: A Dragon Embattled.* 2 vols. New York, 1967.

Cady, John F. *The United States and Burma.* Cambridge, Mass., 1976.

Chassin, Lionel Max. *Aviation Indochine.* Paris, 1954.

———. *The Communist Conquest of China: A History of the Civil War, 1945–1949.* Translated by Timothy Osato and Louis Gelas. Cambridge, Mass., 1965.

Chen, King C. *Vietnam and China, 1938–1954.* Princeton, 1969.

Chennault, Anna. *The Education of Anna.* New York, 1980.

———. *A Thousand Springs.* New York, 1962.

Chennault, Claire L. *Way of a Fighter.* New York, 1949.

Clark, Leonard. *The Marching Wind.* New York, 1954.

Cline, Ray S. *Secrets, Spies, and Scholars.* Washington, D.C., 1976.

Coble, Parks M., Jr. *The Shanghai Capitalists and the Nationalist Government, 1927–1937.* Cambridge, Mass., 1980.

Cohen, Jerome Alan, and Hungdah Chiu, eds. *People's China and International Law: A Documentary Study.* 2 vols. Princeton, 1974.

Colby, William. *Honorable Men: My Life in the CIA.* New York, 1978.

Cook, Blanche Wiesen. *The Declassified Eisenhower.* Garden City, N.Y., 1981.

Cornelius, Wanda, and Thayne Short. *Ding Hao: America's Air War in China, 1937–1945.* Gretna, La., 1980.

Corson, William R. *The Armies of Ignorance.* New York, 1977.

Crozier, Brian. *The Man Who Lost China.* New York, 1976.

Dunlop, Richard. *Behind Japanese Lines: With the OSS in Burma.* Chicago, 1974.

Eisenhower, Dwight D. *Mandate for Change, 1953–1956.* New York, 1963.

Fall, Bernard B. *Hell in a Very Small Place.* New York, 1966.

———. *Street without Joy.* Harrisburg, Pa., 1961.

Ferrell, Robert H., ed. *Off the Record: The Private Papers of Harry S. Truman.* New York, 1980.

Futrell, Robert F. *The United States Air Force in Korea, 1950–1953.* New York, 1961.

———, and Martin Blumenson. *The United States Air Force in Southeast Asia: The Advisory Years to 1965.* Washington, D.C., 1981.

Gillin, Donald G. *Warlord: Yen Hsi-shan in Shansi Province, 1911–1949.* Princeton, 1967.

Gittings, John. *The Role of the Chinese Army.* London, 1967.

Goulden, Joseph C. *Korea: The Untold Story of the War.* New York, 1982.

Grantham, Alexander. *Via Ports.* Hong Kong, 1965.

Herring, George C. *America's Longest War: The United States and Vietnam, 1950–1975.* New York, 1979.

Hunt, E. Howard. *Undercover: Memoirs of an American Secret Agent.* New York, 1974.

Jurika, Stephen, ed. *From Pearl Harbor to Vietnam: The Memoirs of Admiral Arthur W. Radford.* Stanford, 1980.

Kahn, E. J., Jr. *A Reporter in Micronesia.* New York, 1966.

Kirkpatrick, Lyman B., Jr. *The Real CIA.* New York, 1968.

Lampard, David. *A Present from Peking.* New York, 1965.

Leary, William M., Jr. *The Dragon's Wings: The China National Aviation Corporation and the Development of Commercial Aviation in China.* Athens, Ga., 1976.

Liu, F. F. *A Military History of Modern China, 1924–1949.* Princeton, 1956.

MacDonald, Elizabeth P. *Undercover Girl.* New York, 1947.

Mao Tsu-tung. *Selected Works.* Vol. 4: *The Third Revolutionary Civil War Period.* Peking, 1961.

Marchetti, Victor, and John D. Marks. *The CIA and the Cult of Intelligence.* New York, 1974.

McCoy, Alfred W. *The Politics of Heroin in Southeast Asia.* New York, 1972.

Melby, John F. *The Mandate of Heaven: Record of a Civil War, China, 1945–1949.* Toronto, 1968.

Meyer, Cord. *Facing Reality: From World Federalism to the CIA.* New York, 1980.

Millis, Walter, ed. *The Forrestal Diaries.* New York, 1951.

Montross, Lynn, and Nicholas A. Canzona. *The Chosin Reservoir Campaign.* Vol. 3 of *U.S. Marine Operations in Korea, 1950–1953.* Washington, D.C., 1957.

Mosley, Leonard. *Dulles.* New York, 1978.

Parmet, Herbert S. *Eisenhower and the American Crusades.* New York, 1972.

Patti, Archimedes L. A. *Why Vietnam?* Berkeley, 1980.

Peck, Graham. *Two Kinds of Time.* Boston, 1950.

Phillips, David Atlee. *The Night Watch.* New York, 1977.

Pouget, Jean. *Nous étions à Dien-Bien-Phu.* Paris, 1964.

Powers, Thomas. *The Man Who Kept the Secrets: Richard Helms and the CIA.* New York, 1979.

Prados, John. *The Sky Would Fall.* New York, 1983.

Prouty, L. Fletcher. *The Secret Team.* Englewood Cliffs, N.J., 1973.

Rankin, Karl Lott. *China Assignment.* Seattle, 1964.

Rees, David. *Korea: The Limited War.* New York, 1964.

Ridgway, Matthew B. *The Korean War.* New York, 1967.

Robbins, Christopher. *Air America.* New York, 1979.

Romanus, Charles F., and Riley Sunderland. *Stilwell's Command Problems.* Washington, D.C., 1956.

———. *Stilwell's Mission to China.* Washington, D.C., 1953.

———. *Time Runs Out on CBI.* Washington, D.C., 1959.

Rositzke, Harry. *The CIA's Secret Operations.* New York, 1977.

Roy, Jules. *The Battle of Dienbienphu.* New York, 1965.

Schaller, Michael. *The U.S. Crusade in China, 1938–1945.* New York, 1979.

Seagrave, Sterling. *Soldiers of Fortune.* Alexandria, Va., 1981.

Shaplen, Robert. *The Lost Revolution.* New York, 1965.

Skoggard, Bruno. *China Hand*. New York, 1979.

Smith, Joseph B. *Portrait of a Cold Warrior*. New York, 1976.

Smith, R. Harris. *OSS*. Berkeley, 1972.

Spence, Jonathan. *To Change China: Western Advisers in China, 1620–1960*. Boston, 1969.

Stueck, William Whitney, Jr. *The Road to Confrontation: American Policy toward China and Korea, 1947–1950*. Chapel Hill, 1981.

Tang Tsou. *America's Failure in China, 1941–50*. Chicago, 1963.

Taylor, Robert H. "Foreign and Domestic Consequences of the KMT Intervention in Burma." *Data Paper Number 93*. Southeast Asia Program, Department of Asian Studies, Cornell University, Ithaca, N.Y., 1973.

Thompson, Annis G. *The Greatest Airlift*. Tokyo, 1954.

Tong Te-kong and Li Tsung-jen. *The Memoirs of Li Tsung-jen*. Boulder, Colo., 1979.

Topping, Seymour. *Journey between Two Chinas*. New York, 1972.

Troy, Thomas F. *Donovan and the CIA: A History of the Establishment of the Central Intelligence Agency*. Frederick, Md., 1981.

Truman, Harry S. *Memoirs*. 2 vols. Garden City, N.Y., 1955–56.

Tuchman, Barbara. *Stilwell and the American Experience in China, 1911–45*. New York, 1972.

Tunner, William H. *Over the Hump*. New York, 1964.

Van Deurs, George. *Wings for the Fleet*. Annapolis, 1966.

White, Theodore H. *In Search of History*. New York, 1978.

Wise, David, and Thomas B. Ross. *The Invisible Government*. New York, 1964.

Wyden, Peter. *Bay of Pigs*. New York, 1979.

Young, Arthur N. *China and the Helping Hand, 1937–1945*. Cambridge, Mass., 1967.

Articles

Black, Victor. "Chennault's CAT." *Flying* 55 (February 1954):15, 45.

Cedergren, Ernest W. "I Flew at Dien Bien Phu." *Flying* 56 (February 1955):26–27, 66–67.

Christian, George C. "LST Base Keeps Chennault Line Flying." *Aviation Week*, February 2, 1953, pp. 64–66, 68, 70, 72.

Denson, John, and Charlotte Knight. "The World's Most Shot-at Air Line." *Collier's*, August 11, 1951, pp. 35, 65–69.

Dibble, Arnold. "The Nine Lives of CAT." *Saturday Review*, May 11, 1968, pp. 44, 49–50; May 18, 1968, pp. 50, 55–56.

Ford, Corey. "The Flying Tigers Carry On." *Saturday Evening Post*, February 5, 1955, pp. 24–25, 57–58, 60; February 12, 1955, pp. 30, 99–102.

Gray, William P. "Chennault Flies Again." *Life*, June 7, 1948, pp. 13–14, 16, 19.

Hersey, John. "Letter from Shanghai." *New Yorker*, February 9, 1946, pp. 82–90.

———. "A Reporter in China." *New Yorker*, March 23, 1946, pp. 32–36.

Horton, Philip. "The China Lobby." *The Reporter*, April 29, 1952, pp. 5–18.

Leary, William M., Jr. "Aircraft and Anti-Communists: CAT in Action, 1949–52." *China Quarterly* 52 (1972):654–69.

——. "Portrait of a Cold War Warrior: Whiting Willauer and Civil Air Transport." *Modern Asian Studies* 5 (1971):378–88.

Meng, C.Y.W. "Tin Industry in Yunnan." *China Monthly* 8 (1947):314–17.

Paget, William. "C.A.T.—Chennault's Airline." *China Weekly Review*, February 25, 1950, pp. 182–84.

Paterson, Thomas G. "If Europe, Why Not China? The Containment Doctrine, 1947–49." *Prologue* 13 (1981):19–38.

Rosbert, C. Joseph. "Only God Knew the Way." *Saturday Evening Post*, February 12, 1944, pp. 11ff.

Scott, Peter Dale. "The Private War in Laos." *Ramparts* 8 (February 1970):39–42.

Wertenbaker, Charles. "The China Lobby." *The Reporter*, April 15, 1952, pp. 4–24; April 29, 1952, pp. 19–22.

Index